Tappan microwave cooking guide

Over 400 new recipes plus tested microwave techniques and cooking tips, illustrated with 650 step-by-step color photos.

These behind-the-scenes photos were made in the test kitchens and photo studios during the preparation of this cooking guide. All recipes were tested in Tappan Microwave ovens under the supervision of the professional home economists of the Tappan Department of Home Economics.

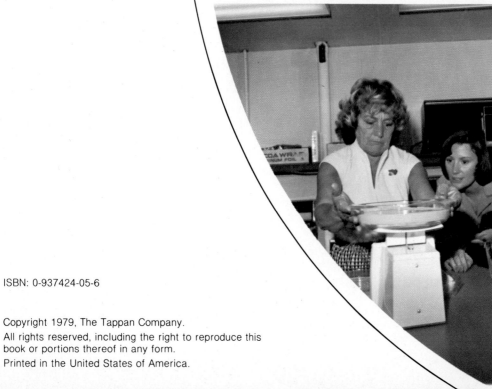

ISBN: 0-937424-05-6

Copyright 1979, The Tappan Company.
All rights reserved, including the right to reproduce this book or portions thereof in any form.
Printed in the United States of America.

A lot of changes have occurred since Tappan first introduced the Microwave Oven for the home in 1955. Tappan engineers and designers have created many new, innovative improvements to make the microwave ovens of today even easier and more convenient to use.

One thing that hasn't changed is Tappan's continuing interest in helping the cook to enjoy more success with every Tappan cooking appliance. That's why we urge you to study and use this new Microwave Cooking Guide.

Microwave cooking is uniquely different. The techniques, the timing, the utensils, even the recipes, are different than those you learned to cook with on conventional ranges and ovens. The hundreds of tried and tested microwave cooking techniques and tips in this guide will help steer you through the learning steps. The over 400 proven step-by-step recipes will enable you to more quickly enjoy the new ease and convenience of using microwave cooking in preparing basic family meals, quick snacks or elegant appetizers and dinners.

TAPPAN®

Serving the cooking experts since 1881

Power Levels used in the recipes	Equivalent Settings on various Selector Controls	Power Level Settings on Touch Controls
HIGH (100%)	NORMAL	*
MEDIUM-HIGH (70%)	MEDIUM-HIGH REHEAT ROAST	7
MEDIUM (50%)	MEDIUM BAKE HIGH DEFROST DEFROST	5
LOW (30%)	SIMMER STEW LOW DEFROST	3
WARM (10%)	LOW KEEP WARM	1
		*100% power is automatic.

POWER LEVEL REFERENCE CHART

The number of "Power Level Settings" available on microwave ovens varies from model to model. The names given to these different power levels also vary.

This chart will help you identify the names and power level settings on your microwave oven with the power levels called for in recipes throughout this book.

PRECAUTIONS TO AVOID POSSIBLE EXPOSURE TO EXCESSIVE MICROWAVE ENERGY

Do not attempt to operate the oven with the door open since open door operation can result in harmful exposure to microwave energy. It is important not to defeat or tamper with the safety interlocks.

Do not place any object between the oven front face and the door or allow soil or cleaner residue to accumulate on sealing surfaces.

Do not operate the oven if it is damaged. It is particularly important that the oven door close properly and that there is no damage to the (1) door (bent), (2) hinges and latches (broken or loosened), (3) door seals and sealing surfaces.

The oven should not be adjusted or repaired by anyone except properly qualified service personnel.

Do not attempt to operate oven with temperature probe assembly caught in door (on models equipped with probe).

Contents

Introduction to microwave cooking

Quick, convenient, clean and cool. That's what microwave cooking is all about. Add to those factors that the microwave oven is also economical and energy efficient, and you've got the perfect kitchen appliance.

It's quick and convenient! The microwave will save you hours in the kitchen. Most foods will be cooked in just minutes or even seconds as compared to the conventional methods. The microwave is ideal for today's fast-paced lifestyles.

It's clean! Microwave cooking puts an end to messy ovens, range tops and spattered walls. Spills or spatters do not get baked on the inside surfaces of the microwave oven. If they do happen, simply wipe them clean with a damp cloth. Cleanup time is reduced because you can prepare, cook and serve many foods in just one container.

It's cool! The only heat in a microwave oven comes from the food itself. The air inside a microwave oven remains at room temperature and may warm just slightly as the food gets hot. You won't heat up the whole kitchen with your microwave.

It's economical and energy efficient! Saving energy is a big concern today. Most of us are looking for any way possible to save energy because that means saving dollars as well. Much of microwave cooking is a one-step process. You'll save energy both in the quick operation of the microwave oven as well as in cleanup.

MICROWAVE OVEN 170 WATTS

CONVENTIONAL RANGE 1,000 WATTS

Approximate
Energy Consumption:
Hamburgers
(1-lb., 4 patties)

An artist's conception of how microwaves enter the oven, then bounce back off the

6

How do "waves" cook food?

Your microwave oven is really similar to a little broadcasting station. Inside the oven is a special power source called a magnetron tube. This tube is activated by electricity which causes it to produce short, high frequency waves, similar to radio waves. Microwaves do not penetrate metal. They are directed along a wave guide in the oven and come in contact with a special metal stirrer. The stirrer is constantly revolving to direct the waves throughout all areas of the oven.

Some waves will go directly toward the food, while others will be reflected off the metal walls and flooring of the oven to be directed towards all the different surfaces of the food. All the microwave energy remains inside the oven. When the door is opened or the oven is turned off, the broadcasting of microwaves stops.

metal walls and bottom to reach all surfaces of the food from every direction.

Microwaves cause heat by friction, just as you create heat when you rub your hands together. As the microwave energy comes into contact with the food, it acts like a magnet on food molecules, causing them to vibrate against each other. As the molecules vibrate, they cause friction which produces instant heat in the food.

7

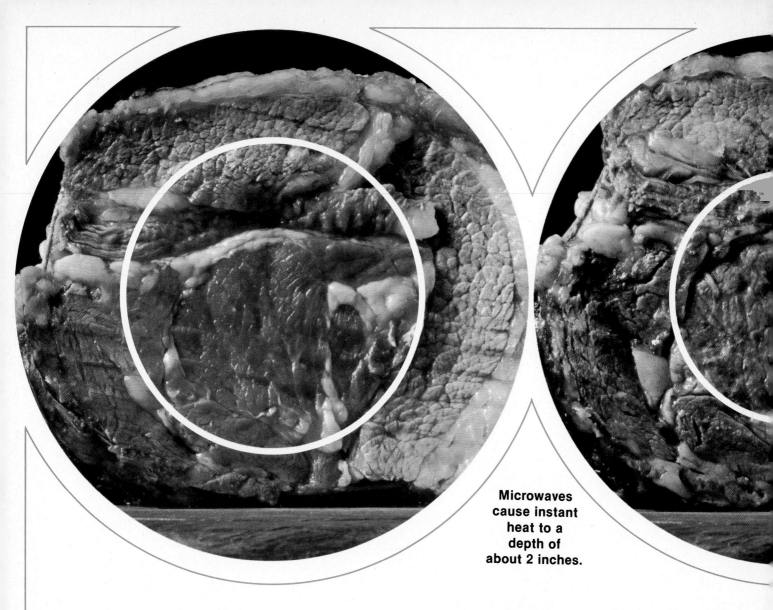

**Microwaves
cause instant
heat to a
depth of
about 2 inches.**

A common misconception

It is a common misconception that foods cooked in the microwave cook from the inside out. Actually, microwaves cause molecules to vibrate only to a depth of about 2 inches in food, depending on the differences in resistance and different types of food. Heat from these vibrating molecules then moves toward the center of the food, and the food becomes cooked.

Foods of small size and low density tend to cook throughout at the same time. In larger, more dense foods, the cooking is started at the outer edges and heat is conducted to the center.

The importance of "standing time"

An important difference between microwave and conventional cooking is the need for "standing time." In microwave cooking, a standing time is usually recommended.

During this standing time, the internal heat causes foods to finish cooking. Temperatures will even out throughout the food. Meat actually is further tenderized during this time. Standing time helps you to avoid overcooking which may tend to toughen some foods.

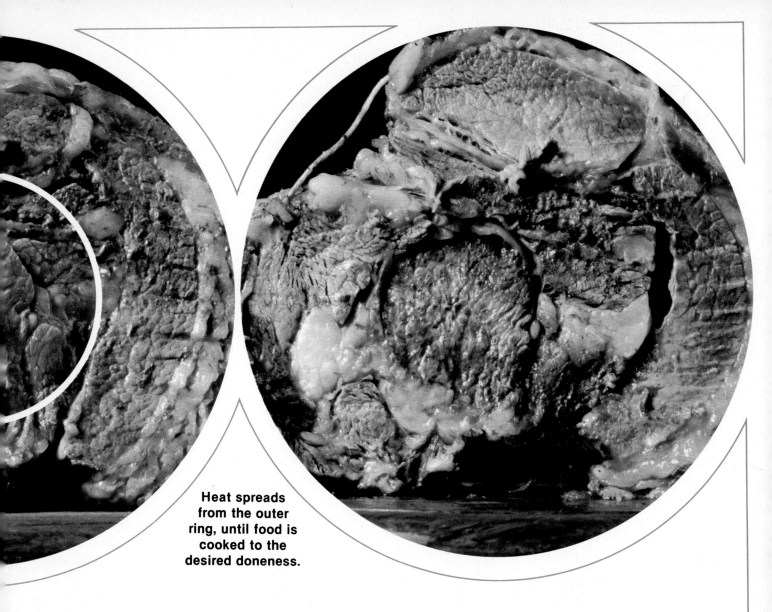

Heat spreads from the outer ring, until food is cooked to the desired doneness.

It's more than an "oven!"

Your microwave oven is called an "oven" but it is really much more than an oven. It can be used for many of the kinds of cooking you are used to doing on top of the range as well as inside the conventional oven.

But in the microwave oven, it is the microwave effect on food molecules which causes the food to heat and to cook — not food contact with a hot pan or hot dry air.

You can boil water, cook bacon, saute or steam foods, make cakes, breads or roasts — all in the microwave!

Life will be easier

The microwave oven will make your life easier. You'll be learning some new cooking techniques as you use this cookbook, and you'll be pleasantly surprised to discover how microwave cooking helps you save energy. In no time at all, you'll even be preparing foods that you might have hesitated to cook in the conventional manner. The microwave oven makes it easy to add variety to your day-to-day meal planning.

The right utensils for microwave cooking

Many of the dishes and utensils in your kitchen are usable in the microwave oven, so you don't have to buy all new cookware. But many new utensils have been specially designed to make microwave cooking easier. Microwaves pass through most materials but not through any metal, so metal containers and utensils should not be used in the microwave oven.

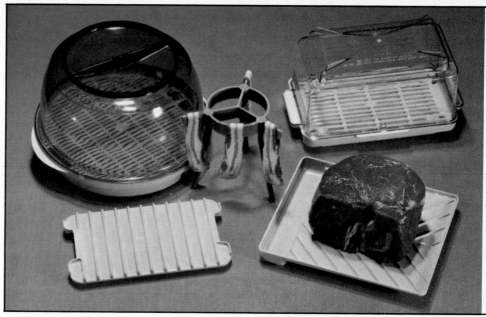

Many new utensils are specially designed to make microwave cooking easier. Pictured above are helpful utensils for cooking meats, for baking, and other microwave cooking.

Wooden tools are very helpful. Unlike metal tools, they can be left in the microwave oven when frequent stirring is necessary.

Dinnerware. Much of today's dinnerware is marked for use in the microwave. When in doubt, use the dish test (see page 12). Don't use metal-trimmed dishes and check to see if a plate may have been signed or decorated with a metal-base paint.

Corning ware is ideal for cooking in a microwave oven. Corning's Corelle dinnerware can be used in the microwave but not Corning's Centura dinnerware.

Glass oven ware. Glassware used in conventional ovens is also good for microwave ovens because it allows microwaves to pass through into the food.

Some plastics are specially made and marked for microwave cooking. Others will become deformed when the food gets hot. Therefore they should only be used for heating foods to serving temperature, not for cooking.

Pottery cookware, without metal trim, is usually fine for microwave cooking. Use the dish test to be sure. Extra thick or colored pottery may require a little extra cooking time.

Ceramics and porcelain are usable. Be sure not to use any with metallic rims or decoration. If the ware is extra thick you may have to add a little extra cooking time.

Seashells. Because microwaves pass through seashells, they're great for cooking seafood casseroles or hot seafood appetizers.

Wood and straw. Wooden dishes and straw baskets can be used for quick reheating of foods but aren't recommended for baking and cooking.

Paper ware. You probably never thought of paper ware as cookware but paper plates, paper towels, wax paper, paper napkins, frozen food cartons, plastic wrap and meat-packing paperboard are all okay for microwave cooking.

Microwave browning dishes and griddles are specially made to let you add a crisp, browned finish to your microwave cooking. The use of a 10'' browning dish and 12'' griddle are described in our recipes.

TESTING DISHES

Place the dish in the microwave along with a glass measuring cup half full of water. Heat on High (100%) for one minute. If the dish feels hot, you shouldn't use it. If it's just slightly warm, you can use it for reheating but not for cooking. If the dish is room temperature, it's okay for microwave cooking.

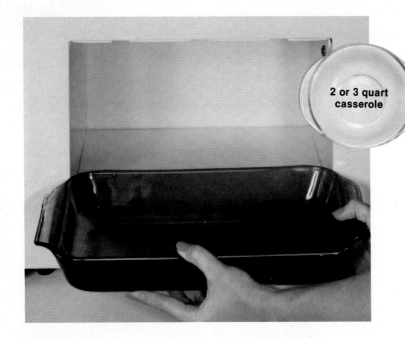

2 or 3 quart casserole

10¼ x 8³/₈ x 2½ inch Corning ware

12 inch pizza or quiche dish

To Substitute Baking Dish Sizes

Our recipes sometimes call for an 11¾ x 7½ x 1¾ inch baking dish. If you have a Space-Saver microwave oven or one with a turntable, instead of this size dish you can substitute: a 10¼ x 8³/₈ x 2½ inch Corning ware dish, a 2 or 3 quart casserole, or a 12 inch round pizza dish or quiche dish. Stir or rearrange foods if necessary.

Do not use metal pots, pans or utensils, metal-trimmed, metallic-decorated or metallic-labeled dishes, foil or foil-lined trays in the microwave oven because microwaves will not pass through these materials to properly cook the food. This includes all kinds of metal: gold, silver, brass, platinum, copper, aluminum or cast iron. Watch for hidden metal such as screws, wire inside paper twisters or metal inside wicker handles.

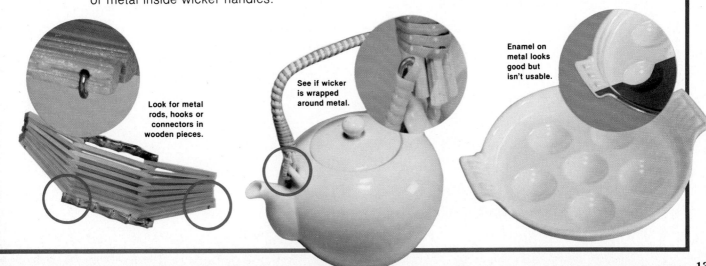

Look for metal rods, hooks or connectors in wooden pieces.

See if wicker is wrapped around metal.

Enamel on metal looks good but isn't usable.

Paper Products are Useful Utensils

Paper products make excellent companions to microwave cooking. Different kinds of paper help obtain different results in cooking. For example, if you want to retain more moisture, you'll probably be covering with plastic wrap.

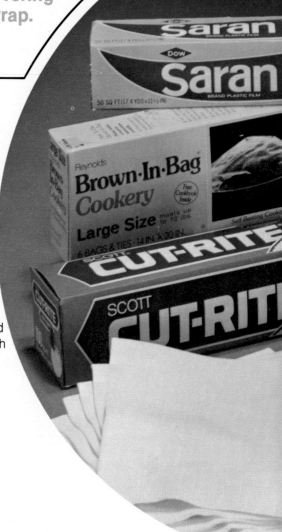

Paper towels and napkins absorb excess moisture and promote even heating when wrapped around a sandwich or used with such foods as bacon, breads or cakes. Steam can escape, and spatters are virtually eliminated.

Do not use colored paper towel or napkins as the color may tend to bleed onto the food.

Waxed paper. Using a light cover of waxed paper when cooking lets you hold in heat and retain some moisture. For fast, even heating use waxed paper for covering some foods.

When less moisture is desired, you may be using waxed paper. Paper towels and napkins are used for heating and serving foods, and as covers for absorbing moisture and cutting down spatters during cooking.

Plastic wrap. A tight covering of plastic wrap allows you to steam and tenderize food. It helps to pleat the plastic wrap covering to allow room for the steam to expand. When removing plastic lift carefully from far end to allow steam to escape.

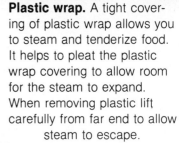

Cooking bags. When used for large cuts of meat, roasts, turkey or chicken, these bags hold in moisture. Sometimes the food may cook even faster. Use string or cut a strip of plastic from the open end to use as a tie for the bag. Halfway through cooking slash a small "X" in the bag to allow some steam to escape.

Boilable freezer bags. These bags hold in moisture so make a small "X" slash in the bag to allow some steam to escape.

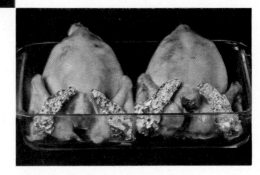

Aluminum foil. Small pieces of aluminum foil are used to protect some spots on food from overcooking. This shielding technique is also used in defrosting. This shielding technique is illustrated whenever appropriate throughout this book.

Using the temperature probe

The temperature probe lets you enjoy carefree cooking and heating without guesswork for many foods. Made of special material, the probe senses the temperature of the food and turns the microwave oven off when the preset temperature is reached. There is no need to set a cooking time.

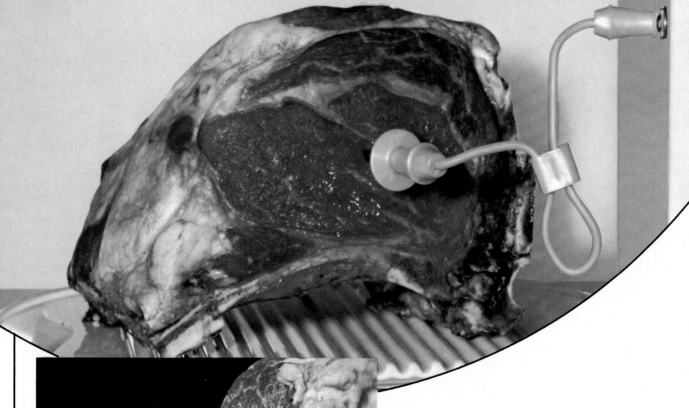

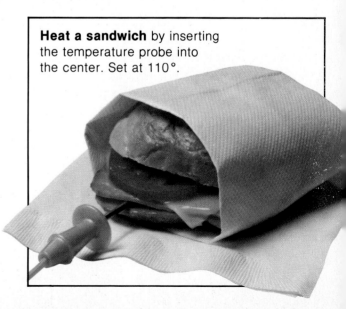

Heat a sandwich by inserting the temperature probe into the center. Set at 110°.

Insert the temperature probe at least 1 inch into food. Ideally the probe should be as horizontal as possible, regardless of the shape or size of the food. Defrost food first. The probe could break if you try to insert it into hard frozen food. When in use, the probe should not be touching plastic or paper, nor the walls, door or floor of the microwave oven. Do not use the probe with a browning dish. The handle of the probe may get hot during cooking, so use a pot holder when removing.

Roast meat to rare, medium or well done with the temperature probe. The probe should be inserted into the center of the meatiest area. The probe tip should not touch bone nor fat.

Cook whole fish with the temperature probe inserted into meatiest area, parallel to the backbone. Set probe at 130°.

Heat soups or beverages with the temperature probe set at 150° to 160°. For milk-base beverages, set at 130° to 140°.

Warm sauces, gravies or dips with the probe. Set the probe at 130° to 140° for sauces, gravies and dips.

Warm baked goods with the temperature probe inserted as horizontally as possible with tip near the center. Set probe at 110° to 120°.

Have hot syrup for pancakes or waffles or toppings for sundaes. Heat in the container or pour syrup or topping into a glass measuring cup. Insert probe and set temperature at 130° to 140°.

Reheat vegetables or leftover mashed potatoes with the probe set at 140° to 150°.

Reheat precooked casseroles or cook casseroles with the temperature probe. Insert probe so tip is in the center of the casserole. Follow recipe for probe setting when cooking casseroles. When reheating, set the probe at 150° to 160°. Stir once during cooking.

Using the
Power levels

The various settings on microwave ovens are called "Power Levels" (rather than "Temperature Settings" as on conventional ovens). The number of "Power Level" settings available and the kinds of controls used, will vary on different models of microwave ovens.

Some models use knobs or dials: turning the pointer adjusts the "Power Level" to the desired setting. As many as seven settings are indicated on some models.

Other models use solid state "Touch" controls: by touching the numbered pads on a panel the desired "Percentage of Power Level" is selected. These models have 10 power settings from 0 to 90%; 100% is automatic.

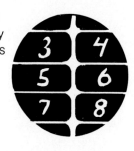

The different power level settings are used for cooking different kinds of foods, as well as for different cooking methods. Therefore the additional power levels available on some models provide additional cooking flexibility, but do not change the basic principles of microwave cooking.

To make it easier to use the recipes in this book the "Power Levels" specified for each recipe have been limited to the five basic settings that are available on most models of microwave ovens:

HIGH (100%) *This is the full power, fastest cooking setting. Generally used for cooking fish, fruits, gravies, sauces, puddings, most soups, cookies, candy, sandwiches and vegetables.*

MEDIUM-HIGH (70%) *Uses 70% of the oven's power, for foods which will require more gentle cooking such as meats, cakes, poultry and some soups.*

MEDIUM (50%) *Uses approximately half the full power when slower cooking and tenderizing is desired for such foods as stews and less tender cuts of meat, eggs, cheese, rice and pasta.*

LOW (30%) *Used when only one-third of the power is required for the delicate kinds of food that need more cooking time. Use this setting for softening cheese and butter, cooking custards and for drying fruits and vegetables. You'll defrost most foods at this power level.*

WARM (10%) *This setting is used primarily for keeping cooked foods warm, for up to a half-hour without causing overcooking.*

Different models of microwave ovens frequently use different words on the Selector Controls to describe the Power Level Settings. Use this reference chart to find the Power Level descriptions on your microwave oven which are equivalent to the five Power Level settings specified in the recipes in this book.

Power Levels used in the recipes	Equivalent Settings on various Selector Controls	Power Level Settings on Touch Controls
HIGH (100%)	NORMAL	*
MEDIUM-HIGH (70%)	MEDIUM-HIGH REHEAT ROAST	7
MEDIUM (50%)	MEDIUM BAKE HIGH DEFROST DEFROST	5
LOW (30%)	SIMMER STEW LOW DEFROST	3
WARM (10%)	LOW KEEP WARM	1
		*100% power is automatic.

TO TEST COOKING TIMES

The cooking times recommended in our recipes were all tested on one or more of our microwave ovens. However house power can vary in different locations of the country, during peak use times or during weather extremes. Such differences in the power supply going to your microwave oven can cause changes in the cooking times required.

It's not difficult to test the cooking time required in your microwave oven against the times used in the recipes in this book.

To make the test, place a measuring cup of room temperature water in your microwave oven. Microwave on HIGH (100%) for 2½ to 3 minutes:

If the water boils within this time, your cooking times should be the same as those we have used in this book.

If the water boils in less time, you'll be able to use slightly less time.

If it takes longer for the water to boil, your cooking times may have to be a bit longer.

When cooking, it's always a good idea to check for doneness at the minimum cooking time. That way you can avoid overcooking or allow extra cooking time if necessary.

Time and energy-saving
Menu planning ideas

Remember when you first began cooking and the hardest thing was getting all the food hot and ready for serving at the same time? With the microwave, you'll soon be a master at quickly preparing whole meals.

When menu planning, keep in mind the importance of good nutrition. Select food from the various food groups. Foods of different color, texture and flavor add appetite and eye-appeal.

Plan your cooking so all foods will not need last-minute attention. Set the table first. Gather ingredients and prepare for cooking.

The first foods to cook are those that need the longest cooking and standing time, or that stay hot longest, such as meats or potatoes. Then move on to those foods such as vegetables and rolls that need the least amount of cooking and standing time.

You can prepare desserts and sauces or foods that reheat quickly earlier in the day when you have extra time. Desserts can be reheated quickly in the microwave while you're clearing away the dinner dishes.

Turn the page for more menu planning ideas.

Let's start cooking!

BREAKFAST FOR 1:

Orange Juice
Hot Oatmeal (page 147)
Sweet Roll (page 51)
Coffee (page 47)

1. Assemble all ingredients and utensils.
2. Set the table and pour the juice.
3. Cook the oatmeal (1½ to 2½ minutes).
4. Heat water for instant coffee (2 to 3 minutes).
5. Heat the sweet roll (15 seconds) while placing food on the table.

BREAKFAST FOR 2:

Hot Breakfast
Grapefruit (page 99)
Scrambled Eggs (page 76)
Bacon (page 139)
Toast
Hot Chocolate (page 49)

1. Assemble ingredients and utensils.
2. Set the table.
3. Measure and prepare foods for cooking.
4. Cook six slices of bacon (4½ to 5½ minutes).
5. Remove bacon from microwave and cover with foil. While bacon is standing, cook four eggs (3 to 3½ minutes).
6. While eggs are standing, cook grapefruit (2 to 3 minutes) and toast bread in your toaster.
7. Heat hot chocolate in microwave (2 to 3 minutes).
8. If necessary, reheat bacon (15 to 30 seconds) while placing food on table.

BRUNCH FOR 4:

Tomato Juice
Eggs Benedict (page 77)
Sour Cream Streusel
Coffeecake (page 52)
Coffee or Tea (page 47)

1. Prepare coffeecake and Hollandaise Sauce (page 107) for Eggs Benedict. If desired do this early in the morning or the day before and keep Hollandaise Sauce refrigerated.
2. Assemble all ingredients and utensils.
3. Set table and pour tomato juice.
4. Measure and prepare foods for cooking.
5. Heat water for instant coffee (6 to 7 min.).
6. Poach four eggs (3½ to 4 minutes) and do English muffins in toaster or broiler.
7. Heat ham on muffins (1½ to 2 minutes) while eggs stand.
8. Reheat sauce (15 to 30 seconds).
9. Assemble Eggs Benedict and place food on the table.

LUNCH FOR 4 TO 6:

Chicken Divan
Sandwich (page 172)
Relishes - carrots, celery, radish
Quick Ambrosia (page 98)
Lemon Meringue Pie (page 149)

1. Make pie early in the day and refrigerate after cooling.
2. Assemble all ingredients and utensils.
3. Set the table.
4. Measure and prepare foods for cooking.
5. Heat sandwiches (8 to 10 minutes).
6. Heat fruit ambrosia (3 to 4½ minutes).
7. Place food on table.

DINNER FOR 4:

Roast Beef (page 129)
Baked Potato (page 188)
Broccoli with Cheese
Sauce (pages 185 and 107)
Tossed Salad
Rolls (page 51)
Upside-Down Cake (page 63)

1. Assemble all ingredients and utensils.
2. Set the table. Toss salad and refrigerate.
3. Prepare upside-down cake (7 to 10 minutes) or prepare cake earlier in the day.
4. Place 3 pound beef roast on trivet, cover and cook (about 30 minutes).
5. While meat is cooking, scrub and pierce potatoes. Clean broccoli and place in dish. Prepare cheese sauce (unless prepared earlier in the day) for cooking.
6. Remove roast from oven and tent with foil. While meat is standing, cook the potatoes (12 to 14 minutes).
7. Remove potatoes from oven and wrap with foil. Allow to stand. Cook broccoli (8 to 10 minutes).
8. While broccoli is standing, reheat sauce (15 to 30 seconds) or cook sauce (3¼ to 4½ minutes).
9. Heat rolls and place food on the table.

DINNER FOR 4 TO 6:

Turkey and Rice Bake (page 163)
Asparagus (page 185)
Tomato slice with mayonnaise
Italian Bread Slice
Baked Apple with
Cinnamon Candies (page 97)

1. Assemble all ingredients and utensils.
2. Set table. Prepare salad and refrigerate.
3. Measure and prepare foods for cooking.
4. Cook casserole (8 to 10 minutes).
5. Remove casserole from oven and cover with foil. While casserole stands, cook asparagus (6 to 8 minutes).
6. Place foods on table. While eating, cook apples (8 to 10 minutes) and allow to stand.
7. Serve apples.

Converting a standard recipe for microwave cooking.

Many of your favorite recipes can be converted to microwave cooking.

The most reliable way to convert a standard recipe is to find a similar microwave recipe or to look for microwave cooking instructions for the main ingredients of your recipe.

Follow the microwave recipe for cooking techniques, power levels, times, seasoning amounts, dish sizes and covering procedures.

If you cannot find a similar microwave recipe, follow these steps:

1 **Check for any special instructions** for the main ingredient of your recipe.

2 **Reduce liquid by about one-half** or add more thickening since there is less evaporation in the microwave. Sometimes liquid may even be omitted.

3 **Use less seasoning.** Usually one-half the seasoning will do. You can adjust to taste after cooking.

4 **Any cooking oils or fats may be reduced** or may not be needed at all because they do not evaporate in the microwave as they would in conventional cooking. Fats tend to attract microwaves away from the food and may cause food to cook longer. Remove any excess grease when possible.

5 **You may wish to precook hamburger** or other meats first and then drain them. This avoids excess fat as well as the overcooking of other foods in the recipe.

6 **Reduce the cooking time** to about:
   one-fourth for High (100%)
   one-third for Medium-High (70%)
   one-half for Medium (50%)
   three-fourths for Low (30%).

7 **Substitute instant or quick cooking ingredients** for those ingredients which may take longer to cook than other foods in the recipe.

8 **Some stirring or rearranging** of food may be necessary during cooking. Stir occasionally when your recipe calls for constant stirring or when you would naturally stir.

---

4 omit or reduce cooking oil.

6 reduce cooking time to one-fourth.

8 stir or rearrange.

Here's what's cookin': SLOPPY JOES   Serves: 6-8

2 tablespoons oil   ½ cup catsup
1½ lbs. ground beef   ¼ cup water
½ cup chopped onion   1 T. Worcestershire sauce
½ cup chopped celery   1/8 tsp. red pepper sauce
½ cup chopped green peppers   1 teaspoon salt

Heat oil in 10 inch skillet. Add meat and onion. Cook until meat is lightly browned. Drain. Stir in remaining ingredients. Cover and cook on low heat for 20 to 25 minutes or until vegetables are just tender. Stir frequently.

2 omit liquid

3 use less seasoning: 1½ tsp. Worcestershire, ½ tsp. salt, dash of pepper

1 cook until slightly pink in center.

Some recipes such as cakes, candies, meat loaves or main dish casseroles may need only a power level and time conversion but no changes in ingredients.

Whenever you convert a recipe, record all changes for future use.

There are a few foods which you will probably prefer to cook in the conventional manner because they are difficult to get satisfactory results when using the microwave. These foods include:

1 **Fried foods** which tend not to get crisp. Also do not deep fat fry in the microwave. Crusty foods such as popovers or French fries tend to get soggy.

2 **Yeast bread recipes** are difficult to convert. It is best to use only those recipes which are specially formulated for microwave cooking.

3 **Souffles** are very delicate and take a long time to make. For easier cooking make souffles in the conventional way.

Be your own test cook. After preparing and serving the converted recipe, you can put a proven microwave recipe in your file.

Here's what's cookin': SLOPPY JOES Serves: 6-8

1½ lbs. ground beef
½ cup chopped onion
½ cup chopped celery
½ cup chopped green peppers
½ cup catsup
1½ tsp. Worcestershire sauce
½ teaspoon salt
Dash of red pepper sauce

Place meat and onion in a casserole or baking dish. Cook on HIGH (100%) until meat is slightly pink in center. Stir halfway through cooking. Drain. Stir in remaining ingredients. Cover. Cook on HIGH for 5 to 7 minutes or until vegetables are just tender. Stir occasionally.

Defrosting with the microwave oven

There are special techniques to learn about defrosting in a microwave oven. These pretty ice penguins help to illustrate what will happen inside frozen foods during defrosting. Remember that ice crystals react rather slowly to microwave energy, but water has a high attraction and heats rapidly. Therefore when the ice crystals start to melt, the water that is formed reacts much faster than remaining ice.

enough ahead to allow time
for meat or another main dish
to defrost, you will
really appreciate the microwave.

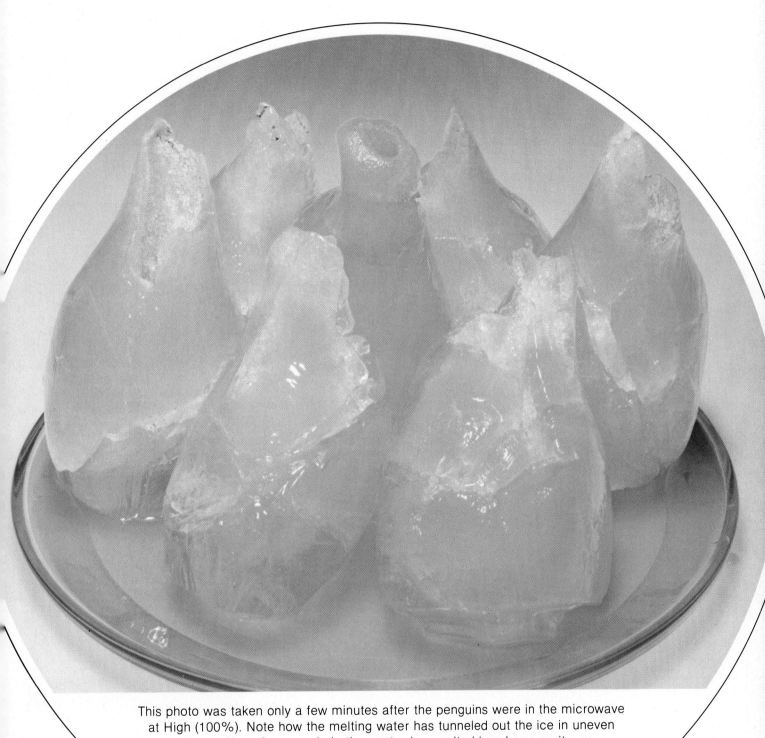

This photo was taken only a few minutes after the penguins were in the microwave at High (100%). Note how the melting water has tunneled out the ice in uneven patterns. Note the penguin in the center has melted less because it was shielded from the microwaves by the surrounding mass. It is important to avoid this uneven defrosting so that's why you'll be defrosting on lower power levels. Study the next pages and the specific defrosting instructions in this cookbook's recipe sections.

DEFROST THOROUGHLY

It is important to thoroughly defrost food before starting to cook. For most food, the Low (30%) power level is recommended for defrosting. At low settings, the microwave oven automatically cycles "on" and "off" which allows the heat to equalize throughout the food. At high power levels, cooking can start on the outside before food is completely defrosted on the inside.

At High (100%) power, this hamburger patty shows signs of cooking before being thoroughly defrosted.

Attempting to defrost at Medium (50%) power still shows signs that cooking has started before meat is thoroughly defrosted.

Using Low (30%) power allows you to thoroughly defrost meat without starting the cooking process.

FROM FREEZER TO THE MICROWAVE

Frozen food in boilable plastic bags can be both defrosted and heated for serving in the microwave. Make an "X" slash in the bag to allow steam to escape.

Freeze food in paper or plastic freezer containers such as those used for margarine or whipped toppings. In the microwave, foods can be defrosted and sometimes reheated in these containers. Greasy foods may cause some plastics to become deformed if the food gets too hot. Do not use foil or foil-lined containers.

You can freeze foods in those special dishes which are designed to be used directly "from freezer to oven to table" in your microwave oven. Foods in such dishes can be defrosted and heated to serving temperature.

It helps to flex frozen food in plastic pouches while defrosting. This distributes heat and makes the defrosting faster.

When defrosting meat, remove any insulated packaging such as Styrofoam trays or paper liners which are used to absorb juices. Such paper products may become saturated with moisture so they will draw microwave energy away from the meat and slow down defrosting.

Remove any metal containers deeper than ¾ inch. Transfer foods in such containers to microwave safe dishes for defrosting.

Stir or break foods apart to distribute heat and speed defrosting.

When defrosting ground meat, it helps to remove meat on the outer edges. This meat could start cooking before the rest of the meat has finished defrosting.

Pouring liquid from foods, such as frozen poultry in a plastic bag will speed up the defrosting time.

Use small pieces of foil to shield any tender parts or spots which may be getting warm during defrosting.

Cover foods with wax paper during defrosting for more even heating and some moisture retention.

When you finish defrosting food in the microwave oven, it may still be slightly icy. You can complete the defrosting by holding such foods as frozen fish or poultry under cold, running water. When properly defrosted and ready for cooking, food should be cool, soft, moist and glossy.

Convenience foods

Convenience foods can be more convenient than ever when heated in your microwave oven. These foods can be brought to serving temperature in less time than would be spent heating in the conventional manner. In fact, many brands now include special microwave instructions right on the package.

If convenience foods come in a thick, metal tray, the food should be transferred to a microwave safe dish such as a casserole or baking dish. TV dinner trays less than ¾ inch thick and frozen juice cans are exceptions.

Convenience foods in boilable plastic pouches can be reheated on a plate. Slash an "X" in the top to allow steam to escape.

Remove the metal lid from one end of a can of frozen juice. Defrost on Medium (50%). Concentrate should be soft and cool after defrosting. If concentrate becomes warm, vitamin C may be lost.

CONVENIENCE FOOD CHART

Item	Power Level	Cooking Time
Canned Meat or Poultry Main Dishes under 16 ounces over 16 ounces	High (100%) High (100%)	4 to 6 minutes 8 to 10 minutes (or temperature probe can be used, set at 150° to 160°)
Frozen Fried Chicken Pieces 2 pounds	High (100%)	8 to 10 minutes
Frozen Fruits 10 to 12 ounces	High (100%)	6 to 8 minutes
Frozen Juices 6 ounces 12 ounces 16 ounces	Medium (50%) Medium (50%) Medium (50%)	2 to 3 minutes 3 to 4 minutes 4 to 6 minutes
Frozen Macaroni & Cheese (or other Pasta Dishes) 12 ounces 32 ounces	High (100%) High (100%)	8 to 10 minutes 14 to 16 minutes
Frozen Meat or Poultry Main Dishes 5 to 8 ounces 8 to 12 ounces 12 to 16 ounces 16 to 32 ounces	High (100%) High (100%) High (100%) High (100%)	3 to 5 minutes 5 to 8 minutes 8 to 10 minutes 10 to 20 minutes
Frozen Vegetables (In Sauce, Au Gratin, Scalloped or Stuffed) 10 to 12 ounces	High (100%)	7 to 9 minutes

Stir and cover foods not in boilable bags.

HOW TO MICROWAVE A TV DINNER

Remove TV dinner from its box. Then remove foil covering from the dinner. We do not recommend heating three-course dinners in the microwave.

Cover dinner with plastic wrap, pleated to allow steam to expand. Unless the foil tray is more than ¾ inch deep, it is not necessary to transfer the food to another dish. It's best to remove porous foods such as brownies or cornbread or sweets such as puddings. Return them to the dinner during the last 15 to 20 seconds of heating.

Microwave on High (100%). Most dinners will thaw and heat to serving temperature in 5 to 7 minutes. Larger portion dinners may take 12 to 15 minutes. When the tray becomes warm on the bottom, the dinner is thoroughly heated. Allow 2 minutes standing time before eating.

You can heat a TV dinner even more quickly if you do transfer the foods to a microwave safe dish.

Make your own TV dinners. Use a divided plastic plate or one of the special divided microwave plates which have their own lids. Arrange food on plate. Cover with lid or plastic wrap. Secure with foil or plastic bag for freezer storage. Remove foil, metal twister or bag (but not plastic wrap or lid) before heating. You can heat these frozen dinners to serving temperature in 3 to 5 minutes on High (100%). Times may vary according to the food you select.

Reheating Techniques

Reheat foods in the microwave without loss of quality, moisture, flavor or texture. Now leftovers will taste fresh, almost like they have just been prepared for the first time.

Most reheating is done using High (100%) power. For more delicate foods, you may wish to reheat on a lower power setting.

When reheating meats, remember that you don't want to restart the cooking process unless you want the meat to be more fully cooked than before it was reheated. You'll also find meat reheats more quickly when sliced into smaller pieces.

Small amounts of food will reheat more quickly than large amounts of food. It's faster to reheat casseroles by spreading the food out in a shallow dish.

Foods in a dish should be of the same starting temperature for reheating. A plate of room temperature food will take about 1 to 1¼ minutes to reheat; a refrigerator temperature plate will take 1½ to 2 minutes. Arrange foods so pieces that take longer to reheat are on the outside while more tender food is towards the inside.

It helps to cover foods when reheating. Waxed paper works best for a plate of food while vegetables or a casserole may benefit most by a covering of plastic wrap or a tight fitting lid.

Breads and sugary foods such as desserts and rolls reheat very quickly and can easily be overcooked. When reheating foods, add these items during the last 15 to 30 seconds.

Stirring foods occasionally during reheating will help to distribute the heat throughout the food and speed the reheating time.

You can add extra flavor and speed up reheating by adding a tablespoon of butter (or margarine) to pasta, rice or vegetables. Adding sauces to meats has the same effect. This is because moisture and fat tend to attract microwave energy to foods.

Use the temperature probe for fast, even reheating. Set it at 150° to 160°.

Appetizers & Hors d'oeuvres

Guests will rave over the hot appetizers you can make in minutes. These treats are easily prepared in advance, to be heated when the company arrives. Or let guests join in the fun and warm their own.

Pierce the thick outer membrane *of oysters and escargots to allow steam to escape and to prevent spattering.*

Cover oysters and escargots completely *with sauce to prevent them from popping out of their shells.*

Place shellfish in a circle *with small tender parts toward the center for even heating without overcooking. Use lower power levels and slowly cook clams, oysters and escargots. You might try using the new microwave paper plates rather than a glass or ceramic serving dish.*

LOBSTER DAINTIES OR ROCK SHRIMP

Power Level: HIGH [100%]
Total Cooking Time: 2½ to 3½ minutes

16 lobster dainties (or rock shrimp)

1. Cut through soft shell side. Place tails, hard shell side up, in a circle with tips toward center on a serving plate. Cover with plastic wrap.

2. Microwave on HIGH (100%) for 2½ to 3½ minutes or until meat is opaque and shell is pink.

3. If desired, serve with melted butter or chili sauce.

Recipe yield: 4 servings

Shellfish

The delicate flavors of shellfish are most delicious when steamed in the microwave oven. Do them in their shells, or in a dish covered with pleated plastic wrap. Cook and serve immediately.

OYSTERS DENNIE

Power Level: HIGH [100%] and MEDIUM [50%]
Total Cooking Time: 5¾ to 7½ minutes

Sauce:
5 tablespoons butter (or margarine)
1 cup chopped celery
¼ cup chopped onion
¼ cup finely chopped green pepper
1 bottle (12 ounces) chili sauce
1 teaspoon brown sugar

Oysters:
2 cups oysters
2 cups milk
1 tablespoon butter (or margarine)
Dash of salt
Dash of pepper
12 to 18 oyster or clam shells

1. Place 5 tablespoons butter, celery, onion and green pepper in a 1 quart casserole. Microwave on HIGH (100%) for 3 to 4 minutes or until vegetables are tender.

2. Stir in chili sauce and brown sugar. Set aside.

3. Pierce oyster membranes. Combine oysters, milk, remaining butter, salt and pepper in a 1½ quart casserole. Microwave on HIGH (100%) for 2 to 2½ minutes or until edges of oysters curl.

4. Place 1 or 2 oysters and 1 teaspoon broth in each shell. Top each with 1 tablespoon sauce making sure oysters are completely covered.

5. Microwave 6 at a time in a circle on MEDIUM (50%) for 45 seconds to 1 minute or until hot and bubbly. Repeat with remaining oysters.

Recipe yield: 4 to 6 servings or 12 to 18 oysters

ESCARGOTS

Power Level: HIGH [100%] and LOW [30%]
Total Cooking Time: About 1¼ minutes per plate

⅓ cup butter (or margarine)
¼ cup lemon juice
1 tablespoon instant minced onion
1 tablespoon chopped parsley
½ teaspoon minced garlic
1 can (4 ounces) medium size escargots (about 24) with shells

1. Place butter, lemon juice, onion, parsley and garlic in a 2 cup measure. Microwave on HIGH (100%) for 45 seconds to 1 minute or until butter is melted. Stir.

2. Drain and rinse escargots. Fill each shell with a small amount of sauce, place snail in loosely and cover with more sauce. (Do not plug hole with snail).

3. Place 6 snails in a circle on each plate. Microwave, one plate at a time, on LOW (30%) for 35 to 40 seconds.*
Repeat with remaining appetizers.

Recipe yield: 4 servings

*Be careful not to overcook because snails will pop out of shells.

CRAB CLAWS

Power Level: HIGH [100%]
Total Cooking Time: 3 to 4 minutes

12 precooked frozen crab claws

1. Place crab claws in a circle with tips toward center on a serving dish. Cover with plastic wrap.

2. Microwave on HIGH (100%) for 3 to 4 minutes or until heated through.

3. If desired, serve with melted butter or chili sauce.

Recipe yield: 3 to 4 servings

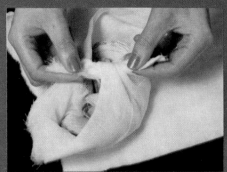

Oysters Dennie have
a delicate flavor.

Clams in Shells
with melted butter.

Place clams in cheesecloth *and tie at top for individual servings. Put bags in a circle for cooking. Melt cups of butter at the same time.*

CLAMS IN SHELLS
Power Level: MEDIUM [50%]
Total Cooking Time: 6 to 8 minutes

24 small soft shell clams

1. Scrub clams thoroughly with a brush. Rinse several times to remove sand.

2. Divide clams onto four pieces of cheesecloth. Tie together at top. Place in a circle in a 10 inch pie dish. Cover with plastic wrap.

3. Microwave on MEDIUM (50%) for 6 to 8 minutes or until shells open. (Clams that do not open are bad and must be discarded.)

4. Serve with melted butter, lemon wedges and broth which collects in shells.

Tip: To eat clams, hold them by the neck, dip into broth to remove any possible sand, then into melted butter. Do not eat neck sheath.

Recipe yield: 4 servings

Each canape spread recipe makes enough for 24 crackers.

Combine ingredients in a small bowl. Spread half the mixture on 12 crackers and arrange on plate. Heat on HIGH (100%) 30 to 60 seconds. Repeat with remaining mixture and crackers.

Place canapes in a circle *for even heating.*

CHEESY ONION SPREAD

1 small onion, chopped
½ cup mayonnaise
  (or salad dressing)
¼ cup grated Parmesan cheese
Dash of paprika

SEAFOOD SPREAD

1 can (6½ ounces) crab, shrimp or
  tuna, rinsed and drained
1 cup grated Swiss cheese
½ cup mayonnaise
  (or salad dressing)
¼ cup sliced green onion
1 teaspoon lemon juice
1 teaspoon Worcestershire sauce
  (or horseradish)
Dash of paprika

HOT TUNA SALAD SPREAD

¾ cup drained tuna
2 tablespoons mayonnaise
  (or salad dressing)
⅓ cup finely chopped celery
⅓ cup finely chopped onion
⅓ cup drained crushed pineapple
Dash of curry powder

WAIKIKI CHICKEN SPREAD

1 can (5 ounces) chicken
¼ cup crumbled cooked bacon
¼ cup lightly drained crushed
  pineapple
¼ cup chopped walnuts (or pecans)
2 tablespoons mayonnaise
  (or salad dressing)
¼ teaspoon salt
Dash of pepper

Cracker Tip

Use dry, crisp crackers as a base. Heat only to serving temperature to keep crackers from becoming soggy with canape spread.

Canapes

Put a little life in the party with taste-tempting spreads and finger foods.

Sprinkle tortilla chips *with cheese for Perky Nachos.*

PERKY NACHOS
Power Level: MEDIUM [50%]
Total Cooking Time: 2 to 2½ minutes

16 large tortilla chips
2 tablespoons chopped chilies
2 tablespoons chopped
**   black olives (optional)**
4 ounces finely grated
**   Cheddar cheese**

1. Place a layer of tortilla chips close together on a waxed paper lined 10 inch plate. Sprinkle with chopped chilies and black olives. Top with Cheddar cheese.

2. Microwave on MEDIUM (50%) for 2 to 2½ minutes or until cheese melts.

Recipe yield: 16 appetizers

A tempting tray of Deviled Eggs, Canape Spreads and Cheese Strips.

Stuffed mushrooms are the stars on any hors d'oeuvres tray.

First wash mushrooms and remove stems. Prepare stuffing mixture and heap into mushroom caps. Arrange stuffed mushroom caps on plate lined with paper towel. Microwave on HIGH (100%) for 3 to 4 minutes.

MUSHROOM VARIATIONS:

SPINACH STUFFED
1 package (10 ounces) frozen
**   spinach souffle, thawed**
⅓ cup grated Parmesan cheese

SAUSAGE STUFFED
¼ cup bulk pork sausage
Dash of paprika

HAM AND CHEESE STUFFED
1 package (3 ounces) cream
**   cheese, softened**
1½ teaspoons butter
**   (or margarine), softened**
¼ cup finely chopped ham
2 tablespoons bread crumbs
2 tablespoons finely chopped
**   onion**
½ teaspoon Worcestershire sauce
¼ teaspoon salt

OYSTER STUFFED
1 can (5 ounces) oysters, chopped
¼ cup crumbled cooked bacon
¼ cup bread crumbs
¼ teaspoon dried parsley
¼ teaspoon instant minced onion
Dash of basil
1 tablespoon oyster liquid

DEVILED EGG FILLING
Power Level: HIGH [100%]
Total Cooking Time: 1 to 1¼ minutes

6 hard cooked eggs, sliced in
**   halves or thirds (cooked on**
**   conventional range)**
2 tablespoons cider vinegar
1 tablespoon butter (or margarine)
1 teaspoon sugar
¼ teaspoon salt
Dash of white pepper
1 tablespoon slaw dressing

1. Mash egg yolks from hard cooked eggs. Set aside.

2. Combine vinegar, butter, sugar, salt, and pepper in a 2 cup measure or small casserole. Microwave on HIGH (100%) for 1 to 1¼ minutes or until boiling.

3. Stir in mashed egg yolks and slaw dressing until smooth.

4. Fill each egg white half with a heaping tablespoon of egg yolk mixture.

Turn dough *onto a chilled pastry board. Roll and cut into strips. Heat half of the strips on a piece of waxed paper.*

CHEESE STRIPS
Power Level: LOW [30%] and
*   HIGH [100%]*
Total Cooking Time: 3¾ to
*   4½ minutes*

2 tablespoons butter (or margarine)
1 cup (4 ounces) grated Cheddar
**   cheese**
½ teaspoon salt
½ teaspoon Worcestershire sauce
1 to 2 drops hot pepper sauce
½ cup all purpose flour
Bacon bits, crushed chopped
chives, sesame seeds or poppy
seeds

1. Place butter in a large bowl. Microwave on LOW (30%) for 45 seconds to 1 minute or until softened. Add cheese, salt, Worcestershire sauce and hot pepper sauce. Mix until well blended.

2. Stir in flour until dough gathers to form a ball.

3. Turn onto a chilled pastry board. Roll out until 1/8 inch thick. Cut into ½ inch wide strips about 2 to 3 inches long.

4. Place half of the strips on a piece of waxed paper. Sprinkle with crushed bacon bits, chopped chives, sesame seeds, or poppy seeds.

5. Microwave on HIGH (100%) for 3 to 3½ minutes. Turn waxed paper a half turn halfway through cooking. Remove strips immediately from waxed paper and place on cooling racks. Repeat with remaining cheese strips.

Recipe yield: 30 appetizers

Remove any foil wrapping. *Place cream cheese in microwave and soften on Low [30%] for slow, even heating.*

Thoroughly blend *all ingredients for best cooking results.*

Use the temperature probe, *set at 130° to 140°. Stir dips at least once during cooking. Remove metal lid from glass jar of chutney and heat contents using probe.*

Dips

Party-pleasing dips can be easily prepared and heated in pretty serving dishes. When making cheese dips, remember cheese gets tough and stringy when overcooked.

HOT CHUTNEY CHEESE DIP

Power Level: HIGH [100%] and LOW [30%]
Total Cooking Time: 8 to 11½ minutes
Temperature Probe: 130° to 140°

1 tablespoon butter (or margarine)
½ pound finely chopped fresh mushrooms
½ cup finely chopped ham
1 package (3 ounces) cream cheese
¼ cup sour cream
¼ teaspoon curry powder
Dash of salt
Dash of pepper
⅔ cup chutney

1. Place butter, mushrooms and ham in a 1 quart casserole. Microwave on HIGH (100%) for 2 to 3 minutes or until mushrooms are tender.

2. Add cream cheese. Microwave on LOW (30%) for 1 to 1½ minutes or until softened. Stir in sour cream and seasonings until smooth.

3. Microwave on HIGH (100%) for 4 to 5 minutes or until bubbly. Stir halfway through cooking.

4. Remove lid from chutney jar. Microwave in glass jar on HIGH (100%) for 1 to 2 minutes. Spread over hot dip.

5. Serve with crackers.

Recipe yield: about 1½ cups

HOT CHEESE SPREAD

Power Level: HIGH [100%] and LOW [30%]
Total Cooking Time: 3 to 4½ minutes

3 thin slices bacon
1 package (8 ounces) cream cheese
2 cups (8 ounces) finely grated Cheddar cheese
¼ cup mayonnaise (or salad dressing)
¼ cup chopped chives

1. Place bacon between paper towels (see page 139) or on bacon grill and cover with paper towel. Microwave on HIGH (100%) for 2 to 3 minutes or until crispy. Crumble and set aside.

2. Place cream cheese in a 1 quart casserole. Microwave on LOW (30%) for 1 to 1½ minutes or until softened.

3. Stir in Cheddar cheese, bacon, mayonnaise and chives until smooth.

4. Spread immediately onto crackers.

Tip: Securely cover cheese spread and store in refrigerator up to 1 week. Before serving, place 10 to 15 crackers on a serving dish. Spread each cracker with 1 tablespoon mixture and microwave on HIGH (100%) for 30 to 45 seconds.

Recipe yield: about 2½ cups

They'll talk about your Creamy Shrimp Dip.

2. Stir in remaining ingredients. Cover with plastic wrap or a tight fitting lid.

3. Microwave on MEDIUM (50%) for 6 to 8 minutes or until hot and bubbly. Stir twice during cooking.

4. Serve with crackers or raw vegetables.

Recipe yield: about 2 cups

ZIPPY SEAFOOD DIP

Power Level: LOW [30%] and MEDIUM [50%]
Total Cooking Time: 5 to 6½ minutes
Temperature Probe: 130° to 140°

1 package (8 ounces) cream cheese
1 can (7 ounces) shrimp, rinsed and drained
2 teaspoons chili sauce
1 teaspoon horseradish
1 teaspoon instant minced onion
1 teaspoon Worcestershire sauce

1. Place cream cheese in a 1 quart casserole. Microwave on LOW (30%) for 1 to 1½ minutes or until softened.

2. Stir in remaining ingredients. Cover with plastic wrap or tight fitting lid.

3. Microwave on MEDIUM (50%) for 4 to 5 minutes or until hot and bubbly. Stir halfway through cooking.

4. Serve with crackers or raw vegetables.

Variation:

CRAB DIP

1 package (8 ounces) cream cheese
1 can (7 ounces) crabmeat, rinsed and drained
2 tablespoons mayonnaise
1 tablespoon instant minced onion
1 tablespoon lemon juice
1 teaspoon horseradish

1. Follow Zippy Seafood Dip as directed.

Recipe yield: about 2 cups

SWEET SOY DIP

Power Level: HIGH [100%]
Total Cooking Time: 2 to 3 minutes
Temperature Probe: 130° to 140°

⅓ cup orange marmalade
¼ cup soy sauce
⅓ cup water
2 tablespoons orange juice
Dash of garlic powder

1. Combine all ingredients in small bowl or 2 cup measure.

2. Microwave on HIGH (100%) for 2 to 3 minutes or until boiling.

3. Serve as a marinade or dip for bite-size meatballs or wieners.

Recipe yield: about 1 cup

Place cream cheese and soup *in 1-quart casserole.*

Stir from outside to inside *halfway through cooking.*

CREAMY SHRIMP DIP

Power Level: MEDIUM [50%]
Total Cooking Time: 4 to 6 minutes

1 package (8 ounces) cream cheese
1 can Cheddar cheese soup
1 small can shrimp, rinsed, drained and chopped
2 tablespoons dry white wine (optional)

2 tablespoons lemon juice
1 teaspoon chopped chives

1. Place cream cheese and soup in a 1 quart casserole.

2. Microwave on MEDIUM (50%) for 4 to 6 minutes or until cream cheese is melted. Stir halfway through cooking.

3. Stir in shrimp, wine, lemon juice and chives until smooth.

4. Serve with crackers or fresh vegetables.

Recipe yield: about 2 cups

TANGY CHEESE DIP

Power Level: MEDIUM [50%]
Total Cooking Time: 10 to 13 minutes
Temperature Probe: 130° to 140°

1 package (8 ounces) cream cheese
1 cup (4 ounces) grated smoked Cheddar cheese
⅓ cup beer
1 tablespoon chopped chives
1 teaspoon horseradish
½ teaspoon dry mustard
Dash of cayenne pepper

1. Place cream cheese and Cheddar cheese in a 1 quart casserole. Microwave on MEDIUM (50%) for 4 to 5 minutes or until melted.

Chafing Dish

Guests will think you spent hours on these sensational appetizers. They're made in minutes in the microwave oven, then elegantly served in the warmth of a chafing dish.

Cover appetizers in the oven to hold in moisture and make cooking faster and more even. The type of covering determines how much moisture is retained.

Easy Chicken Wing Dings [p. 42]
Aloha Pigs [this page]

ALOHA PIGS

Power Level: HIGH [100%]
Total Cooking Time: 6 to 8 minutes
Temperature Probe: 130° to 140°

¾ cup brown sugar
½ cup cider vinegar
½ cup water
1 package (1 pound) wieners, cut each in eighths
1 green pepper, cut in ½ inch squares
1 can (8 ounces) pineapple chunks, undrained

1. Combine all ingredients in a 10 x 6 x 1¾ inch baking dish. Stir well to coat fruit, green pepper and wieners with sauce.

2. Cover with plastic wrap. Microwave on HIGH (100%) for 6 to 8 minutes or until hot and bubbly. Stir halfway through cooking.

HAWAIIAN HAM CUBES

Power Level: HIGH [100%]
Total Cooking Time: 10 to 12 minutes
Temperature Probe: 130° to 140°

1 jar (10 ounces) orange marmalade
1 tablespoon soy sauce
1 pound ham, cut into ½ inch cubes
1 can (8 ounces) pineapple chunks, drained
1 large green pepper, cut into ½ inch squares

1. Mix marmalade and soy sauce in a 2 quart casserole. Stir in remaining ingredients until well coated. Cover with a tight fitting lid or plastic wrap.

2. Microwave on HIGH (100%) for 10 to 12 minutes or until hot and bubbly. Stir halfway through cooking.

Recipe yield: 10 to 12 servings

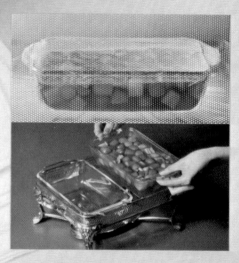

It's convenient *to prepare appetizers right in the dish which fits your chafing dish. Remove from the microwave and elegantly serve to your guests.*

BACON ROLL UPS

WATERMELON

Power Level: HIGH [100%]
Total Cooking Time: 5 to 6 minutes

Watermelon pickles
4 strips sliced bacon, cut in thirds

1. Drain pickles. Pat dry. Cut into bite-size pieces.

2. Wrap each piece with bacon and secure with wooden pick. Place on trivet in a baking dish or on bacon grill. Cover with a paper towel.

3. Microwave on HIGH (100%) for 5 to 6 minutes or until bacon is crisp.

PINEAPPLE

Dust ½ cup fresh pineapple cubes with 1 tablespoon powdered sugar. Pour 2 tablespoons of rum over cubes. Let stand for 30 to 45 minutes. Drain pineapple and pat dry. Continue Watermelon Roll Ups recipe as directed in steps 2 and 3.

BANANA PEANUT BUTTER

Cut 1 ripe banana into bite size slices. Spread with peanut butter and sandwich together. Cut each sandwich in half lengthwise. Continue Watermelon Roll Ups recipe as directed in steps 2 and 3.

SCALLOP

Drain and rinse 12 bite size scallops. Marinate in 1 tablespoon Teriyaki sauce for several hours or overnight. Microwave 6 slices of bacon on HIGH (100%) for 2 to 3 minutes before wrapping scallops. Cut each slice in half. Continue Watermelon Roll Ups recipe as directed in step 2. Microwave roll ups on HIGH (100%) for 2 to 3 minutes or until scallops are tender.

WATER CHESTNUT

Drain 12 small water chestnuts. Marinate in 2 tablespoons brown sugar and 3 tablespoons Worcestershire sauce for several hours or overnight. Continue Watermelon Roll Ups recipe as directed in steps 2 and 3.

MUSHROOM

Clean and trim stems from 12 fresh mushrooms. Continue Watermelon Roll Ups recipe as directed in steps 2 and 3.

OLIVE

Drain 12 stuffed green olives. Wrap bacon around olive. Sprinkle with brown sugar. Continue Watermelon Roll Ups recipe as directed in steps 2 and 3.

SHRIMP AND MUSHROOMS IN BUTTER SAUCE

Power Level: HIGH [100%]
Total Cooking Time: 4 to 5½ minutes

½ cup butter (or margarine)
¼ cup lemon juice
2 tablespoons minced onion
1 tablespoon chopped parsley
½ teaspoon minced garlic
½ teaspoon salt
¼ teaspoon pepper
2 cups (8 ounces) small fresh mushrooms
1 pound medium shrimp, peeled and deveined

1. Combine all ingredients except mushrooms and shrimp in a 2 quart casserole.

2. Microwave on HIGH (100%) for 1 to 1½ minutes or until almost boiling.

3. Add mushrooms and shrimp. Cover with waxed paper. Microwave on HIGH (100%) for 3 to 4 minutes or until shrimp is tender.

4. Serve with cocktail picks in a chafing dish.

Recipe yield: 36 appetizers

TANGY HORSERADISH MEATBALLS

Power Level: HIGH [100%]
Total Cooking Time: 6 to 7 minutes for each dish

1 pound ground beef chuck
1 egg
½ cup dry bread crumbs
1 cup finely chopped celery
2 tablespoons prepared horseradish

1. Mix together all ingredients.

2. Form into 1 inch balls. Place half the meatballs in a baking dish. Cover with waxed paper.

3. Microwave on HIGH (100%) for 6 to 7 minutes or until meatballs are no longer pink. Rearrange meatballs halfway through cooking. Repeat with remaining meatballs.

4. Marinate in Sweet Soy Dip (page 39) for 1 hour. Microwave on HIGH (100%) for 1 to 1½ minutes or until heated through.

Recipe yield: 68 meatballs

Rearrange meatballs *halfway through cooking, bringing outside meatballs to inside and vice versa.*

Cover with plastic wrap or tight fitting lid *to hold in moisture and to steam food. Pleat plastic wrap to allow steam to expand.*

Cover with waxed paper or paper towels. *Waxed paper retains some moisture but not enough to steam food. Towels absorb excess moisture and cut down spattering.*

Stir or rearrange *food halfway through cooking. Bring outside food to center and center food to outside.*

Insert temperature probe *deep into sauce surrounding Hawaiian Ham Cubes or Aloha Pigs. Bring probe to 130° to 140°. When cooked, lift off plastic wrap carefully from far end, allowing steam to escape.*

Separate chicken wings *into three sections by cutting at joints.*

Spear~it Food

For easy pickings, many appetizers can be speared with toothpicks before cooking.

Select a serving dish that will withstand heat. Arrange with tender food toward the center. Spear with plain wooden toothpicks or picks with cellophane frills.

EASY CHICKEN WING DINGS

Power Level: HIGH [100%] and
MEDIUM-HIGH [70%]
Total Cooking Time: 10½ to
12¾ minutes

¼ cup butter (or margarine)
1 dozen chicken wings
½ cup dry bread crumbs
2 tablespoons finely chopped almonds
½ teaspoon salt
½ teaspoon dried parsley
Dash of garlic powder
Dash of pepper
Paprika

1. Place butter in a baking dish. Microwave on HIGH (100%) for 30 to 45 seconds or until melted.

2. Rinse and dry chicken pieces. Cut wings at joints, separating each into three sections. Discard tip sections (or use in soup). Dip remaining sections into melted butter.

3. Combine bread crumbs, almonds, salt, parsley, garlic powder and pepper. Coat chicken pieces.

4. Place half of the Wing Dings in a dish with small end toward middle. Sprinkle with paprika.

5. Microwave, twelve Wing Dings at a time, on MEDIUM-HIGH (70%) for 10 to 12 minutes or until tender. Repeat with remaining Wing Dings.

Recipe yield: 24 appetizers

PEPPERONI CRISP

Power Level: HIGH [100%]
Total Cooking Time: 45 seconds
to 1 minute

8 ounces thinly sliced pepperoni
1 tablespoon lemon juice

1. Place 10 to 12 slices pepperoni in a 9 inch pie plate. Sprinkle with lemon juice. Cover with a paper towel.

2. Microwave on HIGH (100%) for 45 seconds to 1 minute or until sizzling hot.

3. Serve warm or cool with chip dip.

Recipe yield: 4 to 5 dozen appetizers

CHICKEN KIEV APPETIZERS

Power Level: HIGH [100%]
Total Cooking Time: 3 to 4 minutes

2 chicken breasts, cut lengthwise, boned and skinned
¼ cup butter (or margarine), in a stick
2 tablespoons chopped parsley
½ teaspoon onion salt
Butter (or margarine), melted
Paprika
Seasoned salt

1. Pound chicken until ¼ inch thick.

2. Cut butter lengthwise into four sections. Place 1 piece of butter at narrow end of each chicken breast. Sprinkle with parsley and onion salt.

3. Fold over sides to cover butter. Roll up in jelly-roll fashion starting at butter end.

4. Refrigerate for ½ hour.

5. Cut into bite-size pieces and secure with toothpicks.

6. Place in a baking dish. Brush with melted butter. Sprinkle with seasoned salt and paprika. Cover with waxed paper.

7. Microwave on HIGH (100%) 3 to 4 minutes. Allow to stand 3 minutes before serving.

Recipe yield: 28 appetizers

Dip wings *into melted butter. Combine bread crumbs, almonds and seasonings. Coat chicken pieces.*

Arrange chicken wings *with tender parts toward center.*

SEASONED VEGETABLE TRAY

Power Level: HIGH [100%]
Total Cooking Time: About 10½ to 13
minutes for each
plate

⅓ cup butter (or margarine)
½ teaspoon onion salt
¼ teaspoon thyme
¼ teaspoon parsley
1 pound fresh broccoli
1 small head cauliflower
2 medium zucchini
2 medium tomatoes, cut into wedges
¼ cup Parmesan cheese

1. Combine butter, onion salt, thyme and parsley in a 1 cup measure or bowl. Microwave on HIGH (100%) for 45 seconds to 1 minute or until melted. Set aside.

2. Trim and cut broccoli and cauliflower into florets. Alternately arrange groups of the florets around the edge of two 10-inch serving platters. Slice zucchini and fill the center of the plate. Cover with plastic wrap.

3. Microwave each plate on HIGH (100%) for 9 to 11 minutes or until vegetables are almost tender. Drain off excess liquid.

4. Arrange tomato wedges on vegetable platter.

5. Pour butter mixture over vegetables and sprinkle with Parmesan cheese.

6. Microwave uncovered, on HIGH (100%) for 1½ to 2 minutes or until tomatoes are heated. Repeat with second plate.

Recipe yield: 10 to 12 servings

Arrange toothpicks *in a small attractive glass if you choose not to spear each appetizer ahead of time. Guests may select their own pick or use their fingers.*

Variation:

Follow Seasoned Vegetable Tray recipe as directed except in Step 2 place 2 packages (10 ounces each) Brussels sprouts on outside edge of a 10 inch round dish, place 2 medium sliced yellow summer squash towards inside and 1 can (16 ounces) small whole beets (drained) in middle. Continue as directed in Steps 3, 5 and 6.

A refreshing tray of
Seasoned Vegetables

Snacks

Put an extra crunch into snacks by refreshing them in your microwave. Salty snacks such as potato chips, popcorn and pretzels can be quickly converted from stale to crisp.

Occasionally stir party mixes, nuts, seeds and other dry mixtures to evenly distribute heat. Bring the mixture from outside edge to center and center to outside.

Place crackers topped with spreads or cheese in a circle for even heating.

Cut a crisscross slash through chestnut shells to allow steam to escape. This prevents popping.

PIZZA SNACKS

Power Level: HIGH [100%]
Total Cooking Time: 1 to 1½ minutes

2 English muffins, cut in half and toasted
2 tablespoons catsup
16 slices pepperoni
½ cup (2 ounces) grated mozzarella cheese
1 tablespoon Parmesan cheese
½ teaspoon dried Italian seasoning

1. Place English muffins on a paper plate or a paper towel lined dinner plate.

2. Brush each with catsup. Layer with 4 pieces of pepperoni and 2 tablespoons of mozzarella cheese.

3. Mix together Parmesan cheese and Italian seasoning. Sprinkle over each English muffin half. *

4. Microwave on HIGH (100%) for 1 to 1½ minutes or until cheese just begins to melt.

Recipe yield: 4 servings

*Tip: Cut into fourths for smaller snacks.

CHEDDARY BACON GO 'ROUNDS

Power Level: HIGH [100%]
Total Cooking Time: 3 to 4 minutes

5 thin slices bacon, cut in half lengthwise
Mustard or catsup
½ cup fine Cheddar cheese cracker crumbs
10 long bread sticks, any flavor

1. Dredge one side of bacon strips in mustard or catsup.

2. Roll dredged side of bacon around bread stick in "barber pole fashion".

3. Place on two thicknesses of paper towels in microwave.

4. Microwave on HIGH (100%) until bacon is crispy.

5. Roll sticks in cracker crumbs to coat outside.

Amount	Time
2	45 sec.-1 min.
4	1-1½ min.
6	1½-2 min.
10	3-4 min.

Variation:

SWISS BACON GO 'ROUNDS

Follow Cheddary Bacon Go 'Rounds recipe except substitute Swiss cheese cracker crumbs for Cheddar cheese cracker crumbs.

Recipe yield: 10 sticks

WESTERN BEEF JERKY

Power Level: LOW [30%]
Total Cooking Time: 30 to 35 minutes for each half pound

1 pound beef round steak, trimmed
¼ cup liquid smoke
2 teaspoons seasoned salt
¼ teaspoon pepper

1. Freeze meat partially.

2. Trim off fat and cut into ¼ inch thick strips.

3. Layer strips ½ inch deep in a 2 quart casserole. Sprinkle with liquid smoke, salt and pepper. Repeat layers.

4. Place a plate on top of meat. Weigh plate down with several filled cans. Chill overnight.

5. Drain meat and pat dry. Place ½ pound of meat in a single layer on paper towels in microwave.

6. Microwave on LOW (30%) for 30 to 35 minutes or until dried. Rearrange pieces occasionally to dry evenly. Replace paper towels if needed. Continue with the other ½ pound of meat.

PARTY MIX

Power Level: HIGH [100%]
Total Cooking Time: 8 to 10 minutes

3 cups toasted oat cereal
2 cups bite-size wheat square cereal
2 cups bite-size rice square cereal
2 cups thin pretzel sticks
½ pound mixed nuts
½ cup cooking oil
1 tablespoon Worcestershire sauce
2 teaspoons garlic salt
2 teaspoons seasoned salt

1. Mix all ingredients in a 3 quart casserole.

2. Microwave on HIGH (100%) for 8 to 10 minutes or until cereal is hot and crisp. Stir occasionally during cooking.

3. Place in an airtight container. Store in a cool place or freeze.

Recipe yield: about 10 cups party mix

CANDIED PECANS

Power Level: HIGH [100%]
Total Cooking Time: 5½ to
7¾ minutes

¼ cup butter (or margarine)
½ cup brown sugar
1 teaspoon cinnamon
¼ teaspoon ground cloves
2 cups pecan halves

1. Place butter in a 1 quart casserole. Microwave on HIGH (100%) for 30 to 45 seconds or until melted.

2. Stir in sugar, cinnamon and cloves. Microwave on HIGH (100%) for 1 to 2 minutes or until sugar is dissolved.

3. Stir in nuts until well coated. Microwave on HIGH (100%) for 4 to 5 minutes.

4. Spread out on waxed paper to cool.

Recipe yield: ½ pound

BUTTERY WALNUTS

Power Level: HIGH [100%]
Total Cooking Time: 4 to 5 minutes

1 pound walnut halves
1 tablespoon seasoned salt
¼ cup butter

1. Place walnut halves in 1½ quart casserole. Sprinkle with seasoned salt. Dot with butter.

2. Microwave on HIGH (100%) for 4 to 5 minutes. Stir until butter coats the nuts evenly. Serve warm or cool.

Recipe yield: 1 pound

ROASTED NUTS AND SEEDS

Power Level: HIGH [100%]

General Instructions:

1. Place nuts in a single layer in a 10x6x1¾ inch baking dish.

2. Microwave on HIGH (100%) for amount of time given for type of nuts. Stir halfway through cooking.

3. Store in an airtight container.

PUMPKIN AND SQUASH SEEDS

Rinse fibers from 1 cup seeds. Sprinkle a light, even layer of seasoned salt in bottom of baking dish before adding seeds. Drizzle seeds with 1 teaspoon melted butter (or margarine). Microwave for 6 to 7 minutes or until crisp. Shake through sieve or collander to remove excess salt.

SUNFLOWER SEEDS

Sprinkle a light, even layer of salt in bottom of baking dish before adding seeds. Microwave 1 cup hulled sunflower seeds 5 to 6 minutes or until crisp. Shake through sieve or collander to remove excess salt.

PEANUTS

Microwave 1 cup of raw peanuts 6 to 8 minutes. Drizzle with 1 teaspoon cooking oil and sprinkle with seasoned salt. Microwave for an additional 45 seconds to 1 minute or until golden.

ALMONDS

Microwave 1 cup whole or slivered almonds for 6 to 8 minutes or until golden. For added flavor serve sprinkled with salt.

CASHEWS

Microwave 1 cup of raw cashews for 10 to 11 minutes. Drizzle with 1 teaspoon cooking oil and sprinkle with seasoned salt. Microwave for an additional 45 seconds to 1 minute or until golden.

CHESTNUTS

Cut a crisscross slash through the shells of 1½ to 2 dozen chestnuts to prevent popping during cooking. Microwave for 2 to 4 minutes. Allow to stand 5 minutes or until cool enough to peel.

SPICY NUTS AND SEEDS

Drizzle roasted nuts or seeds with 2 teaspoons melted butter (or margarine). Then sprinkle with ½ teaspoon chili powder, ¼ teaspoon paprika, ¼ teaspoon garlic salt and a dash of cayenne pepper. Microwave on HIGH (100%) for an additional 45 seconds to 1 minute or until flavors are well blended. Store in refrigerator.

Candied Pecans, Peanuts, Almonds, Pumpkin and Squash Seeds make wholesome snacks.

Beverages

Chill-chasing beverages are quickly heated right in the cup or serving utensil. Use glass, ceramic, pottery, Styrofoam or "hot drink" paper containers.

Do not use containers made of metal or with metal trim. Also check containers with wicker handles. Many of these are metal wrapped in wicker.

Boil a cup of water in 2½ to 3 minutes. *Cold water will take longer to boil than hot water.*

Arrange cups in a circle *with at least ½ inch space between each cup. This assures even heating.*

Milk-base beverages boil over *rapidly. To avoid boil overs watch these beverages the first time they are heated in your utensils. Record the time for future use.*

Immediately adding *an instant mix to boiling water causes the mixture to boil up and over the cup.* **Wait 15 to 30 seconds,** *then add the instant mix.*

Save that brewed coffee! *When reheated in the microwave, brewed coffee retains its freshness. Heat just until serving temperature.*

BEVERAGE GUIDE

Boiling Water - for coffee, tea, etc.
Power Level: HIGH [100%]

6 oz. cups
1 cup 2-3 min.
2 cups 3½-4½ min.
4 cups 6-7 min.

8 oz. mugs
1 mug 2½-3½ min.
2 mugs 5-6 min.
4 mugs 9-10 min.

Note: Heating 6 cups water in a 2-qt. bowl or utensil takes 12-15 min.

Reheating - to serving temperature coffee, tea, other water based beverages.
Power Level: HIGH [100%]
Temperature Probe: 150° - 160°

6 oz. cups
1 cup 1-1¼ min.
2 cups 1½-2 min.
4 cups 2½-3 min.

8 oz. mugs
1 mug 1½-2 min.
2 mugs 2½-3 min.
4 mugs 5½-6 min.

Milk, Chocolate or high sugar content
Power Level: MEDIUM-HIGH [70%]
Temperature Probe: 130° - 140°

6 oz. cups
1 cup 2-3 min.
2 cups 3-4 min.
4 cups 4½-5½ min.

8 oz. mugs
1 mug 2½-3 min.
2 mugs 3½-4½ min.
4 mugs 6-8 min.

Note: Heating 6 cups milk in a 2-qt. bowl or utensil takes 14-16 min.

Use the temperature probe to *heat beverages to the exact serving temperature. Milk-base beverages are heated to 130° to 140°. Other beverages are heated to 150° to 160°.*

It's easy to prepare and beautifully serve hot beverages that will create a warm, friendly atmosphere at every gathering.

MIX-AND-STORE HOT CHOCOLATE

Power Level: HIGH [100%]
Total Cooking Time: 1¼ to 1½ minutes per cup
Temperature Probe: 130° to 140°

4½ cups instant nonfat dry milk
1 cup plus 2 tablespoons non-dairy creamer
¾ cup cocoa
⅔ cup powdered sugar

1. Combine all ingredients until well blended.

2. Store mix in an airtight container.

To make hot chocolate: Microwave ¾ cup of water on HIGH (100%) for 1¼ to 1½ minutes or until steaming. Stir in ⅓ cup of hot chocolate mix.

Recipe yield: 18 servings or 6 cups mix

HOT EGGNOG

Power Level: MEDIUM-HIGH [70%]
Total Cooking Time: 10 to 12 minutes
Temperature Probe: 130° to 140°

4 eggs, separated
¾ cup sugar
¼ teaspoon salt
3 cups milk
1 teaspoon rum flavoring (or vanilla)

1. Combine egg yolks, ½ cup sugar and salt in a 2 quart mixing bowl or casserole. Beat until thick and lemon colored. Stir in milk and rum flavoring.

2. Microwave on MEDIUM - HIGH (70%) for 10 to 12 minutes or until mixture is steaming. Stir occasionally.

3. Beat egg whites until foamy. Beat in ¼ cup sugar until soft peaks form.

4. Carefully fold milk mixture into egg whites until well blended.

5. Serve topped with grated chocolate or nutmeg.

Recipe yield: 8 to 10 servings

HOT TOMATO COCKTAIL

Power Level: HIGH [100%]
Total Cooking Time: 2 to 3 minutes
Temperature Probe: 150° to 160°

1 cup tomato juice
1 teaspoon lemon juice
¼ teaspoon seasoned salt
Dash of hot pepper sauce
Dash of Worcestershire sauce

1. Mix together all ingredients in an 8 ounce mug.

2. Microwave on HIGH (100%) for 2 to 3 minutes or until steaming.

Hot Eggnog,
Rosy Cranberry Punch
and Mocha Dessert Drink

HOT CHOCOLATE

Power Level: MEDIUM-HIGH [70%]
Total Cooking Time: 1½ to 2 minutes
Temperature Probe: 130° to 140°

⅔ cup milk
1 to 2 tablespoons chocolate syrup
¼ teaspoon vanilla

1. Pour milk into a mug or cup.

2. Stir in chocolate syrup and vanilla. Microwave on MEDIUM-HIGH (70%) for 1½ to 2 minutes or until steaming.

Recipe yield: 1 serving

MOCHA DESSERT DRINK

Power Level: HIGH [100%]
Total Cooking Time: 5 to 6 minutes

1½ cups water
2 tablespoons chocolate syrup
2 teaspoons instant coffee
2 teaspoons powdered sugar
2 cinnamon sticks
Whipped cream or scoop of vanilla ice cream
Ground nutmeg

1. Place water in a 2 cup measure. Microwave on HIGH (100%) for 5 to 6 minutes or until boiling.

2. Stir in chocolate syrup, instant coffee and powdered sugar. Pour into two large mugs.

3. Add cinnamon stick to each mug. Top each with whipped cream or a scoop of ice cream. Sprinkle with nutmeg.

Recipe yield: 2 servings

SPICED TEA

Power Level: HIGH [100%]
Total Cooking Time: 2½ to 3½ minutes
Temperature Probe: 150° to 160°

1½ cups instant tea
1 jar (9 ounces) orange flavored instant breakfast drink
1 package (3 ounces) lemonade mix
¾ cup sugar
1 teaspoon cinnamon
1 teaspoon ground cloves
¾ teaspoon ginger

1. Combine all ingredients until well blended.

2. Store mix in an airtight container.

To make 1 cup of Spiced Tea: Microwave 1 cup of water on HIGH (100%) for 2½ to 3½ minutes or until boiling. Stir in 2 teaspoons of tea mix.

Recipe yield: 64 servings or 3½ cups

SPICY HOT TODDY

Power Level: MEDIUM-HIGH [70%]
Total Cooking Time: 2 to 3 minutes
Temperature Probe: 150° to 160°

1 jigger (3 tablespoons) light rum
¾ cup water
1 tablespoon brown sugar
¼ teaspoon lemon juice
2 whole cloves
1 cinnamon stick

1. Combine rum, water, sugar, lemon juice, cloves, and cinnamon stick in a mug.

2. Microwave on MEDIUM-HIGH (70%) for 2 to 3 minutes or until steaming. Remove spices. Serve immediately.

Recipe yield: 1 serving

IRISH COFFEE

Power Level: HIGH [100%]
Total Cooking Time: 2 to 3 minutes
Temperature Probe: 150° to 160°

1 jigger (3 tablespoons) Irish Whiskey (or Irish Mist liqueur)
¾ cup water
1 tablespoon instant coffee
1 teaspoon sugar
Whipped cream

1. Pour Irish Whiskey into a mug or coffee cup. Add water. Stir in coffee and sugar.

2. Microwave on HIGH (100%) for 1½ to 2 minutes or until steaming. Stir to dissolve sugar.

3. Top with whipped cream.

Recipe yield: 1 serving

SWEET BUTTERED RUM

Power Level: MEDIUM-HIGH [70%]
Total Cooking Time: 3 to 4 minutes
Temperature Probe: 150° to 160°

2 jiggers (6 tablespoons) rum
2 tablespoons honey
1¼ cups water
2 teaspoons butter

1. Combine rum, honey and water in a 16-ounce mug or divide into two 8-ounce mugs. Microwave on MEDIUM-HIGH (70%) for 3 to 4 minutes or until steaming.

2. Stir in butter until melted.

Recipe yield: 1 to 2 servings

Spicy Tip

In some spicy beverages, you can wrap the spices in a small cloth bag and suspend it in the liquid. This eliminates straining out such spices as cloves or cinnamon sticks when serving.

ENGLISH WASSAIL

Power Level: HIGH [100%]
Total Cooking Time: 10 to 12 minutes
Temperature Probe: 150° to 160°

1 quart apple cider
1 tart apple, sliced
½ cup brown sugar
½ cup orange juice
2 tablespoons lemon juice
2 cinnamon sticks
1 teaspoon allspice
½ teaspoon ground cloves
¼ teaspoon nutmeg

1. Combine all ingredients in a 3 quart casserole.

2. Microwave on HIGH (100%) for 10 to 12 minutes or until steaming. Serve immediately.

Recipe yield: 8 to 10 servings

ROSY CRANBERRY PUNCH

Power Level: HIGH [100%] and MEDIUM [50%]
Total Cooking Time: 30 to 35 minutes

1 quart cranberry juice
1 quart apple juice
2 tablespoons lemon juice
2 tablespoons sugar
4 cinnamon sticks each 2" long
¾ teaspoon whole cloves
1 lemon, sliced thin

1. Combine all ingredients, except lemon, in a 3 quart casserole. Cover with a tight fitting lid or plastic wrap.

2. Microwave on HIGH (100%) for 20 to 25 minutes. Stir, then microwave on MEDIUM (50%) for an additional 10 minutes or until flavor is well blended. Remove spices with a slotted spoon.

3. Garnish with lemon slices.

Recipe yield: 14 servings (½ cup each)

MULLED WINE

Power Level: HIGH [100%]
Total Cooking Time: 12 to 14 minutes
Temperature Probe: 150° to 160°

1 quart red wine
2½ cups orange juice
¾ cup sugar
½ cup lemon juice
16 whole cloves
2 cinnamon sticks
1 lemon, sliced

1. Combine all ingredients except lemon in a 3 quart casserole or pitcher.

2. Microwave on HIGH (100%) for 12 to 14 minutes or until steaming.

3. Garnish with lemon slices.

Recipe yield: 8 servings

Breads, rolls, doughnuts and coffee-cakes can be defrosted and heated in one step. Keep in mind that because of their high sugar content, fillings and icings attract microwave energy and are heated very quickly. Avoid overheating which will cause breads to become hard and dry.

CHOCOLATE-CINNAMON ROLLS

Power Level: MEDIUM-HIGH [70%]
Total Cooking Time: 2 to 3 minutes
for four rolls

½ cup chocolate morsels
¼ cup chopped nuts
2 tablespoons honey
1 can (9.5 ounces) refrigerated cinnamon rolls

1. Mix together chocolate morsels, nuts and honey. Place one tablespoon of mixture into 8 individual custard cups.

2. Place one cinnamon roll, cut into fourths, over chocolate chip mixture.

3. Microwave, four at a time, on MEDIUM-HIGH (70%) for 2 to 3 minutes, or until surface springs back when lightly touched. Rearrange halfway through cooking.

4. Invert custard cups immediately onto a serving dish. Leave cups over rolls about 3 minutes, then remove. Serve warm. Repeat with remaining rolls.

Recipe yield: 8 rolls.

GARLIC BREAD

Power Level: LOW [30%] and
HIGH [100%]
Total Cooking Time:1¼ to 1¾ minutes

1 loaf Italian bread
½ cup butter (or margarine)
2 tablespoons Parmesan cheese
1½ teaspoons garlic powder

1. Slice bread, if not already sliced.

2. Place butter in an 8 ounce measuring cup. Microwave on LOW (30%) for 30 to 45 seconds or until softened.

3. Stir in cheese and garlic powder until well blended. Spread slices of bread with butter mixture.

4. Wrap bread in waxed paper. Place in long paper bag. Tie end with yarn or fold under.

5. Microwave on HIGH (100%) for 45 seconds to 1 minute or until warm to the touch.

6. Slash bag with an "X" at top and tear back top. Serve in ready made basket.

Breads

Quick breads and yeast breads are cooked in a jiffy with the microwave. And it takes only seconds to defrost, refresh or reheat breads and rolls.

ROLL O' BREAD

Power Level: MEDIUM [50%]
Total Cooking Time: 7 to 9 minutes

1 can (10 ounces) refrigerated biscuits
1 egg yolk
1 tablespoon water

1. Remove rolls from package but do not separate rolls.

2. Coat entire surface with a mixture of egg yolk and water.

3. Roll in desired topping mixture (see page 53).

4. Place in a 10x6x1¾ inch baking dish.

5. Microwave on MEDIUM (50%) for 7 to 9 minutes or until surface springs back when lightly touched.

6. Remove immediately and place on a cooling rack. Cool completely.

Recipe yield: 1 loaf

PECAN CARAMEL RING

Power Level: HIGH [100%] and
MEDIUM-HIGH [70%]
Total Cooking Time: 10 to 13 minutes

2 tablespoons butter (or margarine)
½ cup dark brown sugar
2 tablespoons light corn syrup
¼ cup maraschino cherries, halved
¼ cup pecan halves
1 roll (10 ounces) refrigerated buttermilk biscuits

1. Dot butter in the bottom of a microwave ring mold.

2. Add brown sugar and corn syrup. Microwave on HIGH (100%) for 2 to 3 minutes or until syrup is formed. Stir to blend.

3. Arrange cherry and pecan halves on syrup.

4. Place biscuits close together in a ring over syrup mixture. Microwave on MEDIUM-HIGH (70%) for 8 to 10 minutes. Turn dish a half turn halfway through cooking.

5. Immediately invert onto serving plate leaving dish over cake for several minutes. Serve warm.

Recipe yield: 6 to 8 servings

┌─ Bread-In-Basket tip ─┐

Dinner rolls can be heated in a napkin-lined straw basket. Microwave only until bread is slightly warm to the touch.

DEFROSTING & REHEATING CHART — Power Level: HIGH (100%)

Room Temperature		Frozen	
Biscuits, muffins, dinner rolls, buns, bagels			
1	10-12 sec.	1	30-40 sec.
2	12-15 sec.	2	45-50 sec.
3	15-20 sec.	3	50-55 sec.
4	20-25 sec.	4	1-1¼ min.
5	25-30 sec.	5	1¼-1½ min.
6	30-45 sec.	6	1½-2 min.
Sweet rolls, doughnuts and toaster pastries			
1	6-8 sec.	1	20-25 sec.
2	10-12 sec.	2	25-30 sec.
3	12-14 sec.	3	40-45 sec.
4	14-16 sec.	4	45-50 sec.
5	16-18 sec.	5	50-60 sec.
6	18-20 sec.	6	1-1¼ min.
Bread Slices			
2	5-10 sec.	2	10-15 sec.
4	10-15 sec.	4	15-20 sec.
6	15-20 sec.	6	30-40 sec.
Bread or buns in pkg.			
12 oz. pkg.	30-45 sec.	12 oz. pkg.	45-60 sec.
1 lb. pkg.	45-60 sec.	1 lb. pkg.	45-60 sec.
Coffeecake			
6½ oz.	30-45 sec.	6½ oz.	1-1½ min.
11-13 oz.	45-60 sec.	11-13 oz.	1½-2 min.
French Toast and Waffles			
1	10-15 sec.	1	30-35 sec.
2	15-20 sec.	2	35-40 sec.
3	20-25 sec.	3	40-45 sec.
4	25-30 sec.	4	45-50 sec.

Do not *use metal twist ties in the microwave. Although the ties may appear to be made of paper or plastic, they usually contain a bit of wire. These ties could cause a fire.*

Place bread *in microwave. Remove any foil wrappers or trays. Defrost on Low [30%] in plastic bag. To allow excess moisture to escape, leave the bag open at one end. For single servings, wrap in paper towel.*

┌─ Slicing tip ─┐

It's easier to slice bread if you allow it to completely cool. Then place bread on its side and cut with a serrated knife.

Bread will feel slightly warm *to the touch when both thoroughly defrosted and reheated.*

QUICK BREADS

Place Irish Soda Bread dough *in greased pie dish. Cut a cross ¼ inch deep on the top of the bread. Brush with a mixture of egg yolk and water. Microwave on Medium-High [70%] for 15 minutes. Meanwhile, preheat conventional oven to 450°. Then place bread in conventional oven and bake for 15 to 20 minutes.*

Test for doneness. *Bread is finished when a wooden skewer or tester inserted near the center comes out clean.*

Remove bread from dish *and allow to finish cooling on rack. When completely cool, wrap bread in plastic wrap so it will not dry out during storage.*

IRISH SODA BREAD

Power Level: MEDIUM - HIGH [70%]
Total Cooking Time: 30 to 35 minutes

4 cups all purpose flour
¼ cup sugar
1 teaspoon salt
1 teaspoon baking powder
2 tablespoons caraway seeds
  (optional)
¼ cup butter (or margarine),
  softened
2 cups raisins
1⅓ cups buttermilk
1 egg
1 teaspoon baking soda
1 egg yolk
1 tablespoon water

1. Mix together flour, sugar, salt and baking powder. Stir in caraway seeds.

2. Cut in butter until crumbly. Stir in raisins.

3. Combine buttermilk, egg and baking soda. Stir into flour mixture until just moistened.

4. Turn dough onto lightly floured surface. Knead until smooth and satiny.

5. Shape into ball and place in greased 2 quart casserole or 9 inch pie dish.

6. Cut a cross ¼ inch deep on the top of the bread. Brush with a mixture of egg yolk and water.

7. Microwave on MEDIUM-HIGH (70%) for 15 minutes, then place in preheated (450°) conventional oven and bake for 15 to 20 minutes or until a tester inserted near center comes out clean.

Recipe yield: 1 loaf

SOUR CREAM STREUSEL COFFEECAKE

Power Level: LOW [30%] and
             MEDIUM-HIGH [70%]
Total Cooking Time: 8½ to
                    10¾ minutes

Batter:
¼ cup butter (or margarine)
1 egg
¾ cup sugar
1 teaspoon vanilla
1½ cups all purpose flour
2½ teaspoons baking powder
¼ teaspoon salt
¾ cup sour cream

Topping:
¼ cup brown sugar
2 tablespoons butter
  (or margarine), softened
2 tablespoons all purpose flour
1 teaspoon cinnamon

1. Place butter in a large glass mixing bowl. Microwave on LOW (30%) for 30 to 45 seconds or until softened. Add

egg, sugar and vanilla. Beat until light and fluffy.

2. Add dry ingredients alternately with sour cream. Beat on medium speed of mixer for 2 minutes.

3. Pour batter into 8 inch round cake dish.

4. Mix together topping ingredients until crumbly. Sprinkle over batter.

5. Microwave on MEDIUM-HIGH (70%) for 8 to 10 minutes or until cake tester inserted near center comes out clean. Turn dish a half turn halfway through cooking.

Recipe yield: 9 to 12 servings

BOSTON STEAMED BROWN BREAD

Power Level: MEDIUM [50%]
Total Cooking Time: 22 to 24 minutes
                    for each loaf

1¼ cups whole wheat flour
1¼ cups cornmeal
1¼ cups rye flour
1 tablespoon baking soda
½ teaspoon salt
2½ cups buttermilk
1 cup dark molasses
1 cup raisins

1. Sift together dry ingredients in a large mixing bowl.

2. Add buttermilk, molasses and raisins. Mix by hand until well blended.

3. Divide into 2 waxed paper lined 10x6x1¾ inch baking dishes. Cover each dish with plastic wrap.

4. Microwave, one loaf at a time, on MEDIUM (50%) for 22 to 24 minutes. Turn dish a half turn halfway through cooking. Remove plastic wrap. Place on a solid surface for 5 to 10 minutes before removing from dish.

Recipe yield: 2 loaves

NUT BREAD

Power Level: LOW [30%],
             MEDIUM-HIGH [70%]
             and HIGH [100%]
Total Cooking Time: 13½ to
                    16¾ minutes

¼ cup butter (or margarine)
¾ cup sugar
1 egg, beaten
½ teaspoon orange peel
½ teaspoon vanilla
2½ cups sifted all purpose flour
1 tablespoon baking powder
¾ teaspoon salt
1¼ cups milk
1 cup chopped nuts

1. Place butter in a large glass mixing bowl. Microwave on LOW (30%) for 30 to 45 seconds or until softened. Stir in sugar, egg, orange peel and vanilla. Beat until light and fluffy.

2. Sift together flour, baking powder and salt. Add alternately with milk, mixing by hand until blended.

3. Stir in nuts.

4. Pour batter into a waxed paper lined 10x6x1¾ inch baking dish. Cover with paper towel.

5. Microwave on MEDIUM-HIGH (70%) for 8 to 10 minutes. Then microwave on HIGH (100%) for 5 to 6 minutes or until tester inserted near center of bread comes out clean. Turn dish a half turn halfway through cooking. Immediately remove paper towel.

6. Allow to stand for 5 to 10 minutes on a solid surface before removing from pan.

Variation:
NUT BREAD RING
Follow Nut Bread recipe as directed except pour batter into a 10-inch baking ring. Microwave on MEDIUM-HIGH (70%) for 14 to 16 minutes.

Recipe yield: 1 loaf

BANANA NUT BREAD
Power Level: LOW [30%],
MEDIUM-HIGH [70%]
and HIGH [100%]
Total Cooking Time: 13½ to
16¾ minutes

¼ **cup butter (or margarine)**
1 **cup sugar**
1 **egg, beaten**
2 **teaspoons vanilla**
1¾ **cups sifted all purpose flour**
1 **tablespoon baking powder**
½ **teaspoon salt**
¾ **cup milk**
1 **cup (3 small) mashed ripe**
   bananas
½ **cup chopped nuts**

1. Place butter in a large glass mixing bowl. Microwave on LOW (30%) for 30 to 45 seconds or until softened. Add sugar, egg and vanilla. Beat until light and fluffy.

2. Sift together flour, baking powder and salt. Add alternately with milk, mixing by hand until well blended.

3. Stir in bananas and nuts.

4. Pour batter into a waxed paper lined 9x5x3 inch loaf dish. Cover with a paper towel.

5. Microwave on MEDIUM-HIGH (70%) for 8 to 10 minutes. Then microwave on HIGH (100%) for 6 to 8 minutes or until tester inserted near center of bread comes out clean. Turn

dish a half turn halfway through cooking.

6. Immediately remove paper towel. Allow to stand for 5 to 10 minutes on a solid surface before removing from pan.

Recipe yield: 1 loaf

TOPPINGS FOR BREADS AND MUFFINS
For Quick Breads and Muffins:
   Sprinkle batter with desired topping.

For Yeast Breads:
   Coat sides and bottom of dough with desired topping and sprinkle remaining topping over top of dough.

BACON
Microwave 4 slices of bacon on HIGH (100%) for 3 to 3½ minutes or until crispy. Let stand 1 minute. Crumble fine.

BACON-CHEESE
Mix ¼ cup grated Cheddar or Parmesan cheese with crumbled bacon.

BACON-ONION-GREEN PEPPER
Microwave 1 tablespoon each finely chopped onion and green pepper in 1 teaspoon butter on HIGH (100%) for 3 to 4 minutes or until tender. Mix with crumbled bacon.

BACON-CHIVE
Mix 2 tablespoons dried chopped chives with crumbled bacon.

ONION
1 can (3 ounce size) French fried onions.

PAPRIKA-CORNMEAL
Mix together 1 tablespoon paprika and 1 tablespoon cornmeal.

SEEDS
¼ cup sesame seeds, poppy seeds or celery seeds.

CINNAMON-SUGAR
Mix ¼ cup sugar and 1 teaspoon cinnamon.

CINNAMON-NUT CRUNCH
Mix ¼ cup flour, 2 tablespoons brown sugar, 2 tablespoons softened butter (or margarine), ¼ cup chopped nuts and 1 teaspoon cinnamon until crumbly.

CEREAL CRUNCH
¼ cup crushed graham cereal, granola cereal, raisin bran cereal or oatmeal.

TOFFEE CRUNCH
2 bars (¾ ounces each) crushed chocolate covered toffee bars.

TOASTED COCONUT
Place ½ cup coconut in a 9 inch pie plate. Microwave on HIGH (100%) for 1½ to 2 minutes stirring occasionally.

Using ingredients with color or adding tasty toppings can make quick breads quite attractive. Because they are not exposed to the hot, dry air of conventional baking, microwave breads tend not to brown or crust. Ingredients such as molasses, dark brown sugar and whole wheat flour add extra color.

CONVENTIONAL

MICROWAVED

FRENCH FRIED ONIONS

POPPY SEEDS

SESAME SEEDS

OATMEAL

MUFFINS

Ingredients with color *such as molasses. dark brown sugar or whole wheat flour can make muffins quite attractive. Or you might add a topping since microwave muffins do not brown or form a crust.*

Test for doneness. *Muffins are done when their surface springs back when lightly touched or when a wooden skewer or tester inserted near center comes out clean.*

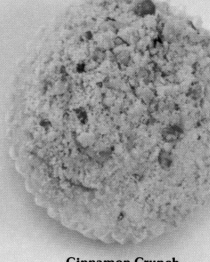

Cinnamon Crunch

Use microwave muffin pans, *6 ounce custard cups or 7 ounce Styrofoam cups. For well formed muffins, line each cup with a cupcake liner. Two liners help absorb any excess moisture.*

Remove muffins *immediately from pan or cups. Place on cooling rack.*

Toasted Coconut

Fill custard cups *or Styrofoam cups with ¼ cup batter. Use 3 tablespoons batter in muffin pan. Arrange individual cups in circle and microwave on Medium-High [70%] according to chart.*

MUFFIN COOKING CHART

Power Level: MEDIUM-HIGH (70%)	
Amount	**Time**
1	30 sec.-1 min.
2	1½-2 min.
3	2-2½ min.
4	3-3½ min.
5	4-5 min.
6	5-6 min.

Microwave

Cinnamon and Sugar

Chopped Nuts

Conventional

COUNTRY CORNBREAD

Power Level: MEDIUM-HIGH [70%]
Total Cooking Time: 8 to 10 minutes

1 cup all purpose flour
1 cup yellow cornmeal
2 tablespoons sugar
4 teaspoons baking powder
½ teaspoon salt
1 egg, beaten
1 cup milk
½ cup cooking oil

1. Sift together flour, cornmeal, sugar, baking powder and salt in a large mixing bowl.

2. Add egg, milk and cooking oil. Beat on medium speed of mixer for 1 minute.

3. Pour batter into a 10 inch ring mold.

4. Microwave on MEDIUM-HIGH (70%) for 8 to 10 minutes or until tester inserted near center of bread comes out clean. Turn dish a half turn halfway through cooking.

5. Remove immediately from pan and place on cooling rack. Serve warm.

Recipe yield: 1 ring

Variation:
CORNBREAD MUFFINS

Follow Country Cornbread as directed except place 3 tablespoons batter in paper lined microwave muffin pan or ¼ cup batter in 6 ounce custard cups or 7 ounce Styrofoam cups. Sprinkle bacon mixture over tops. Microwave on MEDIUM-HIGH (70%) until tester inserted near center comes out clean. (Follow muffin cooking chart on page 54 for times). Rearrange muffins halfway through cooking.

MICRO MUFFINS

Power Level: HIGH [100%] and
MEDIUM-HIGH [70%]

¼ cup butter (or margarine)
1 egg, beaten
1 cup milk
2 cups all purpose flour
⅓ cup sugar
1 tablespoon baking powder
½ teaspoon salt

1. Place butter in a small glass mixing bowl. Microwave on HIGH (100%) for 30 to 45 seconds or until melted.

2. Mix together egg and milk until well blended. Stir into melted butter.

3. Mix together dry ingredients in a large mixing bowl. Make a well in center.

4. Pour liquid mixture into well. Stir just until dry ingredients are moistened. Mixture should appear lumpy.

5. Place 3 tablespoons batter in each paper lined microwave muffin pan or ¼ cup batter in each paper lined 6 ounce custard cup or 7 ounce Styrofoam cup.

6. Microwave on MEDIUM-HIGH (70%) until a tester inserted near center comes out clean. (Follow muffin cooking chart on page 54 for times.) Turn dish or rearrange halfway through cooking.

Recipe yield: 10 custard cup muffins or
18 muffin pan muffins

BRAN MUFFINS

Power Level: MEDIUM-HIGH [70%]

2 cups whole bran cereal
2 cups all purpose flour
1 cup sugar
4 teaspoons baking powder
1 teaspoon salt
½ cup cooking oil
2 eggs
1½ cups milk
1 cup chopped nuts

1. Mix together bran cereal, flour, sugar, baking powder and salt in a large mixing bowl.

2. Mix together eggs, oil and milk. Pour into dry ingredients. Stir just until dry ingredients are moistened. Mixture should appear lumpy.

3. Place 3 tablespoons batter in each paper lined microwave muffin pan or ¼ cup batter in each paper lined 6 ounce custard cup or 7 ounce Styrofoam cup. Sprinkle chopped nuts on top of muffins.

4. Microwave on MEDIUM-HIGH (70%) until a tester inserted near center comes out clean. (Follow muffin cooking chart on page 54 for times). Turn dish or rearrange muffins halfway through cooking.

Variation:
BRAN BREAD

Prepare Bran Muffins recipe as directed in steps 1 and 2. Pour batter into a 10 inch baking ring. Microwave on MEDIUM-HIGH (70%) for 16 to 18 minutes or until tester inserted near center of bread comes out clean. Turn dish a half turn halfway through cooking. Allow to stand on a solid surface for 5 to 10 minutes before removing from pan. Serve warm or cool. Makes 1 (10 inch) ring.

Recipe yield: 10 custard cup muffins or
18 muffin pan muffins

YEAST BREADS

Microwave breads have no crust so it's a snap to make canapes and tea sandwiches. Kids especially enjoy sandwiches made with these special breads.

Place dough in dish. *If desired, first roll dough in a topping mixture. Cover dish with a warm, damp cloth. Place a dry cloth over the damp one. Allow dough to rise [proof].*

Proofing: *Reduce rising time by starting proofing of dough in the microwave. Cover dough [in glass bowl or baking dish] with a warm, damp cloth, then a dry cloth. Microwave on High [100%] for 25 seconds. Turn dough over and allow to stand 2 minutes. Microwave on High [100%] for 25 seconds. Turn dough over and allow to stand 15 minutes. Microwave on High [100%] for 25 seconds. Allow to finish rising in a warm place or in the microwave until dough is double original size. [This time will usually be half of original rising time.]*

You can use this microwave method of proofing bread to shorten your conventional bread baking time as well.

Microwave yeast bread *on lower power settings to achieve the best volume and quality in the finished product.*

Test for doneness. *The surface of the bread will appear dry and will spring back when lightly touched. Overcooking can make bread dry, chewy and hard.*

Remove bread *from microwave and immediately remove bread from dish. Place bread on cooling rack. When completely cool, wrap securely to preserve freshness.*

EASY OATMEAL BREAD
Power Level: HIGH [100%] and
MEDIUM [50%]
Total Cooking Time: 23 to 26 minutes
for each loaf

2 packages active dry yeast
1/2 cup warm water (110°)
1 1/2 cups water
1/3 cup shortening
1 1/4 cups quick cooking oatmeal
1/2 cup light molasses
1 tablespoon salt
1/2 teaspoon cinnamon
6 cups all purpose flour
2 eggs, slightly beaten

1. Sprinkle yeast over 1/2 cup warm water. Stir to dissolve. Set aside.

2. Place remaining water and shortening in a large glass mixing bowl. Cover with plastic wrap. Microwave on HIGH (100%) for 3 to 4 minutes or until boiling. Stir in oatmeal, molasses, salt and cinnamon. Let stand for 15 minutes.

3. Add 4 cups flour, eggs and yeast mixture. Beat on medium speed of mixer for 3 minutes.

4. Stir in remaining flour. By hand, beat until smooth (about 10 minutes).

5. Grease top lightly. Cover with plastic wrap. Refrigerate overnight.

6. Shape into 2 loaves. Place into two 8 1/2x4 1/2x2 1/2 inch dishes. Sprinkle with remaining oatmeal.

7. Cover with damp cloth, then dry cloth. Allow to rise in warm place until double (about 2 hours) in size. (To speed rising, see proofing instructions.)

8. Microwave, one loaf at a time, on MEDIUM (50%) for 20 to 22 minutes or until surface appears dry and will spring back when lightly touched. Turn dish a half turn halfway through cooking.

9. Remove immediately from dish and place on cooling rack.

Recipe yield: 2 loaves

WHITE BREAD
Power Level: HIGH [100%] and
MEDIUM [50%]
Total Cooking Time: 19 to 22 minutes
for each loaf

2 cups milk
2 packages active dry yeast
3/4 cup warm water (110°)
7 1/2 cups all purpose flour
1/4 cup butter (or margarine), softened
1/4 cup sugar
1 tablespoon salt

1. Microwave milk on HIGH (100%) for 4 to 5 minutes or until scalded. Cool to lukewarm (110°).

2. Sprinkle yeast over warm water. Stir to dissolve.

3. Add 4 cups flour, cooled milk, butter, sugar and salt. Mix well.

4. Stir in 3 cups flour and continue mixing until smooth.

5. Knead dough adding remaining flour until smooth and satiny.

6. Place in a greased bowl, turn dough to grease surface. Cover with plastic wrap. Refrigerate overnight.

7. Place into three 8 1/2x4 1/2x2 1/2 inch loaf dishes or 1 1/2 quart casseroles.

8. Cover with a damp cloth then a dry cloth. Allow to rise in a warm place until double in size. (To speed rising, see proofing instructions.)

9. Microwave on MEDIUM (50%) for 15 to 17 minutes or until surface appears dry and will spring back when lightly touched. Turn dish a half turn halfway through cooking.

10. Remove immediately from dish and place on cooling rack.

Recipe yield: 3 loaves.

FROZEN BREAD DOUGH

1 (one pound) loaf frozen bread dough

Defrosting:

1. Place dough into an 8½x4½x2½ inch loaf dish. Turn loaf to grease surface.

2. Cover with a damp cloth then a dry cloth.

3. Microwave on LOW (30%) for 5 to 6 minutes. Turn dish halfway through cooking.

4. Allow to stand 5 to 10 minutes before proofing.

Proofing (Rising):

1. Follow package instructions or to speed rising, see proofing instructions.

Baking:

1. Microwave on MEDIUM (50%) for 15 to 17 minutes or until surface appears dry and will spring back when lightly touched.

2. Remove bread immediately from dish and place on a cooling rack.

Tip: For larger frozen bread dough (1¼ pounds) microwave on MEDIUM (50%) for 18 to 20 minutes.

SWEET ROLL RING

Power Level: LOW [30%] and MEDIUM [50%]
Total Cooking Time: 14 to 16 minutes

1 pound loaf frozen bread dough (or white bread dough)
1 cup brown sugar
1½ teaspoons cinnamon
½ cup butter (or margarine), melted
¾ cup finely chopped nuts (or coconut)

1. Defrost and proof bread dough (see Frozen Bread Dough recipe).

2. Form dough into 1 inch balls.

3. Mix together brown sugar and cinnamon.

4. Dip each ball into melted butter, then brown sugar mixture. Coat with nuts.

5. Layer balls in a 9-inch tube pan leaving ½ inch between each ball.

6. Top with remaining brown sugar mixture, butter and nuts.

7. Cover with a damp cloth then a dry cloth. Allow to rise in a warm place until double in size. (To speed rising, see proofing instructions.)

8. Microwave on LOW (30%) for 10 minutes. Turn dish a half turn halfway through cooking. Microwave on MEDIUM (50%) for 4 to 6 minutes or until surface appears dry and will spring back when lightly touched.

9. Allow to stand 2 minutes. Loosen edges with a knife. Invert onto a serving dish.

It's fun to add toppings to microwave yeast breads for flavor and decoration. Browned butter, a mixture of 1 tablespoon paprika and 1 tablespoon cornmeal or poppy seeds and an egg wash (1 egg yolk plus 1 tablespoon water) made these three breads so pretty. You might try cinnamon and sugar or toasted sesame seeds as well.

Cakes & Icing

Delicious, delectable cakes are a dream
come true with microwave cooking. Cakes turn
out light, fluffy and high when prepared in
the microwave. And it's a one-step process
to mix and cook icing in the same container.
You'll save time and have less cleanup.

*Upside-Down Cake, Orange-Pistachio Cake with
Marshmallow Frosting and Italian Cream Cake
with Quick Cream Cheese Frosting taste as
good as they look.*

SELECTING AND PREPARING THE CAKE DISH

Select an 8 or 9 inch *round glass, ceramic or plastic microwave cake dish or ring mold.*

Ring molds *specially made for microwave ovens can be purchased or you can make your own.*

To make your own ring mold, *prepare cake batter in a large glass mixing bowl. After batter is thoroughly mixed, place a glass or jar [4 to 5 inches high and 1 inch wide] with open end up in the center of the batter, pushing glass to bottom of bowl or cake dish.*

Line bottom of dish *with waxed paper if cake is to be removed from dish. If cake is to remain in dish, this treatment is unnecessary.*

Do not *flour or grease dish surface because this will leave a paper-thin layer on cake.*

PREPARING THE BATTER

Prepare batter *as directed in recipe or mix. Divide batter into cake dishes or pour batter [less 1 cup] into ring mold.*

Gently pat *bottom of dish several times to remove any large air bubbles.*

COVERING

Place a white paper towel *over cake dish. This makes the cake more level and helps to absorb excess moisture. A colored paper towel may bleed onto the cake.*

IN THE MICROWAVE

For layer cakes, *microwave one layer at a time according to recipe.*

Testing for doneness. *Microwave cake for least amount of time given in recipe or chart below. A cake tester or wooden pick inserted near the center of cake will come out clean when cake is done. When cake begins to pull back from dish sides, remove from oven. Cake may still appear moist on surface but it should be removed from microwave. The moisture will disappear during standing.*

CAKE COOKING CHART*	
Power Level: MEDIUM-HIGH (70%)	
Item	**Time**
Layer cake, 8-9 inch round or square	8-10 minutes
Baking ring 10 inch	14-16 minutes
Sheet cake 10x6x1¾ inch (½ of batter)	8-10 minutes
11¾x7½x1¾ inch	16-18 minutes

*Use this chart as a cooking guide. Cakes, such as Angel Food, which are leavened entirely with egg whites, are not included as they tend to give unsatisfactory results. Buttery rich cakes should be cooked on HIGH (100%). Cake times may vary.

REMOVE FROM OVEN

Remove cake from microwave *and immediately remove paper towel from top of cake.*

Allow cake to stand *on a heat-resistant solid surface for 5 to 10 minutes before removing cake from dish. This holds in heat and helps the bottom of cake finish cooking.*

Place a wire rack *over top of cake dish and turn over so cake falls out of dish on rack.*

Cool cake completely. *Remove waxed paper just before frosting cake.*

WHAT ABOUT THE
Difference
IN
Appearance

You'll discover a difference when you first remove your cake from the microwave and compare its appearance to a conventionally baked cake. But that difference disappears when you add icing or a simple topping to the cake.

These luscious looking box cakes — spice, cherry, white and marble — were all prepared in the microwave. In just a fraction of the time you used to spend baking, you'll get these good looking, good tasting results.

A microwave cake will be moist, high and fluffy. With some cakes, you may get even more volume when using the microwave.

The microwave cake does not get a dry, brown crisp surface because it is not exposed to hot, dry air as in a conventional oven. However, when you add a topping or icing, this surface difference does not show.

A cake baked in a conventional oven *has a browned, crusty surface because of its exposure to hot, dry oven air.*

The microwave cake *has a light surface and remains moist and fluffy. There is no hot air in a microwave oven so the cake does not dry out.*

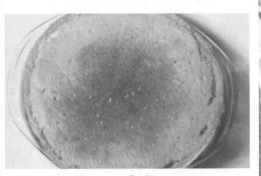

You can obtain a light crust *on a microwave cake if your microwave has a browning element. Use the browning element after the cake has finished cooking.*

Spice

White

Cherry

Marble

CAKE MIX VARIATIONS

SEVEN-UP CAKE WITH PINEAPPLE TOPPING

Power Level: HIGH [100%] and
MEDIUM-HIGH [70%]
Total Cooking Time: 20½ to
24¾ minutes

Topping:
¼ cup butter (or margarine)
2 eggs
1 cup sugar
1 cup (8 ounces) crushed
   pineapple, drained
1 cup flaked coconut

Batter:
1 package (18.5 ounces) yellow
   cake mix
1 package (3¾ ounces) instant
   vanilla pudding
2 eggs
¾ cup cooking oil
1¼ cups diet 7-Up drink

1. Place butter in a 1 quart casserole. Microwave on HIGH (100%) for 30 to 45 seconds or until melted.

2. Stir in eggs and sugar. Microwave on HIGH (100%) for 4 to 6 minutes or until thickened. Stir occasionally. Stir in pineapple and coconut. Set aside.

3. Mix together all batter ingredients except 7-Up in a large mixing bowl until well blended. Stir in 7-Up.

4. Pour batter into an 11¾x7½x1¾ inch baking dish. Tap bottom gently. Cover with a paper towel.

5. Microwave on MEDIUM-HIGH (70%) for 16 to 18 minutes or until a cake tester inserted near center comes out clean. Turn dish a half turn halfway through cooking.

6. Immediately remove paper towel and spread topping over cake. Allow to stand on a solid surface until cooled.

FROST-N-BAKE CAKE

Power Level: HIGH [100%] and
MEDIUM-HIGH [70%]
Total Cooking Time: 10 to 13 minutes

Frosting:
½ cup semi-sweet chocolate morsels,
1 tablespoon water
⅓ cup sweetened condensed milk
½ teaspoon vanilla

Batter:
1⅓ cups biscuit mix
¾ cup sugar
⅔ cup milk
3 tablespoons shortening

1 egg
1 teaspoon vanilla
½ cup chopped nuts (walnuts or
   pecans)

1. Place chocolate in a 2 cup measure. Microwave on HIGH (100%) for 2 to 3 minutes or until melted. Stir in water, sweetened condensed milk and vanilla. Spread in waxed paper lined 8 inch round cake dish. Set aside.

2. Combine all batter ingredients, except nuts in a small mixing bowl. Blend at low speed of a mixer for 30 seconds, then beat 1 minute at medium speed. Pour over chocolate mixture. Tap bottom gently. Cover with paper towel.

3. Microwave on MEDIUM-HIGH (70%) for 8 to 10 minutes or until cake tester inserted near center of cake comes out clean. Turn dish a half turn halfway through cooking.

4. Immediately remove paper towel and invert onto serving plate. leaving dish over cake for several minutes. Sprinkle top with chopped nuts.

BOSTON CREAM PIE

Power Level: HIGH [100%] and
MEDIUM-HIGH [70%]
Total Cooking Time: 13½ to
17½ minutes

Filling:
⅓ cup sugar
2 tablespoons cornstarch
¼ teaspoon salt
1 cup milk
1 egg, slightly beaten
1 tablespoon butter (or margarine)
½ teaspoon vanilla

Batter:
1 package (9 ounces) yellow
   cake mix

Frosting:
1 (1 ounce) square unsweetened
   chocolate
1 cup powdered sugar
¼ cup cream cheese, softened
2 tablespoons butter
   (or margarine), melted
1 tablespoon milk
½ teaspoon vanilla

1. Mix together sugar, cornstarch, salt and milk in a 4 cup measure until smooth. Microwave on HIGH (100%) for 3 to 4 minutes or until thickened. Stir occasionally.

2. Stir a little hot mixture into egg, then stir egg mixture into remaining hot mixture.

3. Microwave on HIGH (100%) for 1½ to 2 minutes or until boiling. Stir in butter and vanilla. Set aside.

4. Prepare batter as directed on package. Pour batter in a waxed paper lined 8 inch round cake dish. Tap bottom gently. Cover with a paper towel.

5. Microwave on MEDIUM-HIGH (70%) for 8 to 10 minutes or until a cake tester inserted near center of cake comes out clean. Turn dish a half turn halfway through cooking.

6. Immediately remove paper towel. Allow to stand on a solid surface for 5 to 10 minutes before removing cake from dish. Cool completely on cooling rack and cut in half lengthwise.

7. Place chocolate in 4 cup measure. Microwave on HIGH (100%) for 1 to 1½ minutes or until melted.

8. Beat in powdered sugar, cream cheese, butter, milk and vanilla until smooth.

9. Spread cooled filling over half of cake. Top with other half of cake. Spread top with frosting. Refrigerate for 2 hours before serving.

JIFFY GINGERBREAD

Power Level: MEDIUM-HIGH [70%]
Total Cooking Time: 10 to 12 minutes

1 package (14 ounces)
   gingerbread mix
3 tablespoons all purpose flour
⅓ cup brown sugar
3 tablespoons cooking oil
1 teaspoon cinnamon
¼ teaspoon ginger
¼ teaspoon ground cloves
1 cup lukewarm water
½ cup chopped nuts

1. Mix together gingerbread mix, flour, brown sugar, oil, cinnamon, ginger and cloves in a large bowl until well blended.

2. Add water, stir until blended. Stir in nuts.

3. Pour batter into a 10x6x1¾ inch baking dish. Tap bottom gently. Cover with paper towel.

4. Microwave on MEDIUM-HIGH (70%) for 10 to 12 minutes or until a cake tester inserted near center comes out clean. Turn dish a half turn halfway through cooking.

5. Immediately remove paper towel. Allow to stand on a solid surface for 5 minutes. Serve warm. Top as desired.

ORANGE-PISTACHIO CAKE

Power Level: MEDIUM-HIGH [70%]
Total Cooking Time: 21 to 24 minutes

½ cup finely chopped almonds
½ cup brown sugar
1 teaspoon cinnamon
1 package (18.5 ounces) yellow
   cake mix
1 package (3½ ounces) instant
   pistachio pudding mix

4 eggs
1 cup sour cream
½ cup orange juice
¼ cup water
¼ cup cooking oil
1 teaspoon vanilla

1. Combine nuts, sugar and cinnamon.

2. Mix together cake mix, pudding mix, eggs, sour cream, juice, water, oil and vanilla in a large mixing bowl until well blended.

3. Pour half the cake batter into 10″ ring mold. Sprinkle half of the nut mixture over batter. Swirl batter gently. Repeat with remaining batter and nuts. Tap bottom gently. Cover with a paper towel.

4. Microwave on MEDIUM-HIGH (70%) for 21 to 24 minutes or until cake tester inserted near center comes out clean. Turn dish a half turn halfway through cooking.

5. Immediately remove paper towel. Allow to stand 5 to 10 minutes on a solid surface before removing from dish.

UPSIDE-DOWN CAKE

Power Level: HIGH [100%] and
MEDIUM-HIGH [70%]
Total Cooking Time: 10 to 13 minutes

1 package (9 ounces) yellow
  cake mix
1 egg
½ cup pineapple juice
  (or apricot juice)
½ cup brown sugar
2 tablespoons butter, melted
6 slices pineapple (or 1 can
  (16 ounces) apricot halves)
6 maraschino cherries
6 pecan halves

1. Combine cake mix, egg, and fruit juice. Blend for 30 seconds, then beat for 3 minutes. Set aside.

2. Mix together brown sugar and melted butter in an 8 inch round cake dish. Microwave on HIGH (100%) for 2 to 3 minutes or until a syrup is formed. Stir halfway through cooking.

3. Arrange pineapple slices, cherries and pecans over syrup. Pour batter over fruit. Cover with a paper towel.

4. Microwave on MEDIUM-HIGH (70%) for 8 to 10 minutes or until cake tester inserted in cake near center of cake comes out clean. Turn dish a half turn halfway through cooking.

5. Immediately remove paper towel and invert cake onto serving plate leaving dish over cake for several minutes.

FUDGE-PUDDING CAKE

Power Level: HIGH [100%] and
MEDIUM-HIGH [70%]
Total Cooking Time: 19 to 22 minutes

1 package (3-1/8 ounces)
  chocolate fudge pudding mix
2 cups milk
1 package (15 ounces) chocolate
  fudge snack cake mix
½ cup semi-sweet chocolate
  morsels
½ cup chopped nuts (walnuts
  or pecans)

1. Mix together pudding mix and ½ cup milk in a 2 quart casserole or mixing bowl. Stir in remaining milk. Microwave on HIGH (100%) for 5 to 6 minutes or until thickened.

2. Stir cake mix into hot pudding. Beat on medium speed of mixer for 2 minutes.

3. Pour into an 11¾x7½x1¾ inch baking dish. Sprinkle chocolate morsels and chopped nuts over top. Tap bottom gently.

4. Microwave on MEDIUM-HIGH (70%) for 14 to 16 minutes or until cake tester inserted near center comes out clean. Turn dish a half turn halfway through cooking. Allow to stand 5 to 10 minutes on a solid surface.

EASY FRUITCAKE

Power Level: LOW [30%] and
WARM [10%]
Total Cooking Time: 88 to 90 minutes

1 package (17 ounces) date quick
  bread mix
1 egg
1 cup water
1½ cups (8 ounces) mixed
  candied fruit
1 cup pecan halves

1. Combine bread mix, egg and water in a large mixing bowl. Blend for 30 seconds, then beat for 3 minutes. Stir in remaining ingredients until thoroughly mixed.

2. Pour into a brown paper lined 10x6x1¾ inch baking dish. Tap bottom gently. Cover with waxed paper.

3. Microwave on LOW (30%) for 40 minutes then on WARM (10%) for 48 to 50 minutes or until cake tester inserted near center comes out clean. Turn dish four times during cooking.

4. Immediately remove waxed paper. Allow to stand for 5 to 10 minutes on a solid surface before removing from dish. Place on cooling rack and cool completely. Wrap tightly in plastic wrap and refrigerate up to 2 months.

CAKES FROM SCRATCH

TOFFEE CRUNCH CAKE

Power Level: MEDIUM-HIGH [70%]
Total Cooking Time: 8 to 10 minutes
  for each layer

Batter:
½ cup shortening
1 cup brown sugar
½ cup sugar
3 eggs
2 teaspoons vanilla
½ cup sugar
2⅓ cups all purpose flour
1½ teaspoons instant coffee
2 teaspoons baking powder
½ teaspoon salt
½ cup sour cream
½ cup water
2 bars (¾ ounces each) chocolate-
  covered toffee candy, crushed

Topping:
¼ cup brown sugar
½ teaspoon instant coffee
2 cups (1 pint) whipping cream
1 tablespoon white creme de cacao
  (optional)
2 bars (¾ ounces each) chocolate-
  covered toffee candy, crushed

1. Cream shortening, sugars, eggs and vanilla in a large mixing bowl until light and fluffy.

2. Sift together flour, coffee, baking powder and salt. Add to creamed mixture.

3. Add sour cream and water. Blend on low speed of mixer for 30 seconds, then on medium speed for 3 minutes.

4. Divide batter into two waxed paper lined 8-inch round cake dishes. Sprinkle with crushed candy. Gently tap each bottom.

5. Microwave, one layer at a time, on MEDIUM-HIGH (70%) for 8 to 10 minutes or until cake tester inserted near center of cake comes out clean. Turn dish a half turn halfway through cooking.

6. Place each layer on a solid surface for 5 to 10 minutes before removing from dish. Finish cooling on cooling racks.

7. Mix together sugar and coffee. Beat whipping cream until thickened. Gradually add sugar mixture until soft, glossy peaks form. Fold in creme de cacao.

8. Spread over cooled cake. Sprinkle with crushed candy. Refrigerate for 3 hours before serving.

SIMPLE CHEESECAKE

Power Level: HIGH [100%] and
LOW [30%]
Total Cooking Time: 6 to 9 minutes

Crust:

¼ cup butter (or margarine)
1 cup graham cracker crumbs

Filling:

1 package (8 ounces) cream cheese
⅓ cup sugar
1 egg
1 tablespoon lemon juice

Topping:

1 cup sour cream
3 tablespoons sugar

1. Place butter in a 9 inch pie dish. Microwave on HIGH (100%) for 30 to 45 seconds or until melted.

2. Stir in crumbs. Press over bottom and up sides of dish. Microwave on HIGH (100%) for 2 to 3 minutes or until set. Cool.

3. Place cream cheese in a large glass mixing bowl. Microwave on LOW (30%) for 30 to 45 seconds or until softened. Beat in sugar and egg until smooth. Stir in lemon juice. Pour mixture into cooled crust.

4. Microwave on HIGH (100%) for 2 to 3 minutes or until set around edges. Turn dish a half turn halfway through cooking.

5. Mix together sour cream and sugar. Spread over cheesecake. Microwave on HIGH (100%) for 1 to 1½ minutes or until topping is heated through.

6. Cool. Keep refrigerated until ready to serve.

Recipe yield: 6 to 8 servings

ITALIAN CREAM CAKE

Power Level: MEDIUM-HIGH [70%]
Total Cooking Time: 6 to 8 minutes
for each layer

Batter:

2 cups sugar
½ cup shortening
½ cup butter (or margarine)
5 eggs, separated
1 tablespoon vanilla
2 cups all purpose flour
1 teaspoon baking soda
½ teaspoon salt
1¼ cups buttermilk
1 cup chopped pecans
1 cup flaked coconut

1. Cream together sugar, shortening, butter, egg yolks and vanilla until light and fluffy.

2. Alternately add dry ingredients with buttermilk. Beat at medium speed of mixer for 3 minutes.

3. Stir in pecans and coconut.

4. Beat egg whites until stiff but not dry. Fold into egg yolk mixture.

5. Pour batter into three waxed paper lined 8 inch round cake dishes. Cover with a paper towel.

6. Microwave, one layer at a time, on MEDIUM-HIGH (70%) for 6 to 8 minutes or until a cake tester inserted near center comes out clean.

7. Immediately remove paper towel. Allow to stand for 5 to 10 minutes on a solid surface before removing from dish.

8. Frost with Quick Cream Cheese Frosting (page 67).

CARROT CAKE

Power Level: HIGH [100%]
Total Cooking Time: 12 to 15 minutes

1½ cups all purpose flour
2 teaspoons cinnamon
1 teaspoon baking soda
½ teaspoon salt
1½ cups sugar
1 cup cooking oil
3 eggs
1½ teaspoons vanilla
2 cups grated raw carrots
½ cup chopped nuts (walnuts or
   pecans)

1. Mix together flour, cinnamon, baking soda and salt. Set aside.

2. Combine sugar, oil, eggs and vanilla in a large mixing bowl. Blend at low speed of mixer for 30 seconds.

3. Add dry ingredients. Mix at medium speed of mixer for 3 minutes.

4. Fold in carrots and nuts.

5. Pour into an 11¾x7½x1¾ inch baking dish. Tap bottom gently. Cover with a paper towel.

6. Microwave on HIGH (100%) for 12 to 15 minutes or until a cake tester inserted near center comes out clean. Turn halfway through cooking.

7. Immediately remove paper towel. Allow to stand on a solid surface until cool.

8. Frost with Quick Cream Cheese Frosting (page 67).

OATMEAL CAKE AND BROILED FROSTING

Power Level: HIGH [100%]
Total Cooking Time: 12½ to
14¾ minutes

Batter:

1 cup quick cooking oats
1 cup + 2 tablespoons boiling
   water
1 cup sugar
1 cup brown sugar
½ cup butter (or margarine),
   softened
2 eggs
1 teaspoon vanilla
1⅓ cups sifted all purpose flour
1 teaspoon baking soda
1 teaspoon cinnamon
¾ teaspoon salt

Topping:

1 cup shredded coconut
½ cup brown sugar
¼ cup milk
¼ cup butter (or margarine)
½ cup chopped nuts

1. Mix together quick cooking oats and boiling water. Let stand for 20 minutes.

2. Cream sugars, butter and eggs until light and fluffy. Add vanilla and oats mixture, blend well.

3. Sift together dry ingredients. Add to creamed mixture. Blend at low speed of mixer for 1 minute.

4. Pour batter in an 11¾x7½x1¾ inch baking dish. Tap bottom gently. Cover with a paper towel.

5. Microwave on HIGH (100%) for 12 to 14 minutes until a cake tester inserted near center comes out clean. Turn dish a half turn halfway through cooking.

6. Immediately remove paper towel. Allow to stand on a solid surface for 5 to 10 minutes.

7. Combine coconut, sugar, milk and butter in 2 cup measure. Microwave on HIGH (100%) for 30 to 45 seconds. Stir in nuts. Spread on top of cake.

8. If microwave has browning element, brown as desired or broil in conventional range broiler for 1 minute or until lightly browned.

Variation:

Increase chopped nuts to 1 cup and omit the coconut.

Milk tip

It's quick to scald milk in the microwave. Use High (100%) power for 3 to 4 minutes.

DEVIL'S FOOD CAKE

Power Level: MEDIUM-HIGH [70%]
Total Cooking Time: 8 to 10 minutes
for each layer

½ cup shortening
1½ cups sugar
1 teaspoon vanilla
3 eggs, separated
2½ cups sifted cake flour
½ cup cocoa
1½ teaspoons baking soda
1 teaspoon salt
1⅓ cups cold water
¼ teaspoon cream of tartar

1. Beat shortening, sugar and vanilla until light.

2. Beat egg yolks slightly. Add to creamed mixture and continue to beat until fluffy.

3. Sift together dry ingredients. Add alternately with water and mix at medium speed of mixer until well blended.

4. Beat egg whites until foamy. Add cream of tartar and continue to beat until soft peaks form. Fold into chocolate mixture.

5. Divide batter into two waxed paper lined 8 inch round cake dishes. Gently tap each bottom. Cover with paper towel.

6. Microwave, one layer at a time, on MEDIUM-HIGH (70%) for 8 to 10 minutes or until a cake tester inserted near center of cake comes out clean. Turn dish a half turn halfway through cooking.

7. Immediately remove paper towel. Allow to stand on a solid surface for 5 to 10 minutes before removing from dish.

Defrosting tip

To defrost a frozen cake, simply place cake on a plate, cardboard or Styrofoam base. Microwave on Medium (50%) for 4 minutes. The cake will be cool and easy to cut.

Devil's Food Cake with Marshmallow Frosting is party perfect.

CUPCAKES

Power Level: HIGH [100%]

1. Use your favorite recipe or box mix.

2. Use microwave muffin pan, ice cream cones (flat bottom), 6 ounce custard cups, or cut off 7 ounce paper or Styrofoam cups. Line with 2 paper cupcake liners. Fill each cup of muffin pan or ice cream cone with 2 tablespoons of batter. Fill each custard cup, paper or Styrofoam cup with ¼ cup of batter.

3. When cooking more than two cupcakes at a time, arrange cupcakes in a circle.

4. Microwave on HIGH (100%) until surface springs back when lightly touched. Always check for doneness at the minimum suggested time. If some cupcakes are done before the others, remove finished cupcakes and continue cooking remaining cupcakes.

─ Brown Sugar Tip ─

Soften hard brown sugar by placing it in a microwave safe container with a slice of apple. Cover. Microwave on High (100%) for 15 to 30 seconds or until softened.

Amount	Time
In custard, cutoff or Styrofoam cups (¼ cup batter)	
1	45 sec.-1 min.
2	1-1¼ min.
3	1½-1¾ min.
4	2½-2¾ min.
5	3½-3¾ min.
6	4-4¼ min.
In muffin pan or ice cream cones (2 tablespoons batter)	
1	30-45 sec.
2	45 sec.-1 min.
3	1-1¼ min.
4	1¼-1½ min.
5	1¾-2 min.
6	2¼-2½ min.

You can make cupcakes in cutoff paper or Styrofoam cups as well as in 6-ounce custard cups or a microwave muffin pan. Place paper cupcake liners inside cups. Using 2 liners helps absorb moisture. Fill each cup with ¼ cup batter. Use 2 tablespoons batter in muffin pan. Arrange cups in a circle and microwave as directed in chart above.

FROSTING

BUTTERCREAM FROSTING
Power Level: LOW [30%]
Total Cooking Time: 1 to 1½ minutes

1 package (1 pound) powdered sugar
½ teaspoon salt
½ cup butter (or margarine)
2 tablespoons milk
1½ teaspoons vanilla

1. Mix sugar and salt in small mixing bowl.

2. Add butter and milk. Do not stir.

3. Microwave on LOW (30%) for 1 to 1½ minutes or until butter is softened.

4. Stir in vanilla. Beat on high speed of mixer until smooth.

Recipe yield: Frosting for two layer cakes or one sheet cake.

QUICK CREAM CHEESE FROSTING
Power Level: LOW [30%]
Total Cooking Time: 1½ to 2 minutes

2 packages (3 ounces each) cream cheese
½ cup butter (or margarine)
4 cups powdered sugar
1 teaspoon almond extract

1. Place cream cheese and butter in a 2 quart casserole.

2. Microwave on LOW (30%) for 1½ to 2 minutes or until softened.

3. Stir in sugar and almond extract until well blended. Beat until spreading consistency.

Variations:
CHOCOLATE CREAM CHEESE FROSTING
Follow Quick Cream Cheese Frosting recipe as directed except microwave 3 ounces chocolate squares on HIGH (100%) for 3 to 4 minutes or until melted, then stir into cream cheese frosting mixture.

PEPPERMINT CREAM CHEESE FROSTING
Follow Quick Cream Cheese Frosting recipe as directed except stir 5 drops of red food color and 3 tablespoons crushed peppermint candy into cream cheese frosting.

COFFEE CREAM CHEESE FROSTING
Follow Quick Cream Cheese Frosting recipe as directed except in step 1, stir 2 tablespoons instant coffee into cream cheese and butter.

Recipe yield: Frosting for 3 layers or a double recipe of bar cookies.

CARAMEL FROSTING
Power Level: HIGH [100%]
Total Cooking Time: 1¾ to 3 minutes

½ cup butter (or margarine)
1 cup brown sugar
4 cups powdered sugar
¼ cup milk
½ teaspoon vanilla

1. Place butter in a 4 cup measure. Microwave on HIGH (100%) for 45 seconds to 1 minute or until melted.

2. Stir in brown sugar. Microwave on HIGH (100%) for 1 to 2 minutes or until boiling. Beat until mixture has cooled and is starting to thicken.

3. Add sugar, milk and vanilla. Beat until spreading consistency.

Recipe yield: Frosting for two layer cake or one sheet cake.

Variation:
CARAMEL FUDGE
Follow Caramel Frosting recipe as directed except add ½ cup chopped nuts and spread into an 8x8x2 inch baking dish. Refrigerate one hour. Cut and serve.

MARSHMALLOW FROSTING
Power Level: HIGH [100%]
Total Cooking Time: 1½ to 2 minutes

2 egg whites
¼ teaspoon salt
¼ cup sugar
¾ cup light corn syrup
1 teaspoon vanilla

1. Beat egg whites and salt in small mixing bowl until foamy. Gradually add sugar, beating until soft peaks form.

2. Microwave corn syrup on HIGH (100%) for 1½ to 2 minutes or until boiling.

3. Slowly pour a thin stream over egg whites, beating until stiff and glossy.

4. Beat in vanilla.

Recipe yield: Frosting for 2 layer cakes or one sheet cake.

Dear Sue,
Cookie roll in refrigerator. Just slice and bake.
Love Mom

Cookies

Cookies are a quick after-school treat that the kids can easily make themselves. Either Mom or the children can prepare the dough in advance. Then it's fun to put just the number you plan to eat in the microwave. In no time at all, you've got warm, fresh cookies for a snack or a simple dessert.

PEANUT BUTTER COOKIES

Power Level: LOW [30%] and
MEDIUM-HIGH [70%]

¼ cup butter (or margarine)
½ cup peanut butter
¼ cup shortening
½ cup sugar
½ cup brown sugar
1 egg, beaten
1 teaspoon vanilla
1½ cups all purpose flour
¼ teaspoon baking soda
¼ teaspoon salt

1. Place butter in a large glass mixing bowl. Microwave on LOW (30%) for 45 seconds to 1 minute or until softened.

2. Add peanut butter, shortening, sugars, egg and vanilla. Beat until light and fluffy.

3. Stir in dry ingredients until well blended.

4. Divide dough in half, roll each half into a 2 inch wide cylinder. Wrap in waxed paper and refrigerate overnight or for 8 hours.

5. Slice each roll into ½ inch thick sections. Slice only amount desired. Place sections in a circle, 2 inches apart on waxed paper. Keep uncut portion refrigerated until ready to use.

6. Microwave on MEDIUM-HIGH (70%) until set, but still moist. Turn paper a half turn halfway through cooking.

Amount	Time
1	1¼-1½ min.
2	1¾-2 min.
4	2¼-2½ min.
6	3-3½ min.
8	3½-4 min.

7. Allow cookies to stand 3 minutes on a solid surface before removing from waxed paper. Repeat with remaining cookies.

Recipe yield: 3 dozen cookies

Place butter *in large mixing bowl. Microwave on Low [30%] about 45 seconds or until soft. Add peanut butter, shortening, sugars, egg and vanilla. Beat until light and fluffy. Stir in flour, soda and salt until well blended.*

Divide dough *in half. Roll each half to form a 2 inch wide cylinder.*

Wrap dough *in waxed paper and refrigerate overnight or for about 8 hours.*

Slice each roll *into ½ inch thick sections or cut off sections according to how many cookies you wish to make.*

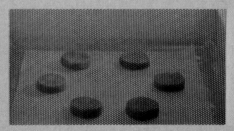

Arrange sections *2 inches apart in a circle. You can microwave as many as eight at a time. Microwave on Medium-High [70%] for 2 to 3 minutes or until set. Turn waxed paper a half turn halfway through cooking. Allow cookies to stand 3 minutes on a solid, heat-resistant surface before removing from waxed paper.*

CHOCOLATE COOKIES

Power Level: HIGH [100%]

1 cup semi-sweet chocolate
   morsels
½ cup butter (or margarine)
1½ cups brown sugar
4 eggs
2 teaspoons vanilla
3¾ cups all purpose flour
1 teaspoon cinnamon
½ teaspoon salt
½ cup finely chopped walnuts
   (or shredded coconut)
Walnut halves

1. Combine chocolate morsels and butter in a large glass mixing bowl. Microwave on HIGH (100%) for 1 to 1½ minutes or until melted. Stir halfway through cooking time.

2. Add sugar, eggs and vanilla. Beat until well blended. Stir in dry ingredients until well blended.

3. Chill dough for 2 to 3 hours. Shape dough into ¾ inch balls. Roll in walnuts. Place desired amount of balls in a circle, 2 inches apart on waxed paper. Place walnut half in center and press down. Keep remaining dough refrigerated until ready to use.

4. Microwave on HIGH (100%) until set but still moist.

Amount	Time
1	45 sec.-1 min.
2	1-1¼ min.
6	2-2¼ min.

5. Allow cookies to stand for 3 minutes on a solid surface before removing from waxed paper. Repeat with remaining cookies. Store cookies in an airtight container.

Recipe yield: 4 to 5 dozen cookies

CRISPY DELIGHTS

Power Level: HIGH [100%]
Total Cooking Time: 2 to 3 minutes

⅓ cup butter (or margarine)
3 cups miniature marshmallows
4 cups crisp rice cereal
1 cup peanuts

1. Place butter and marshmallows in a 2 quart casserole. Microwave on HIGH (100%) for 2 to 3 minutes or until butter and marshmallows are melted. Stir until smooth.

2. Stir in cereal and nuts. Mix until cereal is covered with marshmallow mixture.

3. Pour into a greased 11¾x7½x1¾ inch baking dish. Cool and cut into squares.

Recipe yield: 18 squares

THUMBPRINT COOKIES

Power Level: LOW [30%] and
*   MEDIUM-HIGH [70%]*
Total Cooking Time: 2¾ to
*   3½ minutes*

½ cup butter (or margarine)
½ cup brown sugar
2 eggs
1 teaspoon vanilla
¼ teaspoon salt
1¾ cups all purpose flour
1 cup finely chopped nuts
   (walnuts or pecans)
3 tablespoons sugar
1 egg white, slightly beaten
½ cup preserves

1. Place butter in a large glass mixing bowl. Microwave on LOW (30%) for 45 seconds to 1 minute or until softened.

2. Add brown sugar, eggs, vanilla and salt. Beat until light and fluffy. Gradually stir in flour.

3. Chill dough for 2 to 3 hours or overnight.

4. Mix together nuts and sugar. Shape dough into ¾ inch balls. Dip in egg white, then roll in nut mixture. Place 8 balls in a circle on waxed paper. Indent the center of each cookie with thumb. Keep remaining dough refrigerated until ready to use.

5. Microwave on MEDIUM-HIGH (70%) for 2 to 2½ minutes or until set but still moist. Again indent center of each cookie.

6. Allow cookies to stand 3 minutes on a solid surface before removing from waxed paper.

7. Fill thumbprints with preserves. Repeat with remaining cookies.

Recipe yield: 3 dozen cookies

LEMONY-VANILLA COOKIES

Power Level: LOW [30%] and
*   HIGH [100%]*

⅔ cup butter (or margarine)
1 cup brown sugar
1 egg
1 teaspoon vanilla
½ teaspoon grated lemon rind
2 cups all purpose flour
1½ teaspoons baking powder
¼ teaspoon salt
¾ cup finely chopped nuts
   (walnuts or pecans)

1. Place butter in a large glass mixing bowl. Microwave on LOW (30%) for 45 seconds to 1 minute until softened. Add sugar, egg, vanilla and lemon rind. Beat until light and fluffy.

2. Stir in dry ingredients until well blended.

3. Fold in nuts.

4. Divide dough in half. Roll into a 2 inch wide cylinder. Wrap in waxed paper and refrigerate overnight or for 8 hours.

5. Slice each roll into ½ inch thick sections. Slice only amount desired. Place sections in a circle 2 inches apart on waxed paper. Keep uncut portion refrigerated until ready to use.

6. Microwave on HIGH (100%) until set, but still moist. Turn paper a half turn halfway through cooking.

Amount	Time
1	45 sec.-1 min.
2	1¼-1½ min.
4	2¼-2½ min.
6	3½-4 min.

7. Allow cookies to stand 3 minutes on a solid surface before removing from waxed paper. Repeat with remaining cookies.

Recipe yield: 4½ dozen cookies

Dear Mom,
Took some cookies to Ellen's house
Love
Sue

COCONUT-BUTTERSCOTCH BAR

Power Level: LOW [30%] and
MEDIUM [50%]
Total Cooking Time: 16¾ to 21 min.

½ cup butter (or margarine)
1¼ cups all purpose flour
¼ cup powdered sugar
2 eggs
1 cup brown sugar
2 tablespoons all purpose flour
1 teaspoon vanilla
¾ teaspoon baking powder
¼ teaspoon salt
⅔ cup flaked coconut
⅔ cup sliced almonds

1. Place butter in an 11¾x7½x1¾ inch baking dish. Microwave on LOW (30%) for 45 seconds to 1 minute or until softened. Stir in 1¼ cups flour and powdered sugar until well blended. Press evenly in bottom of dish.

2. Microwave on MEDIUM (50%) for 6 to 8 minutes. Turn dish half turn halfway through cooking.

3. Beat eggs, brown sugar, flour, vanilla, baking powder and salt until light and fluffy. Stir in coconut and almonds. Pour over crust.

4. Microwave on MEDIUM (50%) for 10 to 12 minutes. Turn dish a half turn halfway through cooking time.

5. Allow to stand on a solid surface until completely cool. Refrigerate for 2 to 3 hours, then cut into bars.

Recipe yield: 24 bars.

LEMON SQUARES

Power Level: HIGH [100%] and
MEDIUM-HIGH [70%]
Total Cooking Time: 10¾ to 13 min.

⅓ cup butter (or margarine)
1½ cups vanilla wafer crumbs
1 teaspoon grated lemon rind
1 can (14 ounces) sweetened
condensed milk
½ cup lemon juice

1. Place butter in an 8x8x2 inch baking dish. Microwave on HIGH (100%) for 45 seconds to 1 minute or until melted. Stir in vanilla wafer crumbs and lemon rind until well blended. Remove ¼ cup and set aside. Press remaining mixture evenly in bottom of dish.

2. Beat milk and lemon juice until thick and smooth. Spread evenly over crumb mixture. Sprinkle top with remaining crumb mixture.

3. Microwave on MEDIUM-HIGH (70%) for 10 to 12 minutes. Turn dish a half turn halfway through cooking.

4. Allow to stand on a solid surface until completely cooled. Cut into bars.

Recipe yield: 16 to 24 cookies

BROWNIES

Power Level: HIGH [100%] and
MEDIUM-HIGH [70%]
Total Cooking Time: 8¾ to 11 minutes

½ cup butter (or margarine)
1 cup sugar
2 eggs
1 teaspoon vanilla
¾ cup all purpose flour
½ cup cocoa
¼ teaspoon baking powder
¼ teaspoon salt
½ cup chopped nuts
(walnuts or pecans)

1. Place butter in a large glass mixing bowl. Microwave on HIGH (100%) for 45 seconds to 1 minute or until melted. Add sugar, eggs and vanilla. Beat until creamy.

2. Stir in dry ingredients just until blended.

3. Fold in nuts.

4. Spread evenly into an 8x8x2 inch square baking dish.

5. Microwave on MEDIUM-HIGH (70%) for 8 to 10 minutes or until top appears dry and springs back when lightly touched. Turn dish a half turn halfway through cooking.

6. Allow to stand on a solid surface until completely cool. Cut into bars.

Recipe yield: 16 brownies

S'MORE BARS

Power Level: HIGH [100%]
Total Cooking Time: 1¼ to 2 minutes

⅓ cup light corn syrup
1 tablespoon butter (or margarine)
1 package (5¾ ounces) milk
chocolate chips
½ teaspoon vanilla
4 cups golden grahams cereal
(graham cracker cereal)
1½ cups miniature marshmallows

1. Place corn syrup and butter in a 3 quart casserole. Microwave on HIGH (100%) for 1 to 1½ minutes or until boiling. Stir halfway through cooking.

2. Add chocolate chips and vanilla. Stir until chocolate is melted.

3. Gradually fold in cereal and marshmallows until completely coated with chocolate.

4. Microwave on HIGH (100%) for 15 to 30 seconds or until marshmallows begin to soften. Stir to blend.

5. Pour into a buttered 9x9x2 inch pan. Let stand at room temperature for 1 hour. Cut into bars.

Recipe yield: 4 dozen pieces

OATMEAL CHEWS

Power Level: HIGH [100%] and
MEDIUM [50%]
Total Cooking Time: 7¾ to 11 minutes

½ cup butter (or margarine)
2 cups quick cooking oats
½ cup brown sugar
¼ cup dark corn syrup
1 teaspoon vanilla
¼ teaspoon salt
1 package (6 ounces) milk
chocolate morsels
¼ cup chopped nuts
(walnuts or pecans)

1. Place butter in a large glass mixing bowl. Microwave on HIGH (100%) for 45 seconds to 1 minute or until melted.

2. Stir in oats, sugar, corn syrup, vanilla and salt.

3. Press dough evenly in bottom of a greased 8x8x2 inch baking dish.

4. Microwave on HIGH (100%) for 3 to 4 minutes or until bubbly. Turn dish a half turn halfway through cooking. Spread surface even.

5. Sprinkle chocolate morsels over top. Microwave on MEDIUM (50%) for 4 to 6 minutes or until chocolate morsels are melted.

6. Spread chocolate evenly over crust. Sprinkle with nuts.

7. Chill one hour. Cut into bars.

Recipe yield: 12 bars

CRAZY COOKIES

Power Level: HIGH [100%] and
MEDIUM [50%]
Total Cooking Time: 8¾ to 12 minutes

¼ cup butter (or margarine)
¾ cup graham cracker crumbs
½ cup peanut butter morsels
½ cup chocolate morsels
1 cup shredded coconut
½ cup chopped nuts
(walnuts or pecans)
1 can (14 ounces) sweetened
condensed milk

1. Place butter in an 8x8x2 inch baking dish. Microwave on HIGH (100%) for 45 seconds to 1 minute or until melted.

2. Stir in graham cracker crumbs until well blended. Press evenly in bottom of dish. Microwave on HIGH (100%) for 2 to 3 minutes or until set. Turn dish a half turn halfway through cooking.

3. Layer each of the remaining ingredients in order listed. Microwave on MEDIUM (50%) for 6 to 8 minutes or until bubbly.

4. Allow to stand on a solid surface until completely cooled. Cut into bars.

Recipe yield: 1 dozen bars

FAVORITE FUDGE

Power Level: HIGH [100%]
Total Cooking Time: 14 to 18 minutes

1½ cups sugar
1 can (13 ounces) evaporated milk
¼ cup butter (or margarine)
¼ teaspoon salt
**3 cups miniature marshmallows
   (or 24 large)**
**1 package (12 ounces)
   chocolate chips**
**1 cup chopped nuts (walnuts or
   pecans)**
1 teaspoon vanilla

1. Combine sugar, milk, butter and salt in a 3 quart casserole or mixing bowl. Loosely cover with lid or plastic wrap.

2. Microwave on HIGH (100%) for 4 to 6 minutes or until boiling. Uncover. Microwave on HIGH (100%) for 10 to 12 minutes stirring the last third of cooking every minute, until soft ball stage is reached.

3. Stir in remaining ingredients until marshmallows and chocolate melts. Pour into a well greased 11¾x7½x1¾ inch baking dish. Refrigerate for 2 hours or overnight.

Recipe yield: About 4 dozen
            1-inch pieces

Combine sugar, *milk, butter and salt in a 3 quart casserole or mixing bowl.*

Stir in remaining ingredients *until marshmallows and chocolate melt.*

Microwave, covered, *on High [100%] for 4 to 6 minutes or until boiling. Uncover. Then microwave on high [100%] for another 10 to 12 minutes or to soft ball stage.*

Pour into *a well greased oblong baking dish. Refrigerate for 2 hours or overnight.*

Candies

Candy making is a perfect wedding between old-fashioned goodness and easy, modern cooking. Even beginning cooks will enjoy great success with these treats made so quickly in the microwave. Mixing and cooking are done in the same dish with just a minimum of stirring.

Because microwave energy enters food from all sides, sugar that might collect on the sides of a dish during candy making is dissolved. Thus, candy tends not to crystalize.

Peanut Brittle *syrup mixture has been properly cooked when a few drops form brittle threads when dropped into cold water.*

NUT BRITTLE
Power Level: HIGH [100%]
Total Cooking Time: 17 to 22 minutes

1 cup sugar
½ cup water
½ cup light corn syrup
1 jar (7 ounces) dry roasted peanuts (almonds or cashews)
¾ cup shredded coconut (optional)
1 teaspoon vanilla
1 teaspoon baking soda

1. Stir together sugar, water and syrup in a 2 quart casserole. Microwave on HIGH (100%) for 12 to 14 minutes or until bubbly.

2. Stir in nuts. Microwave on HIGH (100%) for 4 to 6 minutes or until light brown.

3. Stir coconut and vanilla into syrup. Microwave on HIGH (100%) for an additional 1 to 2 minutes or until hard crack stage is reached.

4. Add baking soda. Stir until light and foamy.

5. Pour mixture onto a lightly greased cookie sheet. Spread to ¼ inch thickness.

6. Cool. Break into pieces.

Recipe yield: 1 pound

CHOCOLATE PEANUT BUTTER CLUSTERS
Power Level: HIGH [100%]
Total Cooking Time: 3 to 4 minutes

1 pkg. (6 oz.) chocolate morsels
1 pkg. (12 oz.) peanut butter morsels
1 pkg. (12 oz.) salted Spanish peanuts

1. Combine morsels in a 2 quart casserole. Microwave on HIGH (100%) for 3 to 4 minutes or until melted. Stir halfway through cooking.

2. Stir in peanuts.

3. Drop by teaspoons onto waxed paper. Let set until firm. Store in airtight container.

Recipe yield: 4 to 4½ dozen

ALMOND BARK
Power Level: MEDIUM [50%]
Total Cooking Time: 3 to 5 minutes

1 pound pure chocolate (milk, white or dark)
1 cup almonds

1. Place chocolate in a 2 quart casserole (if solid break into pieces). Microwave on MEDIUM (50%) for 3 to 5 minutes or until melted. Stir halfway through cooking.

2. Stir in almonds.

3. Pour onto waxed paper. Spread to ¼ inch thickness. Cool until hard. Break into pieces. Store in airtight container.

Variation:
NUTTY BARK
Follow Almond Bark recipe as directed except substitute 1 cup cashews or peanuts for almonds.

COCONUT BARK
Follow Almond Bark recipe as directed except substitute 1 cup coconut for almonds.

Recipe yield: 1¼ pounds

CHOCOLATE TURTLES
Power Level: HIGH [100%]
Total Cooking Time: 4 to 6 minutes
for each half dozen

1 pound pecan halves
1 package (14 ounces) caramels
1 package (6 ounces) chocolate morsels
Butter (or margarine)

1. Place pecan halves in 6 groups of three in a ring in a buttered pie plate. Top each group with a caramel. Microwave on HIGH (100%) for 2 to 3 minutes or just until caramels are soft but not melted. Turn dish a half turn halfway through cooking.

2. Place chocolate morsels in a 2 cup measure or mixing bowl. Microwave on HIGH (100%) for 2 to 3 minutes or until morsels are melted. Stir occasionally.

3. Spread about ½ teaspoon of chocolate over each caramel.

4. Chill for 20 to 30 minutes or until set. Repeat with remaining ingredients.

Recipe yield: 4 dozen

NUTTY-CARAMEL APPLES
Power Level: HIGH [100%]
Total Cooking Time: 2 to 3 minutes

25 caramels
1 tablespoon hot water
4 apples
4 wooden sticks
½ cup finely chopped peanuts (optional)

1. Place unwrapped caramels and water in a 1 quart casserole.

2. Microwave on HIGH (100%) for 2 to 3 minutes or until caramels are melted. Stir to make caramels smooth.

3. Insert sticks into core end of apple. Dip each apple into caramel mixture. ***** Turn to coat evenly.

4. Dip each coated apple in chopped peanuts. Turn to coat evenly.

5. Place apples, stick side up, on buttered waxed paper.

Recipe yield: 4 apples

* Tip: If caramel mixture hardens while coating apples, return to microwave and microwave on HIGH (100%) for 30 to 45 seconds or until softened.

Chocolate Peanut Butter Clusters, Nut Brittle, Divinity and Chocolate Turtles are sweet sensations.

DIVINITY

Power Level: HIGH [100%]
Total Cooking Time: 13 to 16 minutes

2¼ cups sugar
½ cup water
½ cup light corn syrup
¼ teaspoon salt
2 egg whites
1½ teaspoons vanilla
½ cup chopped nuts (walnuts or pecans) (optional)
½ cup chopped candied cherries (optional)

1. Mix together sugar, water, corn syrup and salt in a 2 quart casserole.

2. Loosely cover with a lid or plastic wrap. Microwave on HIGH (100%) for 5 to 6 minutes or until boiling. Uncover. Microwave on HIGH (100%) for 8 to 10 minutes or until hard ball stage is reached.

3. Meanwhile, beat egg whites until stiff.

4. Slowly pour hot syrup over egg whites while beating at high speed of mixer. Add vanilla and continue to beat for 4 to 5 minutes or until candy holds its shape.

5. Fold in nuts and cherries.

6. Quickly drop teaspoons of candy onto waxed paper or pour into a buttered 10x6x2 inch baking dish.

Variations:

COCONUT DIVINITY

Follow Divinity recipe as directed except substitute 1 cup coconut for nuts and cherries.

NUT DIVINITY

Follow Divinity recipe as directed except use 1 cup nuts and eliminate cherries.

Recipe yield: about 1 pound

Mix together *sugar, water, corn syrup and salt in a 2 quart casserole. Loosely cover with plastic wrap or lid. Microwave on High [100%] for 5 to 6 minutes or until boiling.*

When the mixture is properly cooked, *you will be able to mold a tiny, hard but pliable ball from a drop of the mixture.*

Uncover *and microwave on High [100%] for 8 to 10 minutes or until hard ball stage is reached. Meanwhile, beat egg whites until stiff.*

Slowly pour *hot syrup over beaten egg whites, beating at high speed of mixer. Add vanilla and continue to beat for 4 to 5 minutes or until candy holds its shape. Fold in nuts and cherries.*

To test for hard ball stage, *drop a few drops of the mixture into very cold water. Use a clean spoon and fresh water for each test.*

Quickly drop *teaspoons of candy onto waxed paper or pour into a buttered 10x6x2 inch baking dish.*

Chocolate tip

It's quick to melt chocolate in the microwave. Melt chocolate squares on High (100%) for 45 seconds to 1 minute per ounce. It takes between 2 and 3 minutes to melt a 6 ounce package of chocolate morsels on High (100%). Remember to use pure chocolate morsels, not chocolate flavored bits. The flavored bits contain paraffin and do not melt properly in the microwave.

Eggs & Cheese

It's a bright new day for cooking eggs and cheese. You'll cook golden cheese dishes like a gourmet chef. And egg dishes that used to be a lot of fuss and bother are fun to fix with the microwave.

Cooking eggs is an excellent illustration of one difference between conventional and microwave cooking. When you conventionally poach or shirr an egg, the outer or white portion cooks first.

But in the microwave, the opposite happens. Because an egg yolk contains more fat than the white, it attracts more energy and cooks faster.

Lower power settings often are used for poached or shirred eggs, omelets and lighter, fluffier scrambled eggs.

The eggs used in these recipes are grade "A" large and at refrigerator temperature.

Do not cook an egg in its shell in the microwave. Steam pressure builds inside the shell, and the egg will spatter. Do not reheat eggs.

FRIED EGGS

Heat empty browning dish *for about 2 minutes. The dish bottom is coated with aluminum or iron ferrite which attracts microwave energy and becomes hot like a skillet.*

Cover eggs *with dish lid and microwave on High [100%] until white is opaque.*

Break each egg *into a custard cup. Pierce yolks with toothpick. Add 1 teaspoon of butter, margarine or bacon drippings per egg to browning dish. Quickly add eggs.*

FRIED EGG CHART	
Amount	**Time**
1	45 seconds to 1 minute
2	1¼ to 1½ minutes

SCRAMBLED EGGS

**1 teaspoon butter (or margarine)
per egg
Large egg(s)
1 tablespoon water (or milk)
per egg**

1. Place butter in container. Microwave on HIGH (100%) until melted.

2. Add egg(s) and desired liquid. Beat until well blended.

3. Microwave on HIGH (100%), stirring occasionally to break apart set portion. If an even fluffier, lighter egg(s) is desired, microwave on MEDIUM (50%).

4. When egg(s) is done, it will be slightly moist.

5. Allow egg(s) to stand 1 to 2 minutes or until completely set.

COUNTRY SCRAMBLED EGGS

Power Level: HIGH [100%]
Total Cooking Time: 6 to 8 minutes

**¼ pound ground pork sausage
6 eggs
½ cup sour cream
½ teaspoon chopped chives
¼ cup chopped mushrooms
Dash of basil**

1. Place sausage in a 1½ quart casserole. Microwave on HIGH (100%) for 2 to 3 minutes or until no longer pink. Drain off excess fat.

2. Stir in eggs, sour cream, chives, mushrooms and basil.

3. Microwave on HIGH (100%) for 4 to 5 minutes or until eggs are set but moist. Stir every minute.

Recipe yield: 4 servings

SCRAMBLED EGGS

Place butter or margarine, *about 1 teaspoon per egg, in glass serving dish or casserole. Microwave on High [100%] for 30 seconds or until butter is melted.*

Add eggs and milk *or water, about 1 tablespoon per egg, and beat.*

SCRAMBLED EGG CHART

Amount	Power Level	Utensil	Time
1	High (100%) Medium (50%)	6 ounce cup	45 sec. to 1 minute 1½ to 2 minutes
2	High (100%) Medium (50%)	10 ounce cup or bowl	1½ to 2 minutes 2½ to 3½ minutes
4	High (100%) Medium (50%)	8 inch round cake dish or 1 quart casserole	3 to 3½ minutes 6 to 7 minutes
6	High (100%) Medium (50%)	8 inch round cake dish or 1½ qt. casserole	4 to 4½ minutes 7 to 8 minutes

Note: The times above are a guide and will vary due to the difference in size, age, grade and temperature of eggs.

Start the morning right with Eggs Benedict.

Stir occasionally *so eggs stay fluffy while heating on High [100%]. For more tender eggs, microwave on Medium [50%]. Remove eggs from oven while still soft, moist and slightly undercooked.*

Allow eggs to stand *for 1 to 2 minutes to finish the cooking process. Overcooking makes eggs tough and rubbery.*

EGGS SUBSTITUTE

Power Level: MEDIUM [50%] and HIGH [100%]
Total Cooking Time: 5 to 6 minutes

1 carton (8 ounces) egg substitute

1. Microwave, in carton, on MEDIUM (50%) for 1½ minutes.

2. Turn carton over and open. Microwave on MEDIUM (50%) for an additional 1½ to 2 minutes or until defrosted, but still icy in center. Stir every 30

seconds. Allow to stand 3 to 5 minutes.

3. Place ½ cup defrosted egg substitute in a 9 inch pie dish.

4. Microwave on HIGH (100%) 2 to 2½ minutes or until set. Stir every 15 seconds.

Recipe yield: 1 serving.

POACHED OR SHIRRED EGGS

Power Level: HIGH [100%]

2 tablespoons water (or 1 teaspoon butter) for each cup
Egg(s)

1. For a poached egg: Place water in each custard cup, coffee cup or cup of a microwave muffin pan.

For shirred egg: Place 1 teaspoon of butter in each custard cup, coffee cup or cup of a microwave muffin pan. Microwave on HIGH (100%) until butter is melted.

2. Slip egg(s) into (cup(s) and pierce the membrane of the yolk with a toothpick or tine of a fork.

3. Cover with a plate or plastic wrap.

4. Microwave on MEDIUM (50%) until white is opaque.

Amount	Time
1	1¼ to 1½ minutes
2	1½ to 2 minutes
4	3½ to 4 minutes

5. Allow egg(s) to stand covered 1 or 2 minutes or until white is set.

6. Remove poached egg onto a slotted spoon.

EGGS BENEDICT *

Power Level: HIGH [100%]
Total Cooking Time: 2¼ to 3 minutes

4 poached eggs
1 package (1¼ ounces) Hollandaise sauce mix or recipe (page 107)
2 English muffins, split and toasted (or 4 Holland Rusks)
8 slices Canadian bacon (or ham)
Paprika
Parsley (optional)

1. Follow Poached Egg recipe as directed.

2. Meanwhile prepare Hollandaise sauce. Follow package directions to prepare packaged Hollandaise sauce except use a 2 cup measure. Microwave on HIGH (100%) for 45 seconds to 1 minute or until thickened. Stir every 15 seconds.

3. Place English muffins on a serving dish. Top each with two slices of Canadian bacon. Microwave on HIGH (100%) for 1½ to 2 minutes or until heated through.

4. Top each with a poached egg. Spoon sauce over eggs. Sprinkle with paprika. Garnish with a sprig of parsley.

Recipe yield: 4 servings

* Tip: To simplify making Eggs Benedict, have all ingredients assembled, measured and prepared, as much as possible, in advance of cooking.

POACHED OR SHIRRED EGGS

For a poached egg, *pour 2 tablespoons of water into a custard cup, coffee cup or cup of a microwave muffin pan.* **For a shirred egg,** *place 1 teaspoon of butter in each custard cup. Microwave on High [100%] until butter is melted.*

Slip egg(s) into cup(s) *and pierce the membrane of the yolk with a toothpick or tine of a fork. This releases steam and keeps the egg from spattering during cooking.*

Cover cups *with plastic wrap or a plate for faster, more even cooking.*

Microwave on Medium (50%) *until white is opaque. Allow egg[s] to stand 1 to 2 minutes or until white is completely set. Remove poached egg onto a slotted spoon.*

OMELETS

Lift omelet edges with spatula *halfway through cooking, allowing uncooked portion to spread evenly. Although shown in a browning dish, omelets can be done in other dishes.*

Sprinkle with cheese *when omelet is set but still glossy in appearance. Continue cooking until cheese melts.*

Loosen omelet with spatula. *Fold in half and gently slide onto serving plate.*

FLUFFY OMELET
Power Level: HIGH [100%] and MEDIUM [50%]
Total Cooking Time: 7 to 9¾ minutes

3 eggs, separated
2 tablespoons sour cream
2 tablespoons mayonnaise
1 tablespoon chopped chives
2 tablespoons butter (or margarine)
½ cup grated Cheddar cheese

1. Beat egg yolks until thick and lemon color. Add sour cream, mayonnaise and chives and continue to beat 1 minute. Set aside.

2. Beat egg whites in a large bowl until soft peaks form. Fold in yolk mixture.

3. Place butter in a 9 inch pie dish. Microwave on HIGH (100%) for 30 to 45 seconds or until melted. Tip to coat plate.

4. Pour egg mixture into pie dish. Microwave on MEDIUM (50%) for 6 to 8 minutes or until set, but still glossy on top. Turn dish a half turn halfway through cooking.

5. Sprinkle with Cheddar cheese. Microwave on MEDIUM (50%) for an additional 30 seconds to 1 minute or until cheese is melted.

6. Loosen edges of omelet from plate with a spatula. Fold omelet in half and slide onto a serving dish. Serve immediately.

Recipe yield: 2 servings

GOLDEN OMELET
Power Level: HIGH [100%]
Total Cooking Time: 2 to 3 minutes

4 eggs
3 tablespoons milk
Dash of salt
Dash of pepper
2 tablespoons butter (or margarine)

1. Beat together eggs, milk, salt and pepper. Set aside.

2. Microwave browning dish on HIGH (100%) for 3 to 4 minutes.

3. Add butter and allow to melt. Pour egg mixture into dish. Cover.

4. Microwave on HIGH (100%) for 2 to 3 minutes or until set but still moist. Halfway through cooking loosen edge of omelet from dish with a rubber spatula.

5. Loosen edge from dish and fold omelet in half. Slide onto a serving dish.

Variation:
GOLDEN COUNTRY OMELET

Add ¼ cup grated Cheddar cheese, ¼ cup crumbled bacon, ¼ cup diced ham or ¼ cup sauteed vegetables the last 30 to 45 seconds of cooking.

Recipe yield: 2 servings

MEXICAN OMELET ROLL
Power Level: HIGH [100%]
Total Cooking Time: 14 to 18 minutes

1 strip of ham, 1½ inches wide and 6 inches long
¼ cup butter (or margarine)
½ cup chopped green pepper
1 medium onion, chopped
5 eggs, beaten
¼ cup water
2 tablespoons chopped pimento

1. Place meat in an 8 x 8 x 2 inch baking dish. Cover. Microwave on HIGH (100%) for 3 to 4 minutes or until heated through. Cover with aluminum foil and allow to stand while cooking omelet.

2. Place butter, green pepper and onion in an 11¾ x 7½ x 1¾ inch baking dish. Microwave on HIGH (100%) for 3 to 4 minutes or until vegetables are tender.

3. Stir together eggs and water. Pour over vegetables. Sprinkle with pimento. Cover with plastic wrap. Microwave on HIGH (100%) for 8 to 10 minutes or until set, but still glossy on top. Turn dish four times during cooking.

4. Remove plastic wrap. Loosen bottom and edges of omelet with a rubber spatula. Cover dish with waxed paper. Place cookie sheet over waxed paper. Flip omelet out onto cookie sheet.

5. Place ham on small end of omelet. Roll ham inside omelet in jelly-roll fashion. Place seam side down on serving dish.

6. If desired, serve topped with cheese sauce. Make sauce by mixing together 1 can (10¾ ounces) Cheddar cheese soup and ½ cup milk. Microwave on HIGH (100%) for 3 to 4 minutes.

Recipe yield: 4 servings

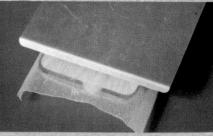

Loosen omelet *around edges and underneath with spatula. Place waxed paper over dish. Place cookie sheet on top and flip over so omelet falls onto waxed paper and sheet. Roll ham inside omelet in jelly-roll fashion.*

MEXICAN EGGS 'N HAM

Power Level: HIGH [100%]
Total Cooking Time: 13½ to 16¾ minutes

3 tablespoons butter (or margarine)
3 tablespoons all purpose flour
¾ teaspoon salt
Dash of pepper
1½ cups half and half
1 tablespoon Worcestershire sauce
1 tablespoon chili sauce
1 teaspoon horseradish
½ teaspoon chili powder
6 hard cooked eggs, peeled and sliced (cook eggs on conventional range)
2 cups finely chopped cooked ham
½ cup chopped ripe olives
¼ cup chopped chilies
1 cup (4 ounces) grated Cheddar cheese
1 can (3 ounces) French fried onions, crushed

1. Place butter in a 4 cup measure or 1 quart casserole. Microwave on HIGH (100%) for 30 to 45 seconds or until melted.

2. Stir in flour, salt and pepper until smooth. Slowly add cream. Microwave on HIGH (100%) for 3 to 4 minutes or until thickened.

3. Stir in Worcestershire sauce, chili sauce, horseradish and chili powder.

4. Place alternate layers of eggs, ham, olives, chilies, cheese and sauce in a 10 x 6 x 1¾ inch glass baking dish. Sprinkle with crushed onions.

5. Microwave on HIGH (100%) for 10 to 12 minutes or until hot and bubbly.

Recipe yield: 6 to 8 servings

Mexican Omelet Roll makes a great brunch.

SAUSAGE STRATA

Power Level: HIGH [100%]
Total Cooking Time: 17 to 21 minutes

1 pound ground pork sausage
8 slices bread, cubed
2 cups grated Cheddar cheese
4 eggs
2 cups milk
1 tablespoon chopped chives
½ teaspoon dry mustard

1. Place sausage in a 1 quart casserole. Microwave on HIGH (100%) for 5 to 6 minutes or until no longer pink. Drain off excess fat.

2. Place alternate layers of bread cubes, sausage and cheese in a greased 11¾ x 7½ x 1¾ inch baking dish, starting and ending with bread cubes.

3. Beat together eggs, milk, chives and mustard. Pour over bread cubes. Cover and refrigerate for 4 hours or overnight.

4. Microwave on HIGH (100%) for 12 to 15 minutes or until knife inserted near center comes out clean.

Recipe yield: 8 servings

HAM & EGGS CREPES

Power Level: HIGH [100%]
Total Cooking Time: 8 to 10 minutes

12 crepes
¼ cup milk
1 can (10½ ounces) condensed cream of chicken soup
4 to 6 hard cooked eggs, peeled and chopped (cook on conventional range)
1½ cups finely chopped cooked ham
1 cup dairy sour cream
1 tablespoon chopped chives
½ teaspoon dry mustard
¼ teaspoon salt
½ cup (2 ounces) grated Cheddar cheese
Paprika

1. Mix together milk and half the soup. Set aside.

2. Combine eggs, ham, sour cream, remaining soup, chives, dry mustard and salt. Place ⅓ cup of mixture on each crepe. Roll up in jelly roll fashion.

3. Place alternate layers of crepes, soup mixture and cheese in an 11¾ x 7½ x 1¾ inch glass baking dish. Sprinkle with paprika.

4. Microwave on HIGH (100%) for 8 to 10 minutes or until hot and bubbly.

Recipe yield: 4 to 6 servings

Cheese

Cheese can be softened, melted or brought to room temperature in the microwave.

Use Low (30%) to bring cheese to room temperature. Be sure to remove any metallic wrappings.

To melt cheese, use Medium (50%). At this setting, you can avoid constant watching, stirring and overcooking.

Because of its high fat content, cheese can quickly overcook and become stringy and tough. To avoid this, use lower power settings. Add cheese at the end of cooking or layer it between other foods.

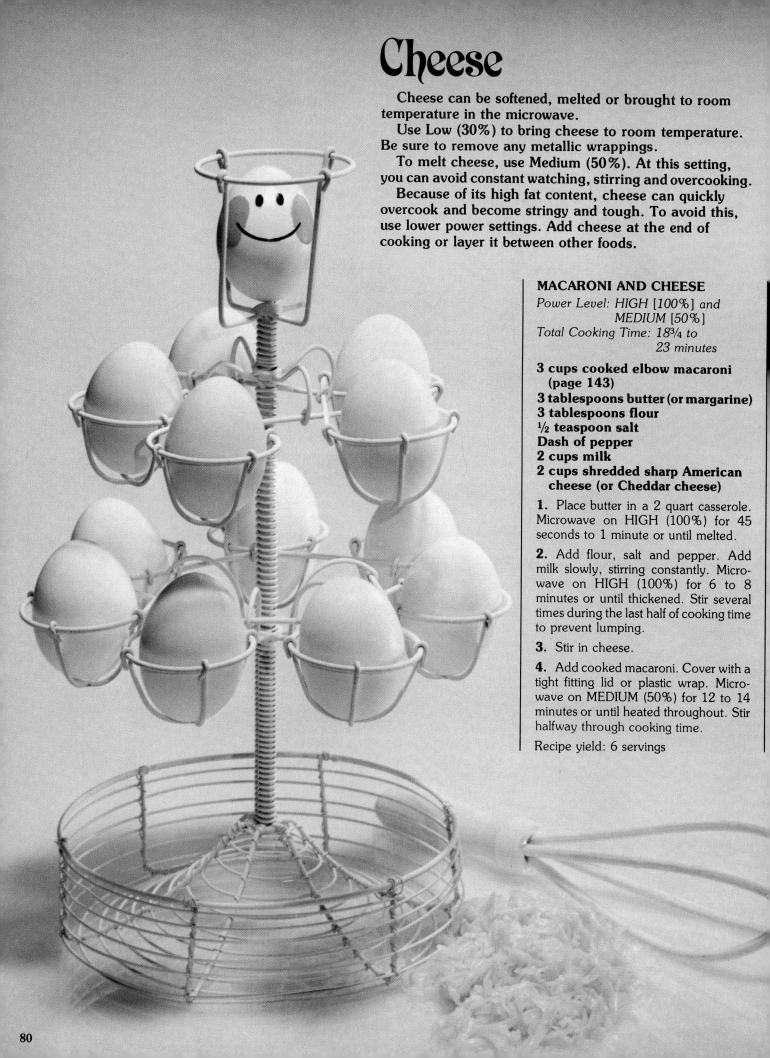

MACARONI AND CHEESE

Power Level: HIGH [100%] and
MEDIUM [50%]
Total Cooking Time: 18¾ to
23 minutes

3 cups cooked elbow macaroni
(page 143)
3 tablespoons butter (or margarine)
3 tablespoons flour
½ teaspoon salt
Dash of pepper
2 cups milk
2 cups shredded sharp American
cheese (or Cheddar cheese)

1. Place butter in a 2 quart casserole. Microwave on HIGH (100%) for 45 seconds to 1 minute or until melted.

2. Add flour, salt and pepper. Add milk slowly, stirring constantly. Microwave on HIGH (100%) for 6 to 8 minutes or until thickened. Stir several times during the last half of cooking time to prevent lumping.

3. Stir in cheese.

4. Add cooked macaroni. Cover with a tight fitting lid or plastic wrap. Microwave on MEDIUM (50%) for 12 to 14 minutes or until heated throughout. Stir halfway through cooking time.

Recipe yield: 6 servings

MACARONI AND CHEESE DINNER

Power Level: HIGH [100%] and MEDIUM [50%]
Total Cooking Time: 19 to 23½ minutes

4 cups water
1 teaspoon salt
1 package (7¼ ounces) macaroni and cheese dinner
¼ cup butter (or margarine)
¼ cup milk

1. Place water and salt in a 2 quart casserole. Cover with a tight fitting lid or plastic wrap. Microwave on HIGH (100%) for 8 to 10 minutes or until boiling.

2. Stir in macaroni. Cover. Microwave on MEDIUM (50%) for 10 to 12 minutes or until tender. Stir halfway through cooking.

3. Immediately drain and rinse with hot water. Return to casserole.

4. Stir in butter, milk and cheese packet. Cover. Microwave on HIGH (100%) for 1 to 1½ minutes or until butter and cheese are melted.

Recipe yield: 3 cups

SWISS CHEESE FONDUE

Power Level: HIGH [100%]
Total Cooking Time: 5 to 8 minutes

¼ cup cornstarch
2 cups dry white wine (or apple juice)
¼ cup water
¼ teaspoon paprika
¼ teaspoon garlic powder
¼ teaspoon salt
Dash of pepper
4 cups (1 pound) grated Swiss cheese

1. Mix together cornstarch, wine, water and seasonings until smooth.

2. Microwave on HIGH (100%) for 4 to 6 minutes or until thickened. Stir occasionally.

3. Stir in cheese until melted. If not completely melted, microwave on HIGH (100%) for 1 to 2 minutes or until melted.

4. Serve hot with French bread cubes.

Recipe yield: about 3 cups

WELSH RAREBIT

Power Level: HIGH [100%] and MEDIUM [50%]
Total Cooking Time: 6½ to 10 minutes
Temperature Probe: 130° to 140°

½ cup beer
1 tablespoon butter (or margarine)
1 teaspoon Worcestershire sauce
½ teaspoon dry mustard
½ teaspoon paprika
Dash of pepper
2 cups (8 ounces) grated Cheddar cheese
2 eggs, slightly beaten
4 slices bread, toasted

1. Combine beer, butter, Worcestershire sauce, dry mustard, paprika and pepper in a 1 quart casserole or 4 cup measure. Microwave on HIGH (100%) for 2 to 3 minutes or until hot.

2. Stir in cheese until melted. If not completely melted, microwave on HIGH (100%) for 30 seconds to 1 minute.

3. Stir a small amount of cheese mixture into eggs, then stir egg mixture into the remaining cheese mixture.

4. Microwave on MEDIUM (50%) for 4 to 6 minutes or until thickened. Stir occasionally. Serve hot over toast.

Recipe yield: 4 servings

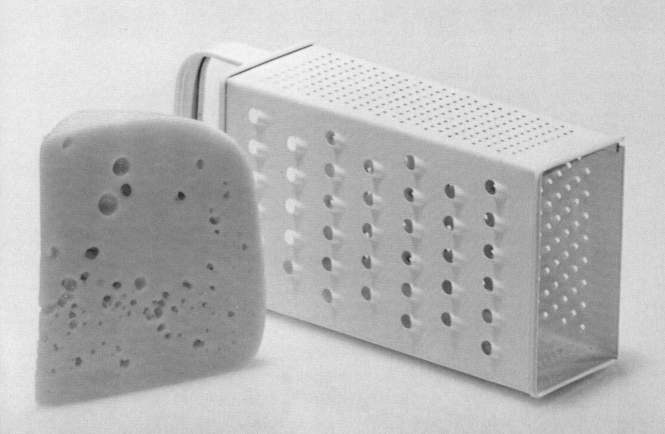

QUICHE

Bake pastry shell *and allow to cool. If shell is not baked first, it will become soggy while quiche is cooking.*

First stir a small amount of hot cream *into eggs to warm the egg mixture. Then add egg mixture to the remaining hot cream.*

Pour mixture over spatula *into pastry shell so as not to disturb cheese filling.*

Test for doneness *by inserting knife near center of quiche. When knife comes out clean, remove quiche from microwave and allow to stand until set.*

HAM AND CHEESE QUICHE
Power Level: HIGH [100%]
Total Cooking Time: 14 to
16½ minutes

1 9-inch baked pastry or
  quiche shell
½ cup grated Cheddar cheese
½ cup grated Swiss cheese
2 cups half and half
1 tablespoon chopped chives
2 teaspoons instant minced onion
½ teaspoon curry powder
¼ teaspoon salt
Dash of hot pepper sauce
4 eggs, slightly beaten
½ cup finely chopped ham

1. Fill cooled shell with cheese. Set aside.

2. Mix together cream, chives, instant minced onion, curry powder, salt and hot pepper sauce in a 4 cup measure or 1 quart casserole.

3. Microwave on HIGH (100%) for 2 to 2½ minutes or until steaming.

4. Stir a small amount of hot cream into eggs, then stir egg mixture into the remaining hot cream. Pour gently into shell. Sprinkle with ham.

5. Microwave on HIGH (100%) for 12 to 14 minutes or until a knife inserted near center comes out clean. Turn dish a half turn halfway through cooking.

6. Allow to stand 10 minutes before cutting or until center is set.

Recipe yield: 6 to 8 servings

CREME LORRAINE
Power Level: HIGH [100%]
Total Cooking Time: 15 to 18 minutes

6 slices bacon
1 egg + 2 egg yolks, beaten
1¼ cups (5 ounces) grated
  Swiss cheese

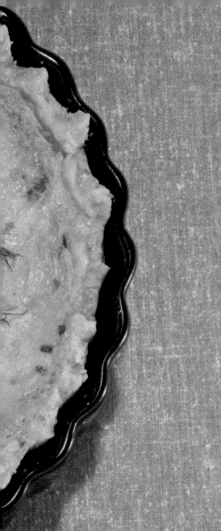

This beautiful Ham and Cheese Quiche deserves its gourmet reputation.

1¼ cups (5 ounces) grated
    Cheddar cheese
½ cup Parmesan cheese
2 cups whipping cream
1 tablespoon chopped chives
Dash of pepper

1. Microwave bacon on HIGH (100%) for 5 to 6 minutes or until crispy. Crumble and set aside.

2. Mix together remaining ingredients. Pour into a buttered 10 inch pie plate or quiche dish. Sprinkle top with crumbled bacon.

3. Microwave on HIGH (100%) for 10 to 12 minutes or until a knife inserted near center comes out clean.

4. Allow to stand 5 minutes or until completely set.

Recipe yield: 6 to 8 servings

PIZZA

Power Level: HIGH [100%]
Total Cooking Time: 11 to 14 minutes
for each pizza

2 cups all purpose flour
2 teaspoons baking powder
1 teaspoon salt
⅔ cup milk
⅓ cup cooking oil
1 tablespoon Worcestershire sauce
1 can (8 ounces) pizza sauce
1 tablespoon Italian seasoning
2 cups cooked and drained
    sausage
3 cups shredded Mozzarella cheese
½ cup Parmesan cheese
¼ cup chopped green pepper
    (optional)

1. Combine flour, baking powder and salt. Add milk, oil and Worcestershire sauce. Stir until dough cleans sides of bowl.

2. Knead dough 4 to 5 times. Divide in half and shape into two balls. Place dough between two pieces of waxed paper. Roll each ball of dough into a 12 inch circle. Remove top sheet of waxed paper. Place one circle, waxed paper side down, in microwave.

3. Microwave on HIGH (100%) for 4 minutes. Turn pizza a half turn halfway through cooking.

4. Carefully turn crust over onto a piece of brown paper cut to the pizza size and peel off waxed paper. Microwave on HIGH (100%) for 2 minutes.

5. Mix together pizza sauce and Italian seasoning in a 2 cup measure. Microwave on HIGH (100%) for 1 to 2 minutes or until steaming.

6. Layer crust with half the sausage, sauce, cheeses and green pepper.

7. Microwave on HIGH (100%) for 4 to 6 minutes or until cheese is melted. Repeat with other pizza.

Recipe yield: two (12 inch) pizzas

INDIVIDUAL PIZZA TREATS

Power Level: MEDIUM HIGH [70%]
Total Cooking Time: 2 to 3 minutes

4 English muffins, split in half
    and toasted
24 slices pepperoni
1 can (5 ounces) pizza sauce
Italian seasoning
1 cup grated Mozzarella cheese

1. Layer pepperoni, pizza sauce, Italian seasoning and Mozzarella cheese on English muffin halves.

2. Place on a paper towel. Microwave on MEDIUM HIGH (70%) for 2 to 3 minutes or until cheese just begins to melt.

Variation:

INDIVIDUAL SAUSAGE PIZZA TREATS

Follow Individual Pizza Treats recipe as directed except substitute ¼ pound browned and well drained sausage for pepperoni. Sprinkle top with chopped green pepper. If desired, place a mound of sauerkraut over sauce for added flavor.

Recipe yield: 6 to 8 servings

CHEESY ENCHILADAS

Power Level: HIGH [100%]
Total Cooking Time: 11½ to
14¾ minutes

2 cups cottage cheese (or ricotta)
1 cup (4 ounces) grated Monterey
    Jack cheese
1 can (4 ounces) chopped chilies
1 egg, beaten
1 teaspoon chili powder
½ teaspoon onion salt
½ teaspoon paprika
8 to 10 tortillas
1 can (10 ounces) enchilada sauce
2 cups (8 ounces) grated
    Cheddar cheese
Sour cream
Chopped green onion

1. Mix together cottage cheese, Monterey Jack cheese, chopped chilies, egg and seasonings.

2. Microwave tortillas on HIGH (100%) for 30 to 45 seconds or until pliable. Place ⅓ cup of filling on each tortilla. Roll up in jelly roll fashion.

3. Place tortillas, seam side down, in an 11¾ x 7½ x 1¾ inch baking dish. Cover with enchilada sauce. Microwave on HIGH (100%) for 10 to 12 minutes or until hot and bubbly.

4. Sprinkle with Cheddar cheese. Microwave on HIGH (100%) for an additional 1 to 2 minutes or until cheese is melted.

5. Garnish with sour cream and green onions.

Recipe yield: 4 to 6 servings

Variation:

CHEESY ENCHILADAS WITH REFRIED BEANS

Follow Cheesy Enchiladas recipe as directed except spread each tortilla with a layer of refried beans before filling.

Fish & Seafood

Fish lovers never had it so good! With its speed and moisture retention, microwave cooking is perfect for preserving the delicate flavor and tenderness of fish and seafood.

Defrosting

Defrost small and large shellfish on Low (30%) power. Always be sure to check them at minimum defrosting time.

SMALL SHELLFISH

Spread small shellfish *loosely in dish, forming a single layer. Defrost on Low [30%] power for half the time. Turn and rearrange pieces midway through defrosting.*

Check after minimum *defrosting time. Shellfish should feel soft and cool and still be translucent.*

Place frozen block *of shellfish in a casserole and cover with plastic wrap or tight-fitting lid. Frozen shellfish in a pouch need not be covered. Defrost on Low [30%] power for half the time.*

BLOCK FISH

Turn block over *and break it up midway through defrosting. Flex shellfish in pouch. The center may still be firm. Continue defrosting, breaking off pieces as they loosen.*

Check after minimum *defrosting time. Pieces should be loose and slightly icy. Let stand to completely defrost.*

LARGE SHELLFISH

Arrange large shellfish *in dish with soft shell side up. Defrost on Low [30%] for half the minimum time.*

Turn back or hard shell side up *halfway through the defrost time.*

Check after minimum *defrosting time. Shellfish should feel cool, be flexible and transparent.*

FROZEN SHELLFISH DEFROSTING CHART

Power Level: LOW (30%)	
Item	**Defrosting Time**
Crab Claws (1 pound) Loose Pack	6-8 min.
Crab Legs (8-10 oz.) 1 or 2 3 or 4	6-8 min. 10-12 min.
Crab Meat (6 ounces) (1 pound) Frozen Block	4-6 min. 7-9 min.
Whole Lobster or Crab (1½ pounds)	18-20 min.
Lobster Tails (8-10 ounces) 1 or 2 3 or 4	8-10 min. 12-14 min.
Lobster Tails (12-16 ounces) 1 or 2	12-14 min.
Oysters (1 pound) Frozen Block	8-10 min.
Scallops (1 pound) Loose Pack	8-10 min.
Scallops (1 pound) Frozen Block	10-12 min.
Shrimp (1 pound) Loose Pack	6-8 min.

Cooking

In the microwave, most shellfish can be steamed without adding water. Just arrange and cover tightly with plastic wrap.

SMALL SHELLFISH

Place clean, deveined shrimp in a ring. Cover with plastic wrap, pleated to allow steam to expand. Also cook clams in a circle.

Check for doneness. Most shellfish turn from translucent to opaque. Clams will partially open. If a clam fails to open, do not eat it.

LARGE SHELLFISH

Cut the hard shell side of lobster tails and loosen meat with fingers, bringing it slightly over the top of shell. Cut into the meat about ¼ inch so meat will "butterfly" over shell.

Arrange lobster tails with meat side up in dish. Brush tails with melted butter, lemon juice and salt.

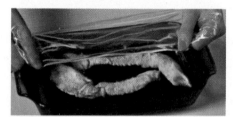

Arrange crab legs in dish with light colored side up.

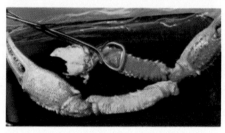

Turn over crab legs so dark side is up midway through cooking. Cover and continue cooking until flesh is opaque. Allow to stand 5 minutes.

WHOLE LOBSTER

Cut into live lobster between the head and first segment, severing the spinal cord which kills the lobster. There may be signs of movement for a few minutes.

Insert a wooden peg lengthwise through the tail to prevent tail from curling. If desired, remove sack near head and dark vein along body.

Place lobster hard shell down in baking dish. Add ½ cup hot water and salt. Cover with plastic wrap, pleated to allow steam to expand. Microwave on High [100%] for 10 to 12 minutes. Turn over halfway through cooking.

Check for doneness. Meat should be opaque, and shell should be pink.

SHELLFISH COOKING CHART

Item	Power Level	Cooking Time
Clams (12)	Med. (50%)	32-36 min.
Crab Legs (8-10 oz.) 1 2 4	Low (30%)	6-8 min. 8-10 min. 10-12 min.
Lobster Tails (8-10 oz.) 1 2 4 (12-16 oz.) 1 2	High (100%)	4-6 min. 8-10 min. 10-12 min. 8-10 min. 12-14 min.
Oysters (1 lb.)	High (100%)	4-6 min.
Scallops (1 lb.)	Med.-Hi. (70%)	6-8 min.
Shrimp (peeled) (1 lb.)	High (100%)	4-6 min.
Whole Lobster (1½ lbs.)	High (100%)	10-12 min.

Butter tip (for seafood)

Use High (100%) power to melt butter in small bowl or glass measure. Heat until bubbly. To clarify, pour off clear liquid.

WHOLE LOBSTER

Power Level: HIGH [100%]
Total Cooking Time: 10 to 12 minutes

1 live lobster
  (about 1¼ to 2 pounds)
½ cup hot water
1 teaspoon salt

1. Sever the lobster's spinal cord by cutting between the head and first section of shell.

2. Insert a wooden skewer lengthwise through tail to prevent curling. If desired, remove sack near head and dark vein along body.

3. Place lobster, hard shell down, in baking dish. Add water and salt. Cover with plastic wrap.

4. Microwave on HIGH (100%) for 10 to 12 minutes or until meat is opaque and shell is pink. Turn over halfway through cooking time.

5. Serve with melted butter and lemon wedges.

LOBSTER TAILS

Power Level: HIGH [100%]

Lobster tails
¼ cup butter (or margarine)
2 tablespoons lemon juice
½ teaspoon salt
Dash of paprika

1. Place butter in a 1 cup measure. Microwave on HIGH (100%) for 30 to 45 seconds or until melted. Stir in lemon juice and salt.

2. Split lobster tails through hard shell. Loosen meat with fingers. Cut into the meat about ¼ inch so meat will "butterfly" over shell. Place, meat side up, in a baking dish. Brush with lemon butter and sprinkle with paprika. Cover with a tight fitting lid or plastic wrap.

3. Microwave on HIGH (100%) until meat is opaque and shell is pink. (See page 86 for cooking times.)

4. Allow to stand 5 minutes.

UNPEELED SHRIMP

Power Level: HIGH [100%]
Total Cooking Time: 9 to 13 minutes

1 pound shrimp (unpeeled)
2½ cups water
1 bay leaf
1 tablespoon lemon juice

1. Place water, bay leaf and lemon juice in a 2 quart casserole. Cover with a tight fitting lid or plastic wrap. Microwave on HIGH (100%) for 6 to 8 minutes or until boiling.

2. Add shrimp. Cover. Microwave on HIGH (100%) for 3 to 5 minutes or until shell turns pink.

3. Drain and rinse. Peel and devein.

Recipe yield: 3 to 4 servings

SEAFOOD NEWBURG

Power Level: HIGH [100%] and
  MEDIUM-HIGH [70%]
Total Cooking Time: 14 to 18 minutes

1 can (10½ ounces) cream of
  shrimp soup
⅔ cup half and half
2 egg yolks, beaten
⅓ cup dry white wine
2 teaspoons lemon juice
1 pound frozen precooked shrimp
6 ounces frozen crabmeat, thawed,
  flaked and cartilage removed
1 cup (8 ounces) grated American
  cheese
6 to 8 patty shells (or toast cups)
Paprika

1. Mix together soup, cream and egg yolks in a 2 quart casserole. Microwave on HIGH (100%) for 8 to 10 minutes or until hot and bubbly. Stir occasionally.

2. Stir in wine, lemon juice, shrimp, crabmeat and cheese. Microwave on MEDIUM-HIGH (70%) for 6 to 8 minutes or until heated through. Stir occasionally. Allow to stand 5 minutes before serving.

3. Serve in toast cups or patty shells and sprinkle with paprika.

Recipe yield: 6 to 8 servings

STEAMED CLAMS WITH BUTTER SAUCE

Power Level: MEDIUM [50%] and
  HIGH [100%]
Total Cooking Time: 20¾ to
  26 minutes

12 hard shell clams
½ cup water
½ cup butter (or margarine)
¼ cup chopped parsley
1 tablespoon lemon juice
1 teaspoon garlic powder

1. Scrub clams thoroughly with a brush to remove sand.

2. Place clams in an 11¾ x 7½ x 1¾ inch baking dish. Add water. Cover with a tight fitting lid or plastic wrap. Microwave on MEDIUM (50%) for 20 to 25 minutes or until all shells are opened. Rearrange halfway through cooking. Reserve clam broth. (Clams that do not open are bad and must be discarded.)

3. Combine butter, parsley, lemon juice and garlic powder in a 1 quart casserole. Microwave on HIGH (100%) for 45 seconds to 1 minute or until melted. Stir to blend.

4. Serve clams with individual serving dishes of clam broth and lemon-butter.

Recipe yield: 4 servings

SHRIMP AND MUSHROOMS

Power Level: HIGH [100%] and
  MEDIUM-HIGH [70%]
Total Cooking Time: 8 to 11 minutes

2 tablespoons butter (or margarine)
2 tablespoons chopped onion
1 tablespoon lemon juice
Dash of garlic powder
1 pound frozen precooked shrimp,
  thawed and drained
1 can (4 ounces) sliced
  mushrooms, drained
¼ cup dry white wine

1. Place butter, onion, lemon juice and garlic powder in a 2 quart casserole. Microwave on HIGH (100%) for 2 to 3 minutes or until onion is tender.

2. Stir in shrimp, mushrooms and wine. Cover with a tight fitting lid or plastic wrap. Microwave on MEDIUM-HIGH (70%) for 6 to 8 minutes or until heated through. Stir halfway through cooking. Allow to stand 5 minutes.

Recipe yield: 4 servings

SHRIMP ORIENTAL

Power Level: HIGH [100%]
Total Cooking Time: 14 to 18 minutes

1 pound frozen uncooked shrimp
1 package (10 ounces) frozen pea
  pods
2 tablespoons cooking oil
1 tablespoon cornstarch
¼ to ½ cup Teriyaki sauce
1 can (8½ ounces) water chestnuts,
  drained and sliced

1. Place shrimp and pea pods in a 2 quart casserole. Cover with a tight fitting lid or plastic wrap. Microwave on HIGH (100%) for 8 to 10 minutes or until shrimp is opaque. Drain.

2. Mix together cooking oil, cornstarch and Teriyaki sauce.

3. Add water chestnuts to shrimp and pea pods. Stir in Teriyaki sauce mixture. Cover. Microwave on HIGH (100%) for 6 to 8 minutes or until hot and bubbly. Stir halfway through cooking. Allow to stand 5 minutes.

4. Serve over rice or chow mein noodles.

Recipe yield: 4 servings

SHRIMP STUFFED SOLE

Power Level: HIGH [100%]
Total Cooking Time: 7¾ to
10½ minutes

1 pound sole fillets
1 tablespoon lemon juice
Dash of onion salt
¼ cup butter (or margarine)
1 can (4½ ounces) shrimp (or
crabmeat), chopped and drained
⅓ cup milk
¼ cup celery
2 teaspoons chopped parsley
1 cup toasted bread cubes
(or croutons)
Dash of paprika

1. Cut fillets in half lengthwise. Sprinkle with lemon juice and onion salt. Set aside.

2. Place butter in a 1 quart casserole. Microwave on HIGH (100%) for 45 seconds to 1 minute or until melted. Remove 2 tablespoons and set aside.

3. Add shrimp, milk, celery and parsley to remaining butter. Cover with tight fitting lid or plastic wrap. Microwave on HIGH (100%) for 1 to 1½ minutes or until steaming. Stir in bread cubes.

4. Spread each fillet with shrimp stuffing. Roll up jelly-roll fashion starting with the small end. Tie rolls together or secure edges with wooden skewers.

5. Place in an 8 x 8 x 2 inch baking dish. Brush with reserved butter and sprinkle with paprika. Cover.

6. Microwave on HIGH (100%) for 6 to 8 minutes or until fish flakes easily with a fork. Rearrange halfway through cooking. Allow to stand 5 minutes before serving.

Recipe yield: 3 to 4 servings

SHRIMP PARMESAN FOR TWO

Power Level: HIGH [100%]
Total Cooking Time: 6¾ to 9 minutes

18 large uncooked shrimp
½ cup butter (or margarine)
2 tablespoons lemon juice
¼ teaspoon garlic powder
½ cup bread crumbs
½ cup grated Parmesan cheese
2 tablespoons dried parsley

1. Butterfly shrimp by cutting the length of the inner curve ¾ of the way through. Spread the sides to form the butterfly shape. Set aside.

2. Place butter in a small bowl. Microwave on HIGH (100%) for 45 seconds to 1 minute or until melted. Stir in lemon juice and garlic powder.

3. Pour half the butter mixture into a baking dish. Arrange shrimp, cut side down and small end toward center, over butter.

4. Mix together bread crumbs. Parmesan cheese and parsley. Sprinkle over shrimp, then drizzle remaining butter over crumb mixture. Cover with waxed paper. Microwave on HIGH (100%) for 6 to 8 minutes or until shrimp is opaque. Allow to stand 5 minutes before serving.

Recipe yield: 2 servings

SOLE AND OYSTER CASSEROLE

Power Level: LOW [30%] and
HIGH [100%] and
MEDIUM-HIGH [70%]
Total Cooking Time: 20¾ to
25 minutes

2 pounds frozen sole fillets
¼ cup butter (or margarine)
1 can (10½ ounces) oyster stew
1 can (3 ounces) sliced
mushrooms, drained
½ teaspoon Worcestershire sauce
¼ teaspoon garlic salt
1½ cups seasoned croutons

1. Microwave fillets on LOW (30%) for 10 to 12 minutes or until defrosted (see page 90).

2. Place fish, thickest end towards outside. in an 11¾ x 7½ x 1¾ inch baking dish. Set aside.

3. Place butter in a 4 cup measure or 1 quart casserole. Microwave on HIGH (100%) for 45 seconds to 1 minute or until melted.

4. Add oyster stew, mushrooms, Worcestershire sauce and garlic salt. Stir until well blended. Pour over fillets. Sprinkle with croutons. Cover with waxed paper.

5. Microwave on MEDIUM-HIGH (70%) for 10 to 12 minutes or until fish flakes easily with a fork. Turn halfway through cooking. Allow to stand 5 minutes before serving.

Recipe yield: 6 to 8 servings

SWEET AND SOUR SHRIMP

Power Level: HIGH [100%]
Total Cooking Time: 12 to 14 minutes

1 pound frozen uncooked shrimp
¼ cup brown sugar
2 tablespoons cornstarch
2 tablespoons soy sauce
2 tablespoons cider vinegar
¼ teaspoon ground ginger
1 can (13¾ ounces) pineapple
chunks, undrained
1 green pepper, cut into ¼ inch
strips
1 medium onion, sliced thin

1. Rinse, drain and pat shrimp dry.

2. Mix together sugar, cornstarch, soy sauce, vinegar and ginger in a 2 quart casserole.

3. Add shrimp, pineapple, green pepper and onion. Cover with a tight fitting lid or plastic wrap.

4. Microwave on HIGH (100%) for 12 to 14 minutes or until shrimp is opaque. Allow to stand 5 minutes before serving.

Recipe yield: 4 servings

OYSTER AU GRATIN CASSEROLE

Power Level: HIGH [100%] and
MEDIUM [50%]
Total Cooking Time: 19½ to
24 minutes

¼ cup butter (or margarine)
2 cups Cheddar cheese cracker
crumbs
1 tablespoon dried parsley
½ teaspoon salt
Dash of paprika
½ cup chopped mushrooms
¼ cup chopped onion
1 egg, slightly beaten
1 pint oysters, pierced and drained,
reserve liquid
1 can (10¾ ounces) cream of
celery soup

1. Place butter in a 1 quart casserole. Microwave on HIGH (100%) for 1½ to 2 minutes or until melted.

2. Mix together 2 tablespoons melted butter, cracker crumbs, parsley, salt and paprika in a large mixing bowl.

3. Add mushrooms and onion to remaining butter. Microwave on HIGH (100%) for 3 to 4 minutes or until onion is tender. Stir halfway through cooking.

4. Mix together egg, oysters, ½ cup oyster liquid and soup. Stir into sauteed vegetables.

5. Line the bottom of a 10 x 6 x 1¾ inch baking dish with half the crumb mixture. Pour oyster mixture over crumbs. Top with remaining crumb mixture.

6. Microwave on MEDIUM (50%) for 15 to 18 minutes or until hot and bubbly. Allow to stand 5 minutes before serving.

Recipe yield: 6 to 8 servings

SCALLOPS IN WINE SAUCE

Power Level: HIGH [100%] and
MEDIUM [50%]
Total Cooking Time: 16¾ to
21 minutes

2 tablespoons butter (or margarine)
2 tablespoons bread crumbs
½ teaspoon dried parsley
½ cup mushrooms, sliced
2 tablespoons thinly sliced celery
1 tablespoon finely chopped onion
1 tablespoon all purpose flour
½ teaspoon salt
Dash of paprika

⅓ cup dry white wine
1 pound scallops
½ cup whipping cream
1 egg yolk

1. Place butter in a 1½ quart casserole. Microwave on HIGH (100%) for 45 seconds to 1 minute or until melted.

2. Mix together 2 tablespoons melted butter, bread crumbs and parsley in a small mixing bowl. Set aside.

3. Add mushrooms, celery and onion to remaining butter. Microwave on HIGH (100%) for 3 to 4 minutes or until celery and onion are tender. Stir halfway through cooking.

4. Stir in flour, salt and paprika. Slowly add wine, mixing until smooth. Add scallops. Cover with a tight fitting lid or plastic wrap. Microwave on MEDIUM (50%) for 8 to 10 minutes. Stir occasionally during cooking.

5. Combine whipping cream and egg yolk. Pour over hot scallops. Sprinkle top with bread crumb mixture. Microwave on MEDIUM (50%) for 5 to 6 minutes or until heated through.

Recipe yield: 3 to 4 servings

FISHERMAN'S STEW OR BOUILLABAISE
Power Level: HIGH [100%]
Total Cooking Time: 28 to 39 minutes

1 medium onion, chopped
1 carrot, chopped
2 tablespoons cooking oil
1 clove garlic, minced
1 pound fish fillets, cut in 3 inch pieces
3 lobster tails, left in shells

½ pound raw shrimp
3 cups water
1 can (8 ounces) tomato sauce
1 bay leaf
1 dozen clams (in shells)
1 cup wine (or beef broth)
1 teaspoon lemon juice
1 teaspoon parsley
½ teaspoon salt
¼ teaspoon saffron (or curry)
Dash of pepper

1. Combine onion, carrot, cooking oil and garlic in a 4 quart casserole. Microwave on HIGH (100%) for 3 to 4 minutes or until onion is tender.

2. Add fish fillets, lobster tails, shrimp, water, tomato sauce and bay leaf. Cover with a tight fitting lid or plastic wrap. Microwave on HIGH (100%) for 15 to 20 minutes or until boiling. Stir halfway through cooking time.

3. Add clams, wine, lemon juice, parsley, salt, saffron and pepper. Cover. Microwave on HIGH (100%) for 10 to 15 minutes or until all seafood is tender.

4. Serve with slices of French bread.

Recipe yield: 6 to 8 servings

Fisherman's Stew brings home the taste of New England goodness.

Defrosting

Fish defrosts quickly so take care that it is still cold when you finish defrosting. Once it gets warm, you have actually started the cooking process.

The shape and weight of both whole and package frozen fish affect defrosting time. Short, thick fish or bulky packages may take longer to defrost than long, thin packages or fish of the same weight.

DEFROSTING CHART

Power Level: LOW (30%)	
Item	**Defrosting Time**
Fish Fillets (1 pound)	10-12 min.
Fish Steak (6 ounces) 1 2	2-4 min. 4-6 min.
Whole Fish (8-10 ounces) 1 2	6-8 min. 12-14 min.
Whole Fish (2-4 pounds)	14-16 min.

FILLETS & STEAKS

Place unopened package directly on the oven floor. Turn package over midway through defrosting. Fillets frozen at home in water should be put in a dish to avoid leakage.

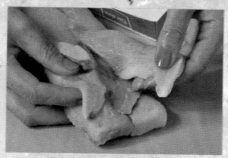

Check fish after minimum defrosting time. Pieces may be starting to loosen, but fish should feel cold.

Hold fish under cold running water until pieces separate and to complete defrosting.

WHOLE FISH

Arrange whole frozen fish in dish. Turn fish over midway through defrosting time.

Check fish after minimum time. It should feel cold.

Rinse fish cavity under cold running water to complete defrosting.

Cooking

There are three basic ways of cooking whole fish, fillets and steaks which can lead to a variety of tasty dishes.

Steaming fish in the microwave actually allows fish to cook in their own juices. You don't have to add any water, but you may like to add a sauce for richer flavor.

Poaching fish is simple and involves actually submerging fish in a liquid.

Or you can scallop the fish by adding crumbs and cream to partially cooked fillets.

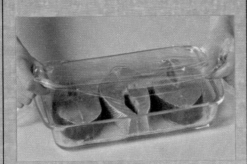

Shield head and tail *areas of whole fish with foil. Insert probe just above the gill into the meatiest area, parallel to the backbone. Probe should not touch the foil or bone. Set probe at 130°.*

For poached fish, *place fish in boiling liquid. Cover with plastic wrap. Microwave on High [100%] 8 to 10 minutes.*

Arrange fillets *and steaks with thickest parts toward the outside of the cooking dish. Brush fish with butter or pour sauce on fillets. For color, brush with soy sauce or other browning agents.*

Cover tightly *with plastic wrap and pleat to allow steam to expand. Be sure to turn fish steaks or fillets once midway through cooking.*

Scallop fish *by spreading crumbs over fillets and pouring in ⅓ cup cream midway through cooking.*

Test for doneness. *Because over-cooking tends to dry and toughen fish, microwave for only the minimum cooking time then check for doneness. Fish will turn from translucent to opaque and will flake easily. The inner areas should still be slightly translucent. They will finish cooking during a 5-minute standing time while the outer areas will remain tender.*

Taste Tip

Cooking fish with wine, ginger, vinegar, onions, garlic or lemon juice minimizes odor and fishy taste.

For a special touch, garnish fish with an orange or lemon slice, chopped green onion, a sprig of parsley, tomato slices or almonds. Spices such as paprika, marjoram or basil complement fish perfectly.

WHOLE FISH

Power Level: HIGH [100%]
Total Cooking Time: 10 to 15 minutes
Temperature Probe: 130°

2 to 4 pound dressed whole fish

1. Place whole fish on a baking dish. Brush fish with melted butter (or margarine). Cover head and tail areas with aluminum foil to shield the thinner areas from overcooking. Cover with plastic wrap.

2. Microwave on HIGH (100%) for 10 to 15 minutes or until fish flakes easily with fork. Turn over halfway through cooking. Allow to stand 5 minutes before serving.

Recipe yield: 4 to 6 servings

BAKED STUFFED WHOLE FISH

Power Level: HIGH [100%]
Total Cooking Time: 10¾ to
                                        16 minutes
Temperature Probe: 130°

½ cup butter (or margarine)
2 to 4 pound dressed whole fish
½ teaspoon salt
2 cups toasted bread cubes
¼ cup finely chopped celery
2 tablespoons chopped onion
2 tablespoons boiling water
½ teaspoon grated lemon peel
½ teaspoon thyme
¼ teaspoon pepper

1. Place butter in a custard cup or small bowl. Microwave on HIGH (100%) for 45 seconds to 1 minute or until melted.

2. Brush inside of fish with 2 tablespoons melted butter. Sprinkle with salt.

3. Toss together remaining ingredients and ¼ cup melted butter.

4. Spoon stuffing into fish cavity. Fasten edges with wooden skewers or lace closed with string and wooden skewers. Cover head and tail areas with aluminum foil to shield the thinner areas.

5. Place fish in a baking dish. Brush with remaining butter. Cover with plastic wrap.

6. Microwave on HIGH (100%) for 10 to 15 minutes or until fish flakes easily with a fork. Allow to stand 5 minutes before serving.

Recipe yield: 4 to 6 servings

SALMON LOAF

Power Level: HIGH [100%]
Total Cooking Time: 10 to 12 minutes

1 can (1 pound) salmon, drained (Remove bone and skin.)
2 eggs
½ cup bread crumbs
½ cup milk
¼ cup finely chopped onion
3 tablespoons chopped ripe olives (optional)
1 teaspoon Worcestershire sauce
1 teaspoon lemon juice
1 teaspoon dried parsley
½ teaspoon salt
Dash of pepper

1. Mix together all ingredients.

2. Place the salmon mixture into a greased 8½ x 4½ x 2½ inch loaf dish or 10 inch ring mold. Cover with waxed paper.

3. Microwave on HIGH (100%) for 10 to 12 minutes or until set. Turn dish a half turn halfway through cooking.

4. Allow to stand 5 minutes then invert onto a serving platter.

5. Serve with Creamy Dill Sauce (page 108).

Variations:
SALMON PATTIES
Follow Salmon Loaf recipe as directed in Step 1 except eliminate milk. Form mixture into 6 patties. Set aside. Microwave browning griddle on HIGH (100%) for 3 to 4 minutes. Add 1 teaspoon cooking oil and patties. Microwave, uncovered on HIGH (100%) for 3 to 4 minutes. Turn patties, microwave for 2 minutes or until lightly browned.

INDIVIDUAL SALMON LOAVES
Follow Salmon Loaf recipe as directed in Step 1. Divide mixture into six greased 6-ounce custard cups. Cover with waxed paper. Microwave, in a circle, on HIGH (100%) for 6 to 8 minutes or until set. Rearrange dishes halfway through cooking. Allow to stand 3 minutes, then invert onto dinner plates or a serving platter.

Recipe yield: 4 to 6 servings

GREEN PEPPERS STUFFED WITH SALMON

Power Level: HIGH [100%]
Total Cooking Time: 15 to 18 minutes

4 green peppers
1 can (1 pound) salmon, drained (remove bone and skin.)
½ cup bread crumbs
¼ cup grated onion
¼ cup finely chopped celery

¼ cup mayonnaise (or salad dressing)
1 egg
1 teaspoon lemon juice
1 teaspoon Worcestershire sauce
¼ teaspoon salt
Dash of hot pepper sauce

1. Remove tops and seeds of green peppers. Place peppers in a 3 quart casserole. Pour enough water into dish to half-cover peppers. Cover with a tight fitting lid or plastic wrap. Microwave on HIGH (100%) for 5 to 6 minutes or until partially cooked. Drain.

2. Mix together remaining ingredients. Spoon into peppers. Cover with waxed paper.

3. Microwave on HIGH (100%) for 10 to 12 minutes or until heated through. Allow to stand 5 minutes before serving.

4. Serve topped with cheese sauce or Sour Cream Sauce (page 107). If desired, garnish with paprika and parsley.

Recipe yield: 4 servings

CREAMY CUCUMBER SALMON STEAKS

Power Level: MEDIUM-HIGH [70%]
Total Cooking Time: 12 to 14 minutes

4 (2 pounds) salmon steaks
½ cup sour cream
¼ cup mayonnaise (or salad dressing)
½ cup chopped cucumber
¼ teaspoon salt
1 teaspoon dill weed
1 teaspoon white vinegar

1. Place salmon steaks, thickest end toward outside, in a baking dish.

2. Mix together remaining ingredients. Spread over fish. Cover with plastic wrap.

3. Microwave on MEDIUM-HIGH (70%) for 12 to 14 minutes or until fish flakes easily with a fork. (The lower power prevents sauce from separating). If desired, garnish with sprigs of parsley.

Recipe yield: 4 servings

Variation:
SOUR CREAM SALMON STEAKS
Follow Creamy Cucumber Steak recipe as directed except substitute 1 tablespoon chopped chives for cucumber and 2 tablespoons butter (or margarine) for mayonnaise.

CRISPY FISH FILLETS

Power Level: HIGH [100%]
Total Cooking Time: 8¾ to 11 minutes

¼ cup butter (or margarine)
1 teaspoon lemon juice
½ cup corn flake crumbs
½ cup dry bread crumbs
¼ cup finely chopped almonds
   (optional)
1 teaspoon salt
Dash of pepper
1 pound fish fillets (sole or
   flounder), cut into serving pieces
Paprika

1. Place butter and lemon juice in an 11¾ x 7½ x 1¾ inch baking dish. Microwave on HIGH (100%) for 45 seconds to 1 minute.

2. Mix together crumbs, almonds, salt and pepper. Dip both sides of fillets in lemon-butter, then coat with crumb mixture. Place fillets in baking dish with remaining butter. Sprinkle with paprika.

3. Microwave, uncovered, on HIGH (100%) for 8 to 10 minutes or until fish flakes easily with a fork. Halfway through cooking turn fish over and sprinkle with paprika. Allow to stand 5 minutes before serving.

Recipe yield: 3 to 4 servings

Variation:

QUICK CRISPY FILLETS

Dip fish in evaporated milk, then coat fish with 1 package (2 ounces) seasoned coating mix for fish and sprinkle with paprika. Continue as directed in step 3 of Crispy Fillets recipe.

Tip: If microwave has a browning element, brown as desired.

Steamed Salmon Steaks are a fish lover's delight, especially when served with Creamy Dill Sauce [page 108].

HALIBUT IN WINE

Power Level: HIGH [100%]
Total Cooking Time: 6½ to
                    8¾ minutes

2 tablespoons butter (or margarine)
¼ cup dry white wine
1 tablespoon chopped chives
¼ teaspoon tarragon
4 (1 pound) halibut fillets
Lemon slices

1. Place butter in a 10 x 6 x 1¾ inch baking dish. Microwave on HIGH (100%) for 30 to 45 seconds or until melted. Stir in wine, chives and tarragon.

2. Arrange fillets, thickest end towards outside, in dish. Cover with plastic wrap.

3. Microwave on HIGH (100%) for 6 to 8 minutes or until fish flakes easily with a fork.

4. Serve topped with lemon slices.

Recipe yield: 4 servings

HADDOCK FILLETS WITH SHRIMP SAUCE

Power Level: LOW [30%] and
              HIGH [100%]
Total Cooking Time: 14 to 18 minutes

1 pound frozen haddock fillets
1 tablespoon lemon juice
1 cup chili sauce
1 tablespoon chopped green onion
1 tablespoon horseradish
½ cup tiny cooked shrimp

1. Microwave fillets on LOW (30%) for 8 to 10 minutes or until defrosted but still icy (see page 90).

2. Place fish, thickest end toward outside, in a 10 x 6 x 1¾ inch baking dish. Sprinkle with lemon juice. Set aside.

3. Mix together remaining ingredients except shrimp. Spread over fish. Cover with plastic wrap.

4. Microwave on HIGH (100%) for 6 to 8 minutes or until fish flakes easily with a fork. Sprinkle with shrimp. Allow to stand, covered, for 5 minutes before serving.

Recipe yield: 3 to 4 servings

FLOUNDER ELEGANT

Power Level: HIGH [100%]
Total Cooking Time: 6½ to
                    8¾ minutes

¼ cup butter (or margarine)
4 (1 pound) flounder fillets
1 medium tomato, peeled and
    chopped
¼ cup chopped mushrooms
1 tablespoon finely chopped onion
1 tablespoon finely chopped
    green pepper
¼ teaspoon garlic salt
¼ cup dry white wine
1 tablespoon lemon juice
Paprika

1. Place butter in a custard cup or small bowl. Microwave on HIGH (100%) for 30 to 45 seconds or until melted.

2. Brush fillets with 2 tablespoons melted butter.

3. Combine tomato pieces, mushrooms, onion, green pepper and garlic salt. Sprinkle over each fillet.

4. Roll up fillets jelly-roll fashion starting with small end. Secure with a string or wooden picks and place in an 8 x 8 x 2 inch baking dish.

5. Mix together remaining butter, wine and lemon juice. Pour over fillets. Sprinkle with paprika. Cover with a tight fitting lid or plastic wrap.

6. Microwave on HIGH (100%) for 6 to 8 minutes or until fish flakes easily with a fork. Rearrange halfway through cooking. Allow to stand 5 minutes before serving.

Recipe yield: 3 to 4 servings

STEAMED FISH

Power Level: HIGH [100%]
Total Cooking Time: 6½ to
                    8¾ minutes

2 tablespoons butter (or margarine)
1 teaspoon lemon juice
1 pound fish fillets (or steaks)
1 teaspoon salt
Dash of pepper
Paprika

1. Place butter and lemon juice in a 10 x 6 x 1¾ inch baking dish. Microwave on HIGH (100%) for 30 to 45 seconds or until melted.

2. Arrange fish pieces, thickest end toward outside, in baking dish. Sprinkle with half the salt, pepper and paprika. Cover with plastic wrap.

3. Microwave on HIGH (100%) for 6 to 8 minutes or until fish flakes easily with a fork. Halfway through cooking turn fish over and sprinkle with remaining salt, pepper and paprika.

Recipe yield: 3 to 4 servings

POACHED FISH

Power Level: HIGH [100%]
Total Cooking Time: 16 to 20 minutes

1¾ cups water
1 tablespoon lemon juice
1 teaspoon salt
Dash of thyme
Dash of marjoram
2 tablespoons finely chopped
    onion
1 teaspoon dried parsley
1 bay leaf
3 peppercorns
1½ pounds fish fillets (or steaks)

1. Combine water, lemon juice, salt, thyme and marjoram in an 11¾ x 7½ x 1¾ inch baking dish. Tie onion, parsley, bay leaf and peppercorns in a cheesecloth bag. Cover with plastic wrap. Microwave on HIGH (100%) for 8 to 10 minutes or until boiling. Remove bag.

2. Place fish in broth, skin side down and thickest end toward outside. Cover.

3. Microwave on HIGH (100%) for 8 to 10 minutes or until fish flakes easily with a fork. Allow to stand 5 minutes before serving.

Variation:
POACHED FISH ITALIAN

Follow Poached Fish recipe as directed except substitute 1 tablespoon olive oil for lemon juice and flavor with ¼ teaspoon minced garlic, ¼ teaspoon basil and ¼ teaspoon oregano instead of thyme, marjoram, bay leaf and peppercorns.

Recipe yield: 4 to 5 servings

SCALLOPED FISH

Power Level: HIGH [100%]
Total Cooking Time: 8¾ to 10 minutes

¼ cup butter (or margarine)
1 cup cracker crumbs
1 tablespoon dried parsley
¼ teaspoon salt
Dash of pepper
1 pound fish fillets (flounder
    or sole)
⅓ cup half and half (or milk)

1. Place butter in a 1 quart casserole. Microwave on HIGH (100%) for 45 seconds to 1 minute or until melted. Stir in cracker crumbs, parsley, salt and pepper until well coated. Set aside.

2. Arrange fish, thickest end toward the outside, in a 10 inch pie dish. Cover with plastic wrap. Microwave on HIGH (100%) for 4 minutes.

3. Turn fish over. Sprinkle with crumb mixture. Pour cream over all. Microwave, uncovered, on HIGH (100%) for 4 to 5 minutes or until fish flakes easily with a fork. Allow to stand 5 minutes before serving.

Recipe yield: 3 to 4 servings

SAUCY FISH STICKS

Power Level: HIGH [100%]
Total Cooking Time: 6 to 8 minutes

1 package (15 ounces) breaded fish
    sticks (or 1 pound fish fillets,
    thawed)
1 can (10¾ ounces) cream of
    celery soup
½ cup milk
1 teaspoon dill weed

1. Place fish in a 10 x 6 x 1¾ inch baking dish.

2. Mix together soup and milk. Pour over fish. Sprinkle with dill weed. Cover with waxed paper.

3. Microwave on HIGH (100%) for 6 to 8 minutes or until sauce is hot and bubbly.

Recipe yield: 4 servings

Variations:
MUSHROOM FISH STICKS

Follow Saucy Fish Sticks recipe as directed except substitute 1 can (10¾ ounces) mushroom soup for celery soup and sprinkle with 1 cup seasoned croutons instead of dill weed. Uncover the last 45 seconds of cooking and sprinkle with grated Cheddar cheese. Continue cooking until cheese just begins to melt.

ITALIAN FISH STICKS

Follow Saucy Fish Sticks recipe as directed except substitute 1 can (15 ounces) of spaghetti sauce (or pizza sauce) for celery soup and milk and Italian seasoning for dill weed. Uncover the last 45 seconds of cooking and add 4 slices of Mozzarella cheese. Continue cooking until cheese just begins to melt.

Recipe yield: 4 servings

TUNA CHOW MEIN CASSEROLE

Power Level: MEDIUM-HIGH [70%]
Total Cooking Time: 10 to 12 minutes

1 can (6½ ounces) tuna, drained
1 can (10¾ ounces) cream of mushroom soup
1 can (8 ounces) water chestnuts, drained and sliced
1 can (4 ounces) sliced mushrooms, drained
½ cup grated onion
½ cup finely sliced celery
¼ cup milk
2 tablespoons soy sauce
1 can (3 ounces) chow mein noodles

1. Combine all ingredients except noodles in a 1½ quart casserole.

2. Stir in ½ cup noodles. Sprinkle top with remaining noodles.

3. Microwave on MEDIUM-HIGH (70%) for 10 to 12 minutes or until hot and bubbly. Allow to stand 5 minutes before serving.

Recipe yield: 4 servings

TUNA-BROCCOLI CASSEROLE

Power Level: HIGH [100%] and MEDIUM-HIGH [70%]
Total Cooking Time: 15 to 19 minutes

1 package (10 ounces) frozen broccoli
1 can (10¾ ounces) cream of mushroom soup
2 hard cooked eggs, chopped (Cook on top of conventional range.)
1 can (4 ounces) chopped mushrooms
¼ cup chopped onion
¼ cup sliced ripe olives
1 can (6½ ounces) tuna, drained
1 cup Cheddar cheese cracker crumbs

1. Place broccoli in a 10 x 6 x 1¾ inch baking dish. Cover with plastic wrap. Microwave on HIGH (100%) for 3 to 4 minutes or until defrosted. Drain.

2. Mix together soup, eggs, mushrooms, onion and olives. Place a layer of tuna and sauce mixture over broccoli.

3. Sprinkle with cracker crumbs.

4. Microwave on MEDIUM-HIGH (70%) for 12 to 15 minutes or until hot and bubbly. Allow to stand 5 minutes before serving.

Recipe yield: 4 servings

CREAMED TUNA

Power Level: HIGH [100%] and MEDIUM-HIGH [70%]
Total Cooking Time: 12 to 15 minutes

3 tablespoons butter (or margarine)
¼ cup finely chopped onion
¼ cup finely chopped celery
¼ cup chopped green pepper
3 tablespoons all purpose flour
2 eggs
1½ cups milk (or half and half)
2 cans (6½ ounces each) tuna, drained
1 can (2 ounces) sliced mushrooms, drained
2 tablespoons chopped pimento
½ teaspoon salt
Dash of pepper

1. Place butter, onion, celery and green pepper in a 2 quart casserole. Microwave on HIGH (100%) for 3 to 4 minutes or until vegetables are tender.

2. Stir together flour, eggs and milk. Add to green pepper mixture. Microwave on HIGH (100%) for 4 to 5 minutes or until thickened. Stir occasionally during the last half of cooking.

3. Add tuna, mushrooms, pimentos, salt and pepper. Cover with a tight fitting lid or plastic wrap. Microwave on MEDIUM-HIGH (70%) for 5 to 6 minutes or until heated through. Stir halfway through cooking. Allow to stand 5 minutes before serving.

5. Serve over rice, noodles or in patty shells.

Recipe yield: 4 to 6 servings

Variation:

CREAMED SEAFOOD

Follow Creamed Tuna recipe as directed except substitute 1 can (4½ ounces) shrimp or crabmeat (rinsed and drained) for tuna and, if desired, add 1 cup grated American cheese the last 2 minutes of cooking.

This beautiful Baked Stuffed Whole Fish was garnished with almonds to enhance the natural flavor.

Fruits

Fruit makes a healthful snack or the ideal end to a perfect meal. Because it's cooked quickly and with little water in the microwave, fruit retains its fresh flavor, color, texture and shape. When done, fruit is tender.

Whether you peel, core, cut or pierce the fruit skin, this natural covering must be opened to allow steam to escape and to avoid spattering.

Microwave fruit on High (100%) unless otherwise specified. Cooking time may vary depending on the age, size and type of fruit. Cover when cooking unless the fruit has a crisp or cobbler topping.

Core, peel or slice *fruit. The skin must be pierced to allow steam to escape and to avoid spattering.*

Add dark brown sugar, *spices or sweets such as grenadine, jelly, cherry juice, cinnamon candies or other crushed candy to enhance color and flavor. Add little or no water to retain nutrients.*

Cover fruit unless *it has a crispy or cobbler topping. Cobbler dishes should be cooked uncovered.*

BAKED WHOLE APPLES

Power Level: HIGH [100%]

1. Wash and core tart cooking apples. If desired, cut lengthwise into sections.

2. Place in dish.

3. Fill each apple with 1½ teaspoons brown sugar, 1 teaspoon softened butter (or margarine) and a dash of cinnamon or other ingredients.

4. Cover with waxed paper.

5. Microwave on HIGH (100%) until tender.

6. Allow to stand 3 to 5 minutes before serving.

Amt.	Utensil	Time
1	6 ounce custard cup or small bowl	1½ to 2½ minutes
2	two 6 ounce custard cups or two small bowls	3 to 4 minutes
4	8 x 8 x 2 inch baking dish or 1 quart casserole	4½ to 5½ minutes
6	10 x 6 x 1¾ inch baking dish or 2 quart casserole	8 to 10 minutes

Times may vary due to size and type of apple(s) being used.

APPLE CRISP

Power Level: LOW [30%] and HIGH [100%]
Total Cooking Time: 10¾ to 13 minutes

4 medium tart cooking apples, peeled and sliced
½ cup butter (or margarine)
¾ cup brown sugar
¾ cup quick cooking oats
½ cup all purpose flour
1 teaspoon cinnamon
½ teaspoon allspice

1. Spread apples evenly in an 8 x 8 x 2 inch baking dish.

2. Place butter in a small glass mixing bowl. Microwave on LOW (30%) for 45 seconds to 1 minute until softened. Add remaining ingredients. Mix until crumbly. Sprinkle over apples.

3. Microwave on HIGH (100%) for 10 to 12 minutes or until apples are tender. Top with whipped cream or ice cream.

Variation:

GRANOLA APPLE CRISP

Follow Apple Crisp recipe as directed except substitute 2 cups granola (packaged or recipe page 146) for butter, brown sugar, oats, flour and spices.

___ Juice Tip ___

To get more juice when you squeeze citrus fruit, Microwave on High (100%) for 15 to 30 seconds.

Test for doneness. *Prick with fork. Fruit should be crispy tender. Allow a 2 to 3 minute standing time to finish the cooking process. Overcooking will make fruit mushy.*

BAKED APPLES WITH CARAMEL SAUCE

Power Level: HIGH [100%]
Total Cooking Time: 7 to 10 minutes

4 cooking apples, cored and cut in half lengthwise
25 vanilla caramels
⅓ to ½ cup milk
¼ cup chopped nuts

1. Place apples, cut side up, in an 8 x 8 x 2 inch baking dish. Cover with a tight fitting lid or plastic wrap.

2. Microwave on HIGH (100%) for 3 to 4 minutes or until apples are just tender.

3. Combine caramels and milk in a 2 cup measure. Microwave on HIGH (100%) for 2 to 3 minutes or until melted. Stir halfway through cooking.

4. Pour caramel sauce over apples and sprinkle with nuts. Microwave, uncovered, on HIGH (100%) for 2 to 3 minutes or until sauce is bubbly and apples are tender. Serve warm.

Variation:

BAKED PEARS WITH CARAMEL SAUCE

Follow Baked Apples with Caramel Sauce recipe as directed except substitute 4 fresh pears for apples.

Recipe yield: 6 to 8 servings

APPLESAUCE

Power Level: HIGH [100%]
Total Cooking Time: 8 to 10 minutes

8 cooking apples, peeled, cored and quartered
¼ to ½ cup water
½ cup brown sugar
½ teaspoon cinnamon (optional)
Dash of ground cloves (optional)

1. Place apples and water in a 2 quart casserole. Cover with a tight fitting lid or plastic wrap. Microwave on HIGH (100%) for 8 to 10 minutes or until apples are soft. Stir halfway through cooking.

2. Puree fruit using either method below:

Sieve or food mill method

Put apple mixture through sieve or food mill. Add remaining ingredients while still very hot. Stir thoroughly.

Food processor or blender method

Place apple mixture in blender or processor container. Add remaining ingredients. Blend until smooth.

Recipe yield: 6 to 8 servings

CHERRIES JUBILEE

Power Level: HIGH [100%]
Total Cooking Time: 4¼ to 6½ minutes

1 can (16 ounces) pitted dark sweet cherries, drained (reserve juice)
½ cup orange marmalade
1 tablespoon sugar
2 teaspoons cornstarch
½ cup brandy (or kirsch)
Ice cream

1. Combine reserved liquid, marmalade, sugar and cornstarch in a 1½ quart casserole. Microwave on HIGH (100%) for 3 to 4 minutes or until thickened. Stir halfway through cooking.

2. Add cherries. Microwave on HIGH (100%) for 1 to 2 minutes or until heated through. Place in chafing dish.

3. Pour brandy in 1 cup glass measure. Microwave on HIGH (100%) for 15 to 30 seconds or until warm. Pour over cherries and ignite. Do not ignite in the microwave. Serve over ice cream.

Recipe yield: 4 to 6 servings

Brandy Tip

For pretty flaming dessert sauces, use brandy of at least 80-proof, kirsch of at least 90-proof or cointreau of at least 80-proof. Rum of 151-proof will give the best flame. Remember, do not ignite the sauce in the microwave oven.

GINGERED PEARS IN SHERRY

Power Level: HIGH [100%]
Total Cooking Time: 8¾ to 11 minutes

4 pears, peeled, halved and cored
¼ cup butter (or margarine)
¼ cup brown sugar
¼ teaspoon cinnamon
¼ teaspoon nutmeg
¼ teaspoon ginger
¾ cup sherry

1. Arrange pears, cut side up, in a baking dish.

2. Place butter in a 1 cup measure. Microwave on HIGH (100%) for 45 seconds to 1 minute or until melted. Stir in brown sugar, cinnamon, nutmeg and ginger. Fill pear cavities with mixture.

3. Pour sherry over pears. Cover with a tight fitting lid or plastic wrap. Microwave on HIGH (100%) for 8 to 10 minutes or until pears are tender.

Recipe yield: 4 to 8 servings

FLAMING BANANAS ROYALE

Power Level: HIGH [100%]
Total Cooking Time: 3 to 4½ minutes

¼ cup butter (or margarine)
⅓ cup brown sugar
1 teaspoon grated orange peel
½ teaspoon cinnamon
¼ teaspoon allspice
4 bananas, sliced
⅓ cup orange flavored liqueur (or rum)
Ice cream

1. Place butter in a 1½ quart casserole. Microwave on HIGH (100%) for 45 seconds to 1 minute or until melted.

2. Stir in brown sugar, orange peel, cinnamon and allspice. Add bananas, stir to coat. Microwave on HIGH (100%) for 2 to 3 minutes or until bubbly. Place in a chafing dish.

3. Pour liqueur in a 1 cup measure. Microwave on HIGH (100%) for 15 to 30 seconds or until warm. Pour over bananas and ignite. Do not ignite in the microwave. Serve over ice cream.

Recipe yield: 4 to 6 servings

QUICK AMBROSIA

Power Level: HIGH [100%]
Total Cooking Time: 5 to 6 minutes

1 jar (17 ounces) chunky salad fruits
½ cup flaked coconut

1. Mix all ingredients in a 1½ quart casserole.

2. Microwave on HIGH (100%) for 5 to 6 minutes or until hot.

Variation:

SPICY AMBROSIA

Follow Quick Ambrosia recipe as directed except mix in ¼ cup chopped walnuts, 1 tablespoon brown sugar, ¼ teaspoon ginger (or curry) and a dash of cinnamon.

Recipe yield: 4 servings

PINEAPPLE CHEESE DESSERT

Power Level: HIGH [100%]
Total Cooking Time: 8 to 10 minutes

2 cups water
1 package (3 ounces) lime gelatin
2 cups miniature marshmallows
  (or 15 large marshmallows)
1 package (3 ounces) cream cheese
1 can (20 ounces) crushed
  pineapple, drained
1 cup whipping cream, whipped

1. Pour water into a large glass mixing bowl. Microwave on HIGH (100%) for 4 to 5 minutes or until boiling.

2. Stir in lime gelatin, marshmallows and cream cheese. Microwave on HIGH (100%) for 4 to 5 minutes. Beat until smooth. Cool.

3. Add pineapple and chill until thickened, but not set.

4. Fold in whipping cream.

5. Pour into a 10 x 6 x 1¾ inch baking dish, 9 x 5 x 3 inch loaf dish or 10 inch ring mold. Chill for 2 hours or until set.

6. When ready to serve, unmold onto serving dish.

Variation:
PINEAPPLE CHEESE SALAD

Follow Pineapple Cheese Dessert recipe as directed except slice and serve over a bed of lettuce.

Recipe yield: 6 to 8 servings

HONEY BAKED PEACHES

Power Level: HIGH [100%]
Total Cooking Time: 5 to 8 minutes

4 fresh ripe peaches, peeled and
  halved*
¼ cup water
⅓ cup honey
2 tablespoons lemon juice
Dash of cinnamon
Coconut (optional)

1. Arrange peach halves in an 8 x 8 x 2 inch baking dish.

2. Combine water, honey, lemon juice and cinnamon. Pour over peaches. Cover with a tight fitting lid or plastic wrap.

3. Microwave on HIGH (100%) for 5 to 8 minutes or until peaches are tender. Stir halfway through cooking.

4. Sprinkle with coconut. Serve warm or cold.

Recipe yield: 8 servings

*Eight canned peach halves can be substituted for fresh peaches. Microwave for only 3 to 4 minutes or until heated through.

Peeling Tip

For easy peeling, microwave peaches on High (100%) for 15 to 30 seconds.

HOT BREAKFAST GRAPEFRUIT

Power Level: HIGH [100%]
Total Cooking Time: 2 to 3 minutes

1 grapefruit, halved
½ cup granola cereal
2 tablespoons honey

1. Seed, core and section grapefruit halves. Place on serving dish.

2. Mix granola and honey. Spread granola mixture over each half.

3. Microwave on HIGH (100%) for 2 to 3 minutes or until heated through.

DEFROSTING FRUIT

Place frozen fruit in bowl, *or if it comes in a plastic pouch, place on a dish. You need not pierce the pouch. Remove any foil or metal from package. Defrost on Med. [50%] for 2 to 5 min.*

Flex package or break up fruit *with fork at minimum time. When properly defrosted, fruit will be cold, firm and slightly icy.*

Quick Ambrosia
has a
heavenly flavor.

FRUIT COOKING CHART

Amount	Additional Ingredients	Covered Casserole	Instructions	Cooking Time
Apples, 2 pounds	¾ cup sugar ½ cup water	2 quart	Peel, core and cut apples into ½ inch slices.	10 to 12 minutes
Apricots, 8.8 ounce package dried	¼ cup sugar 1 cup water	1½ quart	Wash apricots. Combine with other ingredients. Allow to stand 1 hour.	6 to 8 minutes
Peaches, 6 large	¾ cup sugar ¼ cup light corn syrup	2 quart	Blanche peaches in boiling water. Peel. Cut in half. Remove seeds.	6 to 8 minutes
Pineapple, 1 medium	1 cup sugar ⅓ cup water	1½ quart	Peel and cut pineapple into chunks.	8 to 10 minutes
Plums, 2 pounds whole	1 cup water ½ cup sugar ¼ cup light corn syrup	2 quart	Wash and prick skins.	8 to 10 minutes
Prunes, 11 ounce package dried	½ cup water	1½ quart	Wash prunes. Combine with remaining ingredients. Allow to stand 1 hour.	6 to 8 minutes
Rhubarb, 2 cups diced	2 tablespoons water ½ cup sugar Dash salt	2 quart	Wash and dice rhubarb.	6 to 8 minutes

Prepare fruit as directed. Combine fruit and other ingredients in suggested utensil. Cover with a tight fitting lid or plastic wrap. Microwave on High (100%) until tender. Stir halfway through cooking. Allow to stand 5 minutes.

QUICK FRUIT SOUP

Power Level: HIGH [100%]
Total Cooking Time: 30 to 40 minutes

2 packages (6 ounces each) mixed dried fruits
6 cups water
⅔ cup sugar
¼ cup orange juice
1 lemon, sliced thin
1 tablespoon quick cooking tapioca
½ teaspoon salt
½ teaspoon cinnamon

1. Combine all ingredients in a 3 quart casserole. Cover with a tight fitting lid or plastic wrap.

2. Microwave on HIGH (100%) for 15 to 20 minutes or until boiling.

3. Microwave, uncovered, on HIGH (100%) for an additional 15 to 20 minutes. Stir halfway through cooking.

4. Serve hot as a first course or as a dessert dish.

Recipe yield: 6 to 8 servings

STRAWBERRY FLAMBE

Power Level: HIGH [100%]
Total Cooking Time: 2¼ to 3½ minutes

1 quart strawberries, hulled
½ cup orange juice
½ cup sugar
2 tablespoons grated orange peel
1 tablespoon lemon juice
1 tablespoon grated lemon peel
½ cup brandy
Ice cream

1. Place orange juice, sugar, orange peel, lemon juice and lemon peel in a 2 quart casserole. Microwave on HIGH (100%) for 2 to 3 minutes or until steaming.

2. Stir in strawberries to coat thoroughly with syrup. Place in a chafing dish.

3. Pour brandy in a 1 cup measure. Microwave on HIGH (100%) for 15 to 30 seconds or until warm. Pour over strawberries and ignite. Do not ignite in the microwave. Serve over ice cream.

Recipe yield: 4 to 6 servings

LEMON-LIME SOUFFLE

Power Level: HIGH [100%]
Total Cooking Time: 4 to 5 minutes

½ cup sugar
1 tablespoon (1 envelope) unflavored gelatin
¼ teaspoon salt
1 cup water
3 eggs, separated
2 teaspoons grated lemon peel
1 teaspoon grated lime peel
3 tablespoons lemon juice
1 tablespoon lime juice
¼ teaspoon cream of tartar
⅓ cup powdered sugar
1 cup whipping cream, whipped

1. Combine sugar, gelatin, salt and water in a 4 cup measure or 1 quart casserole. Beat in egg yolks.

2. Microwave on HIGH (100%) for 4 to 5 minutes or until mixture begins to boil. Stir occasionally the last half of cooking.

3. Stir in lemon peel, lime peel, lemon juice and lime juice. Cool until thickened, but not set.

4. Beat egg whites and cream of tartar until foamy. Add powdered sugar. Beat until stiff but not dry. Fold in lemon mixture and whipped cream.

5. Pour into a 1 quart souffle dish or casserole. Refrigerate for at least 6 hours.

Recipe yield: 5 to 6 servings

Mixed Fruit Marmalade, Frozen Grape Jelly and Strawberry-Rhubarb Jam are made so quickly and taste so good.

STRAWBERRY MOUSSE

Power Level: HIGH [100%]
Total Cooking Time: 2 to 3 minutes

1 package (10 ounces) frozen strawberries, defrosted
1 envelope unflavored gelatin
¼ cup sugar
½ teaspoon lemon juice
¼ teaspoon lemon peel
2 egg whites
¼ teaspoon cream of tartar
1 cup frozen whipped topping, thawed

1. Mash strawberries, then press through sieve or blend in an electric blender until smooth (pureed).

2. Sprinkle gelatin over pureed fruit. Microwave on HIGH (100%) for 2 to 3 minutes or until gelatin dissolves.

3. Stir in 2 tablespoons sugar, lemon juice and lemon peel. Chill for 20 minutes or until thickened but not set.

4. Beat egg whites and cream of tartar until foamy. Gradually add remaining sugar. Beat until stiff but not dry.

5. Fold beaten egg whites into strawberry mixture. Then fold in whipped topping. Pour into 1 quart serving dish or four individual serving dishes. Refrigerate for 4 hours or until set. Garnish with whipped topping.

Recipe yield: 4 to 6 servings

Jams, Jellies & Relishes

What better way to capture the fresh fruit flavors of summer than with the sweet goodness of sparkling jellies, jams and relishes.

When cooked in the microwave, jams, jellies and relishes retain their fresh flavor and bright color. There is no sticking or scorching because you are heating from all sides, not just from the bottom.

APPLE JELLY

Power Level: HIGH [100%]
Total Cooking Time: 15 to 19 minutes

2½ cups apple juice
1 package (1¾ ounces) fruit pectin
3¼ cups sugar

1. Combine apple juice and pectin in a 3 quart casserole. Cover loosely with a lid or plastic wrap. Microwave on HIGH (100%) for 5 to 6 minutes or until mixture comes to a full boil. Stir occasionally during cooking.

2. Stir in sugar until dissolved. Microwave on HIGH (100%) for 8 to 10 minutes or until mixture again comes to a full boil. Stir occasionally during cooking.

3. Uncover. Microwave on HIGH (100%) for an additional 2 to 3 minutes or until jelly sheets from a spoon. (See page 102.)

4. Skim off foam. Pour into hot sterilized jars. Seal.

Recipe yield: 5 (8 ounce) jars

APPLE-RAISIN CHUTNEY

Power Level: HIGH [100%]
Total Cooking Time: 8 to 10 minutes

2 tart cooking apples, peeled, cored and chopped
½ cup raisins
½ cup brown sugar
⅓ cup cider vinegar
¼ cup chopped onion
¼ cup water
1 teaspoon turmeric
½ teaspoon salt
½ teaspoon ground ginger
¼ teaspoon cinnamon
¼ teaspoon minced garlic
Dash of ground cloves

1. Mix all ingredients in a 1 quart casserole. Cover loosely with lid or plastic wrap.

2. Microwave on HIGH (100%) for 8 to 10 minutes or until thickened. Stir occasionally during cooking. Refrigerate. Serve with meats.

Recipe yield: 1½ cups

JAMS & JELLIES

Use powdered or liquid pectin to insure consistent results. Powdered pectin, used in this book, is added before the sugar to allow it to dissolve. Liquid pectin is added with the sugar.

Select a large container that has at least 4 cups extra space to allow for boil overs. Combine powdered pectin and fruit. Cover loosely with lid or plastic wrap. Microwave on High [100%]. Bring to full boil, stirring occasionally.

PEACH CHUTNEY

Power Level: HIGH [100%] and
            MEDIUM [50%]
Total Cooking Time: 60 to 66 minutes

2 cans (16 ounces each) canned peaches, undrained and chopped
1 tart cooking apple, peeled, cored and chopped
1 cup chopped celery
¾ cup cider vinegar
½ cup sugar
½ cup currants (or raisins)
1 tablespoon candied lemon peel
½ teaspoon salt
¼ teaspoon cinnamon
¼ teaspoon ginger

1. Mix all ingredients in a 3 quart casserole. Cover loosely with lid or plastic wrap. Microwave on HIGH (100%) for 15 to 16 minutes or until boiling.

2. Uncover. Microwave on MEDIUM (50%) for 45 to 50 minutes or until syrup is thickened. Stir occasionally during cooking.

3. Pour into hot, sterilized jars. Cover tightly. Store in refrigerator. Serve with meats.

Recipe yield: 4 (8 ounce) jars

Stir in sugar. Cover and stir occasionally.

Test for doneness. Dip a large spoon into the boiling syrup. The jelling point is reached if the syrup forms a sheet as it runs off the spoon.

PEACH-RAISIN CONSERVE

Power Level: HIGH [100%]
Total Cooking Time: 15 to 19 minutes

3 cups canned peaches, chopped
1 orange, peeled and chopped
½ cup raisins (or currants)
2 tablespoons lemon juice
1 package (1¾ ounces) powdered pectin
5 cups sugar
1 cup chopped walnuts

1. Combine peaches, orange, raisins, lemon juice and pectin in a 3 quart casserole. Cover loosely with lid or plastic wrap. Microwave on HIGH (100%) for 5 to 6 minutes or until mixture comes to a full boil. Stir occasionally during cooking.

2. Stir in sugar until dissolved. Cover. Microwave on HIGH (100%) for 8 to 10 minutes or until mixture again comes to a full boil. Stir occasionally during cooking.

3. Uncover. Microwave on HIGH (100%) for an additional 2 to 3 minutes or until mixture sheets from a spoon.

4. Skim off foam. Stir in walnuts. Allow to stand 5 minutes.

5. Pour into hot, sterilized jars. Seal.

Recipe yield: 6 (8 ounce) jars

Pour into sterilized jars. Wipe off rims and seal with sterile vacuum lids or paraffin. Sterilizing should be done on the regular surface range. Paraffin will not melt in a microwave. Melt carefully on conventional range.

> **Climate Tip**
>
> If you live in a humid or warm southern climate, the U.S. Department of Agriculture recommends you water-bath process the filled and sealed jars of jams and chunky preserves for about 5 minutes.

FROZEN GRAPE JELLY

Power Level: HIGH [100%]
Total Cooking Time: 17 to 22 minutes

3 cups non-sweetened grape juice
1 tablespoon lemon juice
1 package (1¾ ounces) powdered fruit pectin
4¼ cups sugar

1. Place grape juice, lemon juice and pectin in a 3 quart casserole. Cover loosely with lid or plastic wrap. Microwave on HIGH (100%) for 10 to 12 minutes or until mixture comes to a full boil. Stir occasionally during cooking.

2. Stir in sugar until dissolved. Cover. Microwave on HIGH (100%) for 6 to 8 minutes or until mixture again comes to a full boil. Stir occasionally during cooking.

3. Uncover. Microwave on HIGH (100%) for an additional 1 to 2 minutes or until jelly sheets from spoon.

4. Skim off foam. Pour into hot, sterilized jars. Seal. Freeze up to 1 year or refrigerate for 2 to 3 weeks.

Recipe yield: 5 (8 ounce) jars

MIXED FRUIT MARMALADE

Power Level: HIGH [100%]
Total Cooking Time: 24 to 33 minutes

4 oranges
1½ cups water (or fruit juice)
1 package (1¾ ounces) powdered
  fruit pectin
4 pears
4 slices pineapple
5 maraschino cherries
4 cups sugar

1. Cut orange peel in quarters and remove. Scrape and discard about half of the white inner skin. Slice peel into thin strips and measure ¼ cup. Remove seeds and chop fruit into small pieces. Set aside.

2. Combine ¼ cup peel and water in a 3 quart casserole. Cover loosely with lid or plastic wrap. Microwave on HIGH (100%) for 6 to 8 minutes or until peel is tender. Stir halfway through cooking.

3. Meanwhile, chop remaining fruit into small pieces. Add to water mixture. Stir in oranges and pectin. Cover. Microwave on HIGH (100%) for 10 to 12 minutes or until mixture comes to a full boil. Stir occasionally.

4. Stir in sugar until dissolved. Cover. Microwave on HIGH (100%) for 5 to 8 minutes or until mixture again comes to a full boil.

5. Uncover. Microwave on HIGH (100%) for an additional 3 to 5 minutes or until mixture sheets from a spoon.

6. Skim off foam. Allow mixture to stand 5 minutes.

7. Pour into hot, sterilized jars. Seal.

Recipe yield: 6 (8 ounce) jars

CITRUS MARMALADE

Power Level: HIGH [100%]
Total Cooking Time: 24 to 31 minutes

2 oranges
1 grapefruit
1 lemon
1½ cups water
1 package (1¾ ounces) powdered
  fruit pectin
4 cups sugar

1. Cut peel from fruit in quarters and remove. Scrape and discard about half of the white inner skin. Slice peel into thin strips and measure ¼ cup. Remove seeds and chop fruit into small pieces. Set aside.

2. Combine ¼ cup peel and water in a 3 quart casserole. Cover loosely with lid or plastic wrap. Microwave on HIGH (100%) for 6 to 8 minutes or until peel is tender. Stir halfway through cooking.

3. Stir in fruit and pectin. Cover. Microwave on HIGH (100%) for 8 to 10 minutes or until mixture comes to a full boil. Stir occasionally.

4. Stir in sugar until dissolved. Cover. Microwave on HIGH (100%) for 8 to 10 minutes or until mixture again comes to a full boil.

5. Uncover. Microwave on HIGH (100%) for an additional 2 to 3 minutes or until mixture sheets from a spoon.

6. Skim off foam. Allow mixture to stand 5 minutes.

7. Pour into hot, sterilized jars. Seal.

Recipe yield: 6 (8 ounce) jars

FROZEN CHERRY PRESERVES

Power Level: HIGH [100%]
Total Cooking Time: 23 to 28 minutes

1 package (20 ounces) frozen sour
  pitted cherries
1 tablespoon lemon juice
1 cup water
1 package (1¾ ounces) powdered
  fruit pectin
3 cups sugar

1. Combine frozen cherries, lemon juice, water and fruit pectin in a 3 quart casserole. Cover loosely with a lid or plastic wrap.

2. Microwave on HIGH (100%) for 12 to 14 minutes or until mixture comes to a full boil. Stir occasionally during cooking.

3. Stir in sugar until dissolved. Cover. Microwave on HIGH (100%) for 6 to 8 minutes or until mixture again comes to a full boil. Stir occasionally during cooking.

4. Uncover. Microwave on HIGH (100%) for an additional 5 to 6 minutes or until preserves sheet from a spoon.

5. Skim off foam. Allow to cool 5 minutes. Stir. Pour into hot sterilized jars. Seal. Freeze up to 1 year or refrigerate for 2 to 3 weeks.

Recipe yield: 4 (8 ounce) jars

Spoon Frozen Grape Jelly over peanut butter and you've got a real sweet treat.

FROZEN STRAWBERRY JAM

Power Level: HIGH [100%]
Total Cooking Time: 26 to 30 minutes

2 packages (16 ounces each) frozen strawberries, thawed
1 package (1¾ ounces) powdered fruit pectin
2½ cups sugar
1 tablespoon lemon juice

1. Combine strawberries and pectin in a 3 quart casserole. Cover loosely with lid or plastic wrap.

2. Microwave on HIGH (100%) for 12 to 14 minutes or until mixture comes to a full boil. Stir occasionally during cooking.

3. Stir in sugar and lemon juice until sugar is dissolved.

4. Microwave uncovered on HIGH (100%) for 14 to 16 minutes or until jam sheets from a spoon.

5. Skim off foam. Allow to cool. Stir well. Pour into hot sterilized jars. Seal. Freeze up to 1 year or refrigerate for 2 to 3 weeks.

Recipe yield: 3 (8 ounce) jars

STRAWBERRY-RHUBARB JAM

Power Level: HIGH [100%]
Total Cooking Time: 17 to 22 minutes

2½ cups rhubarb, sliced into ½ inch pieces
2½ cups strawberries, hulled and sliced
1 package (1¾ ounces) powdered fruit pectin (3½ tablespoons)
3 cups sugar

1. Combine rhubarb, strawberries and pectin in a 3 quart casserole. Cover loosely with lid or plastic wrap. Microwave on HIGH (100%) for 8 to 10 minutes or until mixture comes to a full boil. Stir occasionally during cooking.

2. Stir in sugar until dissolved. Cover. Microwave on HIGH (100%) for 8 to 10 minutes or until mixture again comes to a full boil. Stir occasionally during cooking.

3. Uncover. Microwave on HIGH (100%) for an additional 1 to 2 minutes or until mixture sheets from a spoon.

4. Skim off foam. Allow to stand 5 minutes.

5. Pour into hot, sterilized jars. Seal.

Recipe yield: 3 (8 ounce) jars

TANGY CORN RELISH

Power Level: HIGH [100%] and LOW [30%]
Total Cooking Time: 27 to 32 minutes

3 cans (12 ounces each) whole kernel corn, drained
1 cup finely chopped cabbage
½ cup finely chopped green pepper
¼ cup finely chopped onion
2 tablespoons finely chopped pimento
1 cup sugar
1 cup cider vinegar
¾ cup water
2 tablespoons cornstarch
1 teaspoon celery seed
1 teaspoon mustard seed
¼ teaspoon dill

1. Combine all ingredients in a 3 quart casserole. Cover with a tight fitting lid or plastic wrap. Microwave on HIGH (100%) for 15 to 20 minutes or until boiling. Stir occasionally during cooking.

2. After mixture begins to boil, microwave on LOW (30%) for an additional 12 minutes to blend flavors.

3. Pour into hot sterilized jars. Seal. Process 15 minutes in boiling water bath on top of conventional range or keep refrigerated.

Recipe yield: 6 (8 ounce) jars

SANDWICH RELISH

Power Level: HIGH [100%]
Total Cooking Time: 9 to 11 minutes

2 tablespoons cooking oil
1 cup finely chopped onion
½ cup finely chopped green pepper
½ cup finely chopped sweet red peppers
4 medium tomatoes, peeled and chopped
2 tablespoons cider vinegar
1 tablespoon brown sugar
1½ teaspoons salt
¼ teaspoon garlic powder
¼ teaspoon dry mustard
Dash of cayenne pepper

1. Place oil, onion and peppers in a 10 inch pie dish. Microwave on HIGH (100%) for 4 to 5 minutes or until vegetables are tender. Stir halfway through cooking.

2. Stir in remaining ingredients. Cover with plastic wrap. Microwave on HIGH (100%) for 5 to 6 minutes or until boiling. Stir halfway through cooking.

3. Pour into hot, sterilized jars. Seal. Process 15 minutes in a boiling water bath on top of conventional range or keep refrigerated. Serve on hot dogs, hamburgers or other sandwiches.

Recipe yield: 3 (8 ounce) jars

BREAD AND BUTTER ZUCCHINI

Power Level: HIGH [100%]
Total Cooking Time: 5 to 6 minutes

2 pounds zucchini*, sliced
2 medium onions, sliced thin
3 tablespoons pickling salt
1 cup brown sugar
1 cup cider vinegar
1 cup water
1 teaspoon mustard seed
½ teaspoon celery seed
½ teaspoon dill weed
Dash of allspice

1. Layer zucchini and onion on a jelly roll pan. Sprinkle each layer with pickling salt. Cover and allow to stand 1 hour.

2. Drain thoroughly and pack in hot sterilized jars.

3. Mix together remaining ingredients in a 4 cup measure. Microwave on HIGH (100%) for 5 to 6 minutes or until boiling.

4. Pour over zucchini. Seal jars. Process 15 minutes in a boiling water bath on top of conventional range or keep refrigerated.

Variation:
BREAD AND BUTTER CUCUMBERS

Follow Bread and Butter Zucchini recipe except substitute 2 pounds of cucumber* for zucchini.

Recipe yield: 6 (8 ounce) jars

*Tip: Zucchini or cucumbers can be peeled or unpeeled.

RELISHES

Combine all corn relish ingredients in a 3-quart casserole. Cover with tight lid or plastic wrap.

Pour relish mixture into hot sterilized jars. Seal.

Process 15 minutes in boiling water bath on the **conventional range** for storage at room temperature.

Or keep refrigerated, storing relish in pretty, sterile containers. The water processing may be omitted if relish is kept refrigerated.

Bread and Butter Zucchini, Peach-Raisin Conserve and Tangy Corn Relish make great "take-alongs" for picnics.

To prepare thickening, *add flour or cornstarch and seasonings to melted butter or heated meat drippings. The mixture is called a roux. Use a bowl double-size the amount of ingredients to avoid boil overs.*

Add the liquid stock, *milk or water slowly to the roux. Beat with a wooden whisk or wooden spoon until smooth.*

Stir 2 or 3 times *while cooking to redistribute heat and to prevent lumpiness. To make it easy, cook uncovered and stir without removing from the microwave.*

Have hot gravy any time. *Prepare sauces in advance or save the leftovers. Heat right in your serving dish or gravy boat, just one minute per cup at High [100%] or use temperature probe set at 130°-140°. Do not use metal or metal trimmed dishes.*

Gravies, Sauces & Salad Dressings

Say goodbye forever to lumpy sauces and gravies. Your microwave takes most of the work out of preparing delicious gravies, sauces and salad dressings. The cooking time is much faster. There is no need for constant stirring, and there are no sticky, scorched or burnt-on pans to clean up.

BASIC GRAVY

Power Level: HIGH [100%]
Total Cooking Time: 4½ minutes to 6¾ minutes

½ cup meat or poultry drippings
1½ cups water (milk or half and half)
3 tablespoons cornstarch
½ teaspoon salt
Dash of pepper

1. Pour drippings in 4 cup measure or 1 quart casserole. Microwave on HIGH (100%) for 30 to 45 seconds until bubbly.

2. Mix together cornstarch, salt, pepper and water until smooth. Stir into drippings. Microwave on HIGH (100%) for 4 to 6 minutes or until thickened. Stir occasionally to prevent lumps.

3. Serve immediately over meat, potatoes or dressing.

Recipe yield: 2 cups

Tip: For a darker color add brown bouquet sauce.

GIBLET GRAVY

Power Level: MEDIUM [50%] and HIGH [100%]
Total Cooking Time: 50 to 58 minutes

Turkey giblets
2 cups water (broth or milk)
½ cup chopped celery
½ cup chopped onion
½ cup turkey drippings
½ cup all purpose flour
1¼ teaspoon salt
¼ teaspoon pepper

1. Pierce membrane of giblets. Place giblets, water, celery and onion in a 1 quart casserole. Cover. Microwave on MEDIUM (50%) for 45 to 50 minutes or until giblets are tender. Reserve liquid. Chop giblets.

2. Pour drippings from roasted turkey into a 4 cup measure. Microwave on HIGH (100%) for 1 to 2 minutes or until hot.

3. Stir in flour, salt and pepper until smooth.

4. Gradually blend in reserved giblet broth. Cover. Microwave on HIGH (100%) for 3 to 4 minutes. Stir occasionally to prevent lumps.

5. Add chopped giblets. Microwave on HIGH (100%) for 1 to 2 minutes or until thickened.

6. Serve over Roast Turkey (page 156).

Recipe yield: 2½ cups gravy

Variation:
CHICKEN GIBLET GRAVY

Follow Giblet Gravy as directed except use chicken giblets and only half the other ingredients.

RICH CREAM GRAVY FOR CHICKEN

Power Level: HIGH [100%]
Total Cooking Time: 6 to 8 minutes

⅓ cup chicken drippings
⅓ cup all purpose flour
¼ teaspoon poultry seasoning
¼ teaspoon salt
Dash pepper
1 cup milk
1 cup half and half

1. Pour drippings into a 4 cup measure. Microwave on HIGH (100%) for 1 to 2 minutes or until hot.

2. Stir in flour, poultry seasoning, salt and pepper until well blended. Slowly blend in milk and cream. Microwave on HIGH (100%) for 6 to 8 minutes until thickened.

3. Serve with Oven-Baked Chicken (page 159).

Recipe yield: 2 cups gravy

SAVORY SAUCE

WHITE SAUCE

Power Level: HIGH [100%]
Total Cooking Time: 3¼ to
4½ minutes

Thin Sauce:
1 tablespoon butter (or margarine)
1 tablespoon all purpose flour
¼ teaspooon salt
1 cup milk
Medium Sauce:
2 tablespoons butter (or margarine)
2 tablespoons all purpose flour
¼ teaspoon salt
1 cup milk
Thick Sauce:
3 tablespoons butter (or margarine)
3 tablespoons all purpose flour
¼ teaspoon salt
1 cup milk

1. Place butter in a 2 cup measure or small bowl. Microwave on HIGH (100%) for 45 seconds to 1 minute or until melted.

2. Stir in flour and salt until smooth. Slowly blend in milk.

3. Microwave on HIGH (100%) for 2½ to 3½ minutes or until thickened. Stir occasionally.

Tip: Use a thin white sauce for soups; a medium white sauce for the base to other sauces or creamed and scalloped foods; and a thick white sauce for croquettes and souffles.

Variations:
CHEESE SAUCE

Follow Medium White Sauce recipe as directed. After sauce has thickened, stir in ½ cup grated Cheddar cheese and ½ teaspoon dry mustard. If cheese does not melt, microwave on HIGH (100%) for 30 seconds to 1 minute or until melted.

SOUR CREAM SAUCE

Follow Thin White Sauce recipe as directed except substitute 1 cup sour cream for milk and add ½ teaspoon lemon juice.

Recipe yield: about 1 cup

HOLLANDAISE SAUCE

Power Level: HIGH [100%]
Total Cooking Time: 1½ to 2¼ minutes

¼ cup butter (or margarine)
2 egg yolks, beaten
¼ cup half and half
1 tablespoon lemon juice (or cider vinegar)
½ teaspoon dry mustard
¼ teaspoon salt

1. Place butter in a 2 cup glass measure or casserole. Microwave on HIGH (100%) for 30 to 45 seconds or until melted.

2. Mix together egg yolks, cream, lemon juice, dry mustard and salt. Stir a little hot mixture into egg mixture, then stir egg mixture into remaining hot mixture. Microwave on HIGH (100%) for 1 to 1½ minutes or until thickened. Stir every 15 seconds. *

3. Remove from microwave and beat until light.

Recipe yield: about ⅔ cup sauce

*Tip: If sauce is overcooked, it will curdle. If sauce starts to curdle, add an ice cube and beat vigorously until light and fluffy.

Hollandaise Sauce over broccoli and Basic Gravy over mashed potatoes.

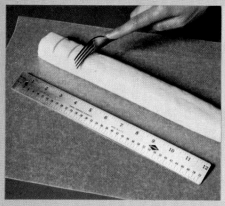

Form a 12-inch roll *from a ball of Stick-of-Sauce dough on waxed paper or plastic wrap. Mark off 1-inch sections.*

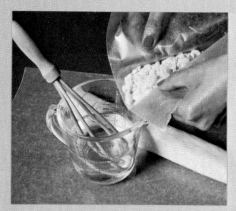

To make the sauce, *crumble just one inch of the stick into one cup of boiling water.*

STICK-OF-SAUCE
Power Level: LOW [30%] and HIGH [100%]
Total Cooking Time: 2½ to 3½ minutes

¾ cup butter (or margarine)
1½ cups nonfat dry milk
¾ cup all purpose flour
¼ cup water
1½ teaspoons salt
¼ teaspoon white pepper

1. Place butter in a 2 quart casserole. Microwave on LOW (30%) for 1½ to 2 minutes or until softened.

2. Stir in milk powder, flour, water, salt and pepper until mixture can be shaped into a ball.

3. Form dough into a 12 inch roll on waxed paper or plastic wrap. Roll can be stored in refrigerator for up to 1 month or in freezer for 3 months.

4. To use: Place ½ cup water in a 2 cup measure. Microwave on HIGH (100%) for 1½ to 2 minutes or until boiling. Crumble a 1 inch section of sauce and stir into water until smooth. Microwave on HIGH (100%) for 1 to 1½ minutes or until boiling. Makes ½ cup of sauce.

Recipe yield: 12 recipes (6 cups)

Variations:

CHEESE SAUCE
Follow Stick-of-Sauce recipe as directed in step 4 except with crumbled sauce add ½ cup grated Cheddar cheese and a dash of hot pepper sauce.

Cheese Stick-of-Sauce tastes great over cauliflower.

QUICK HOLLANDAISE SAUCE
Follow Stick-of-Sauce recipe as directed in step 4 except with crumbled sauce add ¼ cup mayonnaise (or salad dressing), 1 tablespoon lemon juice and a dash of red pepper.

EASY BECHAMEL SAUCE
Follow Stick-of-Sauce recipe as directed in step 4 except substitute ½ cup chicken broth for water and add 1 teaspoon grated onion and a dash of thyme with crumbled sauce.

Tip: Use the sauce stick with your favorite sauce recipe as a substitute for a Basic White Sauce or add crumbled sauce stick to vegetables during the last minute of cooking. If needed, add more liquid.

CREAMY DILL SAUCE
Power Level: HIGH [100%]
Total Cooking Time: 3 to 4 minutes
Temperature Probe: 130° to 140°

1 can (10½ ounces) cream of celery soup
⅔ cup milk
1 tablespoon dried dill weed
1 tablespoon chives
Dash of pepper

1. Mix together all ingredients in a 4 cup measure or 1 quart casserole until well blended.

2. Microwave on HIGH (100%) for 3 to 4 minutes or until hot and bubbly. Stir occasionally.

3. Serve hot over vegetables.

Recipe yield: about 2 cups

ZESTY BARBECUE SAUCE
Power Level: HIGH [100%]
Total Cooking Time: 7 to 9 minutes

1 tablespoon cooking oil
¼ cup chopped onion
2 cups catsup
1 cup water
¼ cup brown sugar
2 tablespoons lemon juice
1 tablespoon Worcestershire sauce
1 teaspoon chili powder
1 teaspoon horseradish
¼ teaspoon salt
Dash of hot pepper sauce
Dash of garlic powder

1. Place oil and onion in a 1 quart casserole. Microwave on HIGH (100%) for 3 to 4 minutes or until onions are tender.

2. Stir in remaining ingredients.

3. Microwave on HIGH (100%) for 4 to 5 minutes or until hot and bubbly.

Recipe yield: about 3 cups

DELICATE MUSHROOM SAUCE

Power Level: HIGH [100%]
Total Cooking Time: 4 to 6 minutes

2 cups sliced mushrooms
¼ cup butter (or margarine)
1 tablespoon cornstarch
¼ teaspoon salt
¼ cup beef broth
¼ cup dry white wine

1. Place mushrooms and butter in a 1 quart casserole. Microwave on HIGH (100%) for 2 to 3 minutes or until mushrooms are tender.

2. Mix together remaining ingredients until smooth. Gradually stir into mushrooms. Microwave on HIGH (100%) for 2 to 3 minutes or until thickened. Stir occasionally.

3. Serve hot over slices of roast, hamburgers or steaks.

Recipe yield: 2½ cups

MUSTARD SAUCE

Power Level: HIGH [100%]
Total Cooking Time: 3 to 4 minutes

2 tablespoons all purpose flour
1 cup water
2 tablespoons sugar
1 tablespoon white vinegar
1 egg, beaten
1 tablespoon horseradish
1½ tablespoons dry mustard
¼ teaspoon salt
Dash of pepper

1. Mix together flour and water in a 2 cup measure or small bowl until smooth. Stir in remaining ingredients.

2. Microwave on HIGH (100%) for 3 to 4 minutes or until thickened. Stir occasionally. Serve hot with ham, wieners, sausage or egg rolls.

Recipe yield: 1½ cups

RAISIN SAUCE

Power Level: HIGH [100%]
Total Cooking Time: 4 to 6 minutes

1 tablespoon cornstarch
2 tablespoons water
1 cup currant jelly
½ cup raisins (or currants)
¼ cup lemon juice

1. Mix together cornstarch and water in a 2 cup measure or small bowl until smooth. Stir in remaining ingredients.

2. Microwave on HIGH (100%) for 4 to 6 minutes or until thickened. Stir occasionally.

3. Serve as a glaze for ham or a sauce over slices of ham or turkey.

Recipe yield: 1¼ cups

SALAD DRESSINGS

CREAMY SALAD DRESSING

Power Level: HIGH [100%]
Total Cooking Time: 2 to 3 minutes

2 tablespoons sugar
2 tablespoons all purpose flour
½ teaspoon salt
½ teaspoon dry mustard
Dash of white pepper
¾ cup half and half
1 egg
2 tablespoons cider vinegar
2 tablespoons water

1. Mix together sugar, flour, salt, mustard, pepper and cream until smooth.

2. Beat egg in a 4 cup measure or 1 quart casserole. Stir in cream mixture, vinegar and water.

3. Microwave on HIGH (100%) for 2 to 3 minutes or until thickened.

Variations:

CREAMY ITALIAN DRESSING

Follow Creamy Salad Dressing recipe as directed except in Step 1 add ½ teaspoon basil, ¼ teaspoon oregano, ¼ teaspoon garlic salt and dash of cayenne pepper.

CREAMY FRENCH DRESSING

Follow Creamy Salad Dressing recipe as directed except in Step 1 add 1 teaspoon paprika, ½ teaspoon instant minced onion and dash of cayenne pepper.

SOUR CREAM DRESSING

Follow Creamy Salad Dressing recipe as directed except substitute ¾ cup sour cream for the half and half and add ½ teaspoon dill (or celery seed) and ¼ teaspoon onion salt.

CREAMY ROQUEFORT DRESSING

Follow Creamy Salad Dressing recipe as directed except substitute ¾ cup sour cream for the half and half. After cooking, add ½ cup Roquefort cheese and 1 tablespoon chopped chives. Beat until smooth.

Recipe yield: about 1½ cups

CREAMY FRUIT DRESSING

Power Level: MEDIUM-HIGH [70%]
Total Cooking Time: 4 to 5 minutes

2 eggs
¼ cup honey
½ cup pineapple juice (or other fruit juice)
¼ cup grapefruit juice (or other fruit juice)
1 tablespoon lemon peel
1 cup whipping cream, whipped

1. Combine all ingredients except cream in a 4 cup measure or 1 quart casserole.

2. Microwave on MEDIUM-HIGH (70%) for 4 to 5 minutes or until thickened. (Do not boil). Stir occasionally during cooking.

3. Refrigerate until cold.

4. Before serving, fold in whipped cream until thoroughly blended.

5. Serve over fruit salads or use as a dip for pieces of sliced fruit.

Recipe yield: about 3 cups

Creamy Salad Dressing will complement your favorite salad.

DESSERT SAUCE

Hot sundae toppings are so easy.
Take the lid off a 12 ounce jar of sundae or fruit sauce and heat in the microwave for 45 seconds to one minute to 130°-140°. These glass jars may not be heat-treated for use in temperatures over 140°. You may wish to use the temperature probe.

Sensational fruit toppings are quickly made from canned pie filling or frozen fruit or berries.

Place your favorite frozen fruit in a 1 quart casserole. Defrost on MEDIUM (50%) for 4 to 6 minutes. Stir in ½ cup water, ¼ cup sugar, 2 tablespoons cornstarch and 1 tablespoon lemon juice.

Heat on HIGH (100%) for 4 to 6 minutes until the sauce is thickened and clear. Stir occasionally. Serve warm over ice cream, cake or pancakes.

For an even quicker fruit sauce, pour one 21 ounce can of prepared pie filling into a small casserole. Microwave on HIGH (100%) for 3 to 4 minutes or until heated through. The temperature probe can be used at 130°.

┌─ **Boil Over Tip** ─────────┐
│ Lightly grease inside of the cooking
│ utensil with shortening or butter to
│ help prevent boil overs.
└─────────────────────────┘

HOT FUDGE SAUCE

Power Level: HIGH [100%]
Total Cooking Time: 3 to 5 minutes

3 squares (3 ounces) unsweetened chocolate
½ cup half and half (or milk)
¾ cup sugar
Dash of salt
¼ cup butter (or margarine)
1 teaspoon vanilla

1. Combine chocolate and cream in a 2 cup measure or a small bowl. Microwave on HIGH (100%) for 2 to 3 minutes or until chocolate melts.

2. Add sugar and salt. Mix well. Microwave on HIGH (100%) for 1 to 2 minutes or until sugar is dissolved. Stir in butter and vanilla.

3. Serve hot over ice cream. If necessary, reheat in microwave before serving. Store in refrigerator.

Recipe yield: approximately ½ cup

LEMON SAUCE

Power Level: HIGH [100%]
Total Cooking Time: 2 to 3 minutes

¾ cup sugar
1 tablespoon cornstarch
Dash of salt
¾ cup boiling water
1 egg, beaten
3 tablespoons lemon juice
1 tablespoon butter (or margarine)

1. Mix together sugar, cornstarch, salt and boiling water in a 2 cup measure or small bowl until smooth.

2. Microwave on HIGH (100%) for 1 to 2 minutes or until thick and clear. Stir halfway through cooking.

3. Stir a small amount of hot mixture into egg, then stir egg mixture into remaining hot mixture. Microwave on HIGH (100%) for 1 minute.

4. Add lemon juice and butter. Beat until smooth.

5. Serve hot or cold over cakes, puddings or fruit desserts.

Recipe yield: about 1½ cups

BUTTERSCOTCH SAUCE

Power Level: MEDIUM-HIGH [70%]
Total Cooking Time: 8 to 10 minutes

1½ cups brown sugar
1 tablespoon cornstarch
½ cup half and half
¼ cup butter (or margarine)
¼ cup light corn syrup
½ teaspoon vanilla (or rum flavoring)

1. Mix together sugar, cornstarch and cream in a 1½ quart casserole until smooth. Add butter and syrup.

2. Microwave on MEDIUM-HIGH (70%) for 8 to 10 minutes or until sauce reaches soft ball stage. Stir often the last half of cooking.

3. Stir in vanilla. Serve hot or cold over cake or ice cream. Store in the refrigerator.

Recipe yield: about 1½ cups

CARAMEL SAUCE

Power Level: MEDIUM-HIGH [70%]
Total Cooking Time: 8 to 10 minutes

1½ cups brown sugar
⅔ cup light corn syrup
⅓ cup half and half
1½ tablespoons butter (or margarine)

1. Mix all ingredients in a 2 quart casserole.

2. Microwave on MEDIUM-HIGH (70%) for 8 to 10 minutes or until sauce reaches soft ball stage. Stir often the last half of cooking.

3. Serve hot or cold over cake or ice cream. Store in the refrigerator.

Recipe yield: about 1½ cups

HOMEMADE SWEETENED CONDENSED MILK*

Power Level: HIGH [100%]
Total Cooking Time: 45 seconds to 1 minute

½ cup cold water
1⅓ cups nonfat dry milk
¾ cup sugar
1 teaspoon vanilla

1. Pour water in a 2 cup measure or small bowl. Stir in milk powder until smooth. Microwave on HIGH (100%) for 45 seconds to 1 minute or until steaming.

2. Stir in sugar and vanilla until sugar is dissolved. Cool completely before using.

*This recipe can be used as a substitute for 1 can (14 ounces) sweetened condensed milk.

Recipe yield: 1⅓ cups

CUSTARD SAUCE

Power Level: MEDIUM-HIGH [70%]
Total Cooking Time: 7 to 8 minutes

4 egg yolks
2 cups milk
¼ cup sugar
1 teaspoon vanilla
Dash of salt

1. Mix together all ingredients in a 4 cup measure or 1 quart casserole until well blended.

2. Microwave on MEDIUM-HIGH (70%) for 7 to 8 minutes or until back of spoon is coated. Stir occasionally during cooking. Chill before serving.

Recipe yield: about 2½ cups

QUICK CHOCOLATE FONDUE

Power Level: HIGH [100%]
Total Cooking Time: 3 to 5 minutes

1 package (12 ounces) semisweet chocolate pieces
4 cups miniature marshmallows (or 32 large)
1 can (14 ounces) sweetened condensed milk
½ cup milk
1 teaspoon vanilla
¼ teaspoon salt

1. Combine all ingredients in a 2 quart casserole.

2. Microwave on HIGH (100%) for 3 to 5 minutes or until chocolate and marshmallows are melted. Beat until smooth and creamy. Pour into a fondue pot.

3. Use to dip pineapple chunks, orange sections, strawberries, apple slices, angel food cake squares or as a sauce over ice cream.

Variations:

BUTTERSCOTCH FONDUE

Follow Quick Chocolate Fondue recipe except substitute butterscotch morsels for semisweet chocolate pieces.

PEANUT BUTTER FONDUE

Follow Quick Chocolate Fondue recipe except substitute peanut butter morsels for semisweet chocolate pieces.

Recipe yield: 2½ cups

Scoop Tip

For easy scooping, soften solidly frozen ice cream in the micro-wave on Low (30%). Heat 1 pint for 25 to 30 seconds; 1 quart for 30 to 35 seconds; ½ gallon for 35 to 40 seconds.

Hot Fudge Sauce is an ice cream lover's favorite.

Meat

Meat probably represents the biggest investment of your food budget. So it deserves your special care and the cooking benefits of the microwave oven.

There are several characteristics of meat which affect the way it cooks. Tenderness is the most important factor. Other factors are temperature, shape and size of meat, amount and position of bone, and the amount and distribution of fat.

Meat cooks much faster in the microwave than in the conventional oven. Keep this in mind so as to avoid overcooking.

Shielding with foil is sometimes helpful in protecting some areas which may overcook.

Because of their fat content, drippings attract microwave energy away from the meat itself. When cooking a roast with an excess amount of drippings, it is helpful to remove the drippings at intervals to speed cooking and to prevent spattering.

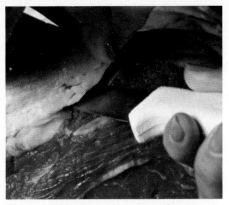

Meat will microwave evenly *when it has even layers of fat along the outside. An even coating of fat helps cook and flavor roasts. If one area has a heavier fat cover, it might cook faster and may overcook. Well marbled meat is more tender than lean meat. Thin veins of interior fat help retain juices, add flavor and give meat a fine grain.*

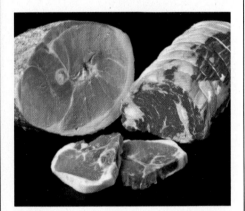

In the microwave, *bone tends not to conduct heat into the surrounding meat as in conventional cooking. Therefore, meat with bone may not cook as evenly as boneless meat. Center bones or bones surrounded by more than 1 inch of meat have little effect on cooking.*

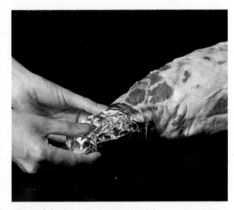

Shield thin portions *of roasts or bony tips with foil. Irregular shaped meat will cook faster in thin areas. Evenly shaped meats such as rolled rib, boneless chuck or rump roast, cook more evenly.*

Thick, whole pieces *of meat are cooked in the center by heat conduction just as in the conventional oven.*

Thin, small pieces *cook faster. When meat is less than 2 inches thick, microwave energy causes complete cooking.*

A long, thin piece *of meat will cook faster than a short, thick piece of equal weight.*

Tender cuts *of meat, such as rolled rib, can be dry roasted on a trivet in the microwave with no liquid added.*

Basic Meat Facts

Less tender cuts, *such as chuck roast, need steam and are cooked slowly and gently with some liquid and covered tightly. Pounding or marinating meat helps tenderize and adds flavor before cooking.*

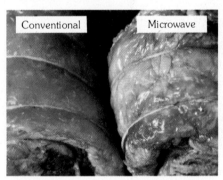

Meat cooked longer *than 10 minutes will begin to brown in the microwave and be similar in appearance to those foods cooked conventionally but will not have a dry surface. Browning of meat occurs in microwave cooking when fat rises to the surface and gets hot enough to partially burn. Browning makes meat more attractive and appetizing.*

--- **Marinade Tip** ---

For a convenient marinade to tenderize meats, try using Italian salad dressing, packaged marinades, tomato juice, wine or teriyaki sauce.

A MEAT THERMOMETER OR TEMPERATURE PROBE HELPS SAVE MEATS

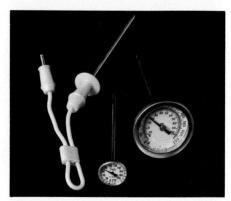

Make sure *any thermometer you use is recommended safe for use in microwave ovens.*

It's easy *to determine the proper depth for the thermometer or probe. Hold it against the outside of the meat. Grasp the probe or thermometer so that the tip reaches the center of the thickest part of the meat. Without changing your grasp, insert the probe to that depth.*

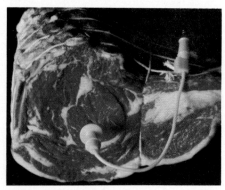

Insert the probe *or thermometer so the tip is in the center of the thickest part of the meat but not touching bone nor resting in a layer of fat. The probe should be set for 15° to 20° less than the final "done" temperature. The oven will shut off automatically.*

THE IMPORTANCE OF

Standing Time

The "standing time" is an important part of cooking meats in a microwave. The internal temperature of most meats will continue to rise as much as 15° to 20° after the meat is taken from the oven. Heat and temperature then become equal throughout the meat. The meat will continue to cook and to tenderize.

Therefore to avoid overcooking, most meats should be removed from the oven when the internal temperature is 15° to 20° below the desired "done" temperature, so that during 20 to 25 minutes of "standing time" meat will finish cooking.

During this standing time the meats will also change appearance and will look more "done" than when first removed from the oven.

INTERNAL TEMPERATURES BEFORE AND AFTER "STANDING TIME"

Meat		Internal temp. when removed from oven	Internal temp. desired after "standing time"
BEEF	Rare	120° - 125°	140°
	Medium	140° - 145°	160°
	Well	150° - 155°	170°
VEAL	Well	150° - 155°	170°
LAMB	Rare	120° - 125°	140°
	Medium	140° - 145°	160°
	Well	150° - 155°	170°
PORK	Well	150° - 155°	170°
HAM	Precooked	120° - 125°	140°
	Raw	150° - 155°	170°

Beef, veal, pork and lamb *toughen and rapidly dry out if overcooked. Standing time completes the cooking and allows these meats to remain juicy. Loosely tent with foil, shiny side down.*

Less tender cuts *remain covered during standing time to hold in steam which tenderizes and softens fibers.*

Defrosting

Defrosting meat is a special time-saving advantage of the microwave oven. Meat also better retains its moisture and quality when microwave defrosted.

It is important to completely defrost meat before cooking. When properly defrosted in the microwave, meat will be cold and moist to the touch. Allow a standing time equal to the defrosting time in the oven to complete the defrosting. There should be no signs of warmth or brownness when meat is removed from the oven as this would indicate the meat has started to cook.

DEFROSTING GROUND MEAT

Place plastic or paper wrapped *ground meat in the microwave. You may wish to begin defrosting in the dish you plan to cook in. Microwave on Low [30%] for time given on chart.*

Halfway through *defrost time, break up meat into dish and cover with waxed paper. Remove any soft pieces of meat so they won't begin to cook. Set soft meat aside on waxed paper.*

Ground meat should be cool *and moist when properly defrosted. Allow about 5 minutes standing time to complete defrosting.*

DEFROSTING CUBED MEAT

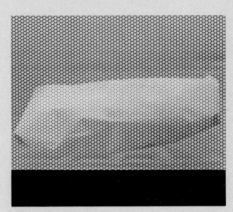

Place package *[paper or plastic wrapped] in the microwave. Defrost half the time on Low [30%].*

Break apart *cubes and spread out in baking dish. Cover with waxed paper.*

Defrost for remaining time. *Allow to stand about 5 minutes then check to see if fully defrosted. Meat should be tender but still cool and moist.*

DEFROSTING SMALL STEAKS, CHOPS AND PATTIES

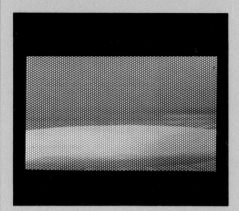

Place steak, chop or patty package *in the microwave. Defrost on Low [30%] for half the time.*

Separate meat pieces *as soon as possible. Turn them over and spread out in baking dish. They should not overlap. Tender parts should be toward the middle. Shield any warm areas with foil. Cover with waxed paper. Defrost for remaining time.*

Allow to stand *about 5 minutes to complete the defrosting process. Meat should be cool and slightly icy toward the center when first removed from the oven.*

DEFROSTING LARGE STEAKS AND FLAT ROASTS

Place steak or flat roast package *in the microwave. Defrost on Low [30%] for half the time.*

Turn meat over *and place in baking dish. Shield any warm areas with foil. Cover with waxed paper. Defrost for remaining time.*

Allow to stand *to complete the defrosting process. Meat should be cool and slightly icy toward the center when first removed from the oven.*

DEFROSTING LARGE ROASTS

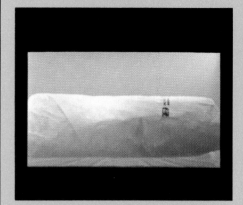

Place roast package *in the oven. Microwave on Low [30%] according to chart.*

Remove from package *and turn over in baking dish halfway through defrosting time. Shield any warm spots. Cover with waxed paper. Very large roasts may need a 15-minute standing time at this point. Defrost for remaining time.*

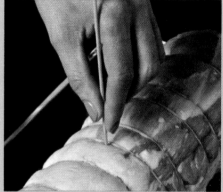

Remove from oven. *Roast should be slightly icy toward center when a wooden skewer is inserted. Allow to stand until skewer can be easily inserted to the roast center.*

MEAT DEFROSTING CHART
Power Level: LOW (30%)
Standing Time Equal to Defrost Time

BEEF

ITEM	DEFROSTING TIME
Ground Beef	
(1 pound)	**8-10 min.**
(2 pounds)	**16-18 min.**
(5 pounds)	**34-36 min.**
Beef Strips and Chunks	
(1 pound)	**8-10 min.**
Beef Patties	
(1 pound)	**6-8 min.**
Cube or Minute Steaks	
(4 ounces each)	
2	**4-6 min.**
4	**6-8 min.**
Steaks:	
Small Steaks	
(Filet Mignon, T-Bone,	
Porterhouse, Rib-Eye)	
¾ to 1 inch thick	
(8 ounces each)	
1	**6-8 min.**
2	**10-12 min.**
4	**16-18 min.**
(16 ounces each)	
1	**10-12 min.**
2	**16-18 min.**
Large Steaks or Flat Roasts	
(Round steak, chuck steak,	
sirloin steak, Swiss steak,	
tenderloin roast, chuck	
roast, shoulder roast,	
brisket)	**4-8 min. per lb.**
Large Roasts	
more than 2 inches thick	
(Rump, sirloin, rolled rib,	
standing rib, sirloin tip)	**6-10 min. per lb.**

LAMB

ITEM	DEFROSTING TIME
Ground Lamb	**6-8 min. per lb.**
Lamb Chops (¾ inch thick)	
2	**4-6 min.**
4	**10-12 min.**
6	**12-14 min.**
8	**14-16 min.**
Lamb Roast	**6-8 min. per lb.**

PORK

ITEM	DEFROSTING TIME
Ground Pork, Ham or Sausage	
(1 pound)	**6-8 min.**
(2 pounds)	**10-12 min.**
(5 pounds)	**24-26 min.**
Pork Chops or Steaks	
(¾ inch thick)	
2	**4-6 min.**
4	**10-12 min.**
6	**12-14 min.**
8	**14-16 min.**
Pork Roast and Ham	**6-8 min. per lb.**
Pork Spareribs	**6-8 min. per lb.**
Pork Steak	**6-8 min. per lb.**
Pork Tenderloin	**6-8 min. per lb.**
Wieners (1 pound)	**3-5 min.**
Bacon Slices	**4-6 min.**
Preformed Sausage Patties (12 ounces)	**2-4 min.**
Link Sausage (10 links)	**2-4 min.**

VEAL

ITEM	DEFROSTING TIME
Ground Veal	**6-8 min. per lb.**
Veal Chops	**6-8 min. per lb.**
Veal Roast	**6-8 min. per lb.**
Veal Steak	**6-8 min. per lb.**

Defrosting tip
Some freezers or freezer compartments freeze foods more solidly than other freezers. This factor may affect the recommended defrosting time, making it slightly longer or shorter. Meat should be completely defrosted before cooking.

Beef

TACO SALAD

Power Level: HIGH [100%]
Total Cooking Time: 7 to 10 minutes

1 pound ground beef chuck
1 medium onion, chopped
1 cup water
1 package (1¾ ounces) taco seasoning mix
1 medium head lettuce, torn into bite size pieces
1 cup grated Cheddar cheese
¼ cup sliced black olives
1 large tomato, cut in wedges
1 package (6 ounces) corn chips

1. Place meat and onion in a 1½ quart casserole. Cover with waxed paper. Microwave on HIGH (100%) for 4 to 6 minutes or until meat is no longer pink. Stir halfway through cooking. Drain off excess grease.

2. Stir in water and taco seasoning. Cover.

3. Microwave on HIGH (100%) for 3 to 4 minutes or until heated through. Stir halfway through cooking.

4. Mix together lettuce, cheese, olives and tomato wedges. Top with meat mixture and corn chips.

Recipe yield: 4 to 6 servings

CHILI

Power Level: HIGH [100%]
Total Cooking Time: 29 to 35 minutes

1 pound ground beef
1 cup chopped onion
½ cup chopped green pepper
1 clove garlic, minced
1 can (1 pound) tomatoes, undrained and chopped
1 can (8 ounces) tomato sauce
1 can (1 pound) kidney beans, undrained
2 to 3 teaspoons chili powder
1 teaspoon salt
½ teaspoon paprika
¼ teaspoon pepper
Dash of cayenne pepper (optional)

1. Place ground beef, onion, green pepper and garlic in a 3 quart casserole. Microwave on HIGH (100%) for 4 to 5 minutes or until beef is no longer pink and vegetables are tender. Stir halfway through cooking time. Drain off excess fat.

2. Stir in remaining ingredients. Microwave on HIGH (100%) for 25 to 30 minutes or until heated through. Stir after cooking.

Recipe yield: 4 to 6 servings

Taco Salad brings a Mexican flair to your dinner table.

Ground Beef

It is easy to precook ground beef in the microwave when using it as a basic ingredient for many main dishes. If you purchase a particularly high quality of ground beef which would be less greasy, you may be able to skip the precooking step.

Crumble 1 pound of ground beef *into a 1½-quart casserole or dish. For more even and faster cooking, cover with pleated plastic wrap or tight fitting lid. Microwave on High [100%] for 6 to 8 minutes.*

Check for doneness. *Meat should be thoroughly crumbled and have only occasional pink spots throughout. If desired, drain off excess grease.*

Stir and break up *meat halfway through cooking.*

For one-step cooking and draining, *select a high-grade plastic colander and place over casserole. Crumble meat into colander. Fat will drain into casserole during cooking.*

CABBAGE ROLLS

Power Level: HIGH [100%] and
MEDIUM-HIGH [70%]
Total Cooking Time: 28 to 35 minutes

12 cabbage leaves
1 cup water
½ pound ground beef
½ pound ground pork sausage
1 egg
½ cup instant rice
¼ cup finely chopped onion
1 teaspoon garlic salt
¼ teaspoon pepper
Dash of hot pepper sauce
1 can (8 ounces) tomato sauce
1 can (6 ounces) tomato paste
1 tablespoon sugar
1 teaspoon basil
1 can (1 pound) sauerkraut,
rinsed and drained

1. Place cabbage and ½ cup water in a 3 quart casserole. Cover with a tight fitting lid or plastic wrap. Microwave on HIGH (100%) for 8 to 10 minutes or until leaves are pliable. Drain. Cut out thick core from each leaf.

2. Mix together ground beef, sausage, egg, rice, onion, garlic salt, pepper, hot pepper sauce and ¼ cup tomato sauce.

3. Place about ¼ cup of meat mixture in the center of each leaf. Fold in edges and roll up from core end.

4. Mix together remaining tomato sauce, tomato paste, remaining water, sugar and basil.

5. Place alternate layers of sauerkraut, cabbage rolls (seam side down) and sauce in an 11¾x7½x1¾ inch baking dish. Cover with a tight fitting lid or plastic wrap.

6. Microwave on MEDIUM-HIGH (70%) for 20 to 25 minutes or until meat is no longer pink and rice is tender. Rearrange rolls halfway through cooking and baste with sauce. Allow to stand 5 minutes.

Recipe yield: 6 servings

GARDENER'S LASAGNA

Power Level: HIGH [100%] and
MEDIUM-HIGH [70%]
Total Cooking Time: 28 to 34 minutes

1¾ pounds zucchini, sliced
lengthwise
1 pound ground beef
1 clove garlic, minced
1 can (8 ounces) tomato sauce
1 teaspoon salt
2 teaspoons Italian seasoning
1 cup small curd cottage cheese
1 egg, beaten

1 tablespoon parsley
½ cup Parmesan cheese
2 cups (8 ounces) grated
Mozzarella cheese
¼ cup bread crumbs

1. Place zucchini in an 11¾x7½x1¾ inch baking dish. Cover with plastic wrap. Microwave on HIGH (100%) for 10 to 12 minutes or until tender crisp. Drain. Set aside.

2. Place beef and garlic in a 1 quart casserole. Microwave on HIGH (100%) for 4 to 6 minutes or until meat is no longer pink. Stir halfway through cooking. Drain off excess grease. Stir in tomato sauce, salt and Italian seasoning.

3. Mix together cottage cheese, egg and parsley.

4. Place alternate layers of zucchini, cottage cheese mixture, ground beef mixture, Parmesan cheese, Mozzarella cheese and bread crumbs in baking dish. Cover with waxed paper.

5. Microwave on MEDIUM-HIGH (70%) for 14 to 16 minutes or until heated through. Allow to stand 10 minutes.

Recipe yield: 6 to 8 servings

STUFFED GREEN PEPPERS

Power Level: MEDIUM-HIGH [70%]
Total Cooking Time: 20 to 25 minutes

1 pound ground beef
½ cup instant rice
1 egg, beaten
1 medium onion, chopped
1 can (15 ounces) tomato sauce
½ cup catsup
1 tablespoon Worcestershire sauce
1 teaspoon seasoned salt
¼ teaspoon seasoned pepper
3 large green peppers, cut in half
lengthwise
⅓ cup water
1 tablespoon sugar

1. Mix together ground beef, rice, egg, onion, ½ cup tomato sauce, catsup, Worcestershire sauce, salt and pepper.

2. Arrange green pepper halves in an 11¾x7½x1¾ inch baking dish. Fill with meat mixture. Mix together remaining tomato sauce, water and sugar. Pour over green peppers. Cover with a tight fitting lid or plastic wrap.

3. Microwave on MEDIUM-HIGH (70%) for 20 to 25 minutes or until meat is no longer pink and green pepper is tender. Allow to stand 5 minutes before serving.

Recipe yield: 4 to 6 servings

HARVEST BEEF CASSEROLE

Power Level: HIGH [100%]
Total Cooking Time: 13 to 17 minutes

1 pound ground beef
1 package (10 ounces) frozen
mixed vegetables in onion sauce
½ cup milk
1 tablespoon butter (or margarine)
1 teaspoon seasoned salt
1 package (8½ ounces) cornbread
mix (Jiffy)

1. Place ground beef in a 2 quart casserole. Microwave on HIGH (100%) for 4 to 6 minutes. Drain off excess grease.

2. Stir in vegetables, milk, butter and salt. Cover. Microwave on HIGH (100%) for 5 to 6 minutes or until vegetables are tender. Stir twice during cooking.

3. Combine cornbread mix as directed on package. Spread evenly around sides of beef mixture.

4. Microwave, uncovered, on HIGH (100%) for 4 to 5 minutes or until wooden pick inserted in cornbread comes out clean.

Recipe yield: 4 to 6 servings

MOCK SALISBURY STEAKS

Power Level: HIGH [100%]
Total Cooking Time: 16 to 18 minutes

2 tablespoons cornstarch
1 can (10¾ ounces) beef
consomme
1 can (4 ounces) sliced
mushrooms, drained
2 teaspoons Worcestershire sauce
¼ teaspoon basil
1½ pounds ground beef
½ cup cooked rice (or soft bread
crumbs)
1 medium onion, chopped
1 egg
1 teaspoon seasoned salt
¼ teaspoon pepper
Parsley

1. Mix together cornstarch and consomme. Stir in mushrooms, Worcestershire sauce and basil. Set aside.

2. Mix together beef, rice, onion, egg, salt and pepper. Shape into 6 patties. Place in a baking dish. Cover with waxed paper.

3. Microwave on HIGH (100%) for 6 minutes. Drain off excess fat. Turn and rearrange patties. Pour sauce over steaks. Cover.

4. Microwave on HIGH (100%) for 10 to 12 minutes or until no longer pink. Allow to stand 5 minutes before serving. Garnish with parsley.

Recipe yield: 6 servings

BEEF PATTIES

Place patties on a microwave safe dish. *If desired, cover with waxed paper to reduce spattering. Microwave on High [100%]. If cooking four or more patties, turn over and rearrange midway through cooking.*

Arrange patties on trivet *for less greasy patties. Microwave on High [100%]. If desired turn patties over midway through cooking.*

Preheat empty browning dish *or griddle. The dish bottom is coated with aluminum or iron ferrite which attracts microwave energy and becomes hot like a skillet. Place patties in dish. Microwave on High [100%]. For four or more patties, turn over and rearrange midway through cooking. If your microwave is equipped with a browning element, use that instead of a browning dish.*

BEEF PATTIES

Power Level: HIGH [100%]
Total Cooking Time: 6 to 8 minutes

1 pound ground beef
2 tablespoons chopped onion
1 teaspoon seasoned salt
¼ teaspoon pepper

1. Mix together all ingredients. Shape into 4 patties.

2. Place in an 8x8x2 inch baking dish. Cover with waxed paper. Microwave on HIGH (100%) for 6 to 8 minutes or until desired doneness.

3. Top with your own choice of sauces and cheeses.

Variations:

ITALIAN PATTIES

Follow Beef Patties recipe as directed except add 1 teaspoon Italian seasoning and a dash of garlic powder. After cooking, top with Mozzarella cheese and a tablespoon of pizza sauce. Microwave on HIGH (100%) for an additional 30 to 45 seconds or until cheese just begins to melt.

GOURMET PATTIES

Follow Beef Patties recipe as directed except add ¼ cup chopped ripe olives and a dash of garlic powder. After cooking, mix together ¼ cup Bleu cheese and ¼ cup sour cream. Spoon cheese mixture over the patties. Microwave on HIGH (100%) for an additional 30 to 45 seconds or until sauce is heated through.

STEAK PATTIES

Follow Beef Patties recipe as directed except add 1 can (2½ ounces) chopped mushrooms (drained), 2 tablespoons Worcestershire sauce and 2 teaspoons parsley.

Tip: For less greasy hamburgers, cook on a trivet.

Recipe yield: 4 servings

— **Surprise Patties Tip** —
Place 2 tablespoons grated cheese, chopped cooked bacon, chopped onion, chopped green pepper or mushrooms on the center of a thin hamburger patty. Top with another thin patty. Pinch and seal around edges. Microwave as directed in ground beef patty chart.

HASH PATTIES

Power Level: HIGH [100%]
Total Cooking Time: 3 to 4 minutes

4 medium potatoes, peeled and shredded
4 cups finely chopped, cooked beef
1 small onion, grated
¼ cup barbecue sauce
2 tablespoons milk
2 tablespoons butter (or margarine)
1 teaspoon salt
¼ teaspoon pepper
2 tablespoons cooking oil

1. Mix together all ingredients except oil. Form into 8 patties.

2. Microwave browning dish on HIGH (100%) for 4 to 5 minutes.

3. Add 1 tablespoon oil. Microwave, 4 patties at a time, on HIGH (100%) for 3 to 4 minutes or until heated through. Turn over halfway through cooking. Remove from dish. Keep warm.

4. Preheat browning dish again for 4 minutes. Repeat Step 3 with remaining 4 patties.

Recipe yield: 8 to 10 patties

BEEF PATTIES COOKING CHART

Power Level: HIGH (100%)

Item	Cooking Time**
Hamburgers * **(¾" thick)** **(4 ounces ea.)**	
1	**2-2½ min.**
2	**3-3½ min.**
3	**4-4½ min.**
4	**5-5½ min.**
5	**6-6½ min.**
6	**6½-7 min.**
Browning griddle	
2	**griddle 6 min.** **patties 3-4 min.**
4	**griddle 8 min.** **patties 5-6 min.**
6	**griddle 10 min.** **patties 6-8 min.**

*For less greasy hamburgers cook on trivet.

**If microwave has a browning element, brown as desired.

MEAT LOAF

Shape meat mixture *into loaf in loaf dish. Avoid overhandling meat as this tends to toughen it. Spread catsup over the top.*

Cover with waxed paper *or pleated plastic wrap for a moister surface on the loaf. For a dry surface, cook uncovered. Microwave on Medium-High [70%] for 20 to 22 minutes.*

Allow meat loaf to stand *5 minutes before serving. Loaf should no longer be pink in center. Internal temperature should be 170°.*

MEAT LOAF

Power Level: MEDIUM-HIGH [70%]
Total Cooking Time: 22 to 24 minutes
Temperature Probe: 150° to 155°

1½ pounds ground beef
1 egg, slightly beaten
1 cup bread crumbs
⅔ cup milk
1 small onion, chopped
1 jar (2½ ounces) sliced
 mushrooms, drained
1 tablespoon Worcestershire sauce
1 teaspoon salt
¼ teaspoon pepper
¼ cup catsup

1. Mix together all ingredients except catsup. Shape into a loaf in a 9x5x3 inch loaf dish. Spread catsup over top. If desired, cover.

2. Microwave on MEDIUM-HIGH (70%) for 22 to 24 minutes or until no longer pink. Allow to stand, covered, 5 minutes before serving.

Variations:
CHEESY MEAT LOAF ROLL

Follow Meat Loaf recipe as directed except pat meat mixture on waxed paper into a 12x9 inch rectangle. Sprinkle with 1 cup grated Cheddar cheese, Swiss cheese or Mozzarella cheese. Roll meat jelly-roll fashion, with aid of waxed paper. Seal seam and ends. Place seam side down in a 10x6x1¾ inch baking dish. If desired, cover.

Roll meat *in jelly-roll fashion. Lift waxed paper along with meat until roll stays firm. Peel back paper to keep it from sticking.*

STUFFED MEAT LOAF RING

Follow Meat Loaf recipe as directed except pat half of mixture into the bottom of a baking ring. Top with a layer of 1 package (10 ounces) chopped broccoli (thawed and well drained), 1 can (2½ ounces) sliced mushrooms (drained) and 1 cup Cheddar cheese, leaving a ½ inch border on both sides. Top with remaining meat loaf mixture. Seal edges. Spread with catsup. If desired, cover.

Recipe yield: 4 to 6 servings

Pat half of meat loaf *mixture into baking ring. Top with broccoli, mushrooms and Cheddar cheese then add remaining meat mixture. If you do not have a baking ring, invert a custard cup in a round casserole.*

Seal edges and smooth top *with spatula. Spread with catsup. If desired, cover with waxed paper or plastic wrap and microwave.*

REUBEN LOAF

Power Level: MEDIUM-HIGH [70%]
Total Cooking Time: 26 to 29 minutes

1 can (11 ounces) spaghetti sauce
1 pound ground beef chuck
1 can (12 ounces) corned beef,
 finely chopped
2½ cups bread crumbs
2 eggs, slightly beaten
2 tablespoons chopped chives
¼ teaspoon salt
¼ teaspoon garlic powder
Dash of pepper
1 cup sauerkraut, finely chopped
 and well drained
½ teaspoon caraway seeds
1 cup grated Swiss cheese
1 teaspoon horseradish
4 slices (about 4 ounces) Swiss
 cheese, cut in 8 triangles

1. Mix together ¼ cup sauce, ground chuck, corned beef, bread crumbs, eggs, chives, salt, garlic powder and pepper.

2. Pat meat on waxed paper into 15x12 inch rectangle.

3. Combine sauerkraut, caraway seeds and cheese. Press into meat to within 1 inch of edges.

4. Roll meat jelly-roll fashion, with aid of waxed paper, starting at short edge. Seal seam and ends.

5. Place loaf seam side down in an 11¾x7½x1¾ inch baking dish. Cover with waxed paper. Microwave on MEDIUM-HIGH (70%) for 18 minutes.

6. Mix together remaining sauce and horseradish. Spoon over loaf. Microwave, uncovered, on MEDIUM-HIGH (70%) for 6 to 8 minutes or until center of meat is no longer pink.

7. Arrange cheese slices over top of loaf, overlapping slightly. Microwave on MEDIUM-HIGH (70%) for 2 to 3 minutes or until cheese just begins to melt. Allow to stand, covered, 5 minutes.

Recipe yield: 6 to 8 servings

MEATBALLS

Arrange meatballs, *evenly spaced apart. If using a round baking dish, place meatballs in a circle. For 12 meatballs, microwave on High [100%] for 6 to 8 minutes.*

If cooking a large amount *of meatballs in an oblong dish, rearrange them midway through cooking. Meatballs in a round dish need not be rearranged.*

Allow to stand *and cool. Drain off grease and add sauce ingredients.*

MEATBALLS
Power Level: HIGH [100%]
Total Cooking Time: 6 to 8 minutes

1 pound ground beef chuck
1 egg
½ cup bread crumbs
1 tablespoon Worcestershire sauce
1 teaspoon instant minced onion
½ teaspoon salt
Dash of pepper

1. Mix together ingredients. Shape into 1½ inch meatballs.

2. Place meatballs in a 10x6x1¾ inch baking dish. Cover with waxed paper.

3. Microwave on HIGH (100%) for 6 to 8 minutes or until no longer pink.

Rearrange halfway through cooking.

Variations:

SWEDISH MEATBALLS
Follow Meatball recipe as directed except after cooking remove meatballs from baking dish (reserve 2 tablespoons drippings). Stir 2 tablespoons all purpose flour, ¼ teaspoon salt and a dash of pepper into drippings until smooth. Gradually stir in ½ cup milk (or half and half) and ½ cup beef broth. Microwave on HIGH (100%) for 4 to 6 minutes or until thickened. Stir in 1 cup sour cream. Add meatballs and 1 can (2½ ounces) sliced mushrooms (drained). Microwave on HIGH (100%) for 1 to 2 minutes or until heated through.

SWEET AND SOUR MEATBALLS
Follow Meatball recipe as directed. After cooking remove meatballs from baking dish (reserve 2 tablespoons drippings). Stir 2 tablespoons cornstarch and ¼ teaspoon ginger into drippings until smooth. Gradually stir in 1 cup beef broth, 2 tablespoons soy sauce, 1 green pepper (thinly sliced) and 1 can (8 ounces) pineapple chunks (undrained). Microwave on HIGH (100%) for 6 to 8 minutes or until thickened. Stir in meatballs. Microwave on HIGH (100%) for 1 to 2 minutes or until heated through.

Recipe yield: about 12 meatballs

Less Tender Cuts

Use lower power settings when cooking less tender cuts of beef in the microwave. These cuts should be cooked slowly in liquid and kept tightly covered.

To help tenderize cuts *such as chuck roast or cubed, round or flank steak, pound the meat first. You might marinate it or cook it in a slightly acidic-base liquid such as tomato sauce or wine.*

BEEF STEW

BEEF STEW
Power Level: HIGH [100%] and
*   MEDIUM [50%]*
Total Cooking Time: 1 hour 50 minutes
*   to 1 hour 56 minutes*

2 cups water
2 pounds beef chuck, cut into
** ½ inch cubes**

2 beef bouillon cubes
1 bay leaf
1 teaspoon salt
2 large potatoes, pared and cut
  into 1/2 inch cubes
2 carrots, cut into 1/4 inch pieces
2 celery stalks, cut into
  1/2 inch pieces
2 onions, sliced

1. Place water in a 3 quart casserole. Cover with a tight fitting lid or plastic wrap. Microwave on HIGH (100%) for 5 to 6 minutes or until boiling.

2. Add meat, beef bouillon, bay leaf and salt. Cover.

3. Microwave on MEDIUM (50%) for 1 hour 30 minutes or until meat is tender. Stir twice during cooking.

4. Add vegetables. Cover. Microwave on HIGH (100%) for 15 to 20 minutes or until vegetables are tender.

Variation:
BEEF STEW AND DILL DUMPLINGS

Follow Beef Stew recipe as directed. Mix together 1 cup flour, 2 teaspoons baking powder, 1/2 teaspoon salt and 1/2 teaspoon dill. Stir in 1/2 cup plus 2 tablespoons milk and 2 tablespoons cooking oil just until dry ingredients are moistened. Drop by tablespoons into hot stew. Cover with a tight fitting lid or plastic wrap. Microwave on HIGH (100%) for 5 to 6 minutes.

Recipe yield: 6 servings

Add meat, *beef bouillon, bay leaf and salt to 2 cups boiling water in a 3-quart casserole. Be sure water is boiling as this helps tenderize the meat.*

Cover with a tight lid *or pleated plastic wrap. Microwave on Medium [50%] for 1 hour 30 minutes or until meat is tender. Stir twice during cooking.*

Add vegetables. *Cover and microwave on High [100%] for 15 to 20 minutes or until vegetables are tender.*

Hobo Stew has the taste they'll love to come home to.

HOBO STEW
Power Level: MEDIUM [50%] and HIGH [100%]
Total Cooking Time: 54 to 65 minutes

1 1/2 pounds (about 4) cube steaks,
  cut into 1 inch cubes
1 can (16 ounces) tomatoes
1 can (8 ounces) tomato sauce
1 medium onion, sliced
1 teaspoon Worcestershire sauce
1 teaspoon salt
1/2 teaspoon basil
1/4 teaspoon rosemary
1/4 teaspoon pepper
4 medium potatoes, cubed (1/2 in.)
1 package (10 oz.) frozen corn,
  thawed
1 green pepper, chopped

1. Combine meat, tomatoes, tomato sauce, onion, Worcestershire sauce and seasonings in a 3 quart casserole. Cover.

2. Microwave on MEDIUM (50%) for 40 to 45 minutes or until meat is tender. Stir twice during cooking.

3. Stir in potatoes. Cover. Microwave on HIGH (100%) for 10 to 15 minutes.

4. Add corn and green pepper. Cover. Microwave on HIGH (100%) for 4 to 5 minutes or until heated through. Stir well before serving.

Recipe yield: 6 servings

BEEF WITH HORSERADISH SAUCE
Power Level: HIGH [100%] and LOW [30%]
Total Cooking Time: 22 to 30 minutes

2 pounds beef round steak,
  cut into 1/2 inch cubes
1 clove garlic, minced
1 tablespoon oil
1 tablespoon Worcestershire sauce
1 teaspoon salt
1/2 teaspoon pepper
1/2 teaspoon dry mustard
1 cup sour cream
2 teaspoons chopped chives
2 teaspoons horseradish sauce

1. Place beef, garlic and oil in a 2 quart casserole. Cover with a tight fitting lid or plastic wrap.

2. Microwave on HIGH (100%) for 6 to 8 minutes or until meat is pink in center. Stir halfway through cooking. Drain excess grease.

3. Stir in Worcestershire sauce, salt, pepper and mustard. Cover. Microwave on LOW (30%) for 15 to 20 minutes or until meat is tender.

4. Stir in sour cream, chives and horseradish sauce. Microwave on HIGH (100%) for 1 to 2 minutes or until heated through. Allow to stand 5 minutes before serving.

Recipe yield: 6 to 8 servings

BEEF STROGANOFF

Power Level: MEDIUM-HIGH [70%]
Total Cooking Time: 16 to 21 minutes

1½ pounds boneless sirloin steak,
trimmed and cut diagonally
into ¼ inch strips
½ pound mushrooms, sliced
1 large onion, chopped
¼ cup butter (or margarine)
1 can (10½ ounces) condensed
cream of chicken soup
2 beef bouillon cubes
¼ cup dry white wine (or beef
broth)
1 teaspoon dill
1 cup sour cream

1. Place beef strips, mushrooms, onion and butter in a 2 quart casserole. Cover. Microwave on MEDIUM-HIGH (70%) for 10 to 12 minutes or until meat is pink in center and vegetables are tender. Stir halfway through cooking. Drain off excess grease.

2. Stir in soup, bouillon cubes, wine and dill. Cover. Microwave on MEDIUM-HIGH (70%) for 4 to 6 minutes or until hot and bubbly. Stir twice during cooking.

3. Stir in sour cream. Microwave, uncovered, on MEDIUM-HIGH (70%) for 2 to 3 minutes or until heated through. Allow to stand, covered, 5 minutes.

4. Serve over buttered noodles.

Variations:

HAMBURGER STROGANOFF

Follow Beef Stroganoff recipe as directed except substitute 1 pound ground beef for sirloin steak and eliminate butter. Microwave on HIGH (100%) for 6 to 8 minutes or until meat is pink in center and vegetables are tender. Drain off excess grease. Stir in soup, wine and dill; continue as directed in steps 2 and 3.

MEATBALL STROGANOFF

Follow Beef Stroganoff recipe as directed except combine 1 pound ground beef, ⅓ cup bread crumbs, ¼ cup chopped onion, 1 can (2½ ounces) drained sliced mushrooms and 1 egg. Form into 1 inch meatballs. Substitute for sirloin steak, onion and mushrooms. Eliminate butter. Microwave on HIGH (100%) for 6 to 8 minutes or until meat is pink in center. Drain off excess grease. Stir in soup, wine and dill; continue as directed in steps 2 and 3.

EASY STROGANOFF

Follow Beef Stroganoff recipe as directed except substitute 1 package (1¾ ounces) stroganoff sauce mix and 1⅓ cups milk for soup and sour cream.

Recipe yield: 4 to 6 servings

SHORT RIBS

Place short ribs *in 3-quart casserole. Stir in sauce and seasonings. Cover with pleated plastic wrap or tight fitting lid.*

Microwave on High (100%) *until boiling. Stir mixture and cover. Microwave on Medium [50%] until meat is fork tender.*

Allow to stand *15 minutes. If desired, thicken gravy with 2 tablespoons of flour.*

SAUCY BEEF SHORT RIBS

Power Level: HIGH [100%] and
MEDIUM [50%]
Total Cooking Time: 1 hour 5 minutes
to 1 hour 12
minutes

3 pounds beef short ribs, cut
in pieces
1 envelope (1½ ounces) dry onion
soup mix
1 green pepper, sliced
1 cup water
1 can (8 ounces) tomato sauce
1 tablespoon Worcestershire sauce
¼ teaspoon thyme

1. Coat spare ribs with onion soup mix. Place in a 3 quart casserole. Stir in green pepper, water, tomato sauce, Worcestershire sauce and thyme. Cover with a tight fitting lid or plastic wrap.

2. Microwave on HIGH (100%) for 10 to 12 minutes or until boiling.

3. Cover. Microwave on MEDIUM (50%) for 55 to 60 minutes or until meat is fork tender. Allow to stand 15 minutes before serving. If desired, thicken gravy with 2 tablespoons of all purpose flour.

Recipe yield: 4 to 6 servings

SWISS STEAK

Coat meat with flour, *salt and pepper mixture. Pour cooking oil into baking dish.*

Arrange meat evenly *in dish. Cover with a tight lid or pleated plastic wrap Microwave on Medium [50%] for 45 to 50 minutes or until meat is pink in center.*

Turn meat over *and add onion and tomatoes. Cover and microwave on Medium [50%] for 25 to 30 minutes or until fork tender. Allow to stand 5 minutes before serving.*

SWISS STEAK

Power Level: MEDIUM [50%]
Total Cooking Time: 1 hour 10 minutes
to 1 hour 20
minutes

1½ pounds beef round steak, cut
½ inch thick
2 tablespoons all purpose flour
1 teaspoon salt
¼ teaspoon pepper
2 tablespoons cooking oil
2 medium onions, sliced thin
1 can (1 pound) tomatoes,
undrained

1. Cut meat into 4 pieces. Combine flour, salt and pepper. Dredge meat in flour mixture.

2. Pour cooking oil into a baking dish. Arrange meat pieces evenly over bottom. Cover with a tight fitting lid or plastic wrap.

3. Microwave on MEDIUM (50%) for 45 to 50 minutes or until meat is pink in center. Turn meat over.

4. Layer onion and tomatoes evenly over meat.

5. Cover. Microwave on MEDIUM (50%) for 25 to 30 minutes or until meat is tender. Allow to stand 5 minutes before serving.

Recipe yield: 4 servings

STUFFED FLANK STEAK

Power Level: HIGH [100%] and
MEDIUM [50%]
Total Cooking Time: 28 to 32 minutes

2 pounds beef flank steak
¼ teaspoon seasoned salt
Dash of pepper
½ cup chopped celery
¼ cup chopped onion
3 tablespoons butter (or margarine)
1½ cups seasoned bread cubes
1 can (10¾ ounces) golden
mushroom soup
1 tablespoon parsley

1. Pound flank steak. Sprinkle with seasoned salt and pepper.

2. Combine celery, onion and butter in a 2 quart casserole. Microwave on HIGH (100%) for 3 to 4 minutes or until vegetables are tender.

3. Stir in bread cubes. Spread evenly over steak. Roll up jelly roll fashion. Secure with string or wooden skewers. Place in an 11¾x7½x1¾ inch baking dish. Cover.

4. Microwave on MEDIUM (50%) for 20 to 22 minutes or until meat is fork tender. Pour soup over meat and sprinkle with parsley. Cover. Microwave on MEDIUM (50%) for an additional 5 to 6 minutes or until heated through. Allow to stand 5 minutes before serving.

Recipe yield: 4 to 6 servings

GINGERED PEPPER STEAK

Power Level: HIGH [100%] and
LOW [30%]
Total Cooking Time: 21 to 29 minutes

1 pound sirloin steak, cut into
strips
½ pound mushrooms, sliced
1 clove garlic, minced
2 tablespoons cooking oil
¼ cup soy sauce
¼ cup water
2 tablespoons cider vinegar
1 tablespoon cornstarch
½ teaspoon salt
¼ teaspoon ginger
Dash of pepper
1 small onion, sliced
1 medium green pepper, cut in
strips

1. Place meat, mushrooms, garlic and oil in a 2 quart casserole. Cover with waxed paper. Microwave on HIGH (100%) for 6 to 8 minutes or until meat is no longer pink. Stir halfway through cooking.

2. Mix together soy sauce, water, vinegar, cornstarch, salt, ginger and pepper until smooth. Stir into meat mixture.

3. Microwave on HIGH (100%) for 5 to 6 minutes or until thickened. Stir occasionally. Add onion and green pepper.

4. Microwave on LOW (30%) for 10 to 15 minutes to blend flavors. Vegetables will be tender crisp.

Recipe yield: 6 to 8 servings

MARINATED STEAK

Power Level: MEDIUM [50%]
Total Cooking Time: 25 to 30 minutes
per pound

1 small bottle Italian salad
dressing or 1 recipe marinade
(below)
1 steak (flank steak, chuck steak,
round steak, or cube steak)

1. Pour marinade into a baking dish.

2. Cut steak in serving pieces. Place in dish and coat thoroughly with marinade. Cover with plastic wrap. Refrigerate overnight. Turn over several times to recoat with marinade.

3. Drain off marinade. Microwave, covered, on MEDIUM (50%) for 25 to 30 minutes per pound. Turn over halfway through cooking time.

TERIYAKI MARINADE

⅓ cup soy sauce
½ cup brown sugar
1 teaspoon ginger
¼ teaspoon garlic powder
Dash of pepper

1. Mix together all ingredients.

RED WINE MARINADE

½ cup red wine
¼ cup cooking oil
¼ cup chopped onion
¼ teaspoon thyme
Dash of pepper

1. Mix all ingredients together.

Gingered Pepper Steak has an Oriental flavor.

COOKING LESS TENDER ROASTS

Arrange roast in 2½-quart casserole. Sprinkle meat with salt and pepper. Pour onion soup over meat. Cover with tight lid or plastic wrap. Microwave on Medium [50%] for 20 minutes.

Turn meat over. Arrange potatoes, carrots and celery around meat. Cover and microwave on Medium [50%] for 55 to 60 minutes or until meat and vegetables are tender.

In a Cooking Bag

Place meat and flour in cooking bag. Shake bag to completely cover meat with flour. Add soup mix, water, salt and pepper. Place bag in baking dish. Cut a strip of plastic from the open end of the bag to tie bag shut or use string or rubber band. Slash bag to allow steam to escape. Microwave on Medium [50%] for 22 to 25 minutes per pound or until meat is tender. Halfway through cooking, turn meat and add vegetables.

POT ROAST
Power Level: MEDIUM [50%]
Total Cooking Time: 1 hour 15 minutes
to 1 hour 20 minutes

3 pound beef chuck roast
¼ teaspoon salt
Dash of pepper
1 can (10¾ ounces) French onion soup
3 small potatoes, quartered
3 carrots, quartered
3 stalks celery, cut into 1 inch pieces

1. Arrange roast in a 3 quart casserole. Sprinkle meat with salt and pepper. Pour undiluted onion soup over meat. Cover with a tight fitting lid or plastic wrap. Microwave on MEDIUM (50%) for 20 minutes.

2. Turn meat over. Arrange potatoes, carrots and celery around meat. Cover. Microwave on MEDIUM (50%) for 55 to 60 minutes or until meat and vegetables are tender.

Recipe yield: 6 to 8 servings

QUICK SAUERBRATEN
Power Level: LOW [30%]
Total Cooking Time: 1 hour 30 minutes
to 1 hour 45 minutes

3 pound beef chuck roast
1 large onion, sliced
2 tablespoons pickling spices
1½ cups water
¾ cup red wine vinegar
1 teaspoon salt
10 gingersnaps, crushed
¼ cup brown sugar

1. Cut meat into 8 pieces. Arrange in a 3 quart casserole. Add onion.

2. Tie pickling spices in a piece of cheesecloth. Mix together remaining ingredients. Pour over meat. Pierce surface of meat several times with fork. Add bag of pickling spices. Cover with a tight fitting lid or plastic wrap. Allow to marinate for 15 minutes.

3. Microwave, covered, on LOW (30%) for 1 hour 30 minutes to 1 hour 45 minutes or until meat is fork tender. Turn meat over halfway through cooking.

Recipe yield: 8 to 10 servings

BEEF BRISKET
Power Level: HIGH [100%] and
MEDIUM [50%]
Total Cooking Time: 1 hour 36 minutes
to 1 hour 48 minutes

3 pounds beef brisket
2 cups water
1 small onion, chopped
1 stalk celery, chopped
1 clove garlic, crushed
2 tablespoons brown sugar
2 tablespoons vinegar
1 teaspoon seasoned salt
½ teaspoon seasoned pepper
1 bay leaf

1. Place meat in a baking dish. Combine remaining ingredients and pour over meat. Cover with plastic wrap.

2. Microwave on HIGH (100%) for 16 to 18 minutes or until boiling.

3. Microwave on MEDIUM (50%) for 1 hour 20 minutes to 1 hour 30 minutes or until meat is fork tender. Turn meat over halfway through cooking.

4. Allow to stand 15 minutes before serving.

Recipe yield: 6 to 8 servings

NEW ENGLAND CORNED BEEF DINNER
Power Level: HIGH [100%] and
MEDIUM [50%]
Total Cooking Time: 1 hour 45 minutes
to 2 hours 7 minutes

3 pound corned beef brisket
3 cups water
2 bay leaves
1 teaspoon dried parsley
1 teaspoon salt
¼ teaspoon pepper
Dash of garlic powder
2 medium potatoes, quartered
2 medium carrots, quartered
1 medium onion, sliced
1 small head cabbage, cut into wedges

1. Place corned beef, water, bay leaves, parsley, salt, pepper and garlic powder in a 3 quart casserole. Cover with a tight fitting lid or plastic wrap.

2. Microwave on HIGH (100%) for 20 to 22 minutes or until boiling. Turn brisket over. Cover.

3. Microwave on MEDIUM (50%) for 1 hour to 1 hour 15 minutes or until tender. Turn over twice during cooking. Remove meat and keep warm by covering with aluminum foil.

4. Add remaining ingredients to brisket broth. Cover. Microwave on HIGH (100%) for 25 to 30 minutes or until vegetables are tender. Stir halfway through cooking.

5. Slice corned beef diagonally into thin slices and serve with vegetables.

Recipe yield: 6 to 8 servings

Tender Cuts

Tenderloin, eye of round, rolled or standing rib, steaks and other tender cuts of beef are perfect for cooking in the microwave oven.

COOKING STEAKS

BROWNING GRIDDLE STEAKS

Microwave browning griddle on HIGH (100%) for 8 minutes. Meanwhile, spread 1 tablespoon butter (or margarine) on each side of steak. Score fat.

Place steak on preheated griddle. Turn over halfway through cooking. Microwave to desired doneness. Times on chart are for medium doneness. Reduce or increase time according to personal preference.

Amt.	Type	Time
1 or 2	Cube or	2-2½ min.
4	Minute (4 oz.)	4-4½ min.
1 or 2	Rib Eye or	5-6½ min.
3	Strip (4 oz.)	8-8½ min.
1	T-Bone or Porterhouse (8 oz.)	4-5 min.

COOKING ROASTS

Roasts may be seasoned before, during or after cooking. Place meat, fat side down, on a rack or trivet in a baking dish to hold the meat out of its drippings. Turn fat side up midway through cooking. With the fat on the top, the meat bastes itself.

Roasts should be cooked up and out of their drippings. Use a trivet or microwave roasting dish. A microwave bacon rack may be used or simply turn a saucer or small dish upside down in a baking dish and place roast on top. Shown above are various kinds of trivets available.

Allow meat to stand before serving to finish the cooking process and so the juices set in the meat. If meat is sliced immediately when removed from the microwave, the juices will run out.

Proper placement of the temperature probe or meat thermometer is especially important in cooking the tender roast cuts. Pictured below are instructions for the best placement in the most popular tender cuts. If you use a meat thermometer instead of a temperature probe be sure it is one that is recommended for use in microwave ovens.

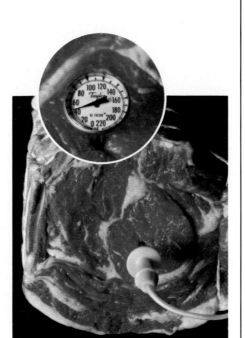

For a standing rib roast, start cooking fat side down. Insert the temperature probe or meat thermometer into the center of the meatiest portion from the front.

For a half tenderloin, begin cooking fat side down. Insert probe or thermometer into the cut end with tip in the meaty center.

For a rolled rib, start cooking fat side down. Insert the probe or thermometer so the tip is in the center, meatiest section.

For eye of round, turn fat side down and insert probe or thermometer into the center of the meatiest portion of the roast.

COOKING TENDER ROASTS	COOKING TENDERLOIN	THE FINISHED PRODUCT

COOKING TENDER ROASTS

Begin cooking meat *with fat side down. Cover with waxed paper, lightly greased with shortening so as to prevent it from sticking to the meat. Microwave on Medium-High [70%].*

Halfway through cooking, *grasp roast with paper towels and turn fat side up. Shield any areas which may be cooking faster. Continue cooking.*

When desired temperature is reached, *tent meat loosely with foil and allow to stand 20 to 25 minutes before serving. Meat should be removed from microwave when it is 15° to 20° less than the desired "done" temperature.*

COOKING TENDERLOIN

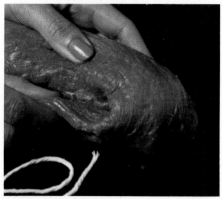

Fold the tenderloin tip under *and secure so as to make meat a uniform shape. Place on trivet in baking dish.*

Shield ends *with foil. Wrap foil down and around the sides if necessary. Microwave on Medium [50%].*

Midway through cooking, *turn tenderloin over. Continue cooking. Allow a standing time of 10 to 15 minutes until desired internal temperature is reached. Tent loosely with foil during standing time.*

THE FINISHED PRODUCT

Rare meat *is brown on the outside and reddish pink throughout with clear, red juice.*

Medium meat *is light pink on the inside with pinkish juice.*

Well done meat *is brown throughout with colorless or slightly yellow juice.*

BEEF ROAST COOKING CHART

Power Level: MEDIUM-HIGH (70%)   **Standing Time: 20 to 25 minutes**

Item	Temperature Probe Setting	Minutes Per Pound	Internal Temperature After Standing
Eye of Round	Rare 120°-125° Medium 140°-145° Well 150°-155°	8-10 min. 10-12 min. 12-14 min.	140° 160° 170°
Rolled Rib	Rare 120°-125° Medium 140°-145° Well 150°-155°	10-12 min. 12-14 min. 14-16 min.	140° 160° 170°
Standing Rib	Rare 120°-125° Medium 140°-145° Well 150°-155°	10-12 min. 12-14 min. 14-16 min.	140° 160° 170°
Tenderloin (Standing Time: 10 to 15 minutes)	Rare 120°-125° Medium 140°-145° Well 150°-155°	6-8 min. 8-10 min. 10-12 min.	140° 160° 170°
Power Level: MEDIUM (50%)			
Rolled Rump	Medium 140°-145°	12-14 min.	160°
Sirloin Tip	Medium 140°-145°	12-14 min.	160°

BEEF COOKING CONVENIENCE CHART

Power Level: HIGH (100%)

Item	Cooking Time	Special Instructions
Canned Beef Main Dish (Under 16 ounces)	4-6 min.	Remove from can and place in 1 quart casserole. Temperature probe 150° to 160°.
(Over 16 ounces)	8-10 min.	Remove from can and place in 1 quart casserole. Temperature probe 150° to 160°.
Dry Casserole Mix (Add hamburger)	14-18 min.	(Hamburger Helper) 1. Microwave crumbled ground beef on HIGH (100%) for 4 to 6 minutes in a 2 quart casserole. Stir halfway through cooking. Drain off excess grease. 2. Add other ingredients following package instructions. Microwave on HIGH (100%) for 10 to 12 minutes. Stir occasionally. 3. Allow to stand, covered, for 5 minutes.
Frozen Beef Main Dish (8 ounces)	4-6 min.	Remove from foil container and place in a 1 quart casserole.
(16 ounces)	10-12 min.	Remove from foil container and place in a 1 quart casserole.
(32 ounces)	18-20 min.	Remove from foil container and place in a baking dish.

ITALIAN LEG OF LAMB

Power Level: MEDIUM-HIGH [70%]
Total Cooking Time:
      Rare: 34 to 36 minutes
      Medium: 40 to 42 minutes
      Well: 52 to 54 minutes
Temperature Probe: ＊
      Rare: 120° to 125°
      Medium: 140° to 145°
      Well: 150° to 155°

6 pound leg of lamb
1 cup wine vinegar
½ cup cooking oil
1 medium onion, chopped
1 clove garlic, crushed
1 tablespoon parsley
1 teaspoon sugar
1 teaspoon basil
1 teaspoon salt
¼ teaspoon oregano
Dash of pepper

1. Score leg of lamb. Place lamb in roasting bag, then in a baking dish.

2. Mix together remaining ingredients. Pour over meat in roasting bag. Cut a strip of plastic from open end of roasting bag. Tie bag closed with strip.

3. Marinate meat in refrigerator 6 to 8 hours or overnight. Turn bag several times to coat meat with marinade.

4. Microwave, fat side down, on MEDIUM-HIGH (70%) until cooked to desired doneness. Turn over halfway through cooking and slash bag to allow steam to escape.

5. Allow to stand 20 to 25 minutes before serving.

Recipe yield: 8 to 10 servings

＊ When using probe or thermometer, push into center of meatiest part until tip touches bone then withdraw it ¼ inch.

ORANGE-GLAZED LAMB CHOPS

Power Level: MEDIUM [50%]
Total Cooking Time: 26 to 28 minutes

¾ cup orange marmalade
2 tablespoons dry sherry
2 tablespoons orange juice
½ teaspoon ginger
4 lamb loin chops, 1 inch thick

1. Mix together all ingredients except chops. Set aside.

2. Arrange lamb chops in an 8 inch round baking dish. Cover. Microwave on MEDIUM (50%) for 14 minutes. Turn chops over halfway through cooking time. Drain off excess grease.

3. Cover. Microwave on MEDIUM (50%) for 12 to 14 minutes or until meat is tender. Turn chops over and top with glaze halfway through cooking.

Recipe yield: 4 servings

Lamb & Veal

Try menu planning with lamb or veal for a pleasant change of taste.

When cooking veal or lamb in the microwave, you may cover either with waxed paper or plastic wrap. Using waxed paper will result in a dry, crisp meat surface while using plastic wrap will keep the surface more moist.

Tender and naturally juicy, lamb has a delicate flavor all its own. It is interesting to substitute lamb for pork in many recipes.

Veal is a drier meat with a delicate and distinct flavor. Because it comes from young beef, it may be necessary to pound veal to tenderize it a little before cooking.

CURRIED LAMB

Power Level: HIGH [100%] and
              MEDIUM [50%]
Total Cooking Time: 28 to 35 minutes

1½ pounds boneless lamb, cut into cubes
1 medium onion, sliced
½ cup chopped celery
2 tablespoons cooking oil
½ cup tomato juice
½ cup beef broth
1 teaspoon lemon juice
½ teaspoon curry powder
¼ teaspoon salt

1. Place lamb, onion, celery and cooking oil in a 1½ quart casserole. Microwave on HIGH (100%) for 8 to 10 minutes or until meat is pink in center. Drain off excess grease.

2. Mix together remaining ingredients. Pour over lamb and vegetables. Cover with a tight fitting lid or plastic wrap.

3. Microwave on MEDIUM (50%) for 20 to 25 minutes or until meat is tender. Stir halfway through cooking.

Recipe yield: 4 to 6 servings

SWEET 'N SPICY GLAZED LAMB CHOPS

Power Level: MEDIUM [50%]
Total Cooking Time: 22 to 24 minutes

½ cup water
3 tablespoons brown sugar
2 tablespoons cider vinegar
1 tablespoon cornstarch
1 tablespoon soy sauce
¼ teaspoon salt
¼ teaspoon parsley
¼ teaspoon dill weed
2 lamb chops (1 inch thick)

1. Mix together all ingredients except chops. Set aside.

2. Arrange lamb chops in a 10x6x1¾ inch baking dish. Cover. Microwave on MEDIUM (50%) for 12 minutes. Turn chops over halfway through cooking. Drain off excess grease.

3. Pour sauce over chops. Cover. Microwave on MEDIUM (50%) for 10 to 12 minutes or until meat is tender. Turn chops over halfway through cooking.

Recipe yield: 2 servings

ROAST VEAL WITH CELERY SAUCE

Power Level: MEDIUM-HIGH [70%]
Total Cooking Time: 46 to 48 minutes
Temperature Probe: 150° to 155°

4 pounds boneless veal shoulder
Dash of garlic salt
Dash of pepper
1 can (10¾ ounces) cream of celery soup
1 medium onion, chopped
2 carrots, sliced
1 bay leaf
¼ teaspoon marjoram

1. Season veal with garlic salt and pepper. Place in a roasting bag.

2. Combine remaining ingredients. Pour around veal.

3. Cut a strip of plastic from open end of bag. Tie bag closed with strip. Place, fat side down, in a baking dish.

4. Microwave on MEDIUM-HIGH (70%) for 46 to 48 minutes or until tender. Turn over halfway through cooking. Slit bag.

5. Allow meat to stand 20 to 25 minutes before serving.

Recipe yield: 8 to 10 servings

VEAL PARMIGIANA

Power Level: HIGH [100%] and MEDIUM [50%]
Total Cooking Time: 20¾ to 25 minutes

4 veal cutlets (½ inch thick)
¼ cup butter (or margarine)
¼ cup bread crumbs
¼ cup grated Parmesan cheese
¼ teaspoon salt
Dash of paprika
1 medium onion, chopped
1 cup (4 ounces) grated Mozzarella cheese
1 can (8 ounces) tomato sauce
½ teaspoon Italian seasoning
Dash of pepper
Parmesan cheese

1. Pound cutlets until ¼ inch thick.

2. Place butter in a 10x6x1¾ inch baking dish. Microwave on HIGH (100%) for 45 seconds to 1 minute or until melted.

3. Mix together bread crumbs, Parmesan cheese, salt and paprika. Dip veal cutlets in butter then coat with crumb mixture.

4. Place in baking dish. Add onion. Microwave on MEDIUM (50%) for 16 to 18 minutes or until meat is pink in center and onion is tender. Drain off excess grease.

5. Sprinkle Mozzarella cheese over cutlets. Spoon tomato sauce over top. Season with Italian seasoning and pepper. Cover.

6. Microwave on MEDIUM (50%) for 4 to 6 minutes or until heated through.

7. Sprinkle Parmesan cheese over top. Allow to stand, covered, 5 minutes before serving.

Recipe yield: 4 servings

VEAL ROLL-UPS

Power Level: HIGH [100%] and MEDIUM [50%]
Total Cooking Time: 28½ to 32¾ minutes

4 boneless veal cutlets (½ inch thick)
1 can (4½ ounces) deviled ham
½ teaspoon dry mustard (or horseradish)
4 slices Swiss cheese
8 to 12 canned asparagus spears
2 tablespoons butter (or margarine)
1 cup dry white wine
2 tablespoons all purpose flour
¼ cup half and half

1. Pound cutlets until ¼ inch thick. Mix together ham and mustard. Spread evenly over cutlets.

2. Top each cutlet with Swiss cheese slices and 2 or 3 asparagus spears. Roll up firmly. Secure with wooden picks or string.

3. Place butter in a baking dish. Microwave on HIGH (100%) for 30 to 45 seconds or until melted.

4. Arrange veal roll-ups in baking dish. Turn to coat with butter. Cover.

5. Microwave on MEDIUM (50%) for 22 to 24 minutes or until meat is tender. Add wine and turn over halfway through cooking.

6. Remove veal roll-ups to serving dish. Cover with aluminum foil to keep warm. Stir flour into liquid in baking dish. Add cream. Microwave on HIGH (100%) for 6 to 8 minutes or until thickened. Stir occasionally. Serve over roll-ups.

Recipe yield: 4 servings

VEAL GOULASH

Power Level: HIGH [100%] and MEDIUM [50%]
Total Cooking Time: 37 to 43 minutes

1½ pounds boneless veal, cut into 1 inch cubes
1 medium onion, chopped
1 can (4 ounces) sliced mushrooms, drained (reserve liquid)
2 tablespoons butter (or margarine)
1 clove garlic, crushed
2 tablespoons all purpose flour
2 teaspoons paprika
½ teaspoon salt
½ cup water and mushroom liquid
½ cup dry white wine
1 teaspoon Worcestershire sauce
½ cup sour cream

1. Place veal, onion, mushrooms, butter and garlic in a 2 quart casserole. Microwave on HIGH (100%) for 8 to 10 minutes or until veal is pink in center. Stir halfway through cooking.

2. Stir in flour, paprika and salt. Add water mixture, wine and Worcestershire sauce. Cover with tight fitting lid or plastic wrap.

3. Microwave on MEDIUM (50%) for 24 to 26 minutes. Stir several times during cooking. Uncover. Microwave on MEDIUM (50%) for 4 to 5 minutes or until meat is tender.

4. Stir in sour cream. Microwave, uncovered, on MEDIUM (50%) for 1 to 2 minutes or until heated through.

5. Serve over noodles.

Recipe yield: 4 to 6 servings

STUFFED VEAL

Power Level: HIGH [100%] and MEDIUM-HIGH [70%]
Total Cooking Time: 33 to 39 minutes

2 pounds boneless veal breast
1 tablespoon cooking oil
4 ounces chopped chicken livers
¼ cup chopped onion
½ teaspoon salt
Dash of pepper
½ package (6 ounces) frozen spinach souffle, thawed
4 slices bacon

1. Pound veal until ¼ inch thick.

2. Microwave browning dish on HIGH (100%) for 4 minutes. Add oil, livers and onion. Microwave on HIGH (100%) for 3 to 4 minutes or until tender. Stir halfway through cooking.

3. Sprinkle salt and pepper on veal. Spread spinach souffle over half of the veal. Spoon chicken livers and onion over spinach. Fold other half of veal over stuffing. Tie together with string. Place on a rack in a baking dish. Top with bacon slices. Cover.

4. Microwave on MEDIUM-HIGH (70%) for 30 to 35 minutes or until tender. Turn roast over halfway through cooking time.

Recipe yield: 4 to 6 servings

LAMB CHOPS COOKING CHART

Power Level: MEDIUM (50%)

Item	Cooking Time
2 Chops	10-12 min.
4 Chops	18-20 min.
6 Chops	24-26 min.

LAMB & VEAL ROASTS COOKING CHART

Power Level: MEDIUM-HIGH (70%)

Item and Temperature Probe	Min. Per Lb.	Internal Temperature after Standing
Lamb Roasts		
Rare: 120-125°	8-9	140°
Med.: 140-145°	9-10	160°
Well: 150-155°	10-12	170°
Veal Roasts		
Well: 150-155°	12-15	170°

Worchestershire Sauce

Cornflake Crumbs

Barbecue Sauce

Pork & Ham

Microwave Pork Chop

Teriyaki Sauce

Today's hogs are bred leaner so pork and ham will benefit by cooking with a moist heat method.

To retain moisture, cover these meats with plastic wrap or use a cooking bag.

It is important to cook pork and fresh ham to a finished temperature of at least 170° throughout.

Meat should be tender and no longer pink or have pink juices in any area of meat.

PORK CHOPS

OVEN-BRAISED PORK CHOPS

Power Level: HIGH [100%] and MEDIUM [50%]
Total Cooking Time: 19 to 26 minutes

4 pork chops (½ inch thick)
½ teaspoon salt
Dash of pepper
¼ cup water

1. Microwave browning dish on HIGH (100%) for 5 to 6 minutes.

2. Add pork chops. Season with salt and pepper.

3. Microwave on HIGH (100%) for 4 to 6 minutes or until meat is golden. Turn over halfway through cooking.

4. Add water. Cover with a tight fitting lid. Microwave on MEDIUM (50%) for

15 to 20 minutes or until tender. Allow to stand for 5 minutes before serving.

Variations:

GERMAN CHOPS AND KRAUT

Follow Oven-Braised Pork Chops recipe as directed except add 2 cups drained sauerkraut, 1 medium onion (chopped), 2 medium apples (chopped), ¼ cup raisins and 2 tablespoons brown sugar with water.

BARBECUED CHOPS

Follow Oven-Braised Pork Chops recipe as directed except add ½ cup barbecue sauce with water.

GARDEN-FRESH CHOPS

Follow Oven-Braised Pork Chops recipe as directed. Substitute tomato juice for water. Halfway through cooking top each chop with a slice of onion and green pepper. Sprinkle with thyme.

MUSHROOM CHOPS

Follow Oven-Braised Pork Chops recipe as directed except halfway through cooking, add 1 can (4 ounces) sliced mushrooms (drained), 1 tablespoon Worcestershire sauce and ½ teaspoon fine herb seasoning (optional).

Recipe yield: 4 to 6 servings

PORK CHOPS COOKING CHART

Power Level: MEDIUM (50%)

1. Arrange chops, small end toward center, in baking dish. Add topping or browning agent. Cover.
2. Microwave on MEDIUM (50%) until no longer pink in center.* Turn over halfway through cooking.
3. Allow to stand, covered, for 5 to 10 minutes.

Item	Cooking Time
Pork Chops (¾" thick)	
2	10-12 min.
3	12-14 min.
4	16-18 min.
6	22-24 min.

*If microwave has a browning element, brown as desired.

PORK CHOPS IN BROWNING DISH OR GRIDDLE

Power Level: HIGH (100%)

1. Microwave browning dish for 5-6 minutes or browning griddle for 8 minutes on HIGH (100%).
2. Add chops. Microwave on HIGH (100%) until no longer pink in center. Turn over halfway through cooking.

Item	Cooking Time
Pork Chops in browning dish or griddle	
2	5-6 min.
4	10-12 min.

Slit pork chops to make a pocket, leaving a 1 inch border at the edge. Fill pork chops with stuffing mixture.

Prepare coating mixture. Dip each pork chop in milk to moisten it. Then dredge chop in the coating mix.

Arrange chops in baking dish with thickest parts toward the outside. Cover with waxed paper or plastic wrap. Microwave on Medium [50%] for about 25 minutes. Turn chops over midway through cooking.

Test for doneness. Chops should be tender and no longer pink. Allow to stand covered for 10 to 15 minutes after cooking.

STUFFED PORK CHOPS

Power Level: HIGH [100%] and MEDIUM [50%]
Total Cooking Time: 30¾ to 36 minutes

½ cup water
¼ cup butter (or margarine)
1½ cups seasoned bread stuffing
½ cup chopped celery
¼ cup chopped onion
½ teaspoon salt
½ teaspoon basil
4 pork chops (about 1 inch thick)
¼ cup evaporated milk
½ cup bread crumbs
1 envelope (1½ ounces) dry onion soup mix

1. Combine water and butter in a 1 quart casserole. Microwave on HIGH (100%) for 45 seconds to 1 minute or until butter is melted. Stir in stuffing, celery, onion, salt and basil.

2. Slit pork chops in half horizontally, leaving a 1 inch border at inside edge. Fill chops with stuffing.

3. Mix together bread crumbs and soup mix. Dip chops in milk. Coat with bread crumb mixture. Place in a baking dish. Cover.

4. Microwave on MEDIUM (50%) for 30 to 35 minutes or until tender. Turn over halfway through cooking. Allow to stand 10 to 15 minutes before serving.

Recipe yield: 2 to 4 servings

PORK PAPRIKA

Power Level: HIGH [100%] and MEDIUM [50%]
Total Cooking Time: 33 to 41 minutes

1½ pounds boneless pork, cut in 1 inch pieces
1 medium onion, sliced
1 cup sliced fresh mushrooms
1 tablespoon cooking oil
½ cup water
1 teaspoon salt
½ teaspoon paprika
¼ teaspoon instant minced garlic
½ cup sour cream

1. Combine pork, onion, mushrooms and oil in a 2 quart casserole. Cover with a tight fitting lid or plastic wrap. Microwave on HIGH (100%) for 6 to 8 minutes. Drain off excess grease.

2. Add water, salt, paprika and garlic. Cover. Microwave on MEDIUM (50%) for 25 to 30 minutes.

3. Stir in sour cream. Microwave on MEDIUM (50%) for 2 to 3 minutes or until heated through. Stir halfway through cooking.

4. Serve over cooked noodles.

Recipe yield: 4 to 6 servings

BARBECUE SPARERIBS

Arrange spareribs *meaty side down in baking dish. Add water and cover with plastic wrap.*

Microwave on Medium (50%) *for 45 to 60 minutes or until tender. Turn ribs over midway through cooking and top with onions. Keep covered during remainder of cooking time.*

Spread barbecue sauce *over ribs when they are tender. Cover with plastic wrap and microwave on Medium [50%] for 10 to 15 minutes to heat sauce through.*

BARBECUED SPARERIBS

Power Level: MEDIUM [50%]
Total Cooking Time: 65 to 75 minutes

3 pounds pork spareribs
2 cups water
1 large onion, sliced thin
1 cup Zesty Barbecue Sauce
(page 108)

1. Place ribs, meaty side down, in a baking dish. Add water. Cover with plastic wrap. Microwave on MEDIUM (50%) for 55 to 60 minutes or until tender. Turn ribs over halfway through cooking and top with onions.

2. Drain. Pour sauce over ribs. Cover. Microwave on MEDIUM (50%) for 10 to 15 minutes or until heated through.

CHEWY SPARERIBS

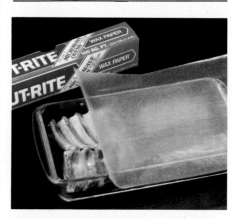

For chewy spareribs, *arrange in dish with meaty side down. Do not add water. Cover with waxed paper. Microwave on High [100%] for 35 to 40 minutes.*

Halfway through cooking, *turn ribs over. Remove grease. Cover with onions and barbecue sauce.*

┌─ **Rib Tip** ─────────
For individual servings, cut into 2 or 3-rib pieces and microwave in a 2 quart covered casserole.
└───────────────────

Variations:
CHEWY SPARERIBS

Follow Barbecued Spareribs recipe as directed except eliminate water; cover with waxed paper and microwave on HIGH (100%) for 30 to 45 minutes or until no longer pink. Drain off excess grease halfway through cooking, turn over, top with onion and barbecue sauce. Cover.

QUICK BARBECUED RIBS

Follow Barbecue Spareribs recipe as directed except substitute 1 bottle (12 ounces) barbecue sauce for Zesty Barbecue Sauce.

Recipe yield: 4 to 6 servings

SWEET AND SOUR SPARERIBS

Power Level: HIGH [100%] and
MEDIUM [50%]
Total Cooking Time: 1 hour 34 minutes
to 1 hour 51 minutes

1 can (20 ounces) pineapple
chunks, drained (reserve syrup)
3 tablespoons cornstarch
¼ cup white vinegar
¼ cup brown sugar
1 tablespoon soy sauce
1 tablespoon Worcestershire sauce
1 teaspoon ginger
1 teaspoon salt
¼ teaspoon pepper
3 pounds pork spareribs, cut into
2 to 3 rib pieces
1 medium onion, sliced
1 green pepper, cut in strips
1 cup water

1. Combine pineapple syrup and cornstarch in 1 quart casserole. Microwave on HIGH (100%) for 4 to 6 minutes or until thickened. Stir occasionally during cooking.

2. Stir in vinegar, brown sugar, soy sauce, Worcestershire sauce, ginger, salt and pepper. Set aside.

3. Place spareribs in a baking dish. Top with pineapple chunks, onion, green pepper and water. Cover with plastic wrap.

4. Microwave on MEDIUM (50%) for 1 hour 30 minutes to 1 hour 45 minutes or until tender. Drain halfway through cooking, rearrange ribs, and pour pineapple syrup mixture over ribs.

Recipe yield: 3 to 4 servings

PORK ROASTS

Insert temperature probe or thermometer *into the center of the meatiest portion of a pork rib end, boneless loin, center cut roast, loin end roast or ham. Push probe or thermometer in until it touches the center bone in a ham. Then withdraw it ¼ inch. The probe should not touch bone nor fat during cooking.*

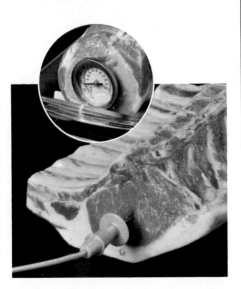

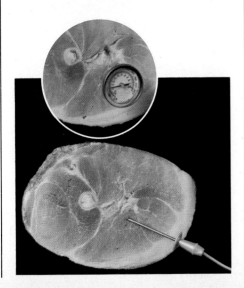

Place rolled loin *fat side down on trivet in baking dish. Add ½ cup of water or other liquid. Cover with plastic wrap. Microwave on Medium [50%].*

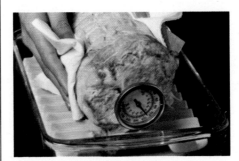

Turn roast over *halfway through cooking. Grasp meat using a double thickness of paper towel. This way you do not have to pierce the meat while turning which would allow juices to escape.*

Remove from microwave *and tent with foil. Let stand about 10 minutes until meat is no longer pink and has reached a finished temperature of 170° in every area of the roast.*

PORK ROAST COOKING CHART

	Power Level: MEDIUM (50%) Temperature probe setting: 170° F Approximate	
Item	**Minutes Per Pound**	
All Roasts	16-20	
In cooking bag	14-18	

In a Cooking Bag

Place pork roast (*fat side down*) *and ½ cup water in cooking bag. Place in baking dish. Secure bag with plastic strip cut from open end of bag or with string. Microwave on Medium [50%]. Turn over halfway through cooking and make a small slit near opening of bag. Remove from microwave and allow to stand until temperature reaches 170° in every area and juice is no longer pink.*

APPLE-STUFFED PORK TENDERLOIN

Power Level: MEDIUM [50%]
Total Cooking Time: 55 to 60 minutes
Temperature Probe: 170° F

2 pound pork tenderloin
1 cup bread crumbs
1 egg, slightly beaten
¼ cup chopped cooking apples
¼ cup chopped nuts (pecans or walnuts)
2 tablespoons chopped onion
1 tablespoon butter (or margarine)
1 teaspoon lemon juice
1 teaspoon Worcestershire sauce
½ teaspoon salt
¼ teaspoon sage
Dash of pepper

1. Cut tenderloin in half lengthwise almost through.

2. Combine remaining ingredients. Toss lightly.

3. Spread stuffing over half the tenderloin. Cover with other half of tenderloin. Tie securely with string shaping in a roll.

4. Place on trivet in a baking dish—add ½ cup water—cover with plastic wrap.

5. Microwave on MEDIUM (50%) for 55 to 60 minutes or until no longer pink. Turn over halfway through cooking.

6. Allow to stand for 10 minutes before serving.

Recipe yield: 6 to 8 servings

PORK LOIN ROAST AND SHERRY SAUCE

Power Level: MEDIUM [50%]
and HIGH [100%]
Total Cooking Time: 70 to 78 minutes
Temperature Probe: 170°

4 pound pork loin roast
2 bay leaves, crushed
1/8 teaspoon thyme
¼ cup all purpose flour
½ teaspoon sugar
1 teaspoon salt
¼ teaspoon pepper
1½ cups water
½ cup sweet sherry

1. Place meat, fat side down, on a trivet in a baking dish. Cover.

2. Microwave on MEDIUM (50%) for 50 minutes.

3. Turn roast fat side up. Cut 4 slits 2 inches deep across the top of roast. Combine crushed bay leaves and thyme. Spoon into slits. Cover.

4. Microwave on MEDIUM (70%) for 20 to 28 minutes until meat and juices are no longer pink.

5. Allow roast to stand for 10 minutes before serving.

6. Meanwhile stir flour, sugar, salt and pepper in meat drippings. Slowly add water and sherry. Microwave on HIGH (100%) for 4 to 6 minutes or until thickened. Serve with pork roast.

Recipe yield: 8 to 10 servings

GINGERED PORK LEG ROAST

Power Level: MEDIUM [50%]
Total Cooking Time: 80 to 90 minutes
Temperature Probe: 170°

5 pound pork leg roast
1 jar (12 ounces) cherry preserves
1 teaspoon ginger
Pineapple slices

1. Place roast, fat side down, on a trivet in a baking dish. Cover.

2. Microwave on MEDIUM (50%) for 55 to 60 minutes.

3. Turn roast fat side up. Mix together preserves and ginger. Brush over roast. Garnish with pineapple. Cover.

4. Microwave on MEDIUM (50%) for 25 to 30 minutes or until meat and juices are no longer pink.

5. Allow to stand 20 to 25 minutes before serving.

IN ROASTING BAG:

1. Brush preserve/ginger mixture over meat and garnish with pineapple. Secure with toothpicks.

2. Place meat in roasting bag, fat side down, then in a baking dish. Cut a strip of plastic from open end of bag. Tie bag closed.

3. Microwave on MEDIUM [50%] for 70 to 90 minutes or until no longer pink. Turn fat side up halfway through cooking and pierce bag.

Recipe yield: 6 to 8 servings

PORK CROWN ROAST

Place pork crown roast *with bone ends down on trivet in baking dish. Season meat. Insert temperature probe or meat thermometer between two ribs so tip is in the meatiest area inside crown, not touching fat or bone. Cover with waxed paper or plastic wrap.*

Microwave on Medium [50%]. *Halfway through cooking turn crown over so bone ends are up. Protect ends with foil. If desired, stuff crown at this time. Cover and microwave until temperature reaches 170° or meat is no longer pink. Remove from microwave and cover loosely with aluminum foil. Allow to stand 10 minutes. All meat and juice should not be pink.*

PORK CROWN ROAST

Power Level: MEDIUM [50%]
Total Cooking Time: 16 to 20 minutes
per pound
Temperature probe: 170°

Pork crown roast
1 teaspoon seasoned salt
¼ teaspoon seasoned pepper

1. Place crown roast, bone ends down, on a baking dish. Season with salt and pepper. Cover.

2. Microwave on MEDIUM (50%). Halfway through cooking, turn roast bone ends up. Protect bone ends with aluminum foil. If desired, fill center with favorite pork stuffing.

3. Cover. Microwave on MEDIUM (50%) until no longer pink.

4. Allow to stand covered with foil for 10 minutes before serving.

SMOKED HAM ROAST

Score ham roast. *Place ham fat side down in baking dish. Add ½ cup water. Shield any small ends with foil. Insert probe or thermometer in until it touches the center bone then withdraw it ¼ inch. Cover with plastic wrap. Microwave on Medium-High [70%].*

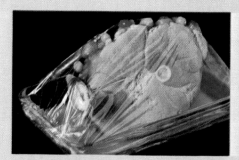

Halfway through cooking, *turn ham fat side up. Remove foil. Decorate or glaze according to personal preference. Cover and microwave until temperature is 15° to 20° below the proper "done" internal temperature.*

Remove from microwave. *Loosely tent with foil and allow to stand until ham reaches 140°, the proper finished temperature.*

In a Cooking Bag

Place ham roast *fat side down in cooking bag in baking dish. Add ½ cup water. Secure bag with plastic strip cut from bag's open end or with a string. Microwave on Medium-High [70%]. Halfway through cooking, turn ham fat side up. Shield as necessary. Cut a small slash in bag near open end. Continue cooking until meat is 15° to 20° below the finished temperature. Remove from microwave and allow to stand until ham reaches "done" temperature, 140°.*

TEMPTING GLAZED HAM

Power Level: MEDIUM-HIGH [70%]
Total Cooking Time: 28 to 30 minutes
Temperature Probe: 120° to 125°

3 pound precooked ham
2 tablespoons prepared mustard
2 tablespoons brown sugar
½ cup ginger ale

1. Score ham and place in a 10x6x1¾ inch baking dish. Brush on mustard and sprinkle with brown sugar. Pour ginger ale on top. Protect small end with aluminum foil. Cover.

2. Microwave, fat side down, on MEDIUM-HIGH (70%) for 28 to 30 minutes or until heated through. Turn over and remove foil halfway through cooking.

3. Allow to stand 20 to 25 minutes before serving.

Variations:

FRUIT GLAZED HAM

Follow Tempting Glazed Ham recipe as directed except substitute a mixture of 1 can (16 ounces) fruit cocktail (drained), ½ cup orange juice and ½ teaspoon ginger for mustard, brown sugar and ginger ale.

QUICK FRUIT GLAZED HAM

Follow Tempting Glazed Ham recipe as directed except substitute a mixture of 1 can (21 ounces) peach or apple pie filling and ¼ cup raisins for mustard, brown sugar and ginger ale.

Recipe yield: 6 to 8 servings

CRANBERRY-CURRANT HAM

Power Level: MEDIUM-HIGH [70%]
Total Cooking Time: 18 to 22 minutes
Temperature Probe: 120° to 125°

2 pound canned ham
1 can (16 ounces) whole cranberry sauce
½ cup currant jelly
2 tablespoons currants (optional)
1 teaspoon allspice

1. Place ham in a 10x6x1¾ inch baking dish.

2. Mix together cranberry sauce, currant jelly, currants and allspice. Pour over ham.

3. Protect small end of ham with aluminum foil. Cover.

4. Microwave on MEDIUM-HIGH (70%) for 18 to 22 minutes or until heated through. Remove foil and turn over halfway through cooking.

5. Allow to stand 10 to 15 minutes before serving.

Recipe yield: 6 to 8 servings

HAM LOAF

Power Level: MEDIUM-HIGH [70%]
Total Cooking Time: 22 to 24 minutes

1 pound ground cooked ham
½ pound ground pork
1 cup bread crumbs
2 eggs
¼ cup brown sugar
¼ cup chopped onion
¼ cup chopped green pepper
¼ cup milk
¼ teaspoon ground cloves

1. Mix together all ingredients. Shape in a 10x6x1¾ inch baking dish. Cover.

2. Microwave on MEDIUM-HIGH (70%) for 22 to 24 minutes or until set. Allow to stand 5 minutes before serving.

3. Serve with Raisin Sauce (page 109).

Variation:

INDIVIDUAL HAM LOAVES

Shape meat mixture into 6 small loaves. Arrange in a baking dish. Cover. Microwave on MEDIUM-HIGH (70%) for 10 to 12 minutes or until set.

Recipe yield: 4 to 6 servings

This glorious Pork Crown Roast is perfect for a festive occasion.

FULLY COOKED HAM COOKING CHART

Power Level:
MEDIUM-HIGH (70%)
Temperature probe setting:
120° to 125°
Internal temperature
after standing: 140°

Item	Minutes Per Pound
All fully cooked ham roast	10-12
In cooking bag	8-10
Ham slice	6-8

HAM SLICES

Slash fat *on edge of ham slice to prevent curling during cooking. Do not cut into meat so as not to release juices.*

Place ham slice *in baking dish and add ½ cup water to keep ham moist. Cover with plastic wrap or waxed paper. Microwave on High [100%] for 8 to 10 minutes.*

HAWAIIAN HAM SLICE
Power Level: HIGH [100%]
Total Cooking Time: 12 to 16 minutes

1 ham slice, 1 inch thick
½ cup crushed pineapple, drained (reserve liquid)
¼ cup chopped maraschino cherries
1 tablespoon brown sugar
1 teaspoon prepared mustard
1 teaspoon cornstarch
¼ cup water
Dash of allspice

1. Place ham slice and pineapple liquid in a 10x6x1¾ inch baking dish. Cover. Microwave on HIGH (100%) for 6 minutes. Drain and reserve drippings.

2. Mix together pineapple, cherries, brown sugar and mustard. Spoon over ham slice.

3. Microwave on HIGH (100%) for 2 to 4 minutes or until meat is tender.

4. Mix together cornstarch, reserved drippings, ¼ cup water and allspice until smooth in a 2 cup measure. Microwave on HIGH (100%) for 4 to 6 minutes or until thickened. Stir occasionally. Pour over ham slice.

Recipe yield: 4 to 6 servings

HAM AND FRUIT KABOBS
Power Level: HIGH [100%]
Total Cooking Time: 4 to 6 minutes

1 cup apricot preserves
½ cup orange juice
1 tablespoon lemon juice
½ teaspoon ginger
1 pound cooked ham, cut into 1 inch cubes
2 bananas, cut into 1 inch slices
1 cup mandarin orange sections
1 cup pineapple chunks

1. Mix together preserves, orange juice, lemon juice and ginger. Set aside.

2. Alternate ham, banana, orange sections and pineapple on 8 wooden skewers. Place horizontally in a baking dish. Brush with sauce.

3. Microwave on HIGH (100%) for 4 to 6 minutes or until ham is heated through. Turn and baste twice during cooking.

Recipe yield: 4 to 6 servings

CREAMY HAM AND POTATO BAKE
Power Level: MEDIUM [50%]
Total Cooking Time: 8 to 10 minutes

2 cups diced cooked potatoes
2 cups cubed cooked ham
1 cup grated Cheddar cheese
½ cup half and half
2 tablespoons chopped pimento
1 teaspoon dry mustard
Dash of cayenne pepper (or hot pepper sauce)

1. Combine all ingredients in a 1½ quart casserole. Cover with waxed paper.

2. Microwave on MEDIUM (50%) for 8 to 10 minutes or until cheese just begins to melt. Stir occasionally.

3. Allow to stand 5 minutes before serving.

Recipe yield: 4 to 6 servings

SMOKED PORK CHOPS

OLD WORLD SAUERKRAUT
Power Level: MEDIUM-HIGH [70%]
Total Cooking Time: 16 to 18 minutes

3 cups sauerkraut, slightly drained
1 can (15¼ ounces) pineapple chunks, undrained
2 small apples, cored and sliced thin
⅓ cup brown sugar
¼ cup raisins
¼ teaspoon salt
Dash of pepper
4 small smoked pork chops
4 pieces knockwurst

1. Mix together sauerkraut, pineapple, apples, brown sugar, raisins, salt and pepper in a 3 quart casserole.

2. Place alternate layers of pork chops, knockwurst and sauerkraut mixture in a 3 quart casserole. Cover.

3. Microwave on MEDIUM-HIGH (70%) for 16 to 18 minutes or until heated through.

Recipe yield: 4 to 6 servings

SMOKED PORK CHOP COOKING CHART

Power Level: HIGH (100%)

1. Arrange chops, small end towards center, in baking dish. Cover.

2. Microwave on HIGH (100%) until heated through. Turn over halfway through cooking.

Item	Cooking Time
Smoked Pork Chops (½" thick)	
2	4-6 min.
4	6-8 min.
6	8-10 min.

BACON

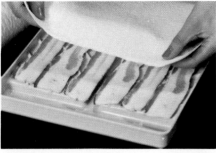

Arrange 6 to 8 bacon strips on rack.
Strips may overlay slightly. Cover with paper towel to avoid spattering. Microwave on High [100%] for 4½ to 5½ minutes or until crisp. You may save the drippings to use in a recipe.

To quickly cook 3 or 4 bacon strips, *place two strips on a double layer of paper towel. Put down another double layer of towel. Place two more bacon strips in the opposite direction as the first strips. Cover with a single layer of paper towel. You may prefer to layer towels and bacon on a paper plate. Microwave on High [100%] for 3 to 4 minutes or until crisp.*

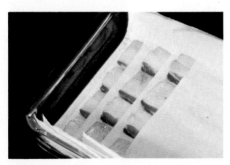

For more than 4 bacon strips, *line a baking dish with a double layer of paper towel. Add a layer of bacon then another layer of towel, then bacon, etc., up to ½ pound of bacon. Microwave on High [100%] for 10 to 12 minutes. Allow to stand 5 minutes. Remember, fat attracts microwave energy so bacon drippings may become very hot.*

CANADIAN BACON

Arrange Canadian bacon slices *in a pie dish. Cover with plastic wrap. Microwave on High [100%] until heated through. Allow 30 seconds per slice. For a whole piece of Canadian bacon, place in baking dish. Glaze or add ¼ cup water. Cover with plastic wrap. Microwave on High [100%] until heated through. Allow 10 to 12 minutes per pound. Turn over halfway through cooking. Add glaze and cover.*

WIENERS & SAUSAGE

Make diagonal slashes *or prick wieners and sausage to keep them from popping.*

Place wieners *on dinner or paper plate. Cover with waxed paper. Microwave on High [100%]. Rearrange halfway through cooking.*

If cooking 6 to 10 wieners, *arrange them in a baking dish. Add ½ cup water. Cover with waxed paper or plastic wrap. Microwave on High [100%].*

WIENERS & SAUSAGE COOKING CHART

Power Level: HIGH (100%)

Item	Cooking Time
WIENERS	
1	30-45 sec.
2	45 sec.-1 min.
4	1½-2 min.
6 to 8	3-4 min.
10 (1 pound)	4-5 min.
BULK PORK SAUSAGE	
4 patties	4-5 min.
8 patties	6-8 min.
SAUSAGE LINKS OR PREFORMED PATTIES (RAW)	
4	2½-3½ min.
6 to 8	3½-4½ min.
BROWN 'N SERVE SAUSAGE LINKS OR PREFORMED PATTIES	
4	1-2 min.
6 to 8	2-3 min.

— Browning Tip —

For extra color, use a browning dish, browning element or browning agent when cooking sausage. For less greasy sausage, place on a trivet when cooking. Cover to retain moisture.

— Casserole Tip —

If sausage is to be used in a casserole, it should be precooked and drained. Some sausage is already fully cooked and only needs to be heated.

— Bacon Tip —

To separate cold bacon, place package of refrigerated bacon in microwave. Microwave on High (100%) for 30 to 45 seconds.

Rice, Pasta & Cereal

Rice and pasta can be the perfect complement to a meal or each can be a meal in itself.

With the microwave, these foods can conveniently be cooked and served in the same dish.

Microwave cooking rice and pasta takes about the same initial amount of time as the conventional method. But you will especially be pleased to find your leftovers restored to their original tenderness and freshness in a matter of seconds.

Adding a little butter or margarine to rice or a little oil to pasta adds flavor and prevents sticking during cooking. Rice and pasta will expand 2 to 3 times its original size when cooked so select a large utensil to allow room for expansion.

Add butter or margarine *to water. Cover with a tight fitting lid or plastic wrap. Microwave on High [100%] until water begins to boil.*

Add instant or quick cooking rice *to boiling water. Cover and allow to stand 5 minutes or until tender. No stirring or additional cooking is necessary.*

Add long-grain or wild rice *to boiling water. Cover and microwave on Medium [50%] until almost tender. Stir once during cooking. Allow rice to stand covered for 5 minutes. Rice will continue to soften.*

SPINACH RICE CASSEROLE

Power Level: HIGH [100%]
Total Cooking Time: 20 to 23 minutes

1 package (10 ounces) frozen
   chopped spinach
3 cups cooked rice
1 cup chicken broth
1 egg, beaten
½ cup chopped onion
¼ cup finely chopped celery
¼ cup butter (or margarine)
3 tablespoons parsley
½ teaspoon salt
Dash of pepper
Dash of garlic powder
1 tablespoon lemon juice

1. Place spinach in an 11¾ x 7½ x 1¾ inch baking dish. Cover with plastic wrap. Microwave on HIGH (100%) for 4 to 5 minutes or until defrosted. Drain. Stir in remaining ingredients except lemon juice.

2. Cover and refrigerate for 4 hours.

3. Microwave, covered, on HIGH (100%) for 16 to 18 minutes or until heated throughout.

4. Allow to stand 5 minutes. Sprinkle with lemon juice before serving.

Recipe yield: 8 servings

ORIENTAL RICE

Power Level: HIGH [100%] and
MEDIUM [50%]
Total Cooking Time: 49 to 56 minutes

1 package (6 ounces) long grain
   and wild rice
¼ cup butter (or margarine)
½ cup water chestnuts, sliced
½ cup sliced mushrooms
1 small onion, sliced
1 tablespoon soy sauce
3 cups chicken broth

1. Place rice, season packet, butter, water chestnuts, mushrooms, onion and soy sauce in a 3 quart casserole. Microwave on HIGH (100%) for 3 to 4 minutes or until onion is tender. Stir halfway through cooking time.

2. Pour in chicken broth. Cover with a tight fitting lid or plastic wrap.

3. Microwave on HIGH (100%) for 6 to 7 minutes or until boiling. Stir, then microwave on MEDIUM (50%) for 40 to 45 minutes or until rice is tender and liquid is absorbed.

Recipe yield: 6 to 8 servings

SPANISH RICE

Power Level: HIGH [100%] and
MEDIUM [50%]
Total Cooking Time: 32 to
41½ minutes

6 slices bacon
1 cup uncooked long grain
   white rice
1 medium onion, chopped
1 can (16 ounces) tomatoes,
   undrained
1 cup tomato juice
¼ cup chopped green pepper
¼ cup parsley
1 teaspoon salt
Dash of pepper

1. Place bacon in a 2 quart casserole. Cover with a paper towel. Microwave on HIGH (100%) for 4 to 4½ minutes or until crispy. Remove bacon, crumble and set aside.

2. Add rice and onion to bacon drippings. Microwave on HIGH (100%) for 3 to 4 minutes or until lightly browned.

3. Stir in remaining ingredients and bacon. Cover with a tight fitting lid or plastic wrap. Microwave on HIGH (100%) for 5 to 8 minutes or until boiling. Stir. Cover, then microwave on MEDIUM (50%) for 20 to 25 minutes or until rice is tender and liquid is absorbed.

Recipe yield: 4 to 5 servings

RICE CHART

Item	Raw Amount	Cooked Amount	Covered Casserole	Water	Power Level	Cooking Time
Instant or Quick-cooking Rice	1 cup	2 cups	1 quart	1 cup	Water HIGH (100%)	2½-3 minutes
Long Grain White Rice	1 cup	3 cups	2 quart	2 cups	Water HIGH (100%) then Rice MEDIUM (50%)	6-8 minutes 14-16 minutes
Brown Rice	1 cup	4 cups	1½ quart	3 cups	Water HIGH (100%) then Rice MEDIUM (50%)	8-10 minutes 24-26 minutes
Wild Rice	1 cup	3½ cups	1½ quart	3 cups	Water HIGH (100%) then Rice MEDIUM (50%)	8-10 minutes 34-36 minutes
White & Wild Rice Mix	6 ounce package	3½ cups	1½ quart	2½ cups	Water HIGH (100%) then Rice MEDIUM (50%)	6-8 minutes 20-22 minutes

Press rice into a buttered microwave baking ring. Cover with plastic wrap.

Place a serving plate across the top of the ring and flip ring so that the molded rice is released onto the plate.

Allow to stand 3 minutes after heated through in the microwave. Loosen rice around edge of ring with knife.

If you don't have a baking ring, use a custard cup inverted in a bowl or casserole to make your own baking ring.

FIESTA RICE RING

Power Level: HIGH [100%] and MEDIUM [50%]
Total Cooking Time: 30 to 38 minutes

¼ cup finely chopped
   fresh mushrooms
¼ cup finely chopped green onion
¼ cup butter (or margarine)
3 cups water
1 tablespoon instant chicken
   bouillon
1 teaspoon salt
¼ teaspoon thyme
Dash of pepper
2 tablespoons finely chopped
   pimento
1½ cups uncooked long grain rice

1. Combine mushrooms, onion and butter in a 2 quart casserole. Microwave on HIGH (100%) for 4 to 5 minutes or until vegetables are tender. Stir halfway through cooking time.

2. Add water, bouillon and seasonings. Cover with a tight fitting lid or plastic wrap. Microwave on HIGH (100%) for 6 to 7 minutes or until boiling.

3. Stir in rice and pimento. Microwave on MEDIUM (50%) for 15 to 20 minutes or until rice is tender.*

4. Refrigerate rice for 1 to 2 hours until chilled. Press into a buttered microwave baking ring. Cover with plastic wrap.

5. Microwave on HIGH (100%) for 5 to 6 minutes or until heated through. Allow to stand 3 minutes, then loosen with knife and invert onto a serving plate. Fill center with favorite vegetable or creamed dish.

Recipe yield: 6 to 8 servings

*If rice is to be served immediately, allow rice to stand 5 minutes. Do not place in baking ring.

Fiesta Rice Ring turns plain rice into spectacular!

PASTA

Add 1 tablespoon oil *and 1 teaspoon salt to water. Cover with a tight fitting lid or plastic wrap. Microwave on High [100%] until water begins to boil.*

Add pasta and cover. *Microwave on Medium [50%] or until tender. Stir once halfway through cooking.*

Immediately pour pasta *into colander to drain and then rinse with hot water.*

HAM AND MACARONI
Power Level: HIGH [100%]
Total Cooking Time: 6 to 8 minutes

4 cups cooked elbow macaroni
1 cup cooked, cubed ham
½ cup sour cream
¼ cup chopped green pepper
2 tablespoons butter (or margarine)
¼ teaspoon salt
Dash of pepper
1 cup grated sharp Cheddar cheese

1. Combine all ingredients except cheese in a 2 quart casserole. Cover.

2. Microwave on HIGH (100%) for 6 to 8 minutes or until hot. Stir halfway through cooking.

3. Stir in cheese. Cover. Allow to stand 5 minutes.

NOODLES ROMANOFF
Power Level: HIGH [100%] and
*   MEDIUM [50%]*
Total Cooking Time: 23 to 29 minutes

4 cups water
1 teaspoon salt
8 ounces (about 4 cups) noodles
1 cup cottage cheese
2 tablespoons butter (or margarine)
¼ cup sliced green onion
¼ teaspoon garlic powder
1 cup sour cream
½ cup grated Parmesan cheese

1. Place water and salt in a 2 quart casserole. Cover with a tight fitting lid or plastic wrap. Microwave on HIGH (100%) for 8 to 10 minutes or until boiling. Stir in noodles. Cover, then microwave on MEDIUM (50%) for 8 to 10 minutes or until noodles are softened. Immediately drain and rinse with hot water. Set aside.

2. Place cottage cheese, butter, onion and garlic powder in casserole. Microwave on HIGH (100%) for 4 to 5 minutes or until hot and bubbly.

3. Stir in cooked noodles and sour cream. Sprinkle Parmesan cheese over top. Microwave on HIGH (100%) for 3 to 4 minutes or until heated throughout.

Recipe yield: 5 to 6 servings

PASTA CHART

Item	Raw Amount	Cooked Amount	Covered Utensil	Water	Power Level	Cooking Time
Spaghetti	7 ounce package	4 cups	2 quart baking dish or casserole	4 cups	Water HIGH (100%) then Spaghetti MEDIUM (50%)	10-12 minutes 8-10 minutes
Spaghetti	16 ounce package	8 cups	2 quart baking dish or casserole	5 cups	Water HIGH (100%) then Spaghetti MEDIUM (50%)	14-16 minutes 10-12 minutes
Egg Noodles	4 cups	4-4½ cups	2 quart casserole	4 cups	Water HIGH (100%) then Egg Noodles MEDIUM (50%)	10-12 minutes 8-10 minutes
Macaroni	2 cups	4 cups	2 quart casserole	3 cups	Water HIGH (100%) then Macaroni MEDIUM (50%)	8-10 minutes 10-12 minutes
Lasagna	8 pieces	8 pieces	3 quart casserole	5 cups	Water HIGH (100%) then Lasagna MEDIUM (50%)	14-16 minutes 14-16 minutes
Manicotti	10-12 pieces	10-12 pieces	2 quart baking dish or casserole	4 cups	Water HIGH (100%) then Manicotti MEDIUM (50%)	10-12 minutes 18-20 minutes

SPAGHETTI WITH MEAT SAUCE

Power Level: HIGH [100%] and
LOW [30%]
Total Cooking Time: 26 to 30 minutes

1 pound ground beef
1 small onion, chopped
1 clove garlic, crushed
1 can (15 ounces) tomato sauce
1 can (6 ounces) tomato paste
1 teaspoon oregano
¼ teaspoon basil
¼ teaspoon salt
Dash of pepper
1 (7 ounce package) spaghetti,
cooked and drained (page 143)
Parmesan cheese

1. Place ground beef, onion and garlic in a 2 quart casserole. Cover with waxed paper. Microwave on HIGH (100%) for 6 to 8 minutes or until meat is pink in center. Stir halfway through cooking. Drain off excess grease.

2. Stir in tomato sauce, tomato paste and seasonings. Microwave on HIGH (100%) for 10 to 12 minutes or until hot and bubbly. Stir halfway through cooking. Microwave on LOW (30%) for 10 minutes to blend flavors.

3. Stir in spaghetti. Sprinkle with Parmesan cheese.

Recipe yield: 4 to 6 servings

Variation:

SPAGHETTI AND MEATBALLS

Follow Spaghetti with Meat Sauce recipe as directed except eliminate Step 1. Substitute cooked meatballs (page 122) for ground beef, onion and garlic. Then add ¼ teaspoon garlic powder to sauce.

SPAGHETTI BAKE

Power Level: HIGH [100%] and
MEDIUM [50%]
Total Cooking Time: 38 to 47 minutes

1 medium onion, chopped
1 can (2½ ounces) sliced
mushrooms, drained
1 tablespoon butter (or margarine)
1 pound ground beef
2 cans (8 ounces each)
tomato sauce
1½ cups water
1½ teaspoons Italian seasoning
1 teaspoon garlic salt
¼ teaspoon pepper
¼ pound uncooked spaghetti,
broken in half
Grated Parmesan cheese (optional)

1. Combine onion, mushrooms and butter in a 2 quart casserole. Microwave on HIGH (100%) for 3 to 4 minutes or until onion is tender.

2. Place ground beef in casserole. Cover with waxed paper. Microwave on HIGH (100%) for 6 to 8 minutes or until meat is pink in center. Stir halfway through cooking. Drain off excess fat.

3. Stir in tomato sauce, water, Italian seasoning, garlic salt and pepper. Cover. Microwave on HIGH (100%) for 4 to 5 minutes or until hot and bubbly.

4. Stir spaghetti noodles into sauce. Cover with a tight fitting lid or plastic wrap. Microwave on MEDIUM (50%) for 25 to 30 minutes or until spaghetti is tender. Stir several times during cooking.

5. Sprinkle with Parmesan cheese before serving.

Recipe yield: 6 servings

Spaghetti Bake
is easy and so tasty.

MANICOTTI

Power Level: HIGH [100%]
Total Cooking Time: 13 to 16 minutes

**8 (¼ pound) manicotti shells,
  cooked and drained (page 143)**
½ pound ground beef
½ cup chopped onion
1 teaspoon salt
1 clove garlic, minced
1 tablespoon parsley
¼ teaspoon basil
¼ teaspoon oregano
1 egg, slightly beaten
**2 cups dry cottage cheese
  (or ricotta cheese)**
⅓ cup grated Parmesan cheese
1 can (8 ounces) tomato sauce
**1 cup (4 ounces) grated
  Mozzarella cheese**

1. Place ground beef in a 1 quart casserole. Add onion, salt, garlic, parsley, basil and oregano. Microwave on HIGH (100%) for 3 to 4 minutes or until meat is no longer pink. Stir halfway through cooking time. Drain off excess grease.

2. Mix together egg, cottage cheese, Parmesan cheese and ground beef mixture.

3. Fill each manicotti shell with cottage cheese-ground beef mixture. Arrange shells in a 10 x 6 x 1¾ inch baking dish. baking dish.

4. Pour tomato sauce over manicotti shells. Cover with plastic wrap. Microwave on HIGH (100%) for 10 to 12 minutes or until hot and bubbly.

5. Top with Mozzarella cheese. Allow to stand covered until cheese melts.

Recipe yield: 4 to 5 servings

QUICK LASAGNA

*Power Level: HIGH [100%] and
            LOW [30%]*
Total Cooking Time: 32 to 38 minutes

1 pound ground beef
1 can (8 ounces) tomato sauce
1 can (6 ounces) tomato paste
1½ cups water
**1 package (1½ ounces) dry
  onion soup mix**
1 teaspoon oregano
½ teaspoon garlic powder
½ teaspoon salt
Dash of pepper
½ teaspoon sugar
10 pieces lasagna noodles, cooked
**1 pound dry cottage cheese
  (or ricotta)**
¾ pound grated Mozzarella cheese
Parmesan Cheese

1. Place ground beef in a 2 quart casserole. Cover with waxed paper. Microwave on HIGH (100%) for 6 to 8 minutes or until pink in center. Stir halfway through cooking. Drain off all but 2 tablespoons grease.

2. Add tomato sauce, tomato paste, water, soup mix, seasonings and sugar. Cover with waxed paper. Microwave on HIGH (100%) for 6 to 8 minutes or until boiling. Stir halfway through cooking. Microwave on LOW (30%) for 10 minutes to blend flavors.

3. Place alternate layers of noodles, cottage cheese, sauce and Mozzarella cheese in an 11¾ x 7½ x 1¾ inch baking dish, ending with sauce. Sprinkle with Parmesan cheese. Cover with waxed paper.*

4. Microwave on HIGH (100%) for 10 to 12 minutes or until heated through. Allow to stand 5 to 10 minutes before serving.

Recipe yield: 6 to 8 servings

*Lasagna can be made through Step 3, then refrigerated up to 2 days. Allow an additional 5 minutes cooking time.

*Manicotti adds an
Italian flair to your meal.*

Cereals

Hot cereals are a quick, fun, one-step process in the microwave. Clean-up is such a snap that Mom won't hesitate to let the children make their own hot breakfast.

Select a bowl *made of glass, paper or micro plastic. Combine all ingredients except raisins.*

Microwave on High [*100%*] *for the recommended time. Cook uncovered for easier stirring. Add raisins the last 5 minutes of cooking.*

GRANOLA

Power Level: HIGH [100%]
Total Cooking Time: 13 to 15 minutes

6 cups quick cooking oats
1 cup shredded coconut
¾ cup wheat germ
⅓ to ⅔ cup honey
½ cup chopped almonds
½ cup shelled sunflower seeds
⅓ cup sesame seeds
⅓ cup brown sugar
⅓ cup salad oil
½ cup raisins

1. Mix together all ingredients except raisins in a 3 quart casserole.

2. Microwave on HIGH (100%) for 13 to 15 minutes. Stir occasionally. Add raisins the last 5 minutes of cooking.

3. Cool. Store in an airtight container.

Recipe yield: About 8 cups

ZIPPY CHEESE GRITS

Power Level: HIGH [100%]
Total Cooking Time: 14 to 19 minutes

2 cups milk
1 cup water
¾ teaspoon salt
1 cup quick cooking grits
1½ cups (6 ounces) grated American cheese
2 eggs, beaten
½ cup butter (or margarine), melted
¼ teaspoon garlic powder
Dash hot pepper sauce
Paprika or chopped chives

1. Place milk, water and salt in a 2 quart casserole. Microwave on HIGH (100%) for 8 to 10 minutes or until boiling.

2. Stir in grits. Microwave on HIGH (100%) for 2 to 3 minutes or until softened.

3. Stir in remaining ingredients except paprika and chives until well blended.

4. Microwave on HIGH (100%) for 4 to 6 minutes or until thickened. Sprinkle with paprika or chopped chives.

Recipe yield: 8 to 10 servings

CEREAL CHART

1. Place all ingredients in cooking utensil. **2.** Microwave on HIGH (100%), uncovered, until softened. Stir occasionally during last half of cooking. **3.** Allow to stand 3 minutes. Stir before serving.

Item	Servings	Cooking Utensil	Cereal	Water	Salt	Cooking Time
Instant Oatmeal or Grits	1 single serving	16 ounce cereal bowl	1 envelope	½ cup	none	1½ minutes
Quick Cooking Oatmeal	1	16 oz. cereal bowl	⅓ cup	¾ cup	1/8 teaspoon	1½ to 2½ minutes
	2	1½ qt. casserole	⅔ cup	1½ cups	¼ teaspoon	2½ to 3½ minutes
	4	2 qt. casserole	1⅓ cups	3 cups	½ teaspoon	5 to 6 minutes
	6	2 qt. casserole	2 cups	4 cups	¾ teaspoon	6 to 8 minutes
Old Fashion Oatmeal	1	16 oz. cereal bowl	⅓ cup	¾ cup	1/8 teaspoon	2 to 3 minutes
	2	1 qt. casserole	⅔ cup	1½ cups	¼ teaspoon	4 to 6 minutes
	4	1½ qt. casserole	1⅓ cups	3 cups	½ teaspoon	6 to 8 minutes
	6	2 qt. casserole	2 cups	4 cups	¾ teaspoon	10 to 12 minutes
Cornmeal	1	16 oz. cereal bowl	3 tablespoons	⅔ cup	1/8 teaspoon	1 to 2 minutes
	2	1 qt. casserole	⅓ cup	1⅓ cups	¼ teaspoon	3 to 4 minutes
	4	1½ qt. casserole	⅔ cup	2⅔ cups	½ teaspoon	4 to 6 minutes
	6	2 qt. casserole	1 cup	4 cups	¾ teaspoon	8 to 10 minutes
Quick Cooking Grits	1	16 oz. cereal bowl	3 tablespoons	¾ cup	1/8 teaspoon	3 to 4 minutes
	2	1½ qt. casserole	⅓ cup	1⅓ cups	¼ teaspoon	4 to 6 minutes
	4	2 qt. casserole	⅔ cup	2⅔ cups	½ teaspoon	8 to 10 minutes
	6	2 qt. casserole	1 cup	4 cups	¾ teaspoon	10 to 12 minutes
Cream of Wheat	1	16 oz. cereal bowl	2½ tablespoons	1 cup	1/8 teaspoon	3 to 4 minutes
	2	1½ qt. casserole	⅓ cup	1¾ cups	¼ teaspoon	4 to 6 minutes
	4	2 qt. casserole	⅔ cup	3½ cups	½ teaspoon	6 to 8 minutes
	6	3 qt. casserole	1 cup	5 cups	¾ teaspoon	8 to 10 minutes
Cream of Rice *	1	16 oz. cereal bowl	3 tablespoons	¾ cup	1/8 teaspoon	2 to 3 minutes
	2	1 qt. casserole	⅓ cup	1⅓ cups	¼ teaspoon	4 to 5 minutes
	4	1½ qt. casserole	⅔ cup	2⅔ cups	½ teaspoon	6 to 8 minutes
	6	2 qt. casserole	1 cup	4 cups	¾ teaspoon	10 to 12 minutes

*Times are for boiling water only. After water comes to a rapid boil, stir in cream of rice. Microwave on High (100%) for 15 to 20 seconds.

Granola gets the morning off to a good start.

CRUMB CRUST

Melt butter in a 9 inch pie dish. Stir in crumbs and sugar.

Use a small cup to press crumb mixture against bottom and sides of dish. Microwave on High [100%] for 2 to 2½ minutes or until heated throughout and set. Turn dish a half turn halfway through cooking.

For easy removal of crust, set pie plate on a warm wet cloth or towel for about 10 minutes.

COOKIE CRUMB CRUST
Power Level: HIGH [100%]
Total Cooking Time: 2½ to
3¼ minutes

⅓ **cup butter (or margarine)**
1½ **cups cookie crumbs (vanilla wafer, graham cracker, chocolate wafer, gingersnaps, etc.)**
3 **tablespoons sugar**

1. Place butter in a 9 inch pie dish. Microwave on HIGH (100%) for 30 to 45 seconds or until melted.

2. Stir in crumbs and sugar until well blended. Press crumb mixture against bottom and sides of dish.

3. Microwave on HIGH (100%) for 2 to 2½ minutes or until heated throughout and set. Turn dish a half turn halfway through cooking time.

4. Cool on cooling rack before filling.

Creme de Menthe Pie tastes as good as it looks!

Pies

Delicious melt-in-the-mouth pies come out light and flaky from the microwave.
You will particularly enjoy the advantages of making pastry with the microwave in the summertime. You won't be heating up your whole kitchen because only the food gets hot.

Pie crusts are done in just 5 to 6 minutes. Remember, always prebake a crust before filling it. Otherwise, moisture in the filling will make the crust soggy.

LEMON MERINGUE PIE

Power Level: HIGH [100%] and MEDIUM [50%]
Total Cooking Time: 8 to 12 minutes

1 baked 9 inch pastry shell
1½ cups sugar
⅓ cup cornstarch
1½ cups water
3 egg yolks, slightly beaten
3 tablespoons butter (or margarine)
¼ cup lemon juice
1 teaspoon grated lemon peel

Meringue:

3 egg whites
¼ teaspoon cream of tartar
6 tablespoons sugar

1. Mix together sugar, cornstarch and water in a 4 cup measure or 1 quart casserole until smooth. Microwave on High (100%) for 4 to 6 minutes or until thickened. Stir occasionally the last half of cooking.

2. Beat a little of the hot mixture into egg yolks, then add the egg yolk mixture to the remaining hot mixture. Microwave on HIGH (100%) for 1 to 2 minutes or until thickened.

3. Blend in butter, lemon juice and lemon peel. Cool. Pour into cooled baked pastry shell.

4. Beat egg whites and cream of tartar until foamy. Gradually add sugar, beating until stiff peaks form. Spread over filling. Seal around rim of pie.

5. Microwave on MEDIUM (50%) for 3 to 4 minutes or until set.*

* If microwave has a browning element, brown as desired.

CREME DE MENTHE PIE

Power Level: HIGH [100%]
Total Cooking Time: 2 to 4 minutes

1 baked 9 inch chocolate wafer crumb crust
3 cups miniature marshmallows (or 32 large marshmallows)
⅔ cup evaporated milk
¼ cup green creme de menthe
1 cup whipping cream
1 teaspoon vanilla

1. Place marshmallows and milk in a 3 quart casserole. Microwave on HIGH (100%) for 2 to 4 minutes or until marshmallows can be stirred smooth.

2. Stir in creme de menthe. Chill for 30 to 45 minutes or until thickened. (Stir occasionally during chilling.)

3. Beat whipping cream and vanilla until soft peaks form. Fold into marshmallow mixture. Pour into cooled crust.

4. If desired, garnish with whipped cream topping and chocolate curls.

Variations:

AMARETTO ALEXANDER PIE

Follow Creme De Menthe pie recipe as directed except substitute 2 tablespoons to ¼ cup Amaretto for creme de menthe. Pour into a vanilla wafer crumb crust. Spread whipped cream topping and slivered almonds over top.

BERRY MALLOW PIE

Follow Creme De Menthe pie recipe as directed except substitute 2 cups sliced fresh strawberries, whole fresh raspberries or whole fresh blueberries for creme de menthe and pour into a graham cracker crumb crust. If desired, garnish with whipped cream topping and berries.

Cut dough in half *to make one crust. Pat dough into a flat, round bun shape. Starting from the center, begin rolling dough out and away from the center.*

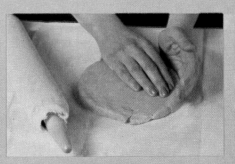

Do not overhandle *the pastry dough as this will make it tough. Continue rolling out dough into a 12 inch circle.*

Roll dough onto rolling pin *and case off into a 9 inch pie dish. Trim off excess dough so about ½ inch hangs over edge of dish. Fold under and pinch edges.*

A pie crust made from plain shortening and done in a microwave oven has a light color and flaky texture.

A pie crust baked in a conventional oven is brown in color due to its exposure to the hot, dry air of the oven.

PIE DEFROSTING CHART

Item	Amount	Power Level	Actual Time
Frozen Cream or Custard Pie	1 to 3 slices (of 14 oz. pie)	Low (30%)	1 to 2 minutes
Frozen Cream or Custard Pie	1 (26 oz.) Whole pie	Low (30%)	4 to 5 minutes
Frozen Cream or Custard Pie	1 (14 oz.) Whole pie	Low (30%)	3 to 4 minutes
Frozen Baked Fruit or Nut Pie	1 to 3 slices (8 inch pie)	Medium (50%)	2 to 4 minutes
Frozen Baked Fruit or Nut Pie	2 slices (8 inch pie)	Medium (50%)	3 minutes
Frozen Baked Fruit or Nut Pie	1 (8 inch) Whole pie	Medium (50%)	4 to 5 minutes

1. Place pie in pie dish or place slices on serving dish.
2. Microwave until defrosted.

A little food coloring can color a plain pie crust. Add a few drops yellow food coloring to water of pastry dough. Prepare dough and microwave.

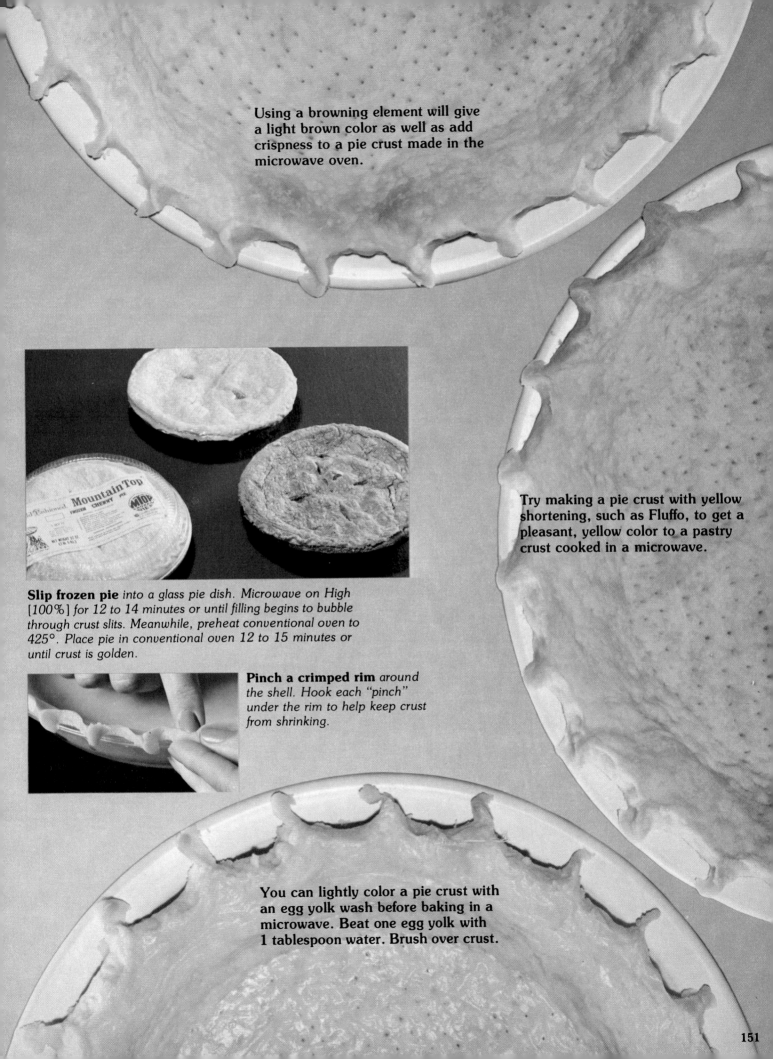

Using a browning element will give a light brown color as well as add crispness to a pie crust made in the microwave oven.

Slip frozen pie *into a glass pie dish. Microwave on High [100%] for 12 to 14 minutes or until filling begins to bubble through crust slits. Meanwhile, preheat conventional oven to 425°. Place pie in conventional oven 12 to 15 minutes or until crust is golden.*

Pinch a crimped rim *around the shell. Hook each "pinch" under the rim to help keep crust from shrinking.*

Try making a pie crust with yellow shortening, such as Fluffo, to get a pleasant, yellow color to a pastry crust cooked in a microwave.

You can lightly color a pie crust with an egg yolk wash before baking in a microwave. Beat one egg yolk with 1 tablespoon water. Brush over crust.

1 CRUST PASTRY SHELL

Prepare package or basic *pie crust mixture. Use a microwave type pie dish. If using a frozen pie crust, transfer it from its metal pan into a pie dish.*

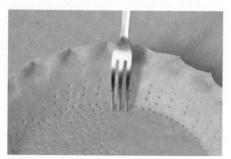

Prick crust *with fork at about 1/8-inch intervals on bottom and sides. Microwave on High [100%] for 5 to 6 minutes. Turn crust halfway through cooking time.*

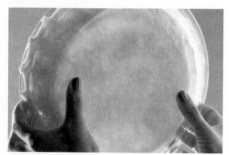

Check for doneness. *The underside should be dry and opaque. The top side will be blistered.*

TART SHELL

Invert custard cup *over rolled out crust. Cut out 6 round crusts, 1 inch larger than the inverted cup.*

Place a paper towel *over the custard cup, then shape the pastry over the towel and cup. Arrange in a circle. Microwave on High [100%] for 7 to 8 minutes. Rearrange cups halfway through cooking.*

Allow finished shell to stand *3 to 4 minutes. Then carefully remove shell from cup.*

PASTRY SHELL FOR 1 CRUST PIE**

Power Level: HIGH [100%]
Total Cooking Time: 5 to 6 minutes

1 cup all purpose flour
½ teaspoon salt
⅓ cup + 1 tablespoon shortening
2 to 3 tablespoons cold water (or milk)

1. Combine flour and salt. Cut in shortening until size of tiny peas. Sprinkle with water, 1 tablespoon at a time, and toss until dough cleans side of bowl. Shape into ball.

2. Roll out on a floured surface to form a circle 1/8 inch thick and 2 inches larger than inverted pie dish.

3. Fold pastry over rolling pin and ease into pie dish. Trim edge of pastry slightly larger than rim of dish. Build up and flute edges. Thoroughly prick bottom and sides of pastry.

4. Microwave on HIGH (100%) for 5 to 6 minutes or until dry and blistery. Turn dish a half turn halfway through cooking.*

5. Cool on cooling rack before filling.

*If microwave has a browning element, brown as desired.

**Double recipe for a 2 crust pie.

Variation:
TART SHELLS
Follow Pastry Shell recipe as directed in Steps 1 and 2. Cut out 6 pastry rounds 1 inch larger than an inverted 6-ounce custard cup. Invert 6 custard cups. Cover each cup with a paper towel, then with a pastry round. Pleat each tart edge in six places. Place in oven in a circle. Microwave on HIGH (100%) for 6 to 8 minutes or until dry and blistery. Rearrange halfway through cooking. Let stand for 3 to 4 minutes, then carefully remove custard cups. Cool before filling.

Recipe yield: 6 tart shells.

COCONUT CRUST
Power Level: HIGH [100%]
Total Cooking Time: 3 to 5 minutes

1 egg white
2 tablespoons sugar
1 tablespoon corn syrup
¼ teaspoon vanilla
¼ teaspoon almond extract
2¼ cups shredded coconut, chopped

1. Beat egg white until stiff. Gradually beat in sugar, corn syrup, vanilla and almond extract. Fold in coconut.

2. Firmly press coconut mixture into the bottom and sides of a 9 inch pie dish.

3. Microwave on HIGH (100%) for 3 to 5 minutes or until set. Turn dish three times during cooking.*

4. Cool on cooling rack before filling.

*If microwave has a browning element, brown as desired.

BAKING POWDER PASTRY SHELL
Power Level: HIGH [100%]
Total Cooking Time: 6 to 8 minutes

1 cup all purpose flour
1 teaspoon baking powder
½ teaspoon salt
¼ cup shortening
4 to 5 tablespoons milk

1. Combine flour, baking powder and salt. Cut in shortening until the size of tiny peas.

2. Sprinkle mixture with milk, 1 tablespoon at a time, and toss lightly until dough begins to clean the side of bowl. Shape into ball.

3. Roll out on a floured surface to form a circle 1/8 inch thick and 2 inches larger than inverted pie dish.

4. Fold pastry over rolling pin and ease into 9 inch pie dish. Trim edges of pastry slightly larger than rim of dish. Build up and flute edges. Thoroughly prick bottom and sides of pastry.

5. Microwave on HIGH (100%) for 6 to 8 minutes or until surface appears dry and blistery. Turn dish a half turn halfway through cooking.*

6. Cool on cooling rack before filling.

*If microwave has a browning element, brown as desired.

IMPOSSIBLE PIE

*Power Level: LOW [30%] and
         MEDIUM [50%]*
*Total Cooking Time: 22¾ to
             25 minutes*

¼ cup butter (or margarine)
4 eggs
2 cups milk
¾ cup sugar
½ cup buttermilk biscuit mix
2 teaspoons vanilla
½ teaspoon salt
1 cup toasted coconut

1. Microwave butter on LOW (30%) for 45 seconds to 1 minute or until softened.

2. Combine softened butter, eggs, milk, sugar, biscuit mix, vanilla and salt in blender container. Mix in blender until well blended. Stir in coconut.

3. Pour into a lightly greased 10" pie plate.

4. Microwave on MEDIUM (50%) for 22 to 24 minutes or until knife inserted near center comes out clean. Turn dish several times during cooking.

VANILLA CREAM PIE

*Power Level: HIGH [100%] and
         MEDIUM [50%]*
Total Cooking Time: 9½ to 14 minutes

1 baked 9 inch pastry shell
½ to ¾ cup sugar
3 tablespoons cornstarch
¼ teaspoon salt
2 cups milk
3 slightly beaten egg yolks
2 tablespoons butter (or margarine)
1 teaspoon vanilla
3 egg whites
¼ teaspoon cream of tartar
6 tablespoons sugar

1. Mix together sugar, cornstarch, salt and ½ cup milk in a 1½ quart casserole until smooth. Stir in remaining milk. Microwave on HIGH (100%) for 5 to 8 minutes or until thickened. Stir occasionally the last half of cooking.

2. Beat a little of the hot mixture into the beaten egg yolks, then add the egg yolk mixture to the remaining hot mixture. Microwave on HIGH (100%) for 1½ to 2 minutes or until thickened. Stir occasionally.

3. Blend in butter and vanilla. Pour into the cooled baked pastry shell.

4. Beat egg whites and cream of tartar until foamy. Gradually add sugar, beating until stiff peaks form. Spread over filling. Seal around rim of pie.

5. Microwave on MEDIUM (50%) for 3 to 4 minutes or until set.*

*If microwave has a browning element, brown as desired.

Variations:
BANANA CREAM PIE

Follow Vanilla Cream Pie recipe as directed except slice 2 medium size bananas in the bottom of the 9 inch baked pastry shell. Pour vanilla cream pie filling over the bananas. Top with meringue.

BUTTERSCOTCH CREAM PIE

Follow Vanilla Cream Pie recipe as directed except substitute the granulated sugar with dark brown sugar and add 3 tablespoons butter instead of the 2 tablespoons butter.

COCOA CREAM PIE

Follow Vanilla Cream Pie recipe as directed except add ⅓ cup cocoa in Step 1 and increase cornstarch to ¼ cup.

COCONUT CREAM PIE

Follow Vanilla Cream pie recipe as directed except add 1 cup coconut to cream pie filling and sprinkle ⅓ cup toasted coconut over the meringue.

Tip: For added variety try these pies in crumb crust or coconut crust.

┌─ **Pie filling tip** ─────────┐

For a quick pie filling, use a pudding and pie filling mix. Microwave on High (100%) for 6 to 8 minutes or until it comes to a full bubbling boil. Stir occasionally during last half of cooking. Pour into baked pie shell.

└────────────────────────────┘

CREAM FILLING

Mix together *sugar, cornstarch, salt and milk. Microwave on High [100%] for 5 to 8 minutes or until thickened. Stir occasionally.*

Beat a little *of the hot mixture into the beaten egg yolks. Then add the yolk mixture to the remaining hot mixture.*

Microwave on High *[100%] for 1½ to 2 minutes or until thickened. Stir occasionally with wooden whisk or spoon. Blend in butter and vanilla.*

Pour mixture *into cooled pastry shell. These basic steps work for banana cream, butterscotch, cocoa and coconut cream pie fillings as well as vanilla.*

Prebake the bottom crust of a two-crust pie before filling. Otherwise, moisture in the filling will prevent the crust from being crisp and flaky.

Cut pastry for the top crust about ½ inch smaller than the pie dish. Gently place top over filling. Vent the crust. Add a pastry design to decorate the top.

FRESH APPLE PIE (FRUIT PIE)

Power Level: HIGH [100%]
Total Cooking Time: 17 to 20 minutes

Pastry for 9 inch 2-crust pie
5 to 6 cups peeled and thinly sliced tart cooking apples (or desired fruit)
¾ to 1 cup sugar
¼ cup all purpose flour
1 teaspoon cinnamon (optional)
¼ teaspoon nutmeg (optional)
2 tablespoons lemon juice
2 tablespoons butter (or margarine)
1 egg yolk
1 tablespoon water

1. Roll half the pastry out to fit a 9 inch pie dish. Trim and flute edge.

2. Thoroughly prick bottom and sides. Microwave on HIGH (100%) for 5 to 6 minutes or until dry and blistery. Cool.

3. Mix together sugar, flour, cinnamon and nutmeg (or desired spices). Add fruit and toss until well coated. Sprinkle with lemon juice.

4. Place in cooled pastry shell. Dot with butter.

5. Roll out remaining pastry ½ inch smaller than pie dish. Place pastry over filling. Vent the crust. Brush with a mixture of egg yolk and water.

6. Microwave on HIGH (100%) for 12 to 14 minutes or until pastry is dry and

blistery and fruit is tender. Turn dish a half turn halfway through cooking.

Variation:

Companion Cooking (Microwave and Conventional)

Follow Fresh Apple Pie (Fruit Pie) recipe as directed except do not prebake bottom shell. Microwave on HIGH (100%) for 8 to 10 minutes or until juices begin to bubble through slits. Meanwhile, preheat conventional oven to 450°. After cooking in microwave, transfer to conventional oven. Bake at 450° for 12 to 15 minutes or until golden.

Sprinkle crumb topping evenly over apple or fruit pie filling.

APPLE STREUSEL PIE

Power Level: HIGH [100%]
Total Cooking Time: 10 to 12 minutes

1 baked 9 inch pastry shell
¾ to 1 cup sugar
¼ cup all purpose flour
1 teaspoon cinnamon
Dash of nutmeg
Dash of salt
5 cups cooking apples, peeled and sliced
2 tablespoons lemon juice
2 tablespoons butter (or margarine)

Crumb Topping:
½ cup all purpose flour (oatmeal, graham cracker crumbs, corn flakes or crisped rice cereal)
¼ cup brown sugar
2 tablespoons butter (or margarine), softened
½ teaspoon cinnamon
¼ cup chopped nuts (optional)
¼ cup shredded coconut (optional)

1. Mix together sugar, flour, cinnamon, nutmeg and salt. Add apples. Toss until well coated. Sprinkle with lemon juice. Place in cooled pastry shell. Dot with butter.

2. Mix together crumb topping ingredients until crumbly. Sprinkle over apples.

3. Microwave on HIGH (100%) for 10 to 12 minutes or until apples are tender.

FRESH STRAWBERRY PIE

Power Level: HIGH [100%]
Total Cooking Time: 7 to 9 minutes

1 baked 9 inch pastry shell
1½ quarts fresh strawberries, stemmed
1 cup sugar
3 tablespoons cornstarch
1 cup water
1 teaspoon lemon juice

1. Place ⅔ cup of strawberries in a 2 quart casserole. Crush strawberries. Cover with a tight fitting lid or plastic wrap. Microwave on HIGH (100%) for 2 to 3 minutes or until boiling.

2. Mix together sugar, cornstarch, water and lemon juice. Stir into strawberry mixture. Microwave on HIGH (100%) for 5 to 6 minutes or until thickened. Stir occasionally during cooking. Cool.

3. Fold strawberries into cooled glaze. Spoon into baked pastry shell. If desired, garnish top with whipped cream.

PEANUT BUTTER PIE

Power Level: HIGH [100%]
Total Cooking Time: 6 to 8 minutes

1 baked 9 inch pastry shell (or vanilla cookie crumb crust)
½ cup chunky peanut butter
¾ cup powdered sugar
1 package (3-1/8 ounces) vanilla pudding and pie filling
1 container (4 ounces) frozen whipped topping, thawed
½ cup chopped peanuts

1. Mix peanut butter and powdered sugar until crumbly. Reserve 2 tablespoons and set aside. Sprinkle remaining mixture on the bottom of cooled pastry shell.

2. Prepare vanilla pudding as directed on package. Microwave on HIGH (100%) for 6 to 8 minutes. Stir occasionally the last half of cooking time.

3. Pour pudding over peanut butter mixture. Cool.

4. Spread whipped topping over pudding. Sprinkle with reserved peanut butter mixture and chopped peanuts. Chill.

— Topping Tip —
Defrost a 4 ounce container of frozen whipped topping in your microwave oven. Microwave on Low (30%) for 20 to 25 seconds. Stir occasionally.

PECAN PIE

Power Level: HIGH [100%] and
MEDIUM [50%]
Total Cooking Time: 12¾ to
16 minutes

1 baked 9 inch pastry shell
¼ cup butter (or margarine)
3 eggs, beaten
¾ cup brown sugar
¾ cup light corn syrup
1 teaspoon vanilla
¼ teaspoon salt
1 cup pecan halves

1. Place butter in a large glass mixing bowl. Microwave on HIGH (100%) for 45 seconds to 1 minute or until melted.

2. Stir a little hot butter into eggs, then stir the egg mixture into the remaining butter. Blend in brown sugar, corn syrup, vanilla and salt.

3. Pour into cooled pastry shell. Place pecans on top.

4. Microwave on MEDIUM (50%) for 12 to 15 minutes or until a knife inserted near center comes out clean. Turn dish a half turn halfway through cooking.

BLACK BOTTOM LIME PIE

Power Level: LOW [30%]
Total Cooking Time: 25 to 30 minutes

1 baked chocolate cookie crumb
crust (page 148)
3 eggs, separated
1 can (14 ounces) sweetened
condensed milk
½ cup lime juice
1 teaspoon grated lime peel
3 to 4 drops green food coloring
¼ teaspoon cream of tartar
1 tablespoon chocolate cookie
crumbs

1. Beat egg yolks until thick and lemon colored. Stir in milk, lime juice, lime peel and food coloring.

2. Beat egg whites and cream of tartar until stiff, but not dry. Fold into lime mixture.

3. Pour lime filling into cooled baked crumb crust. Sprinkle top with crumbs.

4. Microwave on LOW (30%) for 25 to 30 minutes or until a knife inserted near center comes out clean. Turn dish a half turn halfway through cooking.

5. Cool on cooling rack.

SLIPPED CUSTARD PIE

Power Level: HIGH [100%] and
LOW [30%]
Total Cooking Time: 28 to 34 minutes

1 baked 9 inch pastry shell
2½ cups milk
4 eggs
½ cup + 2 tablespoons sugar
¼ teaspoon salt
½ teaspoon vanilla
¼ teaspoon nutmeg

1. Pour milk into a 4 cup measure. Microwave on HIGH (100%) for 3 to 4 minutes or until steaming.

2. Beat together eggs, sugar, salt and vanilla. Stir a small amount of hot milk into egg mixture. then stir egg mixture into remaining hot milk. Pour into a buttered 9 inch pie dish. Sprinkle with nutmeg. Cover with an inverted pie dish for faster cooking.

3. Microwave on LOW (30%) for 25 to 30 minutes or until knife inserted near edge comes out clean. Turn dish a half turn halfway through cooking.

4. Allow to stand 3 minutes. Run knife around edge of custard, then slip into baked pie shell. Cool.

SLIPPED CUSTARD

Microwave custard *in a buttered 9 inch pie dish. Use Low [30%] for 25 to 30 minutes. Turn dish halfway through cooking. Custard is done when knife inserted near edge comes out clean. Let stand 3 minutes.*

Run a knife *around the edge of the custard to loosen.*

Carefully slip *custard into prebaked pie shell.*

Fresh Strawberry Pie and
Fresh Apple Pie will melt
in your mouth.

Poultry

If you haven't tasted poultry cooked in the microwave, you don't know how juicy and tender poultry can really be.

For a gorgeous turkey, *mix together 3 tablespoons butter [or margarine], ½ teaspoon paprika and 8 drops brown bouquet sauce. Microwave on High [100%] for 45 seconds to 1 minute. Baste during cooking.*

Stuff the bird *just before cooking. Fill cavity loosely with stuffing. It will expand during cooking.*
Start trussing *by placing skewers at 1-inch intervals across the opening. Lace tightly around the skewers with string in a crisscross fashion. Tie the drumsticks together.*
After stuffing *the wishbone area, fasten the neck skin to the back with skewers. Bend the wings across the back.*

DEFROSTING POULTRY

When starting with frozen poultry, keep in mind the importance of completely defrosting it before starting to cook. If poultry is not completely defrosted, it will not microwave evenly.

Defrosted poultry should be soft yet still cool to the touch. If it feels warm, you have started the cooking process.

POULTRY DEFROSTING CHART

Power Level: LOW (30%)	
Item	**Cooking Time**
Broiler/Fryer, cut up (2½ to 3½ lbs.)	20-25 min.
Broiler/Fryer, whole (2½ to 3½ lbs.)	20-25 min.
Capon (6 to 8 lbs.)	35-40 min.
Cornish Hens (1 pound) 1	12-14 min.
2	18-20 min.
Duckling (4 to 5 lbs.)	40-45 min.

Turkey - see page 163.

DEFROSTING WHOLE POULTRY

Place the whole wrapped poultry in the oven. Be sure to remove any metal or foil wrappings. Microwave on Low [30%] for half the time.

Unwrap poultry and turn over in a dish. Shield with foil wing tips, leg ends, tail and any other areas which may feel warm or are beginning to change color. Cover with waxed paper. Microwave on Low [30%] for second half of time.

When defrosting Cornish game hens, turn them over midway through defrosting. Hen sides, which were toward the edge of dish, now should be toward center.

Poultry should feel cool and soft when removed from oven. Run cold water inside bird to remove giblets and to complete defrosting.

DEFROSTING PIECES

Place wrapped chicken pieces in oven. Be sure to remove any metal or foil wrappings. Microwave on Low [30%] for half the time.

Unwrap pieces and break apart halfway through defrosting. Turn pieces over and place in baking dish with meaty parts toward the outside. Cover with waxed paper and microwave on Low [30%] for second half of time.

Remove pieces from oven and run under cold water to complete defrosting. Chicken should be soft and still cold.

COOKING POULTRY

When cooking a whole chicken, select a young, tender and plump bird. The skin should be smooth and creamy colored with a slight pink tint. Avoid birds with bumpy, thick skin with large amounts of yellow fat.

Since the poultry skin does not dry out in the microwave, it will not brown. You may wish to use a browning agent to give chicken an attractive color.

Melted butter or a brown bouquet sauce can be used to brown the skin. You might try using equal parts of soy sauce, melted butter and Worcestershire sauce. Or try a mixture of 2 tablespoons shortening and 1 tablespoon paprika.

POULTRY COOKING CHART

Power Level: HIGH (100%)	
Item	**Cooking Time**
Broiler/Fryer, cut up	
1 piece *	2-4 min.
2 pieces *	4-6 min.
4 pieces *	10-12 min.
6 pieces *	14-16 min.
2½ to 3½ lbs. (cut up)	20-25 min.
Power Level: MEDIUM-HIGH (70%)	
Item	**Cooking Time**
Whole Chicken (in cooking bag)	8-10 min. per lb.
Capon (6 to 8 lbs.) (in cooking bag)	8-10 min. per lb.
Cornish Hens 1 (1 lb.)	18-20 min.
2 (2 lbs.)	24-26 min.

*Drumsticks and thighs were used for testing. Times may vary with other pieces.

Turkey - see page 163.

Plain Microwave
Chicken

Oven-Baked
Chicken

Oatmeal
Crunch

Worcestershire,
Soy Sauce
and Butter

Butter and Paprika

Potato and
Parmesan

WHOLE POULTRY

Brush on or rub _browning agent_
into poultry skin.

Turn poultry breast side down _and_
bend back wings. This will expose the
meaty area under wings for more even
cooking.

Shield wing tips and leg ends. _Place_
poultry breast side down on trivet in
baking dish. Cover with waxed paper.
Microwave on Medium-High [70%] for
half the time. Remove shields. Turn
bird over and continue cooking. Re-
move excess grease drippings if cooking
duck or a fatty chicken.

For Cornish hens, _begin cooking_
breast side down. Halfway through
cooking, turn breast side up so that
sides which were to the edge of dish
are now toward center.

Test for doneness. _Cut poultry on_
meatiest part of thigh. Meat should be
tender and easy to remove from bone.
Juices should flow clear.

CHICKEN PIECES

Arrange chicken pieces _in baking_
dish with thick parts toward the outside.
Brush with butter, oil or browning
agent.

Cover with waxed paper. _Microwave_
on High [100%]. Turn pieces over
midway through cooking, keeping
meaty parts toward outside. For crispy
chicken, cook uncovered during
second half of cooking time.

Test for doneness. _Chicken should_
be tender and easy to remove from
bone.

OVEN-BAKED CHICKEN

Power Level: HIGH [100%]
Total Cooking Time: 20¾ to 26 minutes

⅓ cup butter (or margarine)
1 cup cornflake crumbs
1 teaspoon seasoned salt
1 teaspoon paprika
Dash of pepper
2½ to 3½ pound frying chicken, cut up

1. Place butter in an 11¾ x 7½ x 1¾ inch baking dish. Microwave on HIGH (100%) for 45 seconds to 1 minute or until melted.

2. Mix together crumbs, seasoned salt, paprika and pepper.

3. Roll chicken pieces in melted butter, then coat with crumb mixture. Return pieces to dish, placing meaty pieces toward outside. Sprinkle remaining crumbs over chicken.

4. Microwave on HIGH (100%), uncovered, for 20 to 25 minutes or until chicken is fork tender. Allow to stand 5 minutes before serving.

Variations:

SESAME-BAKED CHICKEN

Follow Oven-Baked Chicken recipe as directed except substitute 1 cup bread crumbs for cornflake crumbs and add ¼ cup sesame seeds in Step 2.

POTATO-PARMESAN CHICKEN

Follow Oven-Baked Chicken recipe as directed except substitute 1 cup instant potato flakes for cornflake crumbs and add ¼ cup grated Parmesan cheese in Step 2.

OATMEAL CRUNCH CHICKEN

Follow Oven-Baked Chicken recipe as directed except substitute 1 cup quick-cooking oatmeal (uncooked) for cornflake crumbs, and substitute ½ teaspoon nutmeg and ¼ teaspoon grated orange peel for paprika.

Recipe yield: 4 to 6 servings

CHICKEN AND STUFFING

Power Level: HIGH [100%]
Total Cooking Time: 26¾ to 31 minutes

¼ cup butter (or margarine)
2½ to 3½ pound chicken, cut up
1 package (5 ounces) croutons
1 cup chicken broth
¼ cup chopped onion
½ cup chopped celery
½ teaspoon ground sage
½ teaspoon poultry seasoning
¼ teaspoon pepper
Paprika

1. Place butter in a 1 cup measure. Microwave on HIGH (100%) for 45 seconds to 1 minute or until melted.

2. Arrange chicken pieces, meaty pieces toward the outside, in an 11¾ x 7½ x 1¾ inch baking dish. Brush butter over chicken. Cover with waxed paper. Microwave on HIGH (100%) for 20 to 22 minutes or until fork tender. Remove chicken pieces, set aside. Remove drippings from dish.

3. Combine croutons, chicken broth, onion, celery, sage, poultry seasoning and pepper. Place in baking dish.

4. Arrange cooked chicken pieces over dressing. Sprinkle with paprika. Cover. Microwave on HIGH (100%) for 6 to 8 minutes or until heated through. Allow to stand 5 minutes before serving.

Recipe yield: 4 servings

INDIVIDUAL CHICKEN PIES

Power Level: HIGH [100%]
Total Cooking Time: 21 to 28 minutes

Pastry for a 1 crust pie (page 152)
1 package (10 ounces) frozen mixed vegetables
⅓ cup chopped onion
3 tablespoons butter (or margarine)
¼ cup all purpose flour
1½ teaspoons salt
1½ cups chicken broth
¾ cup milk
2 cups cubed cooked chicken

1. Roll prepared pastry to ¼ inch thick. Cut to fit the tops of four 10-ounce custard cups or individual pie dishes. Prick several times. Set aside.

2. Place frozen vegetables in a 1 quart casserole. Cover with a tight fitting lid or plastic wrap. Microwave on HIGH (100%) for 6 to 8 minutes or until heated through. Drain. Set aside.

3. Place onion and butter in a 2 quart casserole. Microwave on HIGH (100%) for 3 to 4 minutes or until onion is tender. Stir halfway through cooking.

4. Stir in flour and salt until smooth. Slowly add broth and milk. Microwave on HIGH (100%) for 6 to 8 minutes or until thickened.

5. Add chicken and vegetables. Pour into custard cups or dishes and place pastry over filling. Microwave on HIGH (100%) for 6 to 8 minutes or until crust is dry and blistery. *

Recipe yield: 4 servings

*If microwave has a browning element, brown as desired.

CHICKEN IN A BAG

Brush on or rub *browning agent into chicken skin. Rub a little oil on the inside of bag over the breast area to prevent bag from sticking. Cut a thin strip of plastic from the open end of an oven cooking bag.*

Place chicken *breast side down in bag in a microwave safe dish. Add ⅓ cup liquid, water or wine. Tie end of bag with strip or string. Microwave for half the time on Medium-High [70%]. Turn breast side up and make a small slash in bag to release steam. Cook for remainder of time or until done.*

SWEET 'N SOUR CHICKEN

Power Level: HIGH [100%] and MEDIUM-HIGH [70%]
Total Cooking Time: 26 to 30 minutes

2½ to 3½ pounds chicken pieces, skinned
1 can (8¼ ounces) crushed pineapple, undrained
1 envelope (1½ ounces) dry onion soup mix
¼ cup apricot preserves (or jam)
¼ cup barbecue sauce

1. Place chicken pieces in an 11¾ x 7½ x 1¾ inch baking dish. Cover with waxed paper.

2. Microwave on HIGH (100%) for 20 to 22 minutes or until fork tender. Drain off excess grease.

3. Mix together remaining ingredients. Pour over cooked chicken pieces.

4. Cover. Microwave on MEDIUM-HIGH (70%) for 6 to 8 minutes or until heated through.

Recipe yield: 6 to 8 servings

FRUIT STUFFED CHICKEN

Power Level: MEDIUM-HIGH [70%]
Total Cooking Time: 35 to 40 minutes

4 to 5 pound roasting chicken
¼ teaspoon salt
Dash of pepper
2 medium apples, quartered, peeled and cored
2 medium oranges, peeled and sectioned
¼ cup orange marmalade

1. Season inside of chicken with salt and pepper. Fill with apples and oranges. Truss. Place chicken breast side down, on a trivet in a baking dish. Shield wing and leg tips with foil. Brush with half the marmalade. Cover with waxed paper.

2. Microwave on MEDIUM-HIGH (70%) for 35 to 40 minutes or until fork tender. Turn chicken breast side up halfway through cooking and remove shields. Brush with remaining marmalade.

3. Allow to stand 10 to 15 minutes before serving.

Recipe yield: 4 to 6 servings

PARTY LIVER PATE

Power Level: MEDIUM [50%]
Total Cooking Time: 18 to 20 minutes

1 pound chicken livers
2 tablespoons finely chopped onion
2 tablespoons finely chopped celery
1 cup water
½ cup butter (or margarine), softened
2 tablespoons dry sherry
½ teaspoon salt
½ teaspoon dry mustard
¼ teaspoon marjoram
¼ teaspoon hot pepper sauce

1. Pierce chicken livers. Combine chicken livers, onion, celery and water in a 1 quart casserole. Cover with a tight fitting lid or plastic wrap. Microwave on MEDIUM (50%) for 18 to 20 minutes or until tender. Stir halfway through cooking. Drain.

2. Place liver, onion and celery into a blender. Mix until smooth. Add butter and remaining ingredients. Blend well. Spoon into a well greased 2 cup mold. Refrigerate until chilled and firm.

3. Turn onto a serving plate. If desired, garnish with chopped hard cooked egg yolks and parsley.

Recipe yield: 2 cups

CHICKEN LIVERS SAUTE

Power Level: HIGH [100%]
Total Cooking Time: 5 to 6 minutes

½ pound chicken livers
3 tablespoons butter (or margarine)
1 can (2½ ounces) sliced mushrooms, drained
1 medium onion, sliced

1. Pierce chicken livers.

2. Microwave browning dish on HIGH (100%) for 3 to 4 minutes.

3. Add butter, then chicken livers, mushrooms and onion.

4. Microwave on HIGH (100%) for 5 to 6 minutes or until livers are tender. Turn over halfway through cooking.

Recipe yield: 2 to 4 servings

CHICKEN TERIYAKI

Power Level: HIGH [100%]
Total Cooking Time: 20 to 22 minutes

½ cup soy sauce
¼ cup cooking oil
1 tablespoon brown sugar
1 tablespoon sherry (optional)
1 teaspoon garlic powder
½ teaspoon ground ginger
2½ to 3½ pounds chicken, cut up

1. Mix together all ingredients except chicken in an 11¾ x 7½ x 1¾ inch dish. Add chicken and coat with sauce. Marinate for at least 30 minutes or overnight in the refrigerator.

2. Drain off most of the sauce. Cover with waxed paper. Microwave on HIGH (100%) for 20 to 22 minutes or until fork tender. Turn the chicken over and brush with drippings halfway through cooking. Allow to stand 5 minutes before serving.

Recipe yield: 4 to 6 servings

CHICKEN AMARETTO

Power Level: HIGH [100%] and LOW [30%]
Total Cooking Time: 17 to 22 minutes

¼ cup all purpose flour
½ teaspoon salt
¼ teaspoon curry powder
Dash of garlic powder
Dash of pepper
¼ cup butter (or margarine)
3 chicken breasts, boned, skinned and cut into ½ inch cubes
1½ cups chicken broth
¼ cup Amaretto liqueur
1 tablespoon lemon juice
1 tablespoon cornstarch
1 can (2½ ounces) sliced mushrooms, drained
½ cup slivered almonds
6 baked patty shells

1. Mix together flour, salt, curry powder, garlic powder and pepper. Dredge chicken in flour mixture.

2. Microwave browning dish on HIGH (100%) for 5 to 6 minutes.

3. Add butter, then chicken. Microwave on HIGH (100%) for 6 to 8 minutes or until golden. Stir halfway through cooking.

4. Mix together chicken broth, Amaretto, lemon juice and cornstarch until smooth. Stir into chicken. Add mushrooms and almonds. Microwave on HIGH (100%) for 6 to 8 minutes or until thickened.

5. To blend flavors: Microwave on LOW (30%) for 5 to 6 minutes. Spoon into patty shells. If desired, garnish with diced tomatoes and parsley.

Recipe yield: 6 servings

CHICKEN WITH YAM DRESSING

Power Level: HIGH [100%] and MEDIUM-HIGH [70%]
Total Cooking Time: 41 to 48 minutes

½ pound bulk pork sausage
½ cup chopped onion
½ cup chopped celery
1 can (16 ounces) cooked yams, drained
2 cups seasoned bread cubes
1 tablespoon parsley
1 teaspoon salt
¼ teaspoon pepper
4 pound roasting chicken
¼ cup butter (or margarine), melted

1. Place sausage in a 2 quart casserole. Microwave on HIGH (100%) for 3 to 4 minutes or until sausage is slightly pink.

2. Add onion and celery to sausage. Microwave on HIGH (100%) for 3 to 4 minutes or until tender. Drain off excess grease.

3. Stir in yams, bread cubes and seasonings.

4. Fill chicken with stuffing. Truss. Place chicken, breast side down, on a trivet in a baking dish. Shield leg and wing tips with foil. Brush with half the melted butter. Cover with waxed paper.

5. Microwave on MEDIUM-HIGH (70%) for 35 to 40 minutes or until fork tender. Turn chicken breast side up, remove shields and brush with remaining melted butter halfway through cooking.

6. Allow to stand 10 to 15 minutes before serving.

Recipe yield: 4 to 6 servings

CORNISH HEN BAKE

Power Level: HIGH [100%] and MEDIUM [50%]
Total Cooking Time: 1 hour 2 minutes to 1 hour 11 minutes

2 tablespoons butter (or margarine)
1 stalk celery, chopped
1 small onion, chopped
1 package (6 ounces) seasoned long grain and wild rice mix
1 can (10¾ ounces) cream of mushroom soup
1 cup water
2 (1 pound each) Cornish hens, cut in half
1 tablespoon Teriyaki sauce

1. Place butter, celery and onion in an 11¾ x 7½ x 1¾ inch baking dish. Microwave on HIGH (100%) for 3 to 4 minutes or until vegetables are tender.

2. Stir in rice, soup and water. Cover with plastic wrap. Microwave on HIGH (100%) for 6 to 7 minutes or until boiling. Microwave on MEDIUM (50%) for 18 to 20 minutes or until rice is softened.

3. Arrange hen halves, skin side down, over rice mixture. Brush with half of Teriyaki sauce. Cover. Microwave on MEDIUM (50%) for 35 to 40 minutes or until hens are fork tender. Turn hens, skin side up, halfway through cooking and brush with remaining Teriyaki sauce.

Recipe yield: 4 servings

CORNISH HENS WITH ALMOND DRESSING

Power Level: HIGH [100%] and MEDIUM-HIGH [70%]
Total Cooking Time: 43 to 46 minutes

¾ cup chopped almonds
½ cup chopped celery
⅓ cup butter (or margarine)
1 clove garlic, crushed
4 cups bread cubes
⅓ cup milk
1 teaspoon parsley flakes
¼ teaspoon poultry seasoning
Dash of nutmeg
4 (1 pound each) Cornish hens
1 teaspoon salt
¼ cup butter, melted
1 teaspoon paprika

1. Combine almonds, celery, ⅓ cup butter and garlic in a 3 quart casserole. Microwave on HIGH (100%) for 3 to 4 minutes or until celery is tender. Stir halfway through cooking.

2. Stir in bread cubes, milk, parsley flakes, poultry seasoning and nutmeg.

3. Sprinkle inside of hens with salt. Stuff with dressing. Truss. Combine melted butter and paprika. Brush mixture over hens.

4. Place hens, breast side down, in two cooking bags. Place in a baking dish. Cut plastic strip from open ends of cooking bags. Tie bags closed with strips.

5. Microwave on MEDIUM-HIGH (70%) for 40 to 42 minutes or until tender. Turn hens breast side up halfway through cooking. Pierce bag.

6. Allow to stand 10 to 15 minutes.

Recipe yield: 4 servings

HERBED CORNISH HENS

Power Level: MEDIUM-HIGH [70%]
Total Cooking Time: 40 to 42 minutes

1 tablespoon thyme
1 teaspoon garlic powder
1 teaspoon poultry seasoning
1 teaspoon rosemary
½ teaspoon pepper
4 (1 pound each) Cornish hens
2 tablespoons butter (or margarine), melted
¼ cup lemon juice
¼ teaspoon paprika

1. Mix together thyme, garlic powder, poultry seasoning, rosemary and pepper. Place about 1½ teaspoons of seasonings mixture into cavity of each hen. Truss.

2. Combine butter, lemon juice and paprika. Brush mixture over hens.

3. Place hens, breast side down, in two cooking bags. Place in a baking dish. Cut plastic strip from open ends of cooking bags. Tie bags closed with strips.

4. Microwave on MEDIUM-HIGH (70%) for 40 to 42 minutes or until tender. Turn hens breast side up halfway through cooking. Pierce bag.

5. Allow to stand 10 to 15 minutes before serving.

Recipe yield: 4 servings

DUCKLING A L'ORANGE

Power Level: HIGH [100%] and MEDIUM-HIGH [70%]
Total Cooking Time: 56 minutes to 1 hour 1½ minutes

4 to 5 pound ready-to-cook duckling
2 oranges, quartered
1 onion, chopped
1 teaspoon salt
Dash of pepper
¼ cup butter (or margarine)
¼ cup orange marmalade

1. Combine oranges, onion, salt and pepper. Fill duckling with orange mixture. Truss.

2. Place duckling, breast side down, on a trivet in a baking dish. Cover legs and wing tips with aluminum foil.

3. Place butter and marmalade in a 1 cup measure. Microwave on HIGH (100%) for 1 to 1½ minutes or until melted. Brush over duckling.

4. Microwave on MEDIUM-HIGH (70%) for 30 minutes.

5. Remove foil. Turn breast side up. Prick the skin to release fat. Baste duckling with drippings from pan. DRAIN OFF EXCESS GREASE.

6. Microwave on MEDIUM-HIGH (70%) for 25 to 30 minutes or until tender. Allow to stand 10 to 15 minutes before serving.

Recipe yield: 4 to 6 servings

STEWING CHICKEN

Place 2 to 3 pounds of chicken pieces in a 3-quart casserole. Add about 1 quart of water or enough to cover chicken. Add 1 teaspoon salt, 1/4 teaspoon pepper and 1 bay leaf. Chop 2 stalks of celery and one medium onion. Add vegetables to chicken. Cover with tight fitting lid or plastic wrap. Microwave on Medium [50%] for 60 to 70 minutes or until tender. Stir midway through cooking.

CHICKEN FRICASSEE

Power Level: MEDIUM [50%]
Total Cooking Time: 1 hour 5 minutes to 1 hour 10 minutes

2 to 3 pound stewing chicken, cut up
3 carrots, sliced
3 small onions, chopped
3 stalks celery, chopped
2 cups hot water
2 teaspoons salt
1/4 teaspoon pepper
2 bay leaves
3 tablespoons all purpose flour
1/2 cup cold water

1. Combine chicken, carrots, onions and celery in a 3 quart casserole. Add water, salt, pepper and bay leaves. Cover with a tight fitting lid or plastic wrap.

2. Microwave on MEDIUM (50%) for 20 minutes.

3. Mix together flour and water. Stir into stew. Cover. Microwave on MEDIUM (50%) for 45 to 50 minutes or until chicken is fork tender.

Recipe yield: 4 servings

Variations:

CHICKEN FRICASSEE AND CELERY SEED DUMPLINGS

Follow Chicken Fricassee recipe as directed. Mix together 1 cup all purpose flour, 2 teaspoons baking powder, 1/2 teaspoon salt and 1/2 teaspoon celery seed. Stir in 1/2 cup milk, 1 beaten egg and 2 tablespoons cooking oil just until dry ingredients are moistened. Drop by tablespoons into hot stew. Cover with a tight fitting lid or plastic wrap. Microwave on HIGH (100%) for 5 to 6 minutes.

CHICKEN RICE ORIENTAL CASSEROLE

Power Level: HIGH [100%] and MEDIUM-HIGH [70%]
Total Cooking Time: 18 to 22 minutes

1 cup water
2 cubes chicken bouillon
1 cup instant rice
1 tablespoon parsley flakes
1 can (10¾ ounces) cream of celery soup
1 envelope (1½ ounces) dry onion soup mix
1/4 cup dry sherry
3 cups cubed chicken (or turkey)
1 can (4 ounces) sliced mushrooms, drained
1 can (8 ounces) water chestnuts, sliced and drained
1 medium onion, thinly sliced
1 can (8 ounces) bamboo shoots, drained
2 cups grated mild Cheddar cheese
1 cup slivered almonds, toasted *

1. Place water and bouillon cubes in an 11¾ x 7½ x 1¾ inch baking dish. Cover with plastic wrap. Microwave 3 to 4 minutes on HIGH (100%) or until boiling. Stir occasionally to dissolve bouillon.

2. Stir in rice and parsley flakes. Cover and set aside while preparing sauce.

3. Combine cream of celery soup, dry onion soup mix and sherry.

4. Place alternate layers of sauce and remaining ingredients over rice, reserving 1 cup cheese and 1/2 cup almonds. Top with sauce. Sprinkle with reserved cheese and almonds.

5. Microwave on MEDIUM-HIGH (70%) for 15 to 18 minutes or until heated through. Turn dish halfway through cooking.

Recipe yield: 8 to 10 servings

*If microwave has a browning element, brown as desired.

WHOLE TURKEY

Power Level: MEDIUM-HIGH [70%]
Total Cooking Time: 10 to 12 minutes per pound

1 whole turkey
1 tablespoon salt
Stuffing (optional)
1/2 cup oil (melted butter or margarine)

1. Rinse turkey with cold water and pat dry.

2. Salt cavity. If desired, fill turkey with stuffing. Truss.

3. Bend wings around back. Protect wing and drumstick tips with aluminum foil.

4. Place turkey, breast side down, on a trivet in a baking dish. Brush with oil. Cover with waxed paper.

5. Microwave on MEDIUM-HIGH (70%) until tender. Turn turkey breast side up halfway through cooking. Remove foil. Baste frequently with drippings from dish. Remove excess drippings.

6. Allow to stand for 25 to 30 minutes before serving.

7. Serve with Traditional Turkey Dressing (page 163) and Giblet Gravy or Basic Gravy (page 106).

TURKEY DIVAN

Power Level: HIGH [100%] and MEDIUM [50%]
Total Cooking Time: 16 to 20 minutes

1 package (10 ounces) frozen broccoli
10 slices cooked turkey (or chicken)
1 can (10¾ ounces) cream of celery soup
1/4 cup milk
1/4 cup grated Parmesan cheese
1/4 cup grated Cheddar cheese
Dash of paprika

1. Place broccoli in a 1 quart casserole. Cover with a tight fitting lid or plastic wrap. Microwave on HIGH (100%) for 6 to 8 minutes or until tender. Drain.

2. Cover broccoli with turkey slices.

3. Mix together soup and milk. Stir in cheeses. Pour over turkey. Sprinkle with paprika. Cover.

4. Microwave on MEDIUM (50%) for 10 to 12 minutes or until heated through.

Recipe yield: 4 to 6 servings

TRADITIONAL TURKEY DRESSING

Power Level: HIGH [100%]
Total Cooking Time: 8 to 10 minutes

½ cup butter (or margarine)
3 cups chopped celery
1 cup chopped onion
1 cup sliced mushrooms
½ cup chopped parsley
1 tablespoon salt
1 tablespoon poultry seasoning
1 teaspoon paprika
½ teaspoon pepper
2 eggs, slightly beaten
10 cups soft bread cubes

1. Place butter, celery, onion and mushrooms in a large glass mixing bowl. Microwave on HIGH (100%) for 8 to 10 minutes or until tender.

2. Add remaining ingredients. Toss lightly until well mixed.

3. Spoon stuffing into turkey cavity.

Recipe yield: Stuffing for 10 to 12 pound turkey

Variation:
TRADITIONAL CHICKEN DRESSING

Follow Traditional Turkey Dressing recipe except cut all ingredients in half.

TURKEY AND RICE BAKE

Power Level: HIGH [100%]
Total Cooking Time: 8 to 10 minutes

1½ cups cooked rice
3 cups cubed cooked turkey
½ cup chopped celery
¼ cup chopped onion
1 can (8 ounces) water chestnuts, drained and sliced
½ cup slivered almonds
1 can (4 ounces) chopped mushrooms, drained
1 can (10¾ ounces) cream of celery soup
½ cup chicken broth
2 tablespoons chopped pimento
2 tablespoons soy sauce

1. Combine all ingredients in a 3 quart casserole. Cover with a tight fitting lid or plastic wrap.

2. Microwave on HIGH (100%) for 8 to 10 minutes, or until heated through. Stir occasionally.

Recipe yield: 4 to 6 servings

DEFROSTING TURKEY

Defrost turkey 5 to 6 minutes per pound. *First place wrapped turkey in baking dish in oven. It is unnecessary to remove the small metal clasp because of the large mass of food. Microwave on Low [30%] for half defrosting time. Turn turkey over midway through.*

30 Min. Standing Time

Remove turkey *from microwave. Keep wrapped and allow to stand for 30 minutes. Remove wrapping and shield wing tips and legs. Return to oven and microwave on Low [30%] for second half of defrosting time, turning bird over midway through. Remove from microwave and allow turkey to stand another 30 minutes.*

30 Min. Standing Time

Run cold water *into turkey to remove giblets and neck. Turkey should feel soft and cold. Inside, it may still be a bit icy. If turkey has metal clamps on legs, remove at this time.*

COOKING TURKEY

Brush turkey *with butter, oil or browning agent. Shield wing tips and leg ends. Place turkey breast side down on trivet in baking dish. If bird is large, you may be unable to use trivet. Cover with waxed paper. Halfway through cooking, turn turkey breast side up and remove shields.*

If using a roasting bag, *be sure to lightly oil the inside of bag over the breast area to keep it from sticking.*

TURKEY COOKING CHART

Power Level: MEDIUM-HIGH (70%)	
Item	**Cooking Time**
Whole Turkey (10-12 pounds) (In cooking bag)	10-12 min. per lb. 6-8 min. per lb.
Turkey Legs 1 2 4	22-24 min. per lb. 16-18 min. per lb. 10-12 min. per lb.
(In cooking bag) 1 2 4	12-14 min. per lb. 10-12 min. per lb. 8-10 min. per lb.
Turkey Halves (In cooking bag)	10-12 min. per lb. 6-8 min. per lb.
Turkey Breasts (In cooking bag)	16-18 min. per lb. 8-10 min. per lb.
Frozen Turkey Roast (2-4 lbs.) Add ½ cup water DO NOT DEFROST	16-18 min. per lb.

Puddings & Custards

Smooth, creamy custards and perfect puddings are so simple in the microwave.

Baked Custard [page 168], Soft Custard and Rice Pudding are luscious and creamy.

Constant stirring and scorching are things of the past. Because the microwave will not dry or brown those delicate custards, there is no need to set them in a pan of water when cooking.

RICE PUDDING

Power Level: HIGH [100%] and
LOW [30%]
Total Cooking Time: 23 to 29 minutes

2 cups milk
1 cup cooked rice
2 eggs, beaten
½ cup sugar
½ cup raisins
1 teaspoon vanilla
½ teaspoon cinnamon

1. Pour milk in a 4 cup measure. Microwave on HIGH (100%) for 3 to 4 minutes or until steaming.

2. Mix together remaining ingredients in a 2 quart casserole until well blended. Stir in hot milk. Cover with a tight fitting lid or plastic wrap.

3. Microwave on LOW (30%) for 20 to 25 minutes or until a knife inserted near edge comes out clean.

4. Remove cover immediately and allow to stand on a solid surface until center is set. Serve warm or cool.

Recipe yield: 4 to 6 servings

SOFT CUSTARD

Power Level: MEDIUM HIGH [70%]
Total Cooking Time: 7 to 9 minutes

1½ cups milk (or half and half)
⅓ cup sugar
2½ tablespoons cornstarch
3 eggs (or 6 egg yolks), beaten
¼ teaspoon salt
1 teaspoon vanilla

1. Mix together milk, sugar, cornstarch and salt in a 1 quart casserole until well blended. Microwave on HIGH (100%) for 6 to 7 minutes or until thickened.

2. Stir a little hot mixture into eggs, then stir egg mixture into remaining hot mixture. Microwave on MEDIUM-HIGH (70%) for 1 to 2 minutes. Stir mixture occasionally.

3. Stir in vanilla. Chill until ready to serve. Pour into serving dishes or serve as a sauce.

Variation:

FLOATING ISLAND CUSTARD

Follow Soft Custard recipe as directed. Cool custard to room temperature. Leave in casserole or divide into individual serving dishes. Beat together 2 egg whites and ¼ teaspoon cream of tartar until foamy. Gradually beat in ¼ cup sugar until stiff peaks form. Place mounds of meringue on custard(s). Microwave on MEDIUM (50%) for 3 to 4 minutes or until meringue is set.

Recipe yield: 4 to 6 servings

BREAD PUDDING

Power Level: HIGH [100%] and
LOW [30%]
Total Cooking Time: 38 to 44 minutes

3 or 4 slices bread, toasted, buttered and cut into fourths
½ cup raisins (or currants)
2½ cups milk
3 eggs
½ cup brown sugar
1 teaspoon vanilla
¼ teaspoon salt
¼ teaspoon cinnamon

1. Place bread in a greased 2 quart casserole. Sprinkle with raisins. Set aside.

2. Pour milk into a 4 cup measure. Microwave on HIGH (100%) for 3 to 4 minutes or until steaming.

3. Mix together eggs, sugar (reserving 2 tablespoons), vanilla and salt. Stir a little hot milk into egg mixture, then stir the egg mixture into remaining hot milk. Pour over bread and raisins, pressing bread down to absorb liquid. Cover with waxed paper. Allow to stand 10 minutes.

4. Mix together reserved sugar and cinnamon. Sprinkle over custard. Cover.

5. Microwave on LOW (30%) for 35 to 40 minutes or until a knife inserted near edge comes out clean.

6. Remove cover immediately and allow to stand on a solid surface until center is set. Serve warm or cool.

Recipe yield: 4 to 6 servings

TAPIOCA PUDDING

Power Level: HIGH [100%]
Total Cooking Time: 4 to 6 minutes

¼ cup sugar
2 eggs, separated
3 tablespoons quick-cooking tapioca
¼ teaspoon salt
2 cups milk
2 tablespoons sugar
1 teaspoon vanilla

1. Mix together sugar, egg yolks, tapioca, salt and ½ cup milk in a 4 cup measure until smooth. Stir in remaining milk.

2. Microwave on HIGH (100%) for 4 to 6 minutes or until boiling. Stir mixture occasionally during last half of cooking.

3. Beat egg whites until foamy. Gradually beat in 2 tablespoons sugar and vanilla until soft peaks form.

4. Fold in hot tapioca mixture. Serve warm or cold.

Recipe yield: 4 to 6 servings

PUDDINGS

Blend together *sugar, cornstarch, salt and ¹/₂ cup milk. When mixture is smooth and paste-like, add remainder of milk. Microwave on High [100%] until thickened.*

Stir a small amount *of hot pudding into the egg yolks. Then stir egg yolk mixture into the hot pudding. Microwave until mixture begins to boil. Pudding will be thin if overcooked.*

Stir in butter and vanilla. *Chill until ready to serve or pour into individual serving dishes and chill.*

VANILLA PUDDING

Power Level: HIGH [100%]
Total Cooking Time: 5³/₄ to 7 minutes

²/₃ cup sugar
¹/₃ cup cornstarch
¹/₄ teaspoon salt
2 cups milk
2 eggs, slightly beaten
2 tablespoons butter
 (or margarine)
1¹/₂ teaspoons vanilla

1. Mix together sugar, cornstarch, salt and ¹/₂ cup milk in a 4 cup measure until smooth. Stir in remaining milk. Microwave on HIGH (100%) for 5 to 6 minutes or until smooth and thickened. Stir occasionally during last half of cooking.

2. Stir a small amount of hot mixture into eggs, then stir egg mixture into remaining hot mixture. Microwave on HIGH (100%) for 45 seconds to 1 minute or until mixture just begins to boil.

3. Stir in butter and vanilla until well blended. Pour into individual serving dishes. Chill until ready to serve.

Variations:

CHOCOLATE PUDDING

Follow Vanilla Pudding recipe as directed except increase sugar to 1 cup and add 2 squares (1 ounce each) melted unsweetened chocolate in Step 2. To melt chocolate: Microwave on HIGH (100%) for 2 to 2¹/₂ minutes.

BUTTERSCOTCH PUDDING

Follow Vanilla Pudding recipe as directed except substitute brown sugar for sugar and increase butter to 3 tablespoons.

PUDDING SAUCE

Follow Vanilla, Chocolate or Butterscotch recipe as directed except increase milk to 2¹/₂ cups. Serve over pound cake or gingerbread.

Recipe yield: 4 to 6 servings

PEANUT BUTTER CRUNCH PUDDING

Power Level: HIGH [100%]
Total Cooking Time: 4 to 6 minutes

1 package (2¹/₄ ounces)
 custard-flavored dessert mix
¹/₂ cup crunchy-style peanut butter
2 cups milk (or half and half)
¹/₄ cup chopped peanuts

1. Mix dessert mix, peanut butter and ¹/₂ cup milk until smooth. Stir in remaining milk.

2. Microwave on HIGH (100%) for 4 to 6 minutes or until boiling.

3. Pour into six individual serving dishes or 6 ounce custard cups. Garnish with chopped peanuts.

4. Chill until ready to serve.

Recipe yield: 4 to 6 servings

APPLE AND RAISIN BREAD PUDDING DESSERT

Power Level: HIGH [100%]
 and LOW [30%]
Total Cooking Time: 25¹/₂ to
 30³/₄ minutes

¹/₄ cup butter (or margarine)
¹/₂ cup brown sugar
3 cups sliced cooking apples
¹/₂ cup raisins
¹/₂ cup nuts (walnuts or pecans)
2 cups toasted bread cubes
 (or day old)
1¹/₄ cups applesauce
2 eggs, beaten
¹/₄ cup milk
1 teaspoon vanilla
¹/₂ teaspoon cinnamon
¹/₄ teaspoon cloves
¹/₄ teaspoon salt

1. Place butter in a 2 quart casserole. Microwave on HIGH (100%) for 30 to 45 seconds or until melted. Stir in brown sugar, apples, raisins and nuts until apples are coated.

2. Stir in bread cubes, applesauce, eggs, milk, vanilla, cinnamon, cloves and salt until well blended. Cover with a tight fitting lid or plastic wrap.

3. Microwave on LOW (30%) for 25 to 30 minutes or until a knife inserted near edge comes out clean.

4. Remove cover immediately and allow to stand on a solid surface until center is set. Serve warm or cool topped with whipped cream.

Recipe yield: 6 to 8 servings

Apple and Raisin Bread Pudding Dessert is delicious any time.

INDIAN PUDDING

Power Level: HIGH [100%] and
*   MEDIUM-HIGH [70%]*
Total Cooking Time: 27 to 34 minutes

2 cups milk
½ cup cornmeal
2 cups apples, thinly sliced
½ cup raisins (optional)
½ cup sugar
½ cup dark molasses
2 eggs, slightly beaten
2 tablespoons butter
** (or margarine)**
1 teaspoon salt
½ teaspoon ginger
½ teaspoon cinnamon

1. Pour milk into a 2 quart casserole. Microwave on HIGH (100%) for 3 to 4 minutes or until steaming.

2. Add cornmeal. Microwave on MEDIUM-HIGH (70%) for 4 to 5 minutes or until smooth and thickened. Stir halfway through cooking.

3. Stir in remaining ingredients.

4. Microwave on MEDIUM-HIGH (70%) for 20 to 25 minutes or until a knife inserted near center comes out clean. Serve warm.

Recipe yield: 4 to 6 servings

CUSTARDS

Heat milk *in measuring cup on High [100%] for 4 to 5 minutes. Milk should not boil.*

Pour milk into a mixture of sugar, *salt, vanilla and egg. Mix with wooden whisk or spoon.*

Pour into individual custard cups *and garnish with nutmeg or pour into 1½ quart casserole.*

Cover with plastic wrap *or tight fitting lid for fast, even cooking. Microwave on Low [30%]. Slow cooking prevents curdling.*

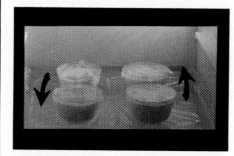

Rearrange cups *once or twice during cooking. Move back cups to front and front cups to back.*

Test for doneness. *Insert a knife ½ inch from edge. Remove from oven when knife comes out clean and custard in center still quivers. Remove cover immediately after taking custard from oven. Place bowl or cups on solid, heat resistant surface until custard center is set.*

BAKED CUSTARD

Power Level: HIGH [100%] and LOW [30%]
Total Cooking Time: 23 to 26 minutes

1¾ cups milk
3 eggs
⅓ cup sugar
¼ teaspoon salt
1 teaspoon vanilla
Nutmeg

1. Place milk in a 2 cup measure. Microwave on HIGH (100%) for 4 to 5 minutes or until steaming.

2. Mix together remaining ingredients, except nutmeg, in a 1½ quart casserole until well blended. Sprinkle with nutmeg. Cover with tight fitting lid or plastic wrap.

3. Microwave on LOW (30%) for 14 to 16 minutes or until a knife inserted near edge comes out clean. Turn dish a half turn halfway through cooking.

4. Remove cover immediately and allow to stand on a solid heat resistant surface until center is set. Serve warm or cool.

Variation:

INDIVIDUAL BAKED CUSTARD

Follow Baked Custard recipe as directed except mix in a 4 cup measure and divide custard into four 6 ounce custard cups. Cover. Microwave on LOW (30%) for 12 to 14 minutes.* Rearrange cups halfway through cooking.

Recipe yield: 4 servings

*Custards may cook at different rates. Remove custards from oven as they finish cooking.

PUDDING AND CUSTARD MIXES
Power Level: HIGH [100%]

1. Combine mix and ½ cup milk. Stir until mix is smooth. Stir in remaining milk.

2. Microwave until thickened and boiling. Stir occasionally during last half of cooking.

3. Pour into individual serving dishes and chill until ready to serve.

Item	Amount of Milk	Utensil	Power Level	Time
Pudding Mix (not instant) (3-1/8 ounces)	2 cups	4 cup measure	High (100%)	6 to 8 minutes
Pudding Mix (not instant) (4¾ ounces)	3 cups	1½ quart casserole	High (100%)	8 to 10 minutes
Golden Egg Custard Mix (4½ ounces)	3 cups	4 cup measure	Medium-High (70%)	7 to 9 minutes

HONEY N' CREME CUSTARD

Power Level: LOW [30%]
Total Cooking Time: 38 to 40 minutes

4 eggs
2½ cups half and half
½ cup honey
¼ teaspoon salt
½ teaspoon vanilla
Cinnamon (optional)

1. Mix all ingredients, except cinnamon, in a 2 quart casserole until well blended. Sprinkle with cinnamon. Cover with a tight fitting lid or plastic wrap.

2. Microwave on LOW (30%) for 38 to 40 minutes or until knife inserted near edge comes out clean. Turn dish a half turn halfway through cooking.

3. Remove cover immediately and allow to stand on a solid surface until center is set. Serve warm or cool.

Variation:

INDIVIDUAL CUSTARDS

Follow recipe as directed except divide custard into eight 6 ounce custard cups. Cover. Microwave on LOW (30%) for 28 to 30 minutes.* Rearrange cups halfway through cooking.

Recipe yield: 6 to 8 servings

*Custards may cook at different rates. Remove custards from oven as they finish cooking.

GERMAN CHOCOLATE MOUSSE

[Illustrated at right]
Power Level: HIGH [100%]
Total Cooking Time: 5 to 8 minutes

1 package (4 ounces) German
** Sweet Chocolate**
1 cup milk (or half and half)
3 eggs, separated
1 envelope unflavored gelatin
¼ teaspoon salt
1 teaspoon vanilla
1 cup whipping cream
⅓ cup sugar

1. Break chocolate into pieces and place in a large mixing bowl. Microwave on HIGH (100%) for 2 to 4 minutes or until melted.

2. Stir in milk, egg yolks, gelatin and salt. Microwave on HIGH (100%) for 3 to 4 minutes or until thickened. Stir occasionally during last half of cooking. Stir in vanilla. Cool.

3. Beat whipping cream into soft peaks. Set aside.

4. Beat egg whites until foamy. Gradually beat in sugar until stiff peaks form.

5. Fold egg whites and whipping cream into cooled chocolate mixture. Pour into serving dishes. Chill.

Recipe yield: 8 servings

169

Sandwiches

Everyone enjoys a hot sandwich. It takes just seconds to warm sandwiches, and heating on paper towels or napkins reduces clean up.

Choose breads that are firm textured or toast the bread first to help keep the sandwich filling from soaking into the bread. Remember bread is porous, so it heats very quickly in a microwave and becomes tough when overheated.

Wrap sandwich *in paper towel or napkin to help absorb the excess moisture which comes to the surface of the bread. Place open faced sandwich on top of paper towel or napkin.*

Cheese cooks quickly *so heat only until it begins to melt. Overheated cheese will get tough and rubbery. Leave at least a half-inch space between each sandwich to assure even heating.*

Thin slices of meat *will heat more evenly and cook faster when you make sandwiches in the microwave.*

Fast food sandwiches *can be brought home and quickly reheated right in the carry-out container. However, do not reheat in a foil or foil lined wrapper.*

In a combination sandwich, *put the cheese between layers of meat or add just for the last 30 to 45 seconds of heating.*

The temperature probe *automatically helps you heat sandwiches to the proper temperature. Be sure the tip of the probe is in the center of the filling. Most sandwiches should be heated at 110°. When not using the temperature probe, heat only until surface feels warm. Overheating causes bread to become tough, rubbery and eventually hard.*

Do not *use plastic or colored toothpicks to hold sandwich together. The plastic can melt. Color from toothpicks or a napkin can seep into the sandwich. Picks with cellophane frills can be used.*

CHICKEN DIVAN SANDWICH
Power Level: HIGH [100%]
Total Cooking Time: 8 to 10 minutes

1 package (10 ounces) frozen
  broccoli spears
1½ cups chopped cooked chicken
  (or turkey)
1 can (10¾ ounces) condensed
  Cheddar cheese soup
4 English muffins, split in half and
  toasted (or 8 slices of toast)
Parsley
Bacon bits

1. Place frozen broccoli spears in a 1
quart casserole. Cover with plastic wrap
or a tight fitting lid. Microwave on HIGH
(100%) for 5 to 6 minutes or until
partially cooked. Drain well.

2. Mix together chicken and cheese
soup.

3. Place toasted English muffin halves
in an 11¾x7½x1¾ inch baking dish.
Top with broccoli and chicken mixture.

4. Microwave on HIGH (100%) for 3
to 4 minutes or until hot and bubbly.
Garnish with parsley and bacon bits.

Recipe yield: 6 to 8 servings

CHILIBURGERS
Power Level: HIGH [100%]
*Total Cooking Time: 14½ to
                    18¾ minutes*

2 pounds ground beef
1 small onion, chopped
1 cup chopped celery
1 can (8 ounces) tomato sauce
1 cup catsup

¼ cup Worcestershire sauce
1 teaspoon sugar
1 teaspoon garlic salt
½ teaspoon chili powder
¼ teaspoon hot pepper sauce
10 to 12 sandwich buns

1. Combine ground beef, onion and
celery in a 2 quart casserole. Microwave
on HIGH (100%) for 6 to 8 minutes or
until meat is pink in center. Stir halfway
through cooking. Drain off excess fat.

2. Stir in remaining ingredients except
sandwich buns. Cover with plastic wrap
or a tight fitting lid.

3. Microwave on HIGH (100%) for 8
to 10 minutes or until hot and bubbly.

4. Remove twister from bun package. Open end. Microwave on HIGH
(100%) for 30 to 45 seconds or until
surface feels warm.

5. Spoon chili sauce into heated buns.

Recipe yield: 10 to 12 servings

TUNA MELT-WICHES
Power Level: HIGH [100%]
Total Cooking Time: 2 to 2½ minutes

4 English muffins, cut in half
  and toasted
Butter (or margarine), softened
1 can (6½ ounces) tuna, drained
1 cup (4 ounces) grated Cheddar
  cheese
2 hard-cooked eggs, chopped
½ cup mayonnaise
¼ cup chopped celery
¼ cup chopped onion
2 tablespoons pickle relish
1 teaspoon prepared mustard
Stuffed green olives (or parsley)

1. Place toasted muffins on a paper
towel on paper plate. Butter cut side.

2. Mix together remaining ingredients.
Spoon filling over muffins.

3. Microwave on HIGH (100%) for 2
to 2½ minutes or until cheese begins to
melt. Garnish with slices of green olives
or pieces of parsley.

Recipe yield: 8 servings

BARBECUED SANDWICHES
Power Level: HIGH [100%]
*Total Cooking Time: 4½ to
                    6½ minutes*

1 cup catsup
¼ cup finely chopped onion
¼ cup brown sugar
2 tablespoons lemon juice
2 teaspoons Worcestershire sauce
¼ teaspoon pepper
¼ teaspoon chili powder
¼ teaspoon onion salt
Dash of hot pepper sauce
Dash of garlic powder
2 cups shredded cooked roast beef
  (or chipped ham)
6 large sandwich buns

1. Mix all ingredients except meat and
buns in a 1 quart casserole.

2. Microwave on HIGH (100%) for 2
to 3½ minutes or until boiling. Stir
occasionally.

3. Stir meat into sauce. Microwave on
HIGH (100%) for 1½ to 2 minutes or
until hot and bubbly.

4. Spoon meat on bottom half of buns
and top with other half of bun. Wrap in
paper towels or napkins, or place on a
paper towel lined plate. Microwave on
HIGH (100%) for 1 minute.

Recipe yield: 6 servings

*Make a lunch
date with our
Italian Hero.*

ITALIAN HERO

Power Level: HIGH [100%]
Total Cooking Time: 5½ to 7 minutes

1 pound ground beef
1 can (8 ounces) tomato sauce
¼ cup grated Parmesan cheese
¼ cup chopped onion
¼ cup chopped ripe olives
  (optional)
1 teaspoon parsley
½ teaspoon oregano
½ teaspoon salt
Dash of pepper
1 loaf Italian bread, unsliced
2 medium tomatoes, sliced
1 package (8 ounces) mozzarella
  cheese, sliced

1. Place meat in a 1 quart casserole. Microwave on HIGH (100%) for 4 to 5 minutes or until no longer pink. Stir halfway through cooking. Drain off excess fat.

2. Stir in tomato sauce, Parmesan cheese, onions, olives and seasonings.

3. Slice Italian bread in half lengthwise and place on paper plate or paper towels. Spread meat sauce over both halves of bread.

4. Top each with tomato slices and mozzarella cheese. Cover with waxed paper. Microwave on HIGH (100%) for 1½ to 2 minutes, or until cheese begins to melt. Slice each half into 4 to 6 sections.

Recipe yield: 8 to 12 servings

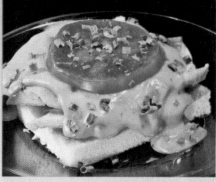

HOT CLUBHOUSE SANDWICHES

Power Level: LOW [30%] and
*   HIGH [100%]*
Total Cooking Time: 3½ to 4¾ minutes

4 slices bread, toasted and
  trimmed
4 slices cooked turkey (or chicken)
4 slices cooked ham
2 tablespoons butter
  (or margarine)
1 can (10½ ounces) condensed
  cream of mushroom soup
2 tablespoons Worcestershire
  sauce
1 medium tomato, sliced
2 tablespoons chopped chives

1. Arrange the slices of toasted bread in an 8x8x2 inch glass dish. Layer turkey and ham on bread.

2. Place butter in a 1 quart casserole. Microwave on LOW (30%) for 30 to 45 seconds or until softened. Stir in soup and Worcestershire sauce until smooth. Pour over sandwiches.

3. Microwave on HIGH (100%) for 3 to 4 minutes or until bubbly.

4. Garnish with tomato slices and chopped chives.

Recipe yield: 4 servings

HAM-SWISS CHEESE BUNS

Power Level: LOW [30%]
*   HIGH [100%]*
Total Cooking Time: 2¾ to 3½ minutes
Temperature Probe: 110°

½ cup butter (or margarine)
¼ cup grated onion
¼ cup prepared mustard
1 tablespoon poppy seeds
6 large sandwich buns
12 slices boiled ham
6 slices Swiss cheese
1 medium tomato, sliced

1. Place butter in a small bowl. Microwave on LOW (30%) for 45 seconds to 1 minute or until softened. Add onion, mustard and poppy seeds. Mix until smooth. Spread on cut side of buns.

2. Place two slices of ham on bottom half of bun. Top with cheese, tomato and other half of bun. Wrap in paper towels or napkins or place on a paper lined plate.

3. Microwave on HIGH (100%) for 2 to 2½ minutes or until cheese begins to melt.

Recipe yield: 6 servings

TOASTED CHEESE SANDWICH

Power Level: MEDIUM-HIGH [70%]

For each sandwich:

1. Toast bread. Butter toast. Sandwich 2 thin slices of cheese between two pieces of toast.

2. Place sandwich(es) on a paper towel lined plate.

3. Microwave on MEDIUM-HIGH (70%).

Amount	Time
1	30 seconds
2	45 seconds
3	1 minute
4	1¼ minutes
6	1½ minutes

HOT HAM SALAD SANDWICH

Power Level: HIGH [100%]
Total Cooking Time: 2 to 2½ minutes
Temperature Probe: 110°

1 cup chopped cooked ham
2 hard-cooked eggs, chopped
  (Cook eggs on conventional range.)
½ cup chopped celery
¼ cup pickle relish
¼ cup mayonnaise
¼ teaspoon dry mustard
¼ teaspoon salt
Dash of pepper
4 sandwich buns, split

1. Mix together all ingredients except sandwich buns.

2. Spread ham salad on bottom half of buns. Top with other half of bun. Wrap in paper towels or napkins.

3. Microwave on HIGH (100%) for 2 to 2½ minutes or until surface feels warm. Serve warm.

Recipe yield: 4 servings

EASY REUBENS

Power Level: HIGH [100%]
Total Cooking Time: 1 to 2 minutes

6 ounces sliced corned beef,
  chopped
½ cup sauerkraut, drained and
  chopped
2 tablespoons salad dressing
½ teaspoon horseradish
¼ teaspoon salt
Dash of hot pepper sauce
2 tablespoons butter
  (or margarine), melted
4 slices rye bread, toasted
4 slices Swiss cheese

1. Mix together corned beef, sauerkraut, salad dressing, horseradish, salt and hot pepper sauce.

2. Butter one side of bread.

3. Spread buttered side of bread with 3 tablespoons of corned beef mixture and a slice of cheese. Place on paper towel or paper plate.

4. Microwave on HIGH (100%) for 1 to 2 minutes or until cheese begins to melt.

Recipe yield: 4 servings

CHEESEBURGER

Power Level: HIGH [100%]
  LOW [30%]
Total Cooking Time: 4½ to
  6¼ minutes

1 pound lean ground beef
¼ cup chopped onion
2 teaspoons Worcestershire sauce
½ teaspoon salt
¼ teaspoon pepper
2 tablespoons butter
  (or margarine)
1 cup grated Cheddar cheese
1 teaspoon prepared mustard
4 sandwich buns, split

1. Combine beef, onion, Worcestershire sauce, salt and pepper. Form into 4 patties. Place in an 8x8x2 inch baking dish.* Cover with waxed paper. Microwave on HIGH (100%) for 3 to 4 minutes.

2. Place butter in a small bowl or a 2 cup measure. Microwave on LOW (30%) for 30 to 45 seconds or until softened. Add cheese and mustard. Mix until smooth.

3. Place hamburger on bottom half of a bun. Top with cheese sauce and other half of bun. Wrap in paper towels or napkins.

4. Microwave on HIGH (100%) for 1 to 1½ minutes or until cheese begins to melt.

*Use a trivet for drier hamburgers.

Recipe yield: 4 servings

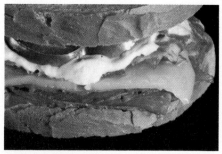

DELI-SPECIAL

Power Level: HIGH [100%]
Total Cooking Time: 2 to 3 minutes
Temperature Probe: 110°

⅓ cup mayonnaise (or salad
  dressing)
1 tablespoon horseradish
¼ teaspoon salt
Dash of pepper
⅓ cup shredded cabbage
¼ pound pastrami, sliced thin
¼ pound Swiss cheese, sliced
¼ pound corned beef, sliced thin
4 large rye rolls (or 8 slices
  rye bread)
1 green pepper, sliced in rings

1. Mix together mayonnaise, horseradish, salt and pepper. Add cabbage and toss until well coated.

2. Place a layer of pastrami, cheese, corned beef and cabbage mixture on the bottom half of each roll. Top with green pepper and other half of roll. Wrap in or place on paper towels or napkins.

3. Microwave on HIGH (100%) for 2 to 3 minutes or until cheese begins to melt.

Recipe yield: 4 servings

Everything you wanted to know about hot dogs

BASIC HOT DOGS

Power Level: HIGH [100%]

1. Score top of wiener(s) with diagonal slashes. This prevents any curling or splitting which may result during rapid cooking. It also adds a decorative touch.

2. Place wiener(s) in bun(s). Top with desired condiment(s) and/or sauce(s).

3. Wrap in a paper towel or napkin to prevent bun from becoming soggy.

4. Follow chart below for basic hot dogs and variations.

Amount	Time
1	30-45 sec.
2	45 sec.-1 min.
3	1-1½ min.
4	1½-2 min.
6	2-2½ min.

FOOT LONGS

Follow hot dog recipe as directed except microwave according to chart below:

Amount	Time
1	45 sec.-1 min.
2	1-1¼ min.
3	1¼-1¾ min.
4	1¾-2 min.

BACONY FRANKS

Wrap each wiener with partially cooked bacon before placing on bun.

MEXICAN FRANKS

Slash wiener(s) lengthwise but not completely through. Place in bun. Spoon chili sauce in center of each wiener. After microwaving, sprinkle with chopped lettuce, chopped onion, grated Cheddar cheese and, if desired, chopped chilies.

GERMAN FRANKS

Slash wiener(s) lengthwise but not completely through. Toast cut side of bun(s) under broiler of conventional range. Butter toasted side. Place wiener, split side down, on bottom half of bun. Layer each wiener with well-drained sauerkraut, a slice of Swiss cheese, Russian dressing and caraway seeds. Top with the other half of bun.

CHEESY FRANKS

Slash wiener(s) lengthwise but not completely through. Place in bun. Fill center of wiener with a ¼ inch thick slice of cheese. Place on a paper towel or napkin.

PIZZA FRANKS

Slash wiener(s) lengthwise but not completely through. Place in a bun. Spread center of each wiener with catsup (or tomato sauce); sprinkle with Italian seasoning and Mozzarella cheese (or Parmesan cheese) and, if desired, top with chopped pepperoni.

CONEY ISLANDS

Slash wiener(s) lengthwise but not completely through. Place in a bun. Spread center of each wiener with mustard; top with canned chili without beans; sprinkle with chopped onions and, if desired, grated Cheddar cheese.

SURPRISE TREATS

Tie a ribbon around the wrapped hot dog. Place on a paper plate and allow each child to cook his own hot dog. Serve with carrot sticks, pickles, celery and radishes.

Soups

Say "Welcome Home!" with a hot bowl of soup for a hearty meal or a quick after-school snack. Save washing extra pots and pans when you prepare, cook and serve the soup in your favorite tureen.

The power level, cooking times and procedures will vary depending on the quantity and consistency of foods used in the soup. Most soups cook faster and more evenly when covered with plastic wrap or a tight-fitting lid. Cream soups are an exception. Cook them uncovered to allow more frequent stirring to evenly distribute the heat.

Allow room for soups to boil by using a larger container than might first appear necessary.

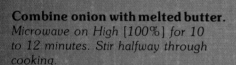

Combine onion with melted butter. *Microwave on High [100%] for 10 to 12 minutes. Stir halfway through cooking.*

Add beef broth. *Worcestershire sauce, soy sauce, salt and pepper. Cover with tight lid or plastic wrap. Microwave on High [100%] for 12 to 15 minutes or until soup begins to boil.*

Garnish each serving *with a piece of toast and Mozzarella cheese. First cut the toast with a large cookie cutter then use a smaller cookie cutter of the same design to cut out the cheese.*

FRENCH ONION SOUP

Power Level: HIGH [100%]
Total Cooking Time: 22¾ to 28 minutes
Temperature Probe: 150° to 160°

4 to 5 large onions, sliced
¼ cup butter (or margarine)
3 cans (13¾ ounces each) condensed beef broth *
1 tablespoon Worcestershire sauce
1 tablespoon soy sauce
¼ teaspoon salt
Dash of pepper
2 slices bread, toasted, buttered and cut into fourths
Grated Parmesan cheese
8 slices Mozzarella cheese

1. Combine onion and butter in a 3 quart casserole. Microwave on HIGH (100%) for 10 to 12 minutes or until onion is tender. Stir halfway through cooking.

2. Add broth, Worcestershire sauce, soy sauce, salt and pepper. Cover with tight fitting lid or plastic wrap.

3. Microwave on HIGH (100%) for 12 to 15 minutes or until soup just begins to boil.

4. Garnish each serving with a piece of toast, Parmesan cheese and a slice of Mozzarella cheese.

5. Microwave, 4 servings at a time, on HIGH (100%) for 45 seconds to 1 minute or until cheese just begins to melt.

Recipe yield: 8 servings

*Tip: Substitute 4 beef bouillon cubes dissolved in 4 cups boiling water for condensed beef broth.

ZUCCHINI SOUP

Power Level: HIGH [100%]
Total Cooking Time: 15 to 20 minutes

3 cups (1½ pounds) zucchini, trim ends and slice thin
1 cup beef broth
1 can (8 ounces) tomato sauce
½ cup chopped onion
2 tablespoons chopped parsley
1 teaspoon salt
¼ teaspoon garlic powder
¼ teaspoon basil
¼ teaspoon oregano
¼ teaspoon pepper
Grated Parmesan cheese

1. Place all ingredients in a 2 quart casserole. Cover with a tight fitting lid or plastic wrap.

2. Microwave on HIGH (100%) for 15 to 20 minutes or until zucchini is tender. Stir halfway through cooking.

3. Garnish each serving with cheese.

Recipe yield: 4 to 6 servings

MEATBALL SOUP

Power Level: HIGH [100%] and
MEDIUM-HIGH [70%]
Total Cooking Time: 51 to 68 minutes

1 pound ground chuck
½ cup dry bread crumbs
¼ cup chopped onion
1 egg
½ teaspoon salt
Dash of pepper
2 quarts water
3 beef bouillon cubes
1 can (1 pound) tomatoes, chopped
1 cup quick cooking barley
2 medium onions, cut into fourths
1 carrot, chopped
1 stalk celery, chopped
1 teaspoon salt

1. Mix together ground chuck, bread crumbs, onion, egg, salt and pepper. Form into 1 inch meatballs. Place in a 4 quart casserole. Microwave on HIGH (100%) for 6 to 8 minutes or until no longer pink. Rearrange halfway through cooking.

2. Add remaining ingredients. Cover with a tight fitting lid or plastic wrap.

3. Microwave on MEDIUM-HIGH (70%) for 45 to 60 minutes or until barley is tender. Stir soup occasionally during cooking.

Recipe yield: 6 to 8 servings

MINESTRONE

Power Level: MEDIUM-HIGH [70%]
Total Cooking Time: 1 hour to
1¼ hours

1 can (16 ounces) tomatoes, undrained
1 can (15½ ounces) kidney beans, undrained
1 can (10¾ ounces) condensed tomato soup
1 cup cubed cooked beef, pork or poultry (optional)
1 cup shredded cabbage
½ cup quick cooking rice
½ cup finely chopped celery
½ cup finely chopped carrots
1 cup water
1 tablespoon Worcestershire sauce
½ teaspoon salt
½ teaspoon marjoram
Dash of pepper
Dash of garlic powder

1. Combine all ingredients in a 2 quart casserole. Cover with a tight fitting lid or plastic wrap.

2. Microwave on MEDIUM-HIGH (70%) for 1 hour to 1 hour 15 minutes or until vegetables are tender. Stir soup occasionally during cooking.

Recipe yield: 8 to 10 servings

Variation:
CANNY MINESTRONE

Follow Minestrone recipe as directed except substitute 2 cans (16 ounces each) mixed vegetables for the cabbage, celery, carrots and water. Microwave on MEDIUM-HIGH (70%) for 20 to 25 minutes or until heated through. Stir occasionally during cooking.

VEGETABLE SOUP

Power Level: MEDIUM [50%] and
HIGH [100%]
Total Cooking Time: 1 hour to 1 hour
10 minutes

2 cups boiling water
½ pound beef chuck, cut into ½ inch cubes
3 cups tomato juice
1 package (10 ounces) frozen mixed vegetables
½ cup chopped onion
½ cup chopped celery
1 tablespoon Worcestershire sauce
2 beef bouillon cubes
1 bay leaf
½ teaspoon celery salt
½ teaspoon garlic salt
¼ teaspoon marjoram
Dash of pepper

1. Place boiling water and meat in a 3 quart casserole. Cover with a tight fitting lid or plastic wrap. Microwave on MEDIUM (50%) for 45 to 50 minutes or until meat is tender.

2. Add remaining ingredients. Cover.

3. Microwave on HIGH (100%) for 15 to 20 minutes or until vegetables are tender.

Recipe yield: 6 to 8 servings

Add meat to boiling water. *Then cover and allow meat to cook until tender. Don't forget to trim fat from the meat to prevent greasy soup.*

Prepare vegetables *by cutting into small, uniform shapes. This makes cooking faster and more even. For easier cutting, try using a food processor.*

Make a meal with
Vegetable Soup.

CREAM OF POTATO SOUP

Power Level: HIGH [100%]
Total Cooking Time: 28 to
        35½ minutes
Temperature Probe: 150° to 160°

4 strips bacon
3 cups potatoes, cut into
  ½ inch cubes
¼ cup chopped onion
¼ cup chopped celery
½ cup water
1 teaspoon salt
2 tablespoons all purpose flour
1½ cups milk
1 cup chicken broth
1 tablespoon chopped parsley

1. Microwave bacon on HIGH (100%) for 3 to 3½ minutes or until bacon is crisp. Crumble and set aside.

2. Combine potatoes, onion, celery, water and salt in a 2 quart casserole. Cover with a tight fitting lid or plastic wrap. Microwave on HIGH (100%) for 10 to 12 minutes or until vegetables are tender.

3. Mix flour, milk, chicken broth and parsley until smooth. Stir into potatoes. Microwave, uncovered, on HIGH (100%) for 15 to 20 minutes or until thickened. Stir occasionally during cooking.

4. Garnish with bacon.

Recipe yield: 4 to 6 servings

Combine potatoes, onion, celery, water and salt in a 2-quart casserole.

Cover with plastic wrap or tight fitting lid for faster and more even cooking.

Mix together flour, milk, chicken broth and parsley until smooth. Stir into potato mixture. When ready to serve, garnish with bacon or stir into mixture.

CLAM CHOWDER

Power Level: HIGH [100%] and
        MEDIUM [50%]
Total Cooking Time: 18 to
        22½ minutes

2 slices bacon, cut in half
1 can (8 ounces) minced clams,
  drained (reserve liquid)
1 large potato, peeled and cut into
  ½ inch cubes
2 tablespoons minced onion
1 tablespoon chopped parsley
1½ teaspoons cornstarch
2 cups milk
1 tablespoon butter
1 teaspoon salt
Dash of pepper
3 to 4 sprigs parsley (optional)

1. Place bacon in a 2 quart casserole. Cover with paper towel. Microwave on HIGH (100%) for 2 to 2½ minutes or until crisp. Remove bacon, crumble and set aside.

2. Add clam liquid, potato, onion and parsley to bacon drippings. Cover with a tight fitting lid or plastic wrap. Microwave on HIGH (100%) for 8 to 10 minutes or until vegetables are tender.

3. Stir in cornstarch until smooth. Add clams, milk, butter, salt and pepper. Cover with a tight fitting lid or plastic wrap. Microwave on MEDIUM (50%) for 8 to 10 minutes or until mixture begins to boil.

4. Garnish each serving with bacon and a sprig of parsley.

Recipe yield: 3 to 4 servings

*Cream of Potato
is a hearty soup
for a cold day.*

CREAM OF ONION SOUP

Power Level: HIGH [100%]
Total Cooking Time: 24 to 27 minutes
Temperature Probe: 150° to 160°

4 medium onions, sliced
¼ cup butter (or margarine)
¼ cup all purpose flour
1 teaspoon salt
¼ teaspoon marjoram
4 cups milk (or half & half)
2 cups chicken broth
2 egg yolks, beaten
1 tablespoon chopped parsley
½ cup croutons

1. Place onions and butter in a 3 quart casserole. Microwave on HIGH (100%) for 8 to 10 minutes or until tender. Stir halfway through cooking.

2. Add flour, salt and marjoram. Blend until smooth. Gradually stir in milk and broth. Microwave on HIGH (100%) for 15 minutes or until thickened. Stir occasionally during cooking.

3. Stir a small amount of hot mixture into egg yolk, then stir egg mixture into hot mixture. Microwave on HIGH (100%) for 1 to 2 minutes. Stir occasionally.

4. Allow to stand 3 to 5 minutes. Garnish top with parsley and croutons.

Recipe yield: 8 servings

CREAM OF CELERY SOUP

Power Level: HIGH [100%]
Total Cooking Time: 14 to 18 minutes
Temperature Probe: 150° to 160°

1½ cups diced celery
¼ cup chopped onion
¼ cup water
3 tablespoons butter
**   (or margarine)**
3 tablespoons all purpose flour
½ teaspoon salt
½ teaspoon dill weed
Dash of pepper
3 cups milk
Chopped parsley

1. Combine celery, onion and water in a 2 quart casserole. Cover with a tight fitting lid or plastic wrap. Microwave on HIGH (100%) for 6 to 8 minutes or until vegetables are tender.

2. Stir in butter, flour, salt, dill weed and pepper until smooth. Add milk.

3. Microwave on HIGH (100%) for 8 to 10 minutes or until thickened. Stir occasionally during cooking.

4. Garnish with chopped parsley.

Recipe yield: 6 servings

Canned & Packaged Soups

A quick and easy way for individual or full family servings.

CANNED SOUP

Power Level: HIGH [100%]
Total Cooking Time: 5 to 6 minutes
Temperature Probe: 150° to 160°

1 can soup

1. Pour soup into a 1½ quart casserole. 2. Add water or milk as directed on can. 3. Cover with a tight fitting lid or plastic wrap. 4. Microwave on HIGH (100%) for 5 to 6 minutes or until hot and bubbly.

SOUP MIX

Power Level: HIGH [100%] without
*   rice or noodles*
*   MEDIUM [50%] with*
*   rice or noodles*
Total Cooking Time: 12 to 15 minutes
Temperature Probe: 150° to 160°

1 envelope dehydrated soup mix

1. Pour water in a 2 quart casserole. Cover with a tight fitting lid or plastic wrap.

2. Microwave on HIGH (100%) for 8 to 10 minutes or until water is boiling.

3. Add soup mix. Cover. For soup without rice or noodles microwave on HIGH (100%) for 4 to 5 minutes. For soup with rice or noodles microwave on MEDIUM (50%) for 4 to 5 minutes or until tender.

4. Allow to stand, covered, 5 minutes before serving.

CREAMY TOMATO SOUP

Power Level: High [100%]
Total Cooking Time: 14 to 18 minutes
Temperature Probe: 150° to 160°

½ cup finely chopped onion
2 tablespoons butter (or margarine)
2 cans (10¾ ounces each)
**   condensed tomato soup**
1½ cups milk (or half & half)
1 teaspoon parsley
½ teaspoon basil
Dash of garlic powder
½ cup sour cream

HOMEMADE SOUP STARTER

Power Level: MEDIUM [50%],
*   HIGH [100%] and*
*   LOW [30%]*
Total Cooking Time: 1 hour 20 min. to
*   1 hour 32 min.*

1 package (6.8 ounces) soup starter
1 pound stew meat
2 cups boiling water
6 cups water

1. Place meat and boiling water in a 3 quart casserole. Cover with a tight fitting lid or plastic wrap. Microwave on MEDIUM (50%) for 55 to 60 minutes or until meat is tender.

2. Add package vegetables, stock and 6 cups water. Cover. Microwave on HIGH (100%) for 10 to 12 minutes or until boiling. Stir, then microwave on LOW (30%) for 15 to 20 minutes or until flavor is well blended.

Recipe yield: 8 servings

┌ Reheating Tip: ┐

Reheat soup quickly in the microwave. Cover. One cup heats in 2 to 2½ minutes. One quart heats in 5 to 7 minutes.

1. Place onion and butter in a 2 quart casserole. Microwave on HIGH (100%) for 3 to 4 minutes or until onion is tender.

2. Mix together soup and milk. Slowly stir into onion mixture. Add seasonings.

3. Microwave on HIGH (100%) for 10 to 12 minutes or until almost boiling. Stir occasionally during cooking.

4. Stir in sour cream. Microwave on HIGH (100%) for 1 to 2 minutes or until heated through. Stir occasionally.

Recipe yield: 4 to 6 servings

Cut vegetables *into small, uniform pieces for faster, more even cooking. Try using a food processor for easier cutting.*

Wrap corn on the cob *in waxed paper or leave in the husk while heating in the microwave. You may secure husk at top with string.*

Put vegetables *in boilable plastic bag or pouch in dish. Slash a small "X" in top of pouch to allow steam to escape.*

Place vegetables *in dish or casserole with thinner or more tender parts toward the center.*

Place frozen vegetables *with icy side up in casserole or serving dish.*

Add about 2 tablespoons of liquid, *butter or margarine to fresh or frozen vegetables. See vegetable chart for exceptions.*

Vegetables

The garden fresh look and taste of vegetables cooked in the microwave will even make vegetable haters say: "More, please!"

More vitamins and nutrients are retained when vegetables are cooked in the microwave because so little liquid is needed. Fresh and frozen vegetables are cooked in just 6 to 8 minutes. Canned and leftover vegetables can be reheated in 2 to 4 minutes in a casserole or on a serving plate.

Do not salt food directly. If placed directly on vegetables, salt tends to cause dark spots and drying out. Salt food after cooking or place in bottom of dish.

Stir vegetables once during cooking to distribute heat and moisture. Bring vegetables at edge of dish to the inside and those inside to the edge. Vegetables are usually cooked on High [100%]. But if in a delicate sauce, cooking on a lower setting will eliminate additional stirring.

Test for doneness after cooking for the least amount of time shown on chart. Vegetables should be slightly firm but crispy tender.

Cover fresh or frozen vegetables with a tight-fitting lid or plastic wrap for faster cooking. Pleat plastic wrap to allow steam to expand. It is unnecessary to cover frozen vegetables in boilable pouch.

Allow vegetables to stand for 3 to 5 minutes to finish cooking and to develop flavor. Usually this is just enough time to get the whole dinner ready for serving.

Carefully remove cover by lifting from the far side to allow steam to escape.

The Zucchini Bake is a golden glory [p. 194].

POTATO

Prick surface *of potato to allow steam to escape.*

On a paper towel, *place potatoes in a circle with at least ½ inch between. Cook potatoes unwrapped for least amount of time on chart.*

Test for doneness. *Potatoes will feel slightly firm. If overcooked, potato will have a withered appearance, and interior will be gummy and yellow.*

Remove from microwave oven *and wrap potato with aluminum foil to retain heat. Allow to stand 5 to 10 minutes to finish cooking and softening.*

ORANGE GLAZED SWEET POTATOES

Power Level: HIGH [100%]
Total Cooking Time: 11 to 14 minutes

4 medium sweet potatoes
¼ cup brown sugar
¼ cup orange marmalade
½ teaspoon grated orange peel
¼ cup butter (or margarine)

1. Wash and pierce surface of potatoes. Microwave on HIGH (100%) for 6 to 8 minutes or until almost tender.

2. Peel sweet potatoes and slice 1/8 inch thick. Place in a 1½ quart casserole.

3. Mix together brown sugar, marmalade and orange peel. Pour over sweet potatoes. Dot with butter. Cover with a tight fitting lid or plastic wrap.

4. Microwave on HIGH (100%) for 5 to 6 minutes or until heated throughout. Stir halfway through cooking.

Recipe yield: 6 servings

TWICE BAKED POTATOES

Power Level: HIGH [100%]
Total Cooking Time: 16 to 19½ minutes

4 medium potatoes
½ cup sour cream (or milk)
2 tablespoons butter (or margarine)
2 tablespoons chives
¼ teaspoon salt
Dash of pepper
½ cup grated Cheddar cheese
2 tablespoons bacon bits

1. Wash and pierce the surface of potatoes. Microwave on HIGH (100%) for 12 to 14 minutes. Wrap in foil and allow to stand 5 minutes.

2. Cut away top of each potato and scoop out inside, being careful not to break shells.*

3. Mash potatoes. Add sour cream, butter, chives, salt and pepper. Beat until smooth and fluffy. Spoon generously into potato shells.

4. Microwave on HIGH (100%) for 3 to 4 minutes or until heated through.

5. Sprinkle with cheese and bacon bits. Microwave for an additional 1 to 1½ minutes or until cheese just begins to melt.

Recipe yield: 4 servings

*Tip: For firmer shells, microwave emptied shells for 2 minutes.

CRUNCHY COATED POTATOES

Power Level: HIGH [100%]
Total Cooking Time: 10½ to 12¾ minutes

3 tablespoons butter (or margarine)
½ cup cornflake cereal, crumbled
¼ cup Parmesan cheese
1 teaspoon dried parsley flakes
1 teaspoon instant minced onion
¼ teaspoon salt
6 to 8 small potatoes, peeled

1. Place butter in an 8 x 8 x 2 inch baking dish. Microwave on HIGH (100%) for 30 to 45 seconds or until melted.

2. Combine cornflake crumbs, Parmesan cheese, parsley flakes, minced onion and salt in a small bowl.

3. Coat potatoes with butter. Then roll in crumb mixture. Place in baking dish. Cover with paper towel.

4. Microwave on HIGH (100%) for 10 to 12 minutes or until potatoes are just tender.

5. Allow to stand 10 to 15 minutes.

Recipe yield: 6 servings

MASHED POTATOES

4 to 6 boiled potatoes
¼ to ½ cup hot milk
1 to 2 tablespoons butter (or margarine)
¼ to ½ teaspoon salt
Dash of pepper

1. Drain for richer mashed potatoes. For more nutritious mashed potatoes do not drain.

2. Mash potatoes. Add milk, butter, salt and pepper. Beat to desired consistency.

Recipe yield: 4 to 6 servings

HOT GERMAN POTATO SALAD

Power Level: HIGH [100%]
Total Cooking Time: 18 to 24 minutes

6 thin strips bacon
4 medium potatoes
½ cup sugar
2 tablespoons all purpose flour
1½ teaspoons salt
½ teaspoon celery salt
¼ teaspoon dry mustard
Dash of pepper
1 cup water
½ cup vinegar
¼ cup chopped onion
¼ cup chopped celery

1. Place bacon in a 2 quart casserole. Cover with a paper towel. Microwave on HIGH (100%) for 4 to 5 minutes or until crispy. Remove bacon from drippings. Crumble and set aside.

2. Wash and pierce surface of potatoes. Microwave on HIGH (100%) for 8 to 10 minutes. Wrap in foil and allow to stand 5 minutes.

3. While potatoes are standing, stir sugar, flour and seasonings into bacon fat until smooth. Add water, vinegar, onion and celery. Microwave on HIGH (100%) for 4 to 6 minutes or until thickened.

4. Peel and slice potatoes 1/8 inch thick or dice into ½ inch cubes. Toss gently into sauce. Sprinkle top with crumbled bacon.

5. Microwave on HIGH (100%) for 2 to 3 minutes or until hot and bubbly.

Recipe yield: 4 to 6 servings

A Twice Baked Potato, a plain baked potato and an Acorn Squash with Apple and Raisin Glaze look pretty and tempting.

ACORN SQUASH WITH APPLE AND RAISIN GLAZE

Power Level: HIGH [100%]
Total Cooking Time: 16 to 20 minutes

2 medium acorn squash
1 medium apple, sliced
2 tablespoons raisins
¼ cup orange juice
2 tablespoons brown sugar
¼ teaspoon nutmeg
2 tablespoons butter
  (or margarine)

1. Pierce the surface of squash. Microwave on HIGH (100%) for 12 to 15 minutes or until almost tender.

2. Cut squash in half and remove seeds. Place open side up on an 11¾ x 7½ x 1¾ inch baking dish.

3. Combine apples, raisins, orange juice, brown sugar and nutmeg. Toss lightly until fruit is coated well. Divide into squash. Dot each with butter.

4. Microwave on HIGH (100%) for 4 to 5 minutes or until sauce is bubbly.

Recipe yield: 4 servings

YAMS ALOHA

Power Level: HIGH [100%]
Total Cooking Time: 5 to 6 minutes

1 can (1 pound) yams, drained
1 small banana, sliced
⅓ cup orange juice
1 teaspoon lemon juice
½ teaspoon salt
Dash of pepper
¼ cup whole pecans
2 tablespoons toasted
  flaked coconut

1. Place yams and bananas in a 1 quart casserole.

2. Stir in orange juice, lemon juice, salt and pepper.

3. Top with pecans and coconut. Cover with a tight fitting lid or plastic wrap.

4. Microwave on HIGH (100%) for 5 to 6 minutes.

Recipe yield: 4 servings

SQUASH

Prick surface of squash to allow steam to escape.

Cut open squash halfway through cooking. This makes cutting easier.

Scoop out seeds. Cover each half squash with waxed paper and cook for least amount of time on chart.

Lift waxed paper and test for doneness. Squash will be tender when pricked with fork. Remove from microwave. Keep covered. Allow a 5 to 10 minute standing time to finish cooking.

CANNED OR REHEATED VEGETABLES

Commercial vegetables are cooked during processing. Therefore, they only need reheating. The same is true for leftover vegetables.

Place vegetables in casserole or on serving plate. Cover tightly with lid or pleated plastic wrap.

Place salt in bottom of dish or salt after heating. Although it enhances the flavor of vegetables, salt will darken and dry them out when placed directly on top. Other seasonings may be added as desired.

Use the temperature probe to heat canned vegetables or to reheat leftovers. Set the probe at 140° to 150°.

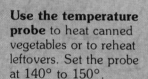

AMOUNT	MINUTES DRAINED	MINUTES UNDRAINED
8 oz. or 1 cup	2 to 2½	2½ to 3
15 oz. or 2 cups	2½ to 3	3 to 4
17 oz.	3 to 4	4 to 5

Cook for the least amount of time given on the chart or reheat using the temperature probe, retaining just a small amount of liquid in bottom of dish.

VEGETABLE COOKING CHART

This vegetable chart is a cooking guide. Your personal preferences as well as vegetable size, texture, age, freshness and temperature are factors which can affect cooking time.

Most vegetables need only 2 tablespoons of liquid, butter or margarine unless specified otherwise. If you prefer a softer vegetable, increase the liquid by about 2 tablespoons and cook about 2 minutes longer.

If cooking double the amount of items given on the chart, increase the amount of cooking time by one-third.

Unless specified otherwise, all vegetables are cooked on High (100%) and should stand covered 2 to 3 minutes before serving.

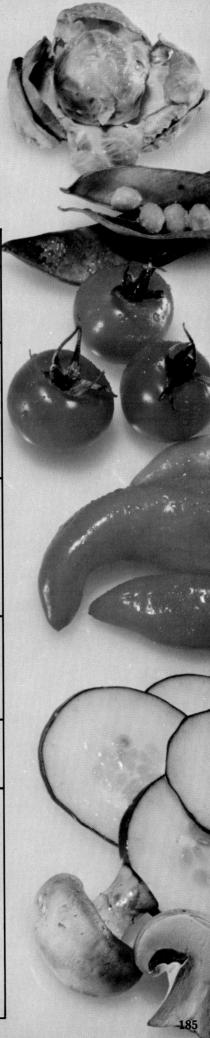

ITEM	AMOUNT	COOKING TIME	UTENSIL	SPECIAL INSTRUCTIONS
Artichoke Fresh	1 med. 2 med.	6-8 min. 8-10 min.	1 qt. covered casserole 2 qt. covered casserole	Place right side up. Add 2 teaspoons lemon juice and 2 tablespoons water.
	4 med.	14-16 min.	3 qt. covered casserole	Add 1 cup water.
Asparagus Fresh (4 inches long)	½ lb.	6-8 min.	10x6x1¾ inch baking dish, covered	Place tender tips toward center. Add ¼ cup water.
	1 lb.	10-12 min.	11¾x7½x1¾ inch baking dish, covered or 2 qt. covered casserole	Place tender tips toward center of dish. Add ¼ cup water.
Frozen	1 (10 oz.) pkg.	6-8 min.	1 qt. covered casserole	Add 2 tablespoons water or butter (margarine). Rearrange halfway through cooking.
Beans - Green and Wax Fresh	1 lb.	12-14 min.	1½ qt. covered casserole	Snip tips and cut beans in half. Add ½ cup water. If desired, add butter (margarine). Stir halfway through cooking.
Frozen	1 (9 oz.) pkg.	10-12 min.	1 qt. covered casserole	Add ¼ cup water. If desired, add butter (margarine). Break apart halfway through cooking.
Beans - Lima Fresh (shelled)	1 lb.	8-10 min.	1½ qt. covered casserole	Add ½ cup water. Break apart halfway through cooking.
Frozen	1 (10 oz.) pkg.	6-8 min.	1 qt. covered casserole	Add ¼ cup water. Break apart halfway through cooking.
Baby Limas in butter sauce	1 (10 oz.) pouch	6-8 min.	1 qt. casserole or serving dish	Cut an "X" in pouch.
Beets - Whole Fresh	4 med.	12-15 min.	1½ qt. covered casserole	Cover with water. Peel after cooking.
	10 small	22-25 min.	1½ qt. covered casserole	Cover with water. Peel after cooking.
Broccoli Fresh	1 (1 lb.) bunch	8-10 min.	11¾x7½x1¾ inch baking dish, covered	Split stalk. Place tender florets towards center of casserole. Add 2 tablespoons water or butter (margarine).
Frozen Spears	1 (10 oz.) pkg.	6-8 min.	1 qt. covered casserole	Add 2 tablespoons water or butter (margarine). Rearrange halfway through cooking.
Chopped	1 (10 oz.) pkg.	6-8 min.	1 qt. covered casserole	Add 2 tablespoons water or butter (margarine). Break apart halfway through cooking.
In butter sauce	1 (10 oz.) pouch	6-8 min.	1 qt. covered casserole or serving dish (covered)	Cut an "X" in pouch.
In cheese sauce	1 (10 oz.) pouch	6-8 min.	1 qt. casserole or serving dish	MEDIUM-HIGH (70%). Cut an "X" in pouch.

ITEM	AMOUNT	TIME	UTENSIL	SPECIAL INSTRUCTIONS
Brussels Sprouts Fresh	1 lb. (3 cups)	6-8 min.	1½ qt. covered casserole	Add 2 tablespoons water or butter (margarine). Rearrange halfway through cooking.
Frozen Regular	1 (10 oz.) pkg.	6-8 min.	1 qt. covered casserole	Add 2 tablespoons water or butter (margarine). Break apart halfway through cooking.
Baby sprouts	1 (10 oz.) pkg.	6-8 min.	1 qt. covered casserole	Add 2 tablespoons water or butter (margarine). Break apart halfway through cooking.
In butter sauce	1 (10 oz.) pouch	6-8 min.	1 qt. casserole or serving dish	Cut an "X" in pouch.
Cabbage Fresh	1 med. head	10-12 min.	3 qt. covered casserole	Cut into wedges. Add 2 tablespoons water or butter (margarine). Rearrange halfway through cooking.
	1 med. head	8-10 min.	2 qt. covered casserole	Finely chop cabbage. Add 2 tablespoons water or butter (margarine). Gently stir halfway through cooking.
Carrots Fresh Whole	6-8 med. (1 lb.)	10-12 min.	10x6x1¾ inch baking dish, covered	Add ¼ cup water. Stir halfway through cooking. Allow to stand, covered, 5 minutes.
Thin strips or sliced	6-8 medium (1 lb.)	10-12 min.	1½ qt. covered casserole	Add ¼ cup water. Stir halfway through cooking. Allow to stand, covered, 5 minutes.
Frozen Sliced	1 (10 oz.) pkg.	6-8 min.	1 qt. covered casserole	Add ¼ cup water. Break apart halfway through cooking. Allow to stand, covered, 5 minutes.
With brown sugar glaze	1 (10 oz.) pouch	4-6 min.	1 qt. casserole or serving dish	Cut an "X" in pouch.
Cauliflower Fresh Whole	1 med. head	8-10 min.	1 qt. casserole or serving dish	Remove outer leaves and wash. Cover with waxed paper or plastic wrap
Florets	1 med. head	8-10 min.	1½ qt. covered casserole	Cut cauliflower into florets. Add 2 tablespoons water or butter (margarine).
Frozen	1 (10 oz.) pkg.	6-8 min.	1 qt. covered casserole	Add 2 tablespoons water or butter (margarine). Break apart halfway through cooking.
In cheese sauce	1 (10 oz.) pouch	6-8 min.	1 qt. casserole or serving dish	MEDIUM-HIGH (70%). Cut an "X" in pouch.
Celery Fresh	4 cups	10-12 min.	2 qt. covered casserole	Cut into 1 inch pieces. Add 2 tablespoons water or butter (margarine). Gently stir halfway through cooking.
Collard Greens Frozen Chopped	1 (10 oz.) pkg.	6-8 min.	1 qt. covered casserole	Add 2 tablespoons water or butter (margarine). Break apart halfway through cooking.
Corn Fresh Cut from cob	2 cups	4-6 min.	1 qt. covered casserole	Add 2 tablespoons water or butter (margarine). Gently stir halfway through cooking.
Frozen	1 (10 oz.) pkg.	4-6 min.	1 qt. covered casserole	Add 2 tablespoons water or butter (margarine). Break apart halfway through cooking.
In butter sauce	1 (10 oz.) pouch	4-6 min.	1 qt. casserole or serving dish.	Cut an "X" in pouch.

ITEM	AMOUNT	TIME	UTENSIL	SPECIAL INSTRUCTIONS
Cream style	1 (10 oz.) pouch	4-6 min.	1 qt. casserole or serving dish.	Cut an "X" in pouch.
Corn (on the cob) Fresh	2 ears 4 ears 6 ears	4-6 min. 6-8 min. 10-12 min.		If desired, butter ears. Wrap ears in waxed paper. Twist ends.
Frozen	2 ears 4 ears	6-8 min. 10-12 min.		
Eggplant Fresh	1 med. or 5 cups	8-10 min.	2 qt. covered casserole	Peel and dice. Add 2 tablespoons water or butter (margarine). Gently stir halfway through cooking.
Fennel Fresh	1 bunch	8-10 min.	1½ qt. covered casserole	Cut into fourths. Add 2 tablespoons water or butter (margarine). Gently stir halfway through cooking.
Kale Frozen	1 (10 oz.) pkg.	6-8 min.	1 qt. covered casserole	Add 2 tablespoons water or butter (margarine). Break apart halfway through cooking.
With onion sauce	1 (10 oz.) pkg.	6-8 min.	1 qt. covered casserole	Add ½ cup milk and 1 table-spoon butter (margarine).
Kohlrabi Fresh	4 med.	8-10 min.	1½ qt. covered casserole	Add ¼ cup water and, if desired, 2 tablespoons butter (margarine).
Mushrooms Fresh	½ lb.	2-4 min.	1 qt. covered casserole	As soon as color begins to darken, remove from oven. Add 2 tablespoons water or butter (margarine). Gently stir halfway through cooking.
	1 lb.	4-6 min.	1½ qt. covered casserole	Add ½ cup water or butter (margarine). Gently stir halfway through cooking.
Mustard Greens Frozen	1 (10 oz.) pkg.	6-8 min.	1 qt. covered casserole	Add 2 tablespoons water or butter (margarine). Break apart halfway through cooking.
Okra Fresh	1 lb.	6-8 min.	1½ qt. covered casserole	Add 2 tablespoons water or butter (margarine). Gently stir halfway through cooking.
Frozen	1 (10 oz.) pkg.	6-8 min.	1 qt. covered casserole	Add 2 tablespoons water or butter (margarine). Break apart halfway through cooking.
Onions Fresh	2 med.	6-8 min.	1½ qt. covered casserole	Cut into eighths. Add 2 tablespoons water or butter (margarine). Gently stir halfway through cooking.
	4 med.	10-12 min.	1½ qt. covered casserole	Cut into eighths. Add 2 tablespoons water or butter (margarine). Gently stir halfway through cooking.
Frozen Small in cream sauce	1 (10 oz.) pouch	6-8 min.	1 qt. covered casserole or serving dish (covered)	MEDIUM-HIGH (70%). Cut an "X" in pouch.
Parsnips Fresh	1 lb. (4 whole)	6-8 min.	2 qt. covered casserole	Peeled or unpeeled. Add 2 tablespoons water or butter (margarine).

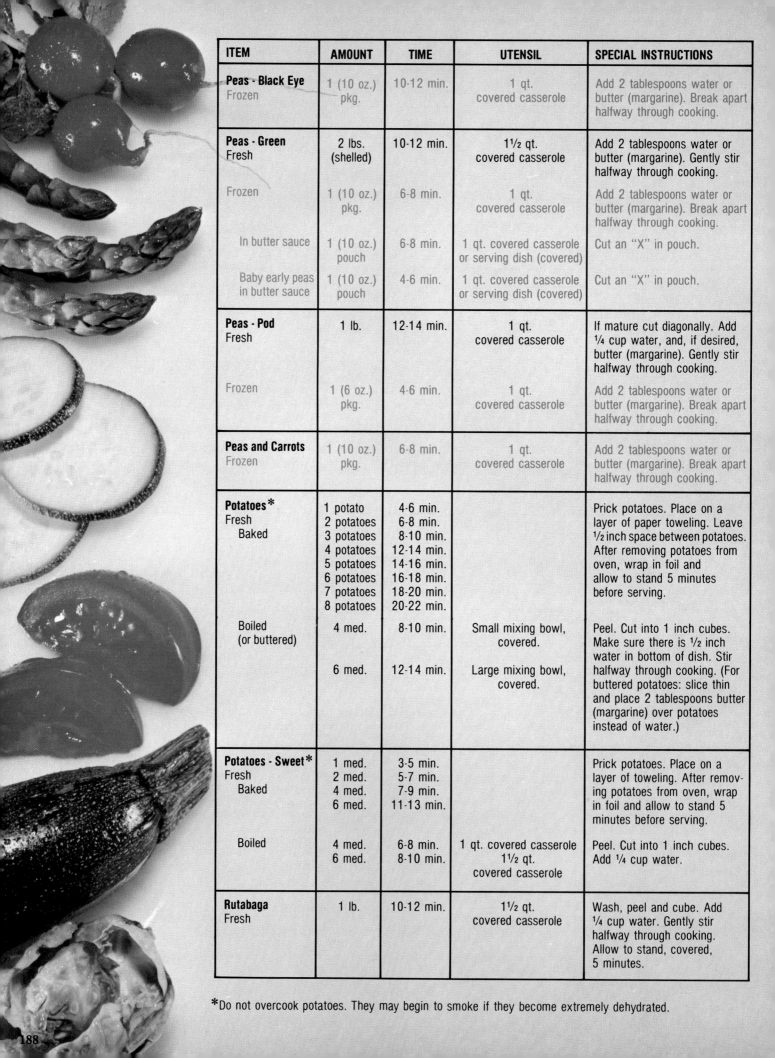

ITEM	AMOUNT	TIME	UTENSIL	SPECIAL INSTRUCTIONS
Peas - Black Eye Frozen	1 (10 oz.) pkg.	10-12 min.	1 qt. covered casserole	Add 2 tablespoons water or butter (margarine). Break apart halfway through cooking.
Peas - Green Fresh	2 lbs. (shelled)	10-12 min.	1½ qt. covered casserole	Add 2 tablespoons water or butter (margarine). Gently stir halfway through cooking.
Frozen	1 (10 oz.) pkg.	6-8 min.	1 qt. covered casserole	Add 2 tablespoons water or butter (margarine). Break apart halfway through cooking.
In butter sauce	1 (10 oz.) pouch	6-8 min.	1 qt. covered casserole or serving dish (covered)	Cut an "X" in pouch.
Baby early peas in butter sauce	1 (10 oz.) pouch	4-6 min.	1 qt. covered casserole or serving dish (covered)	Cut an "X" in pouch.
Peas - Pod Fresh	1 lb.	12-14 min.	1 qt. covered casserole	If mature cut diagonally. Add ¼ cup water, and, if desired, butter (margarine). Gently stir halfway through cooking.
Frozen	1 (6 oz.) pkg.	4-6 min.	1 qt. covered casserole	Add 2 tablespoons water or butter (margarine). Break apart halfway through cooking.
Peas and Carrots Frozen	1 (10 oz.) pkg.	6-8 min.	1 qt. covered casserole	Add 2 tablespoons water or butter (margarine). Break apart halfway through cooking.
Potatoes * Fresh Baked	1 potato 2 potatoes 3 potatoes 4 potatoes 5 potatoes 6 potatoes 7 potatoes 8 potatoes	4-6 min. 6-8 min. 8-10 min. 12-14 min. 14-16 min. 16-18 min. 18-20 min. 20-22 min.		Prick potatoes. Place on a layer of paper toweling. Leave ½ inch space between potatoes. After removing potatoes from oven, wrap in foil and allow to stand 5 minutes before serving.
Boiled (or buttered)	4 med. 6 med.	8-10 min. 12-14 min.	Small mixing bowl, covered. Large mixing bowl, covered.	Peel. Cut into 1 inch cubes. Make sure there is ½ inch water in bottom of dish. Stir halfway through cooking. (For buttered potatoes: slice thin and place 2 tablespoons butter (margarine) over potatoes instead of water.)
Potatoes - Sweet * Fresh Baked	1 med. 2 med. 4 med. 6 med.	3-5 min. 5-7 min. 7-9 min. 11-13 min.		Prick potatoes. Place on a layer of toweling. After removing potatoes from oven, wrap in foil and allow to stand 5 minutes before serving.
Boiled	4 med. 6 med.	6-8 min. 8-10 min.	1 qt. covered casserole 1½ qt. covered casserole	Peel. Cut into 1 inch cubes. Add ¼ cup water.
Rutabaga Fresh	1 lb.	10-12 min.	1½ qt. covered casserole	Wash, peel and cube. Add ¼ cup water. Gently stir halfway through cooking. Allow to stand, covered, 5 minutes.

*Do not overcook potatoes. They may begin to smoke if they become extremely dehydrated.

ITEM	AMOUNT	TIME	UTENSIL	SPECIAL INSTRUCTIONS
Spinach Fresh	1 lb.	4-6 min.	2 qt. covered casserole	Cook in water which clings to leaves. Rearrange halfway through cooking.
Frozen Leaf	1 (10 oz.) pkg.	6-8 min.	1 qt. covered casserole	Add 2 tablespoons water or butter (margarine). Break apart halfway through cooking.
In butter sauce	1 (10 oz.) pouch	6-8 min.	1 qt. casserole or serving dish.	Cut an "X" in pouch.
Chopped	1 (10 oz.) pkg.	4-6 min.	1 qt. covered casserole	Add 2 tablespoons water or butter (margarine). Break apart halfway through cooking.
Squash (winter) Fresh Whole Acorn or Butternut	1 med. 2 med.	8-10 min. 20-22 min.	10x6x1¾ inch baking dish, covered, or 11¾x7½x1¾ inch baking dish, covered.	Pierce squash skin. Microwave half the cooking time. Cut in half. Remove seeds. Add 1 tablespoon butter (margarine) to each half. Cover with waxed paper. Allow to stand covered 5 minutes.
Fresh Hubbard	2 lbs.	14-16 min.	1½ qt. covered casserole	Cut in cubes. Add 2 tablespoons water or butter (margarine). Gently stir halfway through cooking.
	2½-3 lbs.	18-20 min.	8 inch cake dish, covered	Cut in half. Microwave one half at a time.
Frozen	1 (12 oz.) pkg.	6-8 min.	1 qt. covered casserole	Add 2 tablespoons water or butter (margarine). Break apart halfway through cooking.
Squash (summer) Fresh Crookneck Pattypan	1 lb.	10-12 min.	1 qt. covered casserole	Slice or cube. Add ¼ cup water and, if desired, butter (margarine). Stir halfway through cooking.
Zucchini	4 cups	6-8 min.	1½ qt. covered casserole	Cut into ¼ inch slices. Add 2 tablespoons water or butter (margarine). Gently stir halfway through cooking.
Frozen	1 (10 oz.) pkg.	6-8 min.	1 qt. covered casserole	Add 2 tablespoons water or butter (margarine). Break apart halfway through cooking.
Succotash Frozen	1 (10 oz.) pkg.	6-8 min.	1 qt. covered casserole	Add 2 tablespoons water or butter (margarine). Break apart halfway through cooking.
Turnips Fresh	4 med.	10-12 min.	1½ qt. covered casserole	Peel. Cut into eighths. Add 2 tablespoons water or butter (margarine). Rearrange halfway through cooking.
Frozen Greens/chopped	1 (10 oz.) pkg.	8-10 min.	1 qt. covered casserole	Add 2 tablespoons water or butter (margarine). Break apart halfway through cooking.
Greens/chopped (w/diced turnips)	1 (10 oz.) pkg.	8-10 min.	1 qt. covered casserole	Add 2 tablespoons water or butter (margarine). Break apart halfway through cooking.

HOT THREE BEAN SALAD

Power Level: HIGH [100%]
Total Cooking Time: 11 to 14 minutes

3 thin strips bacon
½ cup sugar
1 tablespoon cornstarch
½ teaspoon salt
¼ teaspoon pepper
⅔ cup vinegar
**1 can (15 ounces) red kidney
  beans, drained**
**1 can (1 pound) cut green beans,
  drained**
**1 can (1 pound) cut wax beans,
  drained**
1 medium onion, chopped
**1 jar (2½ ounces) sliced
  mushrooms**

1. Place bacon in a 2 quart casserole. Microwave on HIGH (100%) for 3 to 4 minutes or until crispy.

2. Remove bacon and drain on paper towels. Crumble and set aside.

3. Stir sugar, cornstarch, salt, pepper and vinegar into bacon drippings.

4. Microwave on HIGH (100%) for 3 to 4 minutes or until thickened.

5. Stir in beans, onion and mushrooms. Cover with a tight fitting lid or plastic wrap.

6. Microwave on HIGH (100%) for 5 to 6 minutes. Stir halfway through cooking. Sprinkle with bacon pieces.

Tip: To blend flavors, microwave on LOW (30%) for 10 minutes.

Recipe yield: 6 to 8 servings

CREAMY LIMA BEANS AND MUSHROOMS

Power Level: HIGH [100%]
Total Cooking Time: 8 to 11 minutes

2 tablespoons butter (or margarine)
2 tablespoons chopped onion
1 cup fresh mushrooms, sliced
**1 package (10 ounces) frozen
  lima beans**
½ cup half and half
¼ teaspoon salt
Dash of pepper

1. Place butter, onion and mushrooms in a 1 quart casserole.

2. Microwave on HIGH (100%) for 2 to 3 minutes or until vegetables are tender.

3. Add frozen lima beans, cream, salt and pepper. Cover with a tight fitting lid or plastic wrap.

4. Microwave on HIGH (100%) for 6 to 8 minutes.

Recipe yield: 4 servings

WILTED LETTUCE

Power Level: HIGH [100%]
Total Cooking Time: 5 to 7 minutes

3 thin strips bacon
1 tablespoon sugar
¼ teaspoon dill
¼ teaspoon seasoned salt
Dash of pepper
¼ cup vinegar
¼ cup chopped celery
1 tablespoon sliced green onion
**1 medium head of lettuce (torn
  into bite size pieces)**
**2 hard cooked eggs, peeled and
  sliced thin (Cook eggs on
  conventional range.)**

1. Place bacon in a 3 quart casserole. Microwave on HIGH (100%) for 3 to 4 minutes or until crispy.

2. Remove bacon to paper towels to drain. Crumble. Set aside.

3. Stir sugar, seasonings and vinegar into drippings. Microwave on HIGH (100%) for 2 to 3 minutes or until boiling.

4. Stir in celery and onion.

5. Toss lettuce into hot dressing until each piece is coated and slightly wilted.

6. Top with egg slices and bacon pieces. Serve immediately.

Recipe yield: 8 to 10 servings

GREEN BEANS ORIENTAL

Power Level: HIGH [100%]
Total Cooking Time: 14 to 17 minutes

2 tablespoons butter (or margarine)
3 tablespoons slivered almonds
2 packages (9 ounces each) frozen French-cut green beans
1 can (8 ounces) water chestnuts, drained and sliced
2 tablespoons soy sauce
½ teaspoon ginger

1. Place butter and almonds in a 1½ quart casserole. Microwave on HIGH (100%) for 4 to 5 minutes or until almonds are toasted. Stir occasionally.

2. Add remaining ingredients. Cover with a tight fitting lid or plastic wrap.

3. Microwave on HIGH (100%) for 10 to 12 minutes or until heated throughout.

Recipe yield: 6 to 8 servings

BACON BAKED BEANS

Power Level: HIGH [100%] and MEDIUM [50%]
Total Cooking Time: 24 to 32 minutes

¼ pound thinly sliced bacon
¼ cup chopped onion
¼ cup chopped green pepper
¼ cup chopped celery
2 cans (1 pound each) baked beans
½ cup catsup
2 tablespoons dark molasses
1 tablespoon brown sugar
1 teaspoon dry mustard

1. Place bacon in a 2 quart casserole or 10x6x1¾ inch baking dish. Microwave on HIGH (100%) for 4 to 5 minutes or until crispy. Remove bacon. Cut into 1 inch pieces. Set aside.

2. Add onion, green pepper and celery to bacon drippings. Microwave on HIGH (100%) for 5 to 6 minutes or until tender. Drain off grease.

3. Add bacon and remaining ingredients. Cover with a tight fitting lid or plastic wrap.

4. Microwave on HIGH (100%) for 5 to 6 minutes or until bubbly. Stir, then microwave on MEDIUM (50%) for an additional 10 to 15 minutes.

Recipe yield: 6 to 8 servings

FOUR BEAN BAKE

Power Level: HIGH [100%] and MEDIUM [50%]
Total Cooking Time: 16 to 23 minutes

1 can (30 ounces) pork and beans in tomato sauce
1 can (16 ounces) cut green beans, drained
1 can (15 ounces) garbanzo beans (or chick peas), drained
1 can (16 ounces) lima beans, drained
1 small onion, chopped
½ cup catsup
3 tablespoons brown sugar
1 tablespoon prepared mustard
1 teaspoon vinegar
1 teaspoon cinnamon
3 thin strips bacon, cut into 1 inch pieces

1. Combine all ingredients, except bacon, in a 3 quart casserole. Top with bacon. Cover with a tight fitting lid or plastic wrap.

2. Microwave on HIGH (100%) for 6 to 8 minutes or until bubbly. Stir, then microwave on MEDIUM (50%) for an additional 10 to 15 minutes.

Recipe yield: 8 to 10 servings

Wilted Lettuce and Bacon Baked Beans turn an ordinary picnic into something extra special.

GLAZED CARROTS

Power Level: HIGH [100%]
Total Cooking Time: 8½ to 12 minutes

**3 or 4 medium carrots, cut into
  1 inch pieces
¼ cup water
¼ cup brown sugar
2 tablespoons orange juice
1 teaspoon grated orange peel
1½ tablespoons butter
  (or margarine)**

1. Place carrots and water in a 1 quart casserole. Cover with a tight fitting lid or plastic wrap. Microwave on HIGH (100%) for 6 to 8 minutes or until tender. Allow to stand 5 minutes, then drain.

2. Combine brown sugar, orange juice, orange peel and butter in a 1 cup measure.

3. Microwave on HIGH (100%) for 1½ to 2 minutes or until hot and bubbly. Pour over carrots. Cover.

4. Microwave on HIGH (100%) for 1 to 2 minutes or until heated through.

Recipe yield: 2 to 3 servings

PEAS WITH ONIONS AND MUSHROOMS

Power Level: HIGH [100%]
Total Cooking Time: 6 to 8 minutes

**1 package (10 ounces) frozen peas
  with onions
1 jar (4½ ounces) mushrooms,
  drained
2 tablespoons butter (or margarine)
¼ teaspoon marjoram
¼ teaspoon salt
Dash of pepper**

1. Combine all ingredients in a 1 quart casserole. Cover with a tight fitting lid or plastic wrap.

2. Microwave on HIGH (100%) for 6 to 8 minutes. Stir halfway through cooking.

Recipe yield: 4 servings

*Create colorful flavor
with Glazed Carrots and Peas
with Onions and Mushrooms.*

192

CREAMY PEAS AND ONIONS

Power Level: HIGH [100%]
Total Cooking Time: 7½ to
                     10¾ minutes

2 tablespoons butter (or margarine)
¼ cup dry bread crumbs
½ teaspoon dill weed
1 package (10 ounces) frozen peas
1 package (10 ounces) frozen
  onions in cream sauce
Dash of nutmeg

1. Place butter in a small casserole. Microwave on HIGH (100%) for 30 to 45 seconds or until melted. Stir in bread crumbs and dill weed. Set aside.

2. Combine peas, onions and nutmeg in a 1½ quart casserole. Cover with a tight fitting lid or plastic wrap. Microwave on HIGH (100%) for 6 to 8 minutes or until hot and bubbly. Stir halfway through cooking.

3. Sprinkle bread crumb mixture over peas and onions. Microwave, uncovered, on HIGH (100%) for 1 to 2 minutes or until hot.

Recipe yield: 6 to 8 servings

MARINATED ONIONS

Power Level: HIGH [100%]
Total Cooking Time: 12 to 14 minutes

¾ cup sugar
½ cup brown sugar
¼ cup water
½ cup red wine vinegar
3 cups thinly sliced onion
2 tablespoons butter (or margarine)

1. Mix together sugars, water and vinegar in a 1½ quart casserole. Cover with a tight fitting lid or plastic wrap. Microwave on HIGH (100%) for 4 to 6 minutes or until boiling. Stir halfway through cooking.

2. Add onions. Cover with a tight fitting lid or plastic wrap. Allow to stand 1 hour.

3. Remove onions from marinade and drain well. Place butter and onions in a 9 inch pie dish. Microwave on HIGH (100%) for 8 to 10 minutes or until tender.*Stir halfway through cooking.

4. Serve as a side dish or over meats and sandwiches. Store marinade in refrigerator for future use.

Recipe yield: 4 servings

*If microwave has a browning element, brown as desired.

BROCCOLI WITH CHEESE SAUCE

Power Level: HIGH [100%]
Total Cooking Time: 15½ to
                     19¾ minutes

2 tablespoons butter (or margarine)
2 tablespoons all purpose flour
½ teaspoon salt
Dash of pepper
Dash of paprika
1 cup milk
1 cup grated Cheddar cheese
2 packages (10 ounces each)
  frozen broccoli spears
1 medium tomato, sliced

1. Place butter in a 2 cup measure. Microwave on HIGH (100%) for 30 to 45 seconds or until melted.

2. Stir in flour and seasonings until smooth. Slowly stir in milk. Microwave on HIGH (100%) for 3 to 4 minutes until thickened. Stir in cheese until melted. If cheese has not melted, microwave on HIGH (100%) for 30 seconds to 1 minute. Set aside.

3. Place broccoli in a 1½ quart casserole. Cover with a tight fitting lid or plastic wrap. Microwave on HIGH (100%) for 10 to 12 minutes or until broccoli is tender-crisp. Drain off liquid.

4. Pour cheese sauce over broccoli and garnish with tomato slices. Microwave on HIGH (100%) for 2 to 3 minutes or until hot.

Recipe yield: 6 to 8 servings

CORN PUDDING

Power Level: MEDIUM-HIGH [70%]
Total Cooking Time: 15 to 20 minutes

1 egg
1 can (16 ounces) cream style corn
½ cup milk
¼ cup chopped green pepper
2 tablespoons finely chopped
  onion
1 tablespoon sugar
¾ cup Cheddar cheese cracker
  crumbs
2 tablespoons butter (or margarine)
Paprika

1. Beat egg in 1½ quart casserole. Stir in corn, milk, green pepper, onion, sugar and ½ cup cracker crumbs. Dot with butter and sprinkle with remaining cracker crumbs and paprika.

2. Microwave on MEDIUM-HIGH (70%) for 15 to 20 minutes or until a knife inserted near edge comes out clean. Allow to stand 15 minutes or until center is set.

Recipe yield: 4 servings

ASPARAGUS IN SAUCE

Power Level: HIGH [100%]
Total Cooking Time: 6½ to
                     9 minutes

½ cup fresh mushrooms, sliced
2 tablespoons butter (or margarine)
1 tablespoon all purpose flour
¼ teaspoon salt
Dash of pepper
½ cup milk
1 teaspoon Worcestershire sauce
1 can (15 ounces) asparagus,
  drained
¼ cup bread crumbs

1. Combine mushrooms and butter in a 1 quart casserole. Microwave on HIGH (100%) for 3 to 4 minutes or until mushrooms are tender.

2. Stir in flour, salt and pepper. Slowly stir in milk and Worcestershire sauce until smooth. Microwave on HIGH (100%) for 1½ to 2 minutes. Add asparagus.

3. Sprinkle with bread crumbs.

4. Microwave on HIGH (100%) for 2 to 3 minutes or until heated through.

Recipe yield: 4 to 6 servings

STEWED TOMATOES

Power Level: HIGH [100%]
Total Cooking Time: 6 to 8 minutes

2 medium tomatoes, peeled and
  cut into fourths
  (or one 16 ounce can)
2 tablespoons sugar
1 tablespoon butter (or margarine)
½ teaspoon salt
Dash of pepper
1 tablespoon cornstarch
¼ cup water

1. Combine tomatoes, sugar, butter, salt and pepper in a 1 quart casserole. Cover with a tight fitting lid or plastic wrap.

2. Microwave on HIGH (100%) for 3 to 4 minutes or until tender. Stir halfway through cooking time.

3. Mix cornstarch and water until smooth. Pour over tomato mixture.

4. Microwave on HIGH (100%) for 3 to 4 minutes or until thickened.

Recipe yield: 4 servings

YALE BEETS

Power Level: HIGH [100%]
Total Cooking Time: 7 to 9 minutes

**1 can (16 ounces) sliced beets,
  drained (reserve ¾ cup of liquid)**
¼ cup sugar
1 tablespoon cornstarch
½ teaspoon salt
Dash of pepper
¼ cup vinegar
¼ cup water
¼ teaspoon grated orange peel

1. Place beets in a 1½ quart casserole.

2. Mix together sugar, cornstarch, salt, pepper, reserved beet liquid, vinegar and water until smooth. Pour over beets. Cover with a tight fitting lid or plastic wrap.

3. Microwave on HIGH (100%) for 7 to 9 minutes or until glossy and thick. Stir halfway through cooking.

4. Sprinkle with orange peel before serving.

Recipe yield: 4 servings

STUFFED ARTICHOKES

Power Level: HIGH [100%]
Total Cooking Time: 25 to 31 minutes

1 tablespoon cooking oil
2 small carrots, grated
1 small onion, diced
1 stalk celery, diced
2½ cups water
¼ cup butter (or margarine)
**1 package (8 ounces) seasoned
  stuffing mix (crumb type)**
¼ cup blanched chopped almonds
4 medium artichokes
½ teaspoon salt

1. Combine cooking oil, carrots, onions and celery in a 1½ quart casserole. Cover with a tight fitting lid or plastic wrap. Microwave on HIGH (100%) for 4 to 5 minutes or until vegetables are partially cooked.

2. Add 1½ cups water and butter. Cover. Microwave on HIGH (100%) for an additional 3 to 4 minutes or until boiling.

3. Stir in stuffing mix and almonds. Set aside.

4. Snip off tips of artichoke leaves. Discard tips.

5. Place artichokes, snipped ends up, in a 3 quart casserole. Add remaining water and salt. Cover with a tight fitting lid or plastic wrap.

6. Microwave on HIGH for 14 to 16 minutes.

7. Drain artichokes upside down on a wire rack until partially cooled.

8. Remove center leaves and heart of artichoke. Chop and stir into stuffing mixture. Spoon into artichokes.

9. Replace stuffed artichokes in 3 quart casserole. Microwave on HIGH (100%) for 4 to 6 minutes or until heated throughout.

Recipe yield: 4 servings

HOT CABBAGE SLAW

Power Level: HIGH [100%]
Total Cooking Time: 6 to 8 minutes

4 cups coarsely shredded cabbage
**1 can (16 ounces) cut green beans,
  drained**
½ cup vinegar
⅓ cup sugar
**2 tablespoons instant
  minced onion**
1 teaspoon salt
¼ teaspoon pepper

1. Combine all ingredients in a 2 quart casserole. Cover with a tight fitting lid or plastic wrap.

2. Microwave on HIGH (100%) for 6 to 8 minutes or until cabbage is tender-crisp. Stir halfway through cooking.

Recipe yield: 6 servings

ZUCCHINI BAKE

*Power Level: HIGH [100%] and
             MEDIUM-HIGH [70%]*
Total Cooking Time: 14 to 18 minutes

**4 cups (2 medium) zucchini, cut
  into chunks**
½ cup onion, sliced thin
**1½ cups (6 ounces) grated
  Cheddar cheese**
**1 jar (2 ounces) chopped pimento,
  drained**
½ teaspoon salt
Dash of pepper
4 eggs
Dash of hot pepper sauce

1. Combine zucchini and onion in a 10x6x1¾ inch baking dish. Cover with a tight fitting lid or plastic wrap. Microwave on HIGH (100%) for 6 to 8 minutes or until vegetables are tender. Drain well.

2. Add cheese, pimento, salt and pepper. Toss lightly.

3. Beat together eggs and hot pepper sauce. Pour over zucchini mixture.

4. Microwave on MEDIUM-HIGH (70%) for 8 to 10 minutes or until center is just set. Stir halfway through cooking.

Recipe yield: 4 to 6 servings

EGGPLANT PARMESAN

Power Level: HIGH [100%]
*Total Cooking Time: 15 to
                    17½ minutes*

**1 medium eggplant, peeled
  and sliced 1/8 inch thick**
**2 cans (8 ounces each)
  tomato sauce**
1 teaspoon oregano
1 teaspoon basil
¼ cup Parmesan cheese
**1 package (6 ounces) Mozzarella
  cheese, sliced**

1. Place alternate layers of eggplant, tomato sauce, spices and Parmesan cheese in an 11¾ x 7½ x 1¾ inch baking dish. Cover with a tight fitting lid or plastic wrap.

2. Microwave on HIGH (100%) for 14 to 16 minutes or until eggplant is tender.

3. Add Mozzarella cheese. Microwave on HIGH (100%) for 1 to 1½ minutes or until cheese just begins to melt.

Recipe yield: 4 to 6 servings

Hot Cabbage Slaw and Stuffed Artichokes will bring you compliments at a covered-dish supper.

CHEESY CAULIFLOWER

Power Level: HIGH [100%]
Total Cooking Time: 12 to 16 minutes

1 medium head cauliflower, cut into florets
2 tablespoons water
2 tablespoons butter (or margarine)
1 small onion, chopped
¼ cup finely chopped celery
¼ cup dry bread crumbs
¼ cup grated Cheddar cheese
¼ teaspoon salt
Dash of pepper

1. Place cauliflower and water in a 1½ quart casserole. Cover with a tight fitting lid or plastic wrap. Microwave on HIGH (100%) for 8 to 10 minutes or until tender-crisp. Stir halfway through cooking. Drain.

2. Combine butter, onion and celery in a 1 quart casserole. Microwave on HIGH (100%) for 3 to 4 minutes or until vegetables are tender.

3. Add bread crumbs, cheese, salt and pepper. Mix well. Sprinkle over cauliflower. Microwave, uncovered, on HIGH (100%) for 1 to 2 minutes or until cheese just begins to melt.

Recipe yield: 4 servings

Blanching Vegetables

The backyard gardener will be delighted with the ease of blanching in the microwave.

The gardener can pick small quantities of vegetables when at peak in quality and immediately blanch and freeze them.

The brief heat treatment of blanching is necessary to stop enzyme action and reduce micro-organisms on food which cause undesirable changes in flavor and texture. Blanching before freezing also enhances the color of vegetables.

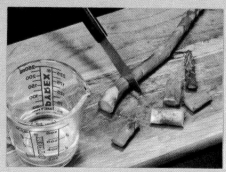

Wash, peel, slice or dice *vegetables. Measure the recommended amount according to chart and place in casserole.*

Drain vegetables *in a colander and immediately plunge colander into ice water to stop the cooking process. Remove vegetables and spread on paper towels. Blot dry.*

Add water *according to the amount on chart. Do not salt. Cover with tight-fitting lid or pleated plastic wrap. Cook for least amount of time given on chart.*

Package in freezer containers *or in boilable bags. Note: 1 pint equals an 8 to 10 oz. package of commercially packed vegetables. Seal, label and date packages.*

Check for doneness. *Vegetables should be evenly bright in color.*

To loose pack vegetables, *spread on a cookie sheet and place in freezer until firm. Then place in freezer containers. Seal, label and date packages. Freeze.*

BLANCHING CHART

Vegetable	Amount	Dish Size	Amount of Water	Cooking Time
Asparagus	1 lb. cut into 1½" pieces	2 qt.	¼ cup	3 to 4 minutes
Beans, green or waxed	1 lb.	1½ qt.	½ cup	6 to 8 minutes
Beans, Lima	1 lb.	1½ qt.	½ cup	4 to 6 minutes
Broccoli	1¼ to 1½ lbs.	3 qt.	¼ cup	4 to 5 minutes
Brussels Sprouts	1 lb.	1½ qt.	¼ cup	4 to 5 minutes
Carrots	1 lbs. cut into ½" pieces	1½ qt.	¼ cup	4 to 6 minutes
Cauliflower	1 head, cut into florets	2 qt.	½ cup	4 to 5 minutes
Corn cut from the cob	4 ears	1 qt.	¼ cup	4 to 5 minutes
Onions	4 medium, cut into fourths	1½ qt.	½ cup	5½ to 6½ minutes
Peas	1 lb. shelled	1 qt.	¼ cup	3½ to 5 minutes
Spinach	1 lb. wash thoroughly	3 qt.	no water	2½ to 3½ minutes
Squash	1 lb. cut into ½" cubes or sliced ½" thick	1½ qt.	¼ cup	3 to 4½ minutes
Zucchini	1 lb. cut into ½" cubes or sliced ½" thick	1½ qt.	¼ cup	4 to 5 minutes

Diet and Health Foods

Whether you are dieting or are simply health food conscious, you will find the microwave oven to be a real asset in the preparation of these foods.

Because you add little or no water when you cook in the microwave, many food nutrients, color and flavor are retained. Calories can be kept to a minimum because you seldom cook in oil. Salty seasonings or butter can be eliminated or decreased as desired.

It's also easier for the dieter to prepare a quick and simple meal in the microwave while simultaneously preparing a larger meal for the rest of the family. But chances are, the whole family will enjoy these "diet-and-health-food" snacks, vegetables, main dishes and desserts.

Main Dish

FISH CREOLE

Power Level: HIGH [100%]
Total Cooking Time: 8 to 10 minutes
Calories: 183 per serving

2 (10 to 12 ounces) fish fillets
½ cup chopped green pepper
¼ cup chopped celery
1 can (2 ounces) sliced mushrooms
¼ cup water
1 tablespoon instant
**   chicken bouillon**
1 cup tomato juice
1 teaspoon chopped pimento
1 teaspoon Worcestershire sauce
Dash of salt
Dash of pepper

1. Place fish fillets, thickest end toward outside, in a 10x6x1¾ inch baking dish.

2. Mix together all remaining ingredients. Pour over fillets. Cover with a tight fitting lid or plastic wrap.

3. Microwave on HIGH (100%) for 8 to 10 minutes or until fish flakes easily with a fork.

Recipe yield: 2 servings

ITALIAN CHICKEN STEW

Power Level: HIGH [100%] and
*   MEDIUM [50%]*
Total Cooking Time: 1 hour 18 minutes
*   to 1 hour 25 minutes*
Calories: 155 per serving

2 cups cooked cubed chicken
1 can (32 ounces) tomato juice
1 cup shredded cabbage
1 cup dried carrots
½ cup dried corn
2 tablespoons dried minced onion
1 teaspoon basil
1 teaspoon dried parsley
½ teaspoon oregano
½ teaspoon salt
Dash of pepper

1. Combine all ingredients in a 2 quart casserole. Cover with a tight fitting lid or plastic wrap.

2. Microwave on HIGH (100%) for 8 to 10 minutes or until boiling. Stir occasionally.

3. Microwave on MEDIUM (50%) for 1 hour 10 minutes to 1 hour 15 minutes or until vegetables are soft.

Recipe yield: 4 to 6 servings

TUNA CASSEROLE

Power Level: HIGH [100%]
Total Cooking Time: 6 to 8 minutes
Calories: 240 per serving

2 cups cooked mashed cauliflower
1 can (6 ounces) tuna, drained
**   and rinsed**
1 can (4 ounces) sliced
**   mushrooms, drained**
2 tablespoons dried minced onion
1 cup tomato juice
Dash of salt
Dash of pepper

1. Layer cauliflower, tuna and mushrooms in a 1 quart casserole. Mix together remaining ingredients. Pour over layers.

2. Microwave on HIGH (100%) for 6 to 8 minutes or until heated through.

Recipe yield: 2 servings

CHILI EGG CASSEROLE

Power Level: MEDIUM [50%] and
*   HIGH [100%]*
Total Cooking Time: 20 to 24 minutes
Calories: 172½ per serving

4 eggs, separated
1 can (4 ounces) chopped chilies,
**   drained**
1 cup grated Monterey Jack cheese
Dash of salt

Sauce:
2 cups tomato juice
1 tablespoon cornstarch
1 teaspoon Italian seasoning
1 teaspoon dried minced onion
¼ teaspoon chili powder
¼ teaspoon garlic powder
Dash of sugar substitute

1. Beat egg whites and salt until stiff peaks form. Beat egg yolks until thick and lemony color. Carefully fold egg yolks into the egg whites.

2. Spread half of egg mixture on the bottom of a lightly greased 8x8x2 inch baking dish. Layer with chilies and cheese. Cover with remaining egg mixture.

3. Microwave on MEDIUM (50%) for 14 to 16 minutes or until knife inserted near center comes out clean.

4. Mix together ingredients for sauce. Microwave on HIGH (100%) for 6 to 8 minutes or until thickened. Pour over Chili Egg Casserole before serving.

Recipe yield: 4 servings

Vegetable

MOCK MASHED POTATOES

Power Level: HIGH [100%]
Total Cooking Time: 8 to 10 minutes
Calories: 16¾ per serving

1 package (10 ounces) frozen
**   cauliflower**
2 tablespoons skim milk
1 teaspoon instant
**   chicken bouillon**
¼ teaspoon butter-flavored salt
Dash of pepper

1. Place cauliflower in a 1 quart casserole. Cover with plastic wrap. Microwave on HIGH (100%) for 8 to 10 minutes or until very tender. Drain off water.

2. Place cauliflower in blender. Add milk, bouillon, salt and pepper. Blend until smooth.

Recipe yield: 4 servings

HONEY GLAZED
CARROTS AND APPLES

Power Level: HIGH [100%]
Total Cooking Time: 12 to
*   15½ minutes*
Calories: 127 per half cup serving

2 cups boiling water
1 cup dried carrots
½ cup dried apple slices
¼ cup honey
2 tablespoons butter (or margarine)
½ teaspoon dried orange peel
¼ teaspoon salt

1. Place water, carrots and apples in a 1½ quart casserole. Cover with a tight fitting lid or plastic wrap. Allow to stand for 1 hour.

2. Microwave, covered, on HIGH (100%) for 10 to 12 minutes or until carrots and apples are tender. Drain, reserving 2 tablespoons water.

3. Mix together honey, reserved water, butter, orange peel and salt in a 1 cup measure. Microwave on HIGH (100%) for 1 to 1½ minutes or until hot and bubbly. Pour over carrots and apples. Cover.

4. Microwave on HIGH (100%) for 1 to 2 minutes or until heated through.

Recipe yield: 2½ cups

┌─ Low-Fat Gravy Tip ─┐

By using a trivet when cooking meat, you can decrease the amount of grease. Then if you place the meat drippings in the refrigerator, the grease will rise to the top and can be skimmed off. Use the remaining drippings to make low-fat gravy.

Dessert

STRAWBERRY PUDDING
Power Level: HIGH [100%]
Total Cooking Time: 4 to 6 minutes
Calories: 137 per serving

**2 packages (10 ounces each)
   frozen strawberries, thawed**
2 tablespoons cornstarch
2 tablespoons lemon juice
½ teaspoon vanilla
Dash of cinnamon
Chopped almonds

1. Drain liquid from strawberries into a 1 quart casserole. Set strawberries aside.

2. Mix together cornstarch, lemon juice, vanilla and cinnamon until smooth. Stir into strawberry liquid.

3. Microwave strawberry liquid mixture on HIGH (100%) for 4 to 6 minutes or until thickened. Stir several times during cooking.

4. Add strawberries to the liquid mixture. Cover with plastic wrap. Chill. Garnish with almonds before serving.

Recipe yield: 6 servings

FRUIT 'N NUT BARS
Power Level: HIGH [100%]
Total Cooking Time: 8 to 10 minutes
Calories: 88 per serving

2 cups chopped, dried appricots
**1 cup chopped walnuts
   (or almonds)**
1 cup raisins
¼ cup shredded coconut
¼ cup honey
1 teaspoon grated orange peel

1. Mix together all ingredients in an 11¾x7½x1¾ inch baking dish.

2. Microwave on HIGH (100%) for 8 to 10 minutes or until fruit softens slightly. Stir several times during cooking to thoroughly blend ingredients.

3. Evenly distribute fruit 'n nut mixture in dish. Cool. Cut into squares. Store in the refrigerator or in an airtight container.

Recipe yield: 20 squares

YOGURT
*Power Level: HIGH [100%] and
            WARM [10%]*
*Total Cooking Time: 1 hour 6 minutes
            to 1 hour 8 minutes*
Temperature Probe: 180° and 110°
Calories: 96 per half cup serving

2 cups milk (skim, low fat, regular)
**2 to 3 tablespoons plain natural
   yogurt, room temperature**

1. Place milk in a 1 quart casserole. Microwave on HIGH (100%) for 5 to 6 minutes or to an internal temperature of 180°.

2. Allow milk to cool in refrigerator for 30 to 35 minutes or until the internal temperature drops to 106° to 110°.

3. Stir in yogurt. Microwave on HIGH (100%) for 1 to 2 minutes or to an internal temperature of 110°.

4. Cover tightly with plastic wrap.

5. Microwave on WARM (10%) for 1 hour.

6. Refrigerate for 5 to 6 hours. Strain through cheesecloth. Add desired fruit.

Recipe yield: 2 cups

*Honey Glazed Carrots
and Apples*

Yogurt

Fruit 'N Nut Bars

BAKED PEACH MELBA

Power Level: HIGH [100%]
Total Cooking Time: 7 to 10 minutes
Calories: 51 per serving

3 large fresh peaches, halved
  (Remove seeds and peel.)
1 cup unsweetened orange juice
1 teaspoon granulated sweetener
  (sugar substitute)
¼ teaspoon allspice
2 tablespoons dietetic raspberry
  preserves

1. Combine orange juice, sweetener and allspice in an 8x8x2 inch baking dish. Microwave on HIGH (100%) for 3 to 4 minutes or until juice is boiling.

2. Arrange peaches in baking dish with sauce. Spoon sauce over peaches. Microwave on HIGH (100%) for 4 to 6 minutes or until peaches are tender.

3. Place peaches, cut side up, on serving dishes. Top with warm liquid and 1 teaspoon of preserves.

Recipe yield: 4 to 6 servings

Italian
Chicken Stew

DIETER'S CHEESECAKE

Power Level: HIGH [100%]
Total Cooking Time: 3 to 4 minutes
Calories: 179¼ per serving

2 envelopes unflavored gelatin
¼ cup granulated sweetener
  (sugar substitute)
1½ cups skim milk
4 eggs, separated
4 cups creamed cottage cheese
1 tablespoon lemon juice
1 teaspoon lemon peel
1½ teaspoons vanilla

1. Combine gelatin, 2 tablespoons sweetener and milk in a 2 quart casserole. Cover with a tight fitting lid or plastic wrap.

2. Microwave on HIGH (100%) for 3 to 4 minutes or until gelatin dissolves and mixture is hot.

3. Beat egg yolks. Stir in a small amount of hot mixture into egg yolks, then stir egg yolk mixture into remaining hot mixture. Cool.

4. Place cottage cheese in blender. Blend until smooth. Add lemon juice, lemon peel and vanilla until smooth. With whisk, stir into cooled milk mixture.

5. Beat egg whites until soft peaks form. Add remaining sweetener. Beat until stiff peaks form. Fold into milk mixture.

6. Pour into an 8 inch spring-form pan. Chill until set. Unmold.

7. If desired, serve with ½ cup fresh strawberries.

Snack

APPLE-RAISIN PARTY MIX

Power Level: HIGH [100%]
Total Cooking Time: 2 to 3 minutes
Calories: 162 per ½ cup serving

¼ cup honey
1 teaspoon cinnamon
¼ teaspoon dried lemon peel
¼ teaspoon dried orange peel
3 cups dried sliced apples
1 cup raisins
1 cup walnuts (or pecans)

1. Mix together honey, cinnamon, lemon peel and orange peel in an 11¾x7½x1¾ inch baking dish. Microwave on HIGH (100%) for 2 to 3 minutes or until heated through. Stir occasionally.

2. Add remaining ingredients, toss to coat.

3. Spread out on waxed paper to dry.

Recipe yield: 5 cups

Apple-Raisin Party Mix

Dieter's
Cheesecake

Speedy Barbecue Ideas

Using microwave cooking with your outdoor grill can speed up barbecue time and give you a better finished product.

Some foods, such as chicken or spareribs, are difficult to get fully cooked on the inside without burning the outside when you are barbecuing. By starting the cooking process in the microwave and finishing it on your grill, you can have a fully cooked food with that outdoor flavor. You can get similar results by combining microwave cooking with your conventional broiler. Total barbecue or broiling time is considerably shorter when you take advantage of the microwave.

Place chicken pieces, *skin side down, in baking dish. Cover with waxed paper. Microwave on High [100%] for 10 to 12 minutes. Turn over halfway through cooking.*

Arrange chicken pieces, *skin side down, on broiler insert rack or barbecue grill. Brush with barbecue sauce or melted butter. Broil or barbecue for 10 to 15 minutes or until chicken is golden brown and fork tender. Turn halfway through cooking.*

ZESTY OUTDOOR DINNER

Power Level: HIGH [100%]
Total Microwaving Time: 20 to 25 minutes

3 pound beef chuck roast
1 bottle (12 ounces) Italian salad dressing
2 potatoes, cut into 1 inch pieces
2 carrots, cut into 1 inch pieces
2 stalks celery, cut into 1 inch pieces
2 medium onions, quartered
1 medium green pepper, cut in rings
½ teaspoon salt
Dash of pepper

1. Place meat in an 11¾x7½x1¾ inch baking dish. Pour salad dressing over meat. Cover with plastic wrap. Refrigerate for 4 to 6 hours. Spoon salad dressing over meat occasionally.

2. Do not drain off salad dressing. Place vegetables around meat. Cover. Microwave on HIGH (100%) for 20 to 25 minutes. Turn meat over halfway through cooking.

3. Drain. Place meat in the center of a double thickness of aluminum foil (2½ feet long). Place vegetables on top of meat. Sprinkle with salt and pepper. Fold foil over and securely seal.

4. Place on insert rack of broiler pan or barbecue grill. Broil or grill for 30 to 45 minutes or until vegetables are tender and meat is to desired doneness.

Recipe yield: 6 to 8 servings

HERB FLAVORED RACK OF LAMB

Power Level: MEDIUM-HIGH [70%]
Total Microwaving Time: 8 to 10 minutes

10 rib rack of lamb
2 tablespoons parsley
2 tablespoons melted butter (or margarine)

1. Place lamb, fat side down, in a baking dish. Cover with waxed paper. Microwave on MEDIUM-HIGH (70%) for 8 to 10 minutes. Turn over halfway through cooking.

2. Meanwhile, mix together parsley and melted butter.

3. Place rack of lamb on barbecue spit. Rotate on spit for 15 to 20 minutes or to desired doneness. Brush with butter mixture occasionally the last 15 minutes of cooking.

Recipe yield: 4 to 6 servings

QUICK BROILED OR BARBECUED CHICKEN

Power Level: HIGH [100%]
Total Microwaving Time: 10 to 12 minutes

2½ to 3 pound chicken, cut up

1. Place chicken pieces, skin side down, in an 11¾x7½x1¾ inch baking dish. Cover with waxed paper.

2. Microwave on HIGH (100%) for 10 to 12 minutes. Turn dish a half turn halfway through cooking.

3. Arrange chicken pieces, skin side down, on broiler insert rack or barbecue grill.

4. Broil or barbecue on grill for 10 to 15 minutes or until golden brown and fork tender. Turn over halfway through cooking and brush with Zesty Barbecue Sauce (page 108), melted butter or other sauce.

Recipe yield: 4 to 6 servings

CRYSTAL GLAZED HAM

Power Level: HIGH [100%]
Total Microwaving Time: 11 to 14 minutes

1 ham slice, 1½ inch thick
1 cup orange juice
1 cup white wine (or white grape juice)
½ cup honey
1 tablespoon white vinegar
2 teaspoons dry mustard
½ teaspoon ginger
¼ teaspoon ground cloves
Dash of cinnamon

1. Slash fat edge of ham. Place ham in a 10x6x1¾ inch baking dish. Add ½ cup orange juice. Cover with plastic wrap. Microwave on HIGH (100%) for 10 to 12 minutes or until tender.

2. Mix together remaining ingredients and remaining orange juice. Pour over ham slice. Cover. Allow to stand 2 hours or refrigerate overnight. Spoon marinade over ham serveral times.

3. Place on insert rack of broiler pan or on barbecue grill. Broil or grill 20 minutes. Turn over halfway through cooking. Baste frequently with marinade.

4. Microwave remaining marinade on HIGH (100%) for 1 to 2 minutes or until heated through. Serve with ham slice.

Recipe yield: 4 to 6 servings

GRILLED BARBECUED RIBS

Power Level: HIGH [100%]
Total Microwaving Time: 15 to 20 minutes

3 pounds pork spareribs, cut in 2 or 3 rib pieces
1 cup barbecue sauce or Zesty Barbecue Sauce (page 108)

1. Arrange ribs in a baking dish. Cover with plastic wrap.

2. Microwave on HIGH (100%) for 15 to 20 minutes. Turn halfway through cooking.

3. Arrange ribs on an insert rack of broiler pan, a barbecue grill or barbecue spit. Brush with barbecue sauce.

4. Broil or barbecue for 10 to 15 minutes or until fork tender. Baste and turn ribs over occasionally.

Recipe yield: 4 servings

Start cooking *your Grilled Barbecued Ribs in the microwave and finish them in quick time on your tabletop grill or your outdoor grill.*

BEER MARINATED BEEF

Power Level: HIGH [100%]
Total Microwaving Time: 15 to 20 minutes

1 can (12 ounces) flat beer
1/3 cup cooking oil
2 tablespoons lemon juice
2 tablespoons brown sugar
1/2 teaspoon salt
1/4 teaspoon instant minced garlic
Dash of ground cloves
3 pound beef chuck roast

1. Mix together all ingredients, except meat, in an 11¾x7½x1¾ inch baking dish. Slash edges of meat to prevent curling. Place meat in dish with marinade. Spoon marinade over meat. Cover with plastic wrap. Refrigerate for 4 to 6 hours. Spoon marinade over meat occasionally.

2. Do not drain off marinade. Microwave, covered, on HIGH (100%) for 15 to 20 minutes. Turn meat over halfway through cooking.

3. Drain and reserve marinade. Place meat on insert rack of broiler pan or barbecue grill. Brush with marinade.

4. Broil or barbecue to desired doneness. Occasionally turn over and brush with marinade.

Recipe yield: 6 to 8 servings

POTATO-ONION BAKE

Power Level: HIGH [100%]
Total Microwaving Time: 8 to 10 minutes

6 large potatoes, scrubbed
1 envelope (1½ ounces) dry onion soup mix
1/4 cup Parmesan cheese
1/4 teaspoon celery salt
1/4 cup butter (or margarine)

1. Pierce potatoes.

2. Arrange potatoes on a paper towel in the microwave oven. Microwave on HIGH (100%) for 8 to 10 minutes. Potatoes should be underdone.

3. Peel and slice potatoes in 1/2 inch thick slices.

4. Place alternate layers of potato slices and onion soup mix on a 20x18 inch double thickness of aluminum foil. Sprinkle with cheese and celery salt. Dot with butter. Wrap.

5. Place on insert rack of broiler pan, on barbecue grill or directly on coals. Broil or grill for 25 to 30 minutes or until tender.

Recipe yield: 4 to 6 servings

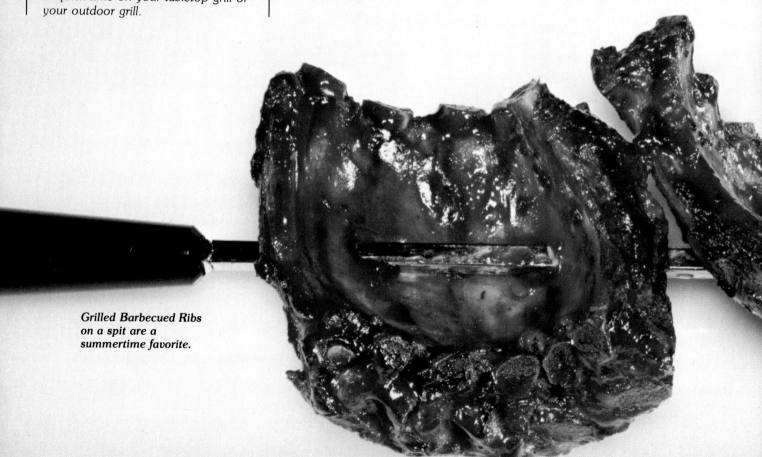

Grilled Barbecued Ribs on a spit are a summertime favorite.

BROCCOLI AND MUSHROOM GRILL

Power Level: HIGH [100%]
Total Microwaving Time: 6 to 8 minutes

2 packages (10 ounces each) frozen broccoli
1 can (4 ounces) sliced mushrooms, drained
1 teaspoon lemon juice
¼ teaspoon salt
Dash of pepper
½ cup grated Cheddar cheese
½ cup bread crumbs

1. Place broccoli and mushrooms in a 2 quart casserole. Microwave on HIGH (100%) for 6 to 8 minutes or until defrosted. Drain.

2. Place on a double thickness of aluminum foil. Sprinkle with lemon juice, salt and pepper.

3. Mix together cheese and bread crumbs. Sprinkle over broccoil and mushrooms. Wrap.

4. Place on insert rack of broiler pan or barbecue grill.

5. Broil or grill for 15 to 20 minutes or until heated through.

Recipe yield: 6 to 8 servings

ZIPPY BARBECUED PORK CHOPS

Power Level: HIGH [100%]
Total Microwaving Time: 15 to 19 minutes

½ cup tomato sauce
2 tablespoons light corn syrup
2 tablespoons instant beef bouillon
1 tablespoon cider vinegar
1 tablespoon finely chopped onion
½ teaspoon dry mustard
½ teaspoon celery salt
Dash of chili powder
Dash of pepper
4 pork chops, ¾ inch thick

1. Mix together all ingredients except pork chops in a 2 cup measure. Microwave on HIGH (100%) for 3 to 4 minutes or until hot and bubbly.

2. Place pork chops in an 8x8x2 inch baking dish. Cover with plastic wrap. Microwave on HIGH (100%) for 12 to 15 minutes. Turn over halfway through cooking.

3. Place on insert rack of broiler pan or barbecue grill. Brush with sauce.

4. Grill or barbecue for 12 to 15 minutes. Baste and turn chops over occasionally.

Recipe yield: 4 servings

Variation:
GRILLED PORK CHOPS

Follow Zippy Barbecued Pork Chops recipe as directed except do not use sauce.

Recipe yield: 4 servings

GRILLED STEAKS

Power Level: HIGH [100%]
Total Microwaving Time: 3 to 4 minutes

At the end of the season: Grill steaks, freeze, store and enjoy grilled steaks any time of the year.

1. Choose thick, tender steaks. Place steaks on barbecue grill.

2. Grill steaks on each side almost to desired doneness. Steaks should be underdone. Allow to cool.

3. Wrap steaks in freezer bags. Freeze until ready to use.

4. To Microwave: Defrost steaks. Place in baking dish. Cover with waxed paper. Microwave on HIGH (100%) for 3 to 4 minutes to desired doneness.

Variation:
GRILLED HAMBURGERS

Follow Grilled Steaks recipe as directed except substitute hamburger patties for steaks.

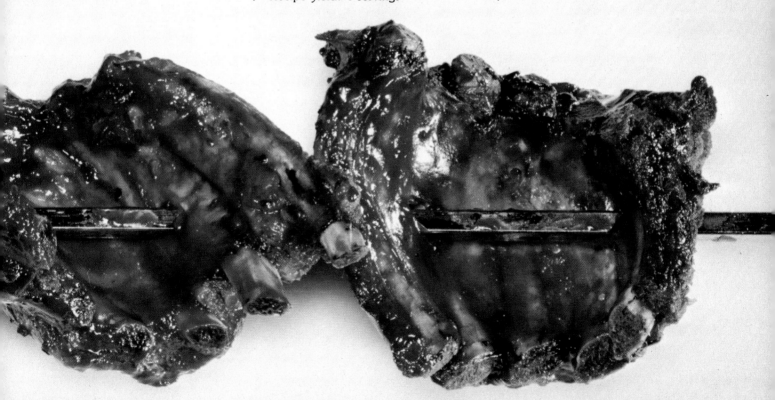

Drying Herbs, Fruits and Vegetables

Preserving herbs, fruits and vegetables is simply "cut and dried" with the microwave. It's quick and easy to clean and cut up these foods and then dehydrate them in the microwave. Dehydration is the process of removing moisture from foods for longer storage.

The microwave is ideal for drying small quantities of fruits, herbs and vegetables. When you have a few extras on hand, use your microwave.

It is best to schedule your drying on clear, sunny days when humidity is low. On rainy or humid days, foods tend to reabsorb moisture as soon as they are removed from the microwave. Then longer drying times may become necessary. The foods may take on a scorched flavor and color if they become too hot.

How To Dry Fruits and Vegetables

Wash, dry and cut up *fruit or vegetable. Peel if necessary. Evenly spread pieces on a double thickness of paper towel. Microwave on Low [30%] until properly dry. Rearrange several times during drying.*

Remove from the microwave *and spread pieces on clean paper towel. Cover with another clean paper towel. Allow to stand until fruit or vegetable pieces are thoroughly dry, showing no signs of moisture.*

Store dried fruit or vegetables *in an air-tight container in a dark, cool, dry place. You may prefer to use glass containers. Fruits treated with sulphite should not be stored in metal containers as the sulphite may react with the metal.*

DRYING APPLES
Power Level: LOW [30%]
Total Cooking Time: 1¾ to 2 hours

4 medium apples

1. Peel and core apples. Cut into ¼ inch slices.

2. Combine 1¾ teaspoons sulphite powder and 2 quarts water. Place apple slices in sulphite mixture for 15 minutes.

3. Remove apple slices and pat dry.

4. Place apples in a single layer on paper towels. Microwave on LOW (30%) for 1 hour 45 minutes to 2 hours. Rearrange apples every 15 minutes.

5. Test for doneness: Leathery; when cut in half no moist area in center.

6. Place on paper towels, then cover with paper towels. Allow to stand until all moisture is gone. Store in refrigerator, freezer or at room temperature in an air-tight container.

DRYING LEMON OR ORANGE RIND
Power Level: LOW [30%]
Total Cooking Time: 30 minutes

2 lemons or 2 oranges

1. Grate rind only, not white membrane.

2. Place grated rind in a single layer on paper towels.

3. Microwave on LOW (30%) for 30 minutes. Rearrange every 5 minutes.

4. Test for doneness: Hard.

DRYING CARROTS
Power Level: LOW [30%]
Total Cooking Time: 1½ to 1¾ hours

2 cups thinly sliced carrots

1. Peel and thinly slice carrots.

2. Place carrot slices in a single layer on paper towels.

3. Microwave on LOW (30%) for 1 hour 30 minutes to 1 hour 45 minutes. Rearrange carrots every 15 minutes.

4. Test for doneness: Tough, leathery.

5. Place on paper towels, then cover with paper towels. Allow to stand until all moisture is gone. Store in refrigerator, freezer, or at room temperature in an air-tight container.

DRYING TOMATOES
Power Level: LOW [30%]
Total Cooking Time: 1½ to 1¾ hours

3 medium tomatoes (24 slices)

1. Do not peel tomatoes. Cut in ¼ inch slices.

2. Place tomato slices in a single layer on paper towels.

3. Microwave on LOW (30%) for 1 hour 30 minutes to 1 hour 45 minutes. Carefully rearrange tomato slices every 15 minutes.

4. Test for doneness: Dry.

5. Place on paper towels, then cover with paper towels. Allow to stand until all moisture is gone. Store in refrigerator, freezer or at room temperature in an air-tight container.

DRYING CORN
Power Level: LOW [30%]
Total Cooking Time: 1¾ to 2 hours

4 medium ears corn

1. Remove husks and silk. Wash. Cut corn off cob.

2. Place corn in a single layer on towels.

3. Microwave on LOW (30%) for 1 hour 45 minutes to 2 hours. Rearrange corn every 10 minutes.

4. Test for doneness: Dry, brittle.

5. Place on paper towels, then cover with paper towels. Allow to stand until all moisture is gone. Store in refrigerator, freezer or at room temperature in an air-tight container.

DRYING ONIONS
Power Level: LOW [30%]
Total Cooking Time: 1½ to 1¾ hours

2 cups finely chopped onions

1. Place onions in a single layer on paper towels.

2. Microwave on LOW (30%) for 1 hour 30 minutes to 1 hour 45 minutes. Rearrange every 15 minutes.

3. Test for doneness: Dry, brittle.

4. Place on paper towels, then cover with paper towels. Allow to stand until all moisture is gone. Store in refrigerator, freezer or at room temperature in an air-tight container.

How To Dry Herbs

Wash and pat dry herbs. *Remove leaves from stems and measure 1½ to 2 cups of leaves.*

Evenly spread leaves *on a double thickness of paper towel. Microwave on High [100%] for 4 to 6 minutes. Stir several times during drying.*

When properly dried, *herbs will be brittle and will rattle when stirred. Store in an air-tight container in a cool, dry place.*

CELERY
Commonly used in:
Stock, bouillon, pickles, salads, salad dressings, seafood and vegetables.

MINT ORANGE
Commonly used in:
Fruit cups, coleslaw, peas, zucchini, lamb, veal, cream cheese, teas, chocolate combinations, jellies, juleps and as garnishes.

CHIVES
Commonly used in:
Soups, cottage cheese, scrambled eggs, softened butter, salads and salad dressings.

OREGANO
Commonly used in:
Sausages, stews, tomato dishes, lamb, pork, chicken, omelets, eggs, pizza, cabbage, green beans, minestrone and salads.

PARSLEY
Commonly used in:
Vegetables, main dishes and as garnishes.

SWEET MARJORAM
Commonly used in:
Sausages, stews, salads, tomato dishes, lamb, pork, chicken, omelets, eggs, pizza, cabbage, minestrone, green beans and lima beans.

ROSEMARY
Commonly used in:
Marinades, lamb, duck, capon, veal, pizza, peas, spinach, boiled potatoes, turnips, cauliflower, beef and fish.

TARRAGON FRENCH
Commonly used in:
Eggs, mushrooms, tomatoes, sweetbreads, mustard sauces, fish and chicken.

SAGE
Commonly used in:
Sausages, duck, goose, rabbit, cheese and chowders, omelets and stuffing.

THYME
Commonly used in:
Veal, pork, rabbit, poultry, creole, beets (pickled), tomatoes (pickled), stuffings, fat fish dishes and stews.

Drying Flowers

It used to take weeks to dry flowers. Now you'll have them in no time at all.

Some flowers lend themselves perfectly to drying while others may change color or fade. Don't be afraid to experiment. Our information is meant to serve as a guide to get you started.

It's a good idea to start with flowers of a lighter color because most flowers tend to darken during drying. Brightly colored flowers such as roses, daffodils, daisies and carnations work best. Yellow flowers retain color especially well. White flowers tend to become dull, gray-brown. Thick flowers such as iris or saucer magnolia do not dry well.

Cut flowers that are cool and dry, usually in the early morning, late afternoon or evening. Do not cut flowers that are wet with rain or dew.

The flowers should be about half open and firm. Flowers in full bloom may lose their petals when dried.

Dry flowers as soon as possible after cutting to preserve their color. If you can't dry them when first cut, store flowers in a refrigerator or cool place until you're ready.

Here are the materials you'll need: scissors, silica gel (available at florist shops), shoe boxes (not those with metal staples), glass bowls or casseroles, wire (florist's wire is best), floral tape, glue or florist's adhesive spray, toothpick, delicate brush to remove silica gel, hair spray, plastic spray or artist's protective spray.

Preparing The Flowers

Pour silica gel into container to a depth of about 2 inches.

Cut flower stems to a length of 1 inch. Flowers should be about half open and firm.

Insert flowers right side up, spacing them so they do not touch each other or the container sides. Use a toothpick to separate the petals and to help petals retain their original shape.

Gently sift silica gel over the flowers until covered, working it up and around so silica gel is in contact with all flower parts. Gently tapping the container helps the grains fill in around the petals.

Drying The Flowers

Place container of flowers in the microwave with a cup of water. Use High [100%] power according to flower chart. Because microwaves act quickly on the flowers, more color is retained than when flowers are air dried or dried for many days in silica gel only. Using the water in the microwave keeps the flowers from becoming brittle.

After heating for the specific time, it helps to leave the container undisturbed in the microwave overnight. If desired, you may carefully remove the container and cover with foil. But moving may dislodge silica gel crystals around the flowers which may affect their final color.

Test for dryness. Before removing flowers, gently move away enough silica gel to touch the petals. If they do not seem completely dry, you may wish to recover the flower and return the container to microwave for one minute. All flowers dry somewhat differently.

Drying Tip

If the blue crystals in the silica gel begin to turn pink, the gel is losing its capability to absorb moisture. To reconstitute the gel, just heat in the microwave for a few minutes until the blue color returns. By doing this, you can use the same silica gel over for several years.

Removing The Flowers

Tip the container gently so the silica gel crystals begin to slowly flow off the flowers. As flowers become exposed, carefully slide two fingers under the flower to remove. Gently shake off excess crystals.

Place flowers in a "dry box" for three to five days for longer lasting dried flowers. Use a metal or plastic container. Add silica gel to a depth of about 1 inch. Insert flowers so just the stems are in the silica gel. Cover with a tight fitting lid.

If you are not going to use the flowers immediately, storing them in a box of shredded newspaper or tissue paper will help them hold their shape until needed. Keep them in a dry place. Adding a teaspoon of silica gel in the container corners helps keep flowers dry.

Use a fine soft brush to carefully dust off any remaining crystals.

Adding The Stems

Use floral tape to bind the flower to a piece of wire. Different weight wire for stems is available at florist shops. The size and weight will depend on the size of the flower and how you plan to use it. Wind and stretch the tape around the base of the flower and down around the wire.

Lightly spray flowers with hair spray or artist's protective or plastic spray. This will help keep moisture out of the flower.

Flower Drying Times and Tips

Flowers in the same family as these listed here will dry
with about the same results. Use this chart as a guide.
Experiment and have fun with flowers.

African Daisy
3 minutes
Color retention is good, but petals may curl if exposed to humidity without protective spray.

Aster
2½ minutes
Cover thoroughly with silica gel.

Calendula
2½ minutes
Petals may fall off if flowers are too old, but you can glue the petals back.

Carnations
1 minute
Be sure silica gel gets down inside the petals. These flowers last longer when allowed to stay in the silica gel overnight.

Clematis
3 minutes
White flowers may turn brownish. Deep colors may come out even darker.

Chrysanthemum
3 minutes
Cover thoroughly with silica gel.

Coral Bells
3 minutes
Lay on side in box so stems dry horizontally.

Daffodil
2½ minutes
Add silica gel so it is well distributed both inside and outside of the flower. Flowers last longer when allowed to stay in the silica gel overnight.

Dahlia
5 to 7 minutes
Pompon types come out best. Others may get droopy when exposed to air. These last longer when given both the overnight and "dry box" treatments.

Delphinium (Larkspur)
4 to 5 minutes
Place flower stalks on their side in a long box. Small cardboard props with notches placed at intervals will help support the stalks when silica gel is poured on top. Colors may fade in bright light.

Dianthus
3 minutes
Petals tend to shrink so the dried specimen looks a little different than the fresh flower.

Dogwood
2½ minutes
After heating, take the container out of the oven and let stand for a few minutes to cool. Take the flowers out immediately and lay flat. If left in longer, they may become too fragile to remove.

Marigold
3 minutes
Use the "dry box" method. Color often fades and may become gray. Do not dry them if the centers are green.

Pansy
2½ to 3 minutes
Petals may shrink. Dark purple varieties tend to turn almost black. Use light and bright pansies. When covering with silica gel, use a toothpick to separate petals so the flower does not become flattened.

Peony
3 to 4 minutes
Single peonies work better than double peonies. White peonies may turn grayish.

Poppy
2½ to 3 minutes
May tend to droop when exposed to air. Plastic spray will help keep them firm.

Rose
1½ minutes
Rotate container halfway through drying time. Allow them to remain in silica gel overnight and use the "dry box" method for best results. Yellow roses may fade, and dark red roses may get darker. Pink roses work well. Use colors several shades lighter than the desired finished color. Select buds and flowers before they are in full bloom or old because older roses may lose their petals. Broken petals can be glued back on with care and patience. You might want to dry a few rose leaves as well and add them to the stems.

Salvia
3 minutes
Place flower stalk horizontally in container, either straight or curved, depending on how you want the finished flower to look.

Scillia
2½ minutes
They last longer when allowed to remain in silica gel overnight. Remove and hang until the stems are dry.

Tithonia (Mexican Sunflower)
5 to 6 minutes
Color remains bright, but petals may be a bit more transparent. They last longer when allowed to remain in silica gel overnight. Use the "dry box" method for best results. Times may vary with humidity.

Tulip
3 minutes
These are very difficult to dry. Be sure silica gel is added evenly both inside and outside the flower. Allow to remain in silica gel overnight and use the "dry box" method for best results.

Violet and Violas
2½ to 3 minutes
Flowers tend to shrink a little. The overnight and "dry box" methods bring best results.

Zinnia
4 to 5 minutes
Use light colored varieties if possible as dark red zinnias tend to get very dark. Petals often shrink a little.

Be a Cut-Up

Lovely fresh table bouquets year 'round. Brighten up any table setting with a bouquet from natures' carrots, radishes, turnips, olives and celery. After creating your flowers, keep them fresh in a large bowl of ice water until you are ready to make your arrangement.

1. Press out a flower from a thin 1/8" turnip slice with a cookie cutter. Cut a stuffed olive in half for a center.

2. Dye a turnip slice in yellow food coloring. Cut around a daisy pattern, made from paper, to form the flower.

3. Attach the olive centers to flower section with florist wire. Then attach wire to a wooden pick to make stem.

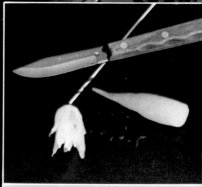

4. Make a white radish flower by cutting thin lengthwise slices to within ½" from bottom. Thread florist wire through bottom and attach wire to wooden pick.

Equipment needed: paring knife, scissors, florist wire and wood skewers.

CROWN ROAST DAISY FRILLS

Have fun making these paper frills. Add process American cheese centers and you have created delightful daisies . . . a fitting garnish for the Royal Crown Roast.

1. Cut strips of white paper 6" x 1½". Fold each strip in half, then in half again.

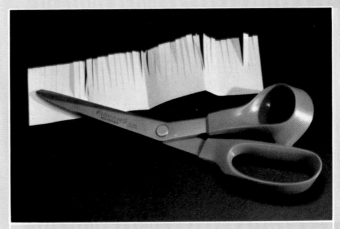

2. While still folded, cut 1/8"-wide strips about half-way down.

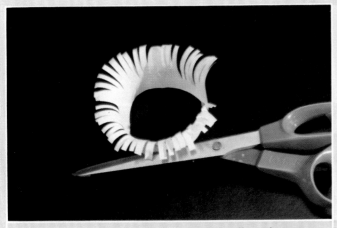

3. Unfold cut strips. Curl the ends by pulling the cut ends between your thumb and the back edge of the scissors.

4. Roll the strip around a finger and fasten with a piece of scotch tape.

5. Using the cap end of a pen, press out the centers from a thin slice of the cheese. Place in center of frills.

6. Step back and admire your handiwork.

KID STUFF
Let your children join in the cooking fun. They'll really enjoy creating fancy toppings on cupcakes. Colored sugars, sprinkles, nuts, maraschino cherries and tiny candies are easy and fun to decorate with.

More Cut-Ups

TOMATO ROSE
Starting at top of unpeeled tomato, form petals with level teaspoon of softened cream cheese. Overlap petals around tomato. Clean spoon in water after making each petal. Make at least 2 rows of petals. Use diced cooked egg yolk for flower center.

CUCUMBER CUP
Cut 2" cross section from each end of cucumber. Cut thin slice off end so cup will stand. Hollow out center 1½" deep. Cut ½" strips down to ¼" from bottom. Place seafood sauce in center.

LEMON TWISTS
Cut lemons into ¼" slices.
Cut through to center. Twist.

FLUTED MUSHROOMS
Cut shallow wedges around the cap of the mushroom. To help keep mushrooms looking appetizingly white, boil them for 3 minutes in water with one tablespoon of salt and one tablespoon of lemon juice.

TO FROST A GRAPE
"Paint" the grapes with a mixture of two egg whites and 2 tablespoons of water. Then sprinkle the grapes with granulated sugar.

PIE TOP DECORATION
Add a special touch by cutting a fruit or flower design out of pastry dough. Place the cutout in a pie dish and microwave on High (100%) until done. Place it on top of your finished pie as shown on page 155.

POTATO FRILLS
It's easy to make Twice-Baked Potatoes (page 182) look extra special. Place potato mixture in a pastry bag and create a flowered effect. Use a straw to cut flower centers from a slice of cheese.

LEMON BASKET
Cut a wedge on both sides of lemon leaving a ¼" "handle" in the middle of the basket.

RADISH ROSES
For the radish on the left cut thin slices starting at stalk up to the top. Cut off top tip. To make the middle radish cut petals starting at the stalk and make 4 cuts around base. For next layer of petals overlap the cuts in alternating pattern. Cut off top tip of radish. For the radish on the right make 6-8 cuts lengthwise through a radish from base to stalk. Put the radishes in a bowl of ice water until they open like flowers.

TOMATO CUP
With sharp-pointed paring knife, cut "lion teeth" all around tomato. Cut deep enough to go to core of tomato.

WEIGHTS AND MEASURES

a dash = less than 1/8 teaspoon
60 drops = 1 teaspoon
1½ teaspoons = ½ tablespoon
3 teaspoons = 1 tablespoon
2 tablespoons = 1/8 cup or 1 fluid ounce
4 tablespoons = ¼ cup
5⅓ tablespoons = ⅓ cup
8 tablespoons = ½ cup
10⅔ tablespoons = ⅔ cup
12 tablespoons = ¾ cup
16 tablespoons = 1 cup

2 cups = 1 pint or 16 fluid ounces
2 pints = 1 quart or 32 fluid ounces
4 cups = 1 quart
4 quarts = 1 gallon
8 quarts = 1 peck
4 pecks = 1 bushel
16 ounces = 1 pound
3/8 cup = ¼ cup plus 2 tablespoons
5/8 cup = ½ cup plus 2 tablespoons
7/8 cup = ¾ cup plus 2 tablespoons
1 cup = 8 fluid ounces
1 jigger = 1½ fluid ounces (3 tablespoons)

COMMON EQUIVALENTS

Baking Powder . . . . 1 tsp. = ¼ tsp. soda plus ½ cup soured
milk or buttermilk
Butter or margarine . . . 1 stick (¼ lb.) = ½ cup
Buttermilk . . . . . 1 cup = 2 tbsp. vinegar plus sweet milk
to fill 1 cup
Chocolate (unsweetened) . 1 square = 3 tbsp. cocoa plus 1 tbsp. butter
Cream, heavy . . . . 1 cup = 2 cups whipped
Egg whites . . . . . 1 cup = 8 to 10 whites
Egg yolks . . . . . 1 cup = 12 to 14 yolks
Eggs, whole . . . . . 2 large = 3 small, 1 cup = 5
Flour . . . . 1 lb. all-purpose = 4 cups sifted
. . . . . . 1 lb. cake = 4¾ cups sifted
. . . . . . 1 cup all-purpose = 1 cup plus 2 tbsp.
cake flour
. . . . . . 1 cup cake = 1 cup minus 2 tbsp.
all-purpose flour
Lemon juice and rind . . 1 med. lemon = 2 tbsp. juice and 2 to 3
tsp. grated rind
Nuts in shell . . . . . 1 lb. = 1 to 1¾ cups shelled
Nut meats . . . . . ¼ lb. = 1 cup (approx.)
Orange juice and rind . . 1 med. orange = ⅓ cup juice and 1 to 2
tbsp. grated rind
Salad Oil . . . . . . ½ lb. (8 oz.) = 1 cup
Shortening . . . . . 1 lb. = 2½ cups
Sugar . . . . 1 lb. brown = 2¼ cups (firmly packed)
. . . . 1 lb. confectioners' = 4 to 4½ cups sifted
. . . . 1 lb. granulated = 2¼ cups

COMMON SIZES OF CANS

Of the different sizes of cans used by commercial canners, the most common are:

Size	Approximate Weight	Average Contents
8 oz.	8 oz.	1 cup
picnic	10½ to 12 oz.	1¼ cups
no. 300	14 to 16 oz.	1¾ cups
no.1 tall	1 lb.	2 cups
no.303	16 to 17 oz.	2 cups
no.2	1 lb.4 oz.or 1 pt.2 fl.oz.	2½ cups
no.2½	1 lb.13 oz.	3½ cups
no.3	3 lb.3 oz. or 1 qt.14 fl.oz.	5¾ cups
no.10	6½ lb.to 7 lb.5 oz.	12 to 13 cups

CONVERSION TABLES FOR METRIC EQUIVALENTS

1 gram = 0.035 ounces
1 kilogram = 2.21 pounds
1 ounce = 28.35 grams
1 pound = 453.59 grams

1 teaspoon = 4.9 milliliters
1 tablespoon = 14.8 milliliters
1 cup = 236.6 milliliters
1 liter = 1.06 quarts or
1,000 milliliters

DRY INGREDIENTS

Ounces	Grams	Grams	Ounces
1	28.35	1	0.035
2	56.70	2	0.07
3	85.05	3	0.11
4	113.40	4	0.14
5	141.75	5	0.18
6	170.10	6	0.21
7	198.45	7	0.25
8	226.80	8	0.28
9	255.15	9	0.32
10	283.50	10	0.35
11	311.85	11	0.39
12	340.20	12	0.42
13	368.55	13	0.46
14	396.90	14	0.49
15	425.25	15	0.53
16	453.60	16	0.57

Pounds	Kilograms	Kilograms	Pounds
1	0.454	1	2.205
2	0.91	2	4.41
3	1.36	3	6.61
4	1.81	4	8.82
5	2.27	5	11.02
6	2.72	6	13.23
7	3.18	7	15.43
8	3.63	8	17.64
9	4.08	9	19.84
10	4.54	10	22.05
11	4.99	11	24.26
12	5.44	12	26.46
13	5.90	13	28.67
14	6.35	14	30.87
15	6.81	15	33.08

LIQUID INGREDIENTS

Liquid Ounces	Milliliters	Milliliters	Liquid Ounces
1	29.573	1	0.034
2	59.15	2	0.07
3	88.72	3	0.10
4	118.30	4	0.14
5	147.87	5	0.17
6	177.44	6	0.20
7	207.02	7	0.24
8	236.59	8	0.27
9	266.16	9	0.30
10	295.73	10	0.33

Quarts	Liters	Liters	Quarts
1	0.946	1	1.057
2	1.89	2	2.11
3	2.84	3	3.17
4	3.79	4	4.23
5	4.73	5	5.28
6	5.68	6	6.34
7	6.62	7	7.40
8	7.57	8	8.45
9	8.52	9	9.51
10	9.47	10	10.57

Gallons	Liters	Liters	Gallons
1	3.785	1	0.264
2	7.57	2	0.53
3	11.36	3	0.79
4	15.14	4	1.06
5	18.93	5	1.32
6	22.71	6	1.59
7	26.50	7	1.85
8	30.28	8	2.11
9	34.07	9	2.38
10	37.86	10	2.74

Index

Photography and design by
Richland Graphics,
Mansfield, OH 44901